D1860140

A VOCABULARY
ENGLISH BURMESE, HINDUSTANI & TAMIL
IN ENGLISH CHARACTERS
WITH THE
BURMESE ALSO IN THE NATIVE LETTERS

A VOCABULARY

ENGLISH BURMESE, HINDUSTANI & TAMIL

IN ENGLISH CHARACTERS

WITH THE

BURMESE ALSO IN THE NATIVE LETTERS

TO WHICH ARE ADDED A FEW SENTENCES LIKELY TO BE USEFUL IN DAILY LIFE

DESIGNED FOR THE USE OF VISITORS AND OTHERS WHO ARE NOT FAMILIAR WITH THE LANGUAGES SPOKEN IN BURMA.

COMPILED BY

WILLIAM HENRY BEGBIE

AND

ABRAHAM JOSEPH

GYAN

Published by

GYAN

Gyan Publishing House
5, Ansari Road
Daryaganj, New Delhi-110002
Phone: 011-47034999, 9811692060
E-mail: books@gyanbooks.com

Distribution Network
gyanbooks.com
India, USA, Canada, UK, Australia, France

© **Publisher**
All rights reserved. No part of this work may be reproduced, stored, adapted, or transmitted in any form or by any means, electronic, mechanical, photocopying, micro-filming, recording or otherwise, or translated in any language, without the prior written permission of the copyright owner and the publisher.

ISBN : 978-81-212-3091-9 (PB)
First Published, Rangoon, 1877

2nd Impression 2020

Printed at: Gyan Press, Delhi.

The book is sold subject to the condition that it shall not, by way of trade or otherwise, be lent, resold, hired out, or otherwise circulated without the prior publisher's written consent.

A Vocabulary
English Burmese, Hindustani & Tamil
In English Characters
Author: William Henry Begbie and Abraham Joseph

A VOCABULARY

ENGLISH, BURMESE, HINDUSTANI & TAMIL.

IN ENGLISH CHARACTERS.

WITH THE

BURMESE ALSO IN THE NATIVE LETTERS.

To which are added a few Sentences likely to be usefsl in daily life.

Designed for the use of Visitors and others who are not familiar with the Languages spoken in Burma.

COMPILED BY

WILLIAM HENRY BEGBIE,

SECOND MASTER *S. John's College, S. P. G.*

AND

ABRAHAM JOSEPH.

FIRST EDITION.

PUBLISHED AND SOLD BY ABRAHAM JOSEPH.

Copyright Registered.

RANGOON:

Printed at the Albion Press.

1877.

Copies can be had at the ALBION PRESS,

AND AT

S. JOHN'S COLLEGE, S. P. G. Rangoon.

AND ALSO FROM

Messrs. HIGGINBOTHAM & Co. Madras.

LIST OF SUBSCRIBERS.

—:o:—

A. Rivers Thompson Esqr. C. S. I. Chief Commissioner of British Burma, & Agent to His Excellency the Viceroy and Governor-General of India — 2 Copies.
Colonel Horace A. Browne, Commissioner of Pegu — 1
The Most Revd. the Lord Bishop of Calcutta — 6

	Copies.
Abraham, Marcar Esqr. Macobin	10
Abdoolcadar Naik Mahomed	1
Adlard, J. H. B. Esqr.	1
Ah Shoung, H. Mr.	1
Ah Saing, Mr.	1
Alan Ker, Esqr.	1
Beatson, Walter W. G. Esqr.	1
Briddon, John. F. Esqr.	1
Brooke Deedes, Revd.	2
Brown, C. J. Esqr.	1
Cassim Thobath	1
Cauder Moideen	1
Catherasen Pillay, V. Vaccinator	1
Chundee Churn Nagth	1
Cohen Brothers, & Co. Messrs.	1
Colbeck, J. A. Revd.	2
Coun Goay, C. Mr.	1
Cowie, Chas. R. Esqr.	1
Darwood, J. Esqr.	5
Dawson, Advocate G. Esqr.	1
Dawson, J. N. Esqr.	1
D'Cruze, A. B. Esqr.	1
Dickmann, F. Esqr.	1
Dobson, F. H. Esqr.	1
Ebrahim Hassum Arriffjee	1
Esmailjee Ebramjee	1
Evanson, R. C. Capt. Magistrate	1
Ferreiro, Emmanuel, Mr.	1
Fforde, T. F. Esqr. Supt. of Police Amherst District Moulmein	1
Foon Foung, T. Mr.	1
Frame, J. Esqr.	1
Francis, C. M. Mr. No. 61 Q. O. S. & Miner D. Company.	1
Francis, M. Mr.	1
Franks, R. Mr. Signaller R. T. Dpt.	1
French, William Mr.	1

	Copies.
Gwyther, H. T. Esqr. Asst. Engr.	1
Haden, A. Esqr.	1
Hagens, H. Esqr.	1
Hardinge, J. J. C. Esqr.	1
Hedderwick, S. G. Mr.	1
Henzadah S. P. G. School	1
Hill, T. C. Esqr.	1
Hintze, J. Esqr.	1
Hpo Thaw	1
Hpo Mhyin	1
Hpay Htoon	1
Hpo Thong, Merchant	1
Htoon Hlah	1
Jodonauth Doss	1
Jordan, V. J. Esqr.	1
Kaly Doss Mukip	1
Knapp, C. Esqr.	1
Kruger, & Co. Messrs.	1
Kulenkampff, L. Esqr.	1
Kyah Bwin	2
Kynoch, G. C. Esqr.	1
Little, Thomas Esqr.	1
Luckett, G. F. Mr.	1
Macfie, F. W. Esqr.	1
MacCarthy, Welbore Revd.	1
Mamoojee Moosajee	1
Mariadossen. Francis Mr.	1
Mark's, Philips Revd. Ceylon	1
Marks, J. E. Revd.	2
Melville, James. Esqr.	2
Mia Ahmed Abdoolvahab	1
Milne, William. Mr.	1
Morrison, D. G. Esqr.	1
Mutter, William Mr.	1
Moollah Mahomed	2
Moung Tsan Phaw Oo	1
Moung Shway Choon	1
Moung Kyay	1

	Copies.
Moung Boa	1
Moung Oung Ming	1
Moung Kho	1
Moung Paw Htoon	1
Moung Htoon Oung, Advocate	1
Moung Ngyain	1
Moung Choe	1
Moung Oung Shway	1
Moung Kho, S.	1
Moung Tho Myah	1
Moung Hpay, Clerk	1
Moung Tha Oh	1
Moung Loo Glay	1
Moung Tha Myat	1
Moung Tha Oo	2
Moung Pho Mhyin Foremen	1
Moung Pho Thoung	1
Moung Myah	1
Moung Hpo Khin	1
Moung Tsain Boo	1
Moung Shwe Oung	1
Moung Hpay, Clerk Forest Office	1
Moung Ohn Ghine	1
Moung Pho Shain, Clerk	1
Neezamut Alley,	1
Noyce, W. F. Esqr.	1
Oung Zay, C. Mr.	3
Peter Jacob, M. Dubash Mr.	1
Preo Nath Mitter, Mr.	1
Rahamathoollah Saib M. S.	1
Rungiah Naidoo, T.	1
Schumacher, B. & Co. Messrs.	1
Scott, J. George Esqr. S. John's College	2
Shain Yen, L. Mr.	1
Shoay Lin, L. Mr.	1
Sleigh, A. D. Esqr. High School	1
Soobrathee, C. R. Mr.	1
S. John's College, S. P. G.	2
S Mary's School S. P. G.	1
Stone, C. Esqr.	1
Swee Keng, Y. Mr.	1
Thaddeus, G. C. Mr.	1
Thayetmyo S. P. G. School	1
Thongchie,	1
Unserkhan, Sahib M.	1
Unwin, D. W. Esqr.	1
Webster, Esqr. Charles S.	1
Wootten, W. H. Esqr.	1
Wright, R. P. S. W. Mr.	1
Yeo Swee Choon Merchant	1
Yeo Swee Sain, Merchant, Prome	1
Young George, Esqr.	1

STUDENTS OF S. JOHN'S COLLEGE, S. P. G. RANGOON.

		Copies.
Abraham, R.	3rd class	1
Aviot A. J.	1st Class	1
Ah Htun C.	2nd class	1
Chimbie	do	1
David Samuel In Nee	8th Master	1
Hasshim	2nd class	1
Hurror Chandre, Dey Michael		1
Henri Ravalo	3rd class	1
Jokelin, O.	6th class	1
Ku Taw	2nd class	1
Lyons, Mr. T. W.	3rd Master	1
Moung Bah Hpay	2nd class	1
Moung Bah Thain	do	1
Moung Chit Oo	4th class	1
Moung Hpo Hlah	do	1
Moung Hpo Yane.	1st class	1
Moung Hpo Tsin	3rd class	1
Moung Hpo Thet	2nd class	1
Moung Hpo Htoon	~~5th class~~	1
Moung Hpo Yin	2nd class	1
Moung Hpo Thin	4th class	1
Moung Hpo Tsun	2nd class	1
Moung Hpo Win	3rd class	1
Moung Hpo Hun	4th class	1
Moung Hpo Khin	3rd class	1
Moung Hpo Thain	do	1
Moung Hpo Tsee	5th master	1
Moung Htoon Hlah	5th class	1
Moung Htoon Oung	do	1
Moung Htoon Aye	2nd class	1
Moung Bah	6th class	1
Moung Chyone	1st class	1
Moung Chain	2nd class	1
Moung Dway	do	1
Moung Goon (Mandalay Royal School).		1
Moung Gyee	5th class	1
Moung Hpay	do	1
Moung Hpay 6th Master		1
Moung Htoon Oung	1st class	1
Moung Moung	do	1
Moung Thain	do	1

		Copies.
MoungShway Hmeh,	Master	1
Moung Myat Thin	2nd class	1
Moung Ney Doon	3rd class	1
Moung Oung Thah	5th class	1
Moung Shway Koo,	1st class	1
Moung Shway Utt	4th class	1
Moung Shway Noo	2nd class	1
Moung Swee Gwan	do	1
Moung Thah Hpo	4th class	1

		Copies.
Moung Kyaw Hpay	3rd class	1
Moung You Swai	2nd class	1

STUDENTS OF KEMENDINE BAPTIST COLLEGE, RANGOON.

Kyah Zan	1st class	1
Shway Hpo	do	1
Yond Daing	do	1

INTRODUCTION.

The work has been compiled to meet a want which is greatly felt in this Province by all whose duties bring them in contact with the natives in business or social life.

There are very few persons who are familiar with English, Burmese, Hindustani and Tamil. People from India often know one or both of the native languages but are unable to converse in the third. Their stay here is generally too short to render their acquisition of Burmese either desirable or useful—though whilst here they have frequent occasions to wish to make themselves understood by Burmans or others.

To aid such is one of the purposes of this work. In its preparation the Revd. F. Poynder's Dictionary, published by the Christian Knowledge Society has been employed. From that Dictionary all words in common use have been incorporated into the Vocabulary in alphabetical order.

A few useful sentences, on the plan of Forbes's Hindustani Manual, have been added.

The Burmese is given in the native character as well as in English. It has not been the design of the compilers to adopt any new system of transliteration but they ~~have tried~~ so to spell the words that an ordinary English reader will be able to pronounce them.

In the preparation of this work the compilers feel that they have striven to supply a real want. They are conscious of many imperfections in their performance, but they send forth their book with every confidence that it will be found useful. Its defects they will endeavour to rectify in future editions.

The accents are not intended to *divide syllables*, but simply to show on what syllable stress is to be laid. Whenever an accent is placed *directly over a vowel*, that vowel has its own full sound. The following abbreviations will be found in the Vocabulary :—

a. Adjective.
adv. Adverb.
conj. Conjunction.
interj. Interjection.
n. Neuter.
part. Participle.
pass. Passive.
pl. Plural.
poss. Possessive.
pr. Preposition.
pret. Preterite.
pron. Pronoun.
rel. Relative.
s. Substantive.
v. a. Verb Active.
v. n. Verb Neuter.
Fr. French.
Gr. Greek.
Ital. Italian.
Lat. Latin.

John's College, S. P. G.
RANGOON.

With regard to the Burmese words in English characters. The pronunciation adopted is that in use in England and *not* the continental mode.

ah is the open English sound in bah or the French â in chăr

ă is the short do păpa do ă in părole

aw is the broad do săw do or ĕ in ĕntrez

ee is the long do see do ī in autruī

e (final) is the short do be do ĭ in luĭ
or the final y in city

ĕ (medial) bed do ĕ in pĕrdrix

ĭ is the short English sound in pin do i in mĭnuir

oh is the long English sound of o in stone do eau in morceau

o is the short English word in stop do ŏ in monnaie

uy is the long English sound of uy in buy, ei in German, *mein*, or long ī in mīne.

y is the ordinary *consonant* English sound of y in yes *e, g,* kyin *pron.* kee-in.

m' n' th' etc. is the expression of these consonants, without any vowel between them and the next letter.

w at the begining of a syllable is used as a consonant.

ow has the ordinary English sound as in town.

u has the short English sound of u in bun.

h before m (as in hmyah, *pron. h'meah*) the lips to be closed and a rough breathing through the nose.

ng *initial* as ng in fli*ng*.

hng *initial* as ng in fli*ng* preceeded by the rough breathing.

h before a consonant is the guttural sound not used in English but like the *ch* in Scotch, or in German *suchen*.

The Days of the Week.

Sunday တနင်္ဂနွေနေ့။
tă-nin-ngă-nooay-nay
Monday တနင်္လာနေ့။
tă-ning-lah-nay
Tuesday အင်္ဂါနေ့။
in-gah-nay
Wednesday ဗုဒ္ဓဟူးနေ့။
boodh-d'hoo-nay
Thursday ကြာသပတေးနေ့။
kyah-thă-p'day-nay
Friday သောက်ကြာနေ့။
thowk-khyah-nay
Saturday စနေနေ့။
tsă-nay-nay

☞ The English Months have no Burmese names.

Numerals.

1 ၁ တစ်။
tit
2 ၂ နှစ်။
hnit
3 ၃ သုံး။
thohn
4 ၄ လေး။
lay
5 ၅ ငါး။
ngah
6 ၆ ခြောက်။
chyowk
7 ၇ ခုနှစ်။
koon-hnit
8 ၈ ရှစ်။
shitt
9 ၉ ကိုး။
koh
10 ၁၀ တဆယ်။
tă-seh'
11 ၁၁ တဆယ်တစ်။
tă-seh-tit
12 ၁၂ တဆယ်နှစ်။
tă-seh-hnit
13 ၁၃ တဆယ်သုံး။
tă-seh-thohn
14 ၁၄ တဆယ်လေး။
tă-seh-lay
15 ၁၅ တဆယ်ငါး။
tă-seh-ngah
16 ၁၆ တဆယ်ခြောက်။
tă-seh-chyowk
17 ၁၇ တဆယ်ခုနှစ်။
tă-seh-koon-hnit
18 ၁၈ တဆယ်ရှစ်။
tă-seh-shitt
19 ၁၉ တဆယ်ကိုး။
tă-seh-koh
20 ၂၀ နှစ်ဆယ်။
hnit-seh
21 ၂၁ နှစ်ဆယ်တစ်။
hnit-seh-tit
22 ၂၂ နှစ်ဆယ်နှစ်။
hnit-seh-hnit
23 ၂၃ နှစ်ဆယ်သုံး။
hnit-seh-thohn
24 ၂၄ နှစ်ဆယ်လေး။
hnit-seh-lay
25 ၂၅ နှစ်ဆယ်ငါး။
hnit-seh-ngah
26 ၂၆ နှစ်ဆယ်ခြောက်။
hnit-seh-chyowk
27 ၂၇ နှစ်ဆယ်ခုနှစ်။
hnit-seh-koon-hnit
28 ၂၈ နှစ်ဆယ်ရှစ်။
hnit-seh-shitt
29 ၂၉ နှစ်ဆယ်ကိုး။
hnit-seh-koh
30 ၃၀ သုံးဆယ်။
thohn-seh
31 ၃၁ သုံးဆယ်တစ်။
thohn-seh-tit
32 ၃၂ သုံးဆယ်နှစ်။
thohn-seh-hnit

33 ၃၃ သုံးယ်သုံး။
thohn-seh-thohn

34 ၃၄ သုံးဆယ်လေး။
thohn-seh-lay

35 ၃၅ သုံးဆယ်ငါး။
thōhn-seh-ngah

36 ၃၆ သုံးဆယ်ခြောက်။
thohn-seh-chyowk

37 ၃၇ သုံးဆယ်ခုနှစ်။
thohn-seh-koon-hnit

38 ၃၈ သုံးဆယ်ရှစ်။
thohn-seh-shitt

39 ၃၉ သုံးဆယ်ကိုး။
thohn-seh-koh

40 ၄၀ လေးဆယ်။
lay-seh

41 ၄၁ လေးဆယ်တစ်။
lay-seh-tit

42 ၄၂ လေးဆယ်နှစ်။
lay-seh-hnit

43 ၄၃ လေးဆယ်သုံး။
lay-seh-thohn

44 ၄၄ လေးဆယ်လေး။
lay-seh-lay

45 ၄၅ လေးဆယ်ငါး။
lay-seh-ngah

46 ၄၆ လေးဆယ်ခြောက်။
lay-seh-chyowk

47 ၄၇ လေးဆယ်ခုနှစ်။
lay-seh-koon-hnit

48 ၄၈ လေးဆယ်ရှစ်။
lay-seh-shitt

49 ၄၉ လေးဆယ်ကိုး။
lay-seh-koh

50 ၅၀ ငါးဆယ်။
ngah-seh

51 ၅၁ ငါးဆယ်တစ်။
ngah-seh-tit

52 ၅၂ ငါးဆယ်နှစ်။
ngah-seh-hnit

53 ၅၃ ငါးဆယ်သုံး။
ngah-seh-thohn

54 ၅၄ ငါးဆယ်လေး။
ngah-seh-lay

55 ၅၅ ငါးဆယ်ငါး။
ngah-seh-ngah

56 ၅၆ ငါးဆယ်ခြောက်။
ngah-seh-chyowk

57 ၅၇ ငါးဆယ်ခုနှစ်။
ngah-seh-koon-hnit

58 ၅၈ ငါးဆယ်ရှစ်။
ngah-seh-shitt

59 ၅၉ ငါးဆယ်ကိုး။
ngah-seh-koh

60 ၆၀ ခြောက်ဆယ်။
chyouk-seh

61 ၆၁ ခြောက်ဆယ်တစ်။
chyouk-seh-tit

62 ၆၂ ခြောက်ဆယ်နှစ်။
chyouk-seh-hnit

63 ၆၃ ခြောက်ဆယ်သုံး။
chyouk-seh-thohn

64 ၆၄ ခြောက်ဆယ်လေး။
chyouk-seh-lay

65 ၆၅ ခြောက်ဆယ်ငါး။
chyouk-seh-ngah

66 ၆၆ ခြောက်ဆယ်ခြောက်။
chyouk-seh-chyowk

67 ၆၇ ခြောက်ဆယ်ခုနှစ်။
chyouk-seh-koon-hnit

68 ၆၈ ခြောက်ဆယ်ရှစ်၊
chyouk-seh-shitt

69 ၆၉ ခြောက်ဆယ်ကိုး။
chyouk-seh-koh

70 ၇၀ ခုနှစ်ဆယ်။
koon-hnit-seh

71 ၇၁ ခုနှစ်ဆယ်တစ်။
koon-hn t-seh-tit

72 ၇၂ ခုနှစ်ဆယ်နှစ်။
koon-hnit-seh-hnit

73 ၇၃ ခုနှစ်ဆယ်သုံး။
koon-hnit-seh-thohn

74 ၇၄ ခုနှစ်ဆယ်လေး။
koon-hnit-seh-lay

75 ၇၅ ခုနှစ်ဆယ်ငါး။
koon-hnit-seh-ngah

76 ၇၆ ခုနှစ်ဆယ်ခြောက်။
koon-hnit-seh-chyowk

77 ၇၇ ခုနှစ်ဆယ်ခုနှစ်။
koon-hnit-seh-koon-hnit

78 ၇၈ ခုနှစ်ဆယ်ရှစ်။
koon-hnit-seh-shitt

79 ၇၉ ခုနှစ်ဆယ်ကိုး။
koon-hnit-seh-koh

80 ၈၀ ရှစ်ဆယ်။
shitt-seh

81 ၈၁ ရှစ်ဆယ်တစ်။
shitt-seh-tit

82 ၈၂ ရှစ်ဆယ်နှစ်။
shitt-seh-hnit

83 ၈၃ ရှစ်ဆယ်သုံး။
shitt-seh-thohn

84 ၈၄ ရှစ်ဆယ်လေး။
shitt-seh-lay

85 ၈၅ ရှစ်ဆယ်ငါး။
shitt-seh-ngah

86 ၈၆ ရှစ်ဆယ်ခြောက်။
shitt-seh chyowk

87 ၈၇ ရှစ်ဆယ်ခုနှစ်။
shitt-seh-koon-hnit

88 ၈၈ ရှစ်ဆယ်ရှစ်။
shitt-seh-shitt

89 ၈၉ ရှစ်ဆယ်ကိုး။
shit-seh-koh

90 ၉၀ ကိုးဆယ်။
koh-seh

91 ၉၁ ကိုးဆယ်တစ်။
koh seh-tit

92 ၉၂ ကိုးဆယ်နှစ်။
koh-seh-hnit

93 ၉၃ ကိုးဆယ်သုံး။
koh-seh-thohn

94 ၉၄ ကိုးဆယ်လေး။
koh-seh-lay

95 ၉၅ ကိုးဆယ်ငါး။
koh-seh-ngah

96 ၉၆ ကိုးဆယ်ခြောက်။
koh-seh-chyowk

97 ၉၇ ကိုးဆယ်ခုနှစ်။
koh-seh-koon-hnit

98 ၉၈ ကိုးဆယ်ရှစ်။
koh-seh-shitt

99 ၉၉ ကိုးဆယ်ကိုး။
koh-seh-koh

100 ၁၀၀ တရာ။
tă-yah

125 ၁၂၅ တရာနှစ်ဆယ်ငါး။
tă-yah-hnit-seh-ngah

150 ၁၅၀ တရာငါးဆယ်။
tă-yah-ngah-seh

175 ၁၇၅ တရာခုနှစ်ဆယ်ငါး။
tă-yah-koon-hnit-seh-ngah

200 ၂၀၀ နှစ်ရာ။
hnit-yah

250 ၂၅၀ နှစ်ရာငါးဆယ်။
hnit-yah-ngah-seh

275 ၂၇၅ နှစ်ရာခုနှစ်ဆယ်ငါး။
hnit-yah-koon-hnit-seh-ngah

300 ၃၀၀ သုံးရာ။
thohn-yah

350 ၃၅၀ သုံးရာငါးဆယ်။
thohn-yah-ngah-seh

400 ၄၀၀ လေးရာ။
lay-yah

1,000 ၁,၀၀၀ တထောင်။
t-towng

10,000 ၁၀,၀၀၀ တသောင်း။
t'thowng.

100,000 ၁၀၀,၀၀၀ တသိန်း။
t'thayn

1,000,000 ၁,၀၀၀,၀၀၀ တသန်း။
t'thun

10,000,000 ၁၀,၀၀၀,၀၀၀ တကုဋေ။
t'tkoo-day

Fractions.

¼ လေးပုံတပုံ။ or တစိတ်။
lay-pohn-t'bohn *or* t'zayt

½ တဝက်။
t'wet

¾ လေးပုံသုံးပုံ။
lay-pohn-thohn-bohn

1 ၁ တစ်။
tit

SCHEME OF LETTERS.

SCHEME OF LETTERS

ADOPTED IN THE ROMANIZED HINDUSTANI WORDS OF THE FOLLOWING VOCABULARY.

---

a, a—as in arm, balm, calm.
e, e—as in bey, dey, obey.
ee, ee—as in eel, bee, see, lee, feel, keel, reel, seem.
i, i—as in din, fin, sin.
o, o—as in lo, lobe, lore, so.
oo, oo—as in ooze, fool, tool.
oo, oo—as in foot, good, hood.
u, u—as in but, cut, hut, fun, pun.
ou, ou—as in our, sour.
ch, ch—as in choose, chop, church, rich.
chh, chh—with aspirate.
d, d—soft dental, nearly as in dew, and formed by placing the tongue against the upper front teeth.
g, g—as the english hard g in gob, gone, got, jugular.
gh, gh—with aspirate.
gh, gh—guttural, like the Northumbrian r, *or* the sound made in gargling.
kh, kh—with aspirate.
k, k—a deep liquid lingual, as in the peculiar and common cry of the raven; and articulated by raising the root of the tongue towards the throat.
kh, kh—a peculiar guttural sound, as in the scotch word loch.
n—nasal, as in the french words bon, sans.
ph, ph—with aspirate.
r—harsh palatial, formed by placing the tongue against the palate, and then striking it against the lower teeth.
s, s—with the hissing sound of s in seen sun.
sh, sh—as in shin, ship, rush.
t, t—soft dental, pronounced by placing the tongue slightly between the upper front teeth.
th, th—the aspirate of the above.
th, th—with aspirate.
y, y—as in yawn, yoke, your, my. type, tyro.
z, z—as in azure, *or* as s in pleasure.

The remaining Letters retain their ordinary sounds.

PREFIXES AND AFFIXES.

WITH EXAMPLES OF THEIR APPLICATION IN THE KEY WHICH FOLLOWS IN THE NEXT PAGE.

All-, -bhur.
Dis-. be- bud-, la-, na-, u'.
Castle of—, -gurh.
City of—, -a'bad, -nug'ur, -poor.
Country of—, -a'bad, -is'tan, -stan.
Deed of—, -na'mu.
Double-, do-.
Evil-, bud-.
Fort of—, -gurh.
Flower-, gool-.
Garden of—, -is'tan, -stan.
Heart-, dil-.
Il-, khil'af-, un-.
Ill-, bud-,
Im-, be-, bud-, ghyr-, khil'af-, la-, na-, u', un-.
In-, be-, bud-, ghyr-, la-, na-, nir-, u'.
Inhabitant of—, -wal.
Ir-, be-, bud-, na-.
Letter-, na'mu-.
Low-, bud-, kum-.
Mis-, be-.
Native of—, -wal.
Power of—, -na'mu.
Reader of—, khwan-.
Rose-, gool-.
Town of—, -a'bad, -nug'ur, -poor.
Two-, do-.
Un, un-, be-, bud-, kum-, khil'af-, la-, na-, nir-.

-ant, -dan.
-ate, -mund.
-bazaar, -ba'zar.
-bearer, -bur'dar, -dar.
-binder, -bund.
-borough, -burgh, } v. City, Ttown.
-box, -dan.
-carrier, -bur'dar.
-case, -dan.
-dealer, -ha'ra.
-deed, -na'mu.
-doer, -kar.
-ed, -wunt, -wur.
-er, -ban, -gar, -gur, -saz, -wan, -wal.
-fighter, -baz.
-ful, -bhur, -ka, -man, -mund, -saz, -wunt.
-holder, -dan, -dar.
-grain-market town *or* village, -gunj.
-hood, -pun.
-house, -kha'nu, -ghur.
-heart, -dil.
-keeper, -ban, -dar, -wan.
-land, -is'tan, stan.
-less, be-, kum-, la-, na-, nir, u'.
-maid, -we'lee.
-maker, -bund, -saz.
-man, -ban, 'ee, ha'ra, -kar, wa'la, -wan.
-master, -wa'la.
mart, *or* -market, } -ba'zar.—*v.* grain-market
-ness, 'ee, -gee, -pun.
-or, -dar,
-office, kha'nu.
-place, -kha'nu.
-player, -baz.
-room, -kha'nu.
-seller, -ha'ra.
-ship, -pun.
-shop, kha'nu.
-smith, -gur, -kar.
-stand, -dan.
-speaker, -go.
-teller, khwan.
-worker, -gur,
y (final) 'a, -man, -mund, -wur.

KEY, ILLUSTRATING THE APPLICATION OF THE FOREGOING.

be- (without.) Im-, In-, Ir-, Mis-, Un-; -less; as be-subr, *a.* Impatient. be-sub'ree, *s.* Im-patience. —be-it'i'kad, *a.* In-credulous.—be-iti'kad'ee, *f.* In-credulity.—Be-ee'man, *a.* Im-pious, Ir-religious. —be-nus'eeb'ee, *f.* Mis-fortune.—be-muk'door, *a.* Un-able. be-a'-ram, *a.* Un-easy, Rest-less.—be-fikr, *a.* Thought-less.

bud- (*a.* bad, evil, vicious, wicked.) Dis-, Evil-, Ill-, Im-, In-, Ir-, Low-, Un-; as bud-li'haz, *a.* Dis-, respectful.—bud-un'desh, *a.* Evil-minded.—bud-soo'rut. *a.* Ill-favoured.—bud-kes, *a.* Im-pious, Irreligious.—bud-nam, *a.* Infamous; bud-nam'ee, In-famy.—bud-usl, *a.* Low-born.—bud-bukht, *a.* Unfortunate, Un-lucky.

dil-, -dil, } Heart-, -heart, } as dil-a'ram, *a.* Heart-easing; dil-a'zar, *a.* Heart-tormenting. (*s. m. f.* Sweet-heart.)—sung-dil, *a.* Stone- (*or* hard-) hearted. mom-dil, *a.* Wax- (*or* tender-) hearted.

do-, *a.* Two-, Double-; as do-pa'-yuh, *a.* Two-legged; do-chund, *a.* Two-fold.—do-a'tush'u, *a.* double-distilled, (from a'tush, Fire.) do-ta'ra, *a.* Double-threaded.

ghyr- (*a.* other, another, different, foreign.—*adv.* besides, without, except, different from, reverse of.) Im-; In-; as ghyr-moom'kin, *a.* Im-possible. ghyr-su'heeh, Incorrect.

gool-, Flower-, Rose-; as gool-cheen, Flower-gather-er.—gool-rung, *a.* Rose-coloured

khil'af-(opposition, contrariety, contradiction;—*a.* reverse, false.) Il-, Im-, Un-; as khil'af-shur'u, *a.* Illegal, Un-just.—khil'af-ki'yas, *a.* Im-probable.—khil'af-ukl, *a.* Unreasonable.

kum- (deficiency,—*a.* deficient, wanting, few, less, little, rare, seldom.) Un-, -less; as kum-hou'sil'u, *a.* Un-ambitious. kum-nus'eeb, *a.* Un-fortunate. kum-ukl, *a.* Senseless.

la- (no, not, without.) Dis-, Im-, In-, Un-, -less; as la-ghur'uz, *a.* Disinterested.—la-zu'wal, *a.* Im-perishable.—la-hul, *a.* In-dissoluble. —la-ha'sil, *a.* Un-productive, Profit-less.—la-char, *a.* Help-less.

na- (no, not.) Dis-, Im-, In-, Ir-, Un-. -less; as na-khoosh, *a.* Displeased.—na-dee'dun'ee, *a.* Imperceptible, In-visible.—na-hum'-war, *a.* Ir-regular, Un-even.—na-huk. *a.* Il-legal, Im-proper, Un-just.—na-oom'med, *a.* Hopeless.

nir- (out, without, on the outside; without, not having.) Un-, -less; as nir-mul, *a.* Un-sullied.—nir-as, *a.* Hope-less.

u'-(an inseparable particle of negation, privation, *or* diminution.) Dis-, Im-, In-. -less; as u'lug, *a.* Dis-joined, Dis-connected.—u'-mur, *a.* Im-mortal.—u'mit, Indelible.—u'par, *a.* Shore-less, u'-chook, *a.* Fault-less.

un- Un-, It-, Im-; as un-dho'a, *a.* Un-washed. un-pur'ha, *a.* Unlearned, Il-literate.—un-ho'na, *a.* Im-possible.

'a. the final y, as myl'a, *a.* Filth-y, from myl, Filth. bhookh'a *a.* Hungr-y, from Bhookh, Hunger.

-a'bad, (*a.* cultivated, inhabited, populated.) City of—Town of—as il'ah-a'bad, the City of GOD. uz'-eem-a'bad, the Town of Uzeem; i. e. Prince Uzeem, its founder.

-bhur, (*a.* full, as much as, as far as, up to, whole, all, bulk, size, every, each, as,) All-, -ful; as rat-bhur, All-night,—chum'chu-bhur, Spoon-ful.

-ban, (affix in compos. guardian.) —Keeper, -man, -er; as dur-ban, Door-keeper, sug-ban, Dog-keeper.—pasban, Watch-man.—bagh-ban, Garden-er.

-baz, -player, -fighter; as shut'runj-baz, Chess-player. moorgh-baz, Cock-fighter.

-bund, -binder, -maker; as dus'tar-bund, Turband-binder (*or* maker.) ny'chu-bund, hook'ku-snake mak-er.

-bur'dar, -carrier, -bearer; as ni'-shan- (*or* ul'um-) bur'dar, Stand-ard-bearer.

-dan, -case, -holder, -cellar; as kul'-um-dan, Pen-case *or* holder.—num'uk-dan, Salt-cellar.— -ant, as his'ab-dan, Account-ant.

-dar, (possessor, lord, master,) -bear-er, -holder, -keeper; as chob-dar. Mace-bearer,—his'su-dar, Share-holder. zum'een-dar, Land-holder. —doo'kan-dar, Shop-keeper. ab-dar, Water-keeper.

-dil. *v.* Heart-.

'ee, -ness, -man; as bhul'a'ee, khoob'-ee, Good-ness, from bhul'a, khoob, *a.* Good.—sip'ah'ee, lush'kur'ee, Army-man (Soldier) from sip'-ah, lush'kur, Army.

-gar, (doer) -er; as tul'ub-gar, Search-er; goon'ah-gar, Sinn-er; from tul'ub, Search; goon'ah, Sin.

'gee, -ness; as ta'zu-gee, Fresh-ness; gun'du'gee, Fetidness; from ta'zu, *a.* Fresh; gun'du, *a.* Fetid.

-go, speaker; as dur'ogh-go, a speaker of lies, a Liar; rast-go, a speaker of truth; from durogh, Lie; rast, *a.* True.

-gunj, (a granary, heap, treasure,) grain-market town *or* village, as ba'kur-gunj, from ba'kur the name of its probable founder.

-gur, (maker, workman,) -er, -smith; as ruf'oo-gur, Darn-er, from ruf'oo, Darn; se'kul-gur, Polish-er, from se'kul, Polish.—zur-gur, Gold-smith.

-gurh, Castle of—Fort of—as fut'ih-gurh (Futtyghur.)

-ha'ra, (doer, dealer,) -man, -seller, -er; as luk'ur-ha'ra, Wood-man, *or* Wood-seller, from lu'kur, Wood.

-is'tan, *or* -stan, (place, station,) Country of—Garden of—as uf-ghan-i'stan, the Country of the Afghans. hin'doo-stan, the Country of the Hindoos.—bo-stan, the Garden of Fragrance.

-ka, (post-pos. of belonging to,) -ful, as kam'ka, *a.* Use-ful.

-kar, (business, profession, labour, work,)-doer, -man, -smith; as bud-kar, Evil-doer,—pesh-kar, Fore-man —sa'du-kar, Silver-smith. (lit. white-smith.)

-kha'nu, -place, -house, -room, -office, -shop; as a'tush-kha'nu, Fire-place.—feel-kha'nu. Elephant-house.—ba'wur'chee-kha'nu, Cook-room.

-khwan, (repeater,) -teller, Reader of—as kis'sa-khwan, Story-teller; —kit'ab-khwan, Reader of the Kooran. misl-khwan, Reader of the papers of cases before a judge.

-man, -ful, -y; as goon-man, *a.* Skilful. bhag-man, Lucky.

-mund, endowed with, having; as ukl-mund, *a.* Sensible; from ukl, Sense. dou'lut-mund, *a.* Rich, Wealthy; from dou'lut, Rich.

-na'mu, letter, deed, warrant, power; as na'mu-bur, Letter bearer. ra'-zee-na'mu, Deed of assent. moo-kht'ar-na'mu, Power of attorney.

-nug'ur, City of—Town of—as chun'dun-nug'ur, the City *or* town of chun'dun (the moon)—krishn-nug'ur, the City *or* town of krishn.

-poor, City *or* town of—as lukh'ee-poor, the City *or* town of lukh'ee. gha'zee-poor, the City of gha'zee, (the Conqueror.)

-pun, pun'a, -hood, -ness, -ship; as lur'ka-pun, Child-hood. boor'a-pun, Bad-ness.

-stan, *or* -sthan, *v.* -istan.

-saz, -maker, -er, -ful; as ghur'ee-saz, Clock- (*or* watch-) maker.—rung-saz, Paint-er.—hee'lu-saz, *a.* Deceit-ful.

-wal, *or* wa'la, (agent, keeper,) -man, -master, -maker, -er, in-

habitant of—as na'o-wa'la, Boatman,—ghur-wa'la, House-master. -eent-wa'la, Brick-maker.—koth'-ee-wal, Bank-er.—deh lee-wal, (*or* -wa'la) Inhabitant of deh'lee.
-wan, (possessed of—possessor, keeper,) -man, -er; as gar'ee-wan, Coach-man, Cart-er.—dhun-wan, *a.* Rich, from dhun, Riches.
-wunt, -ful, -ed; as bul-wunt, *a.* Power-ful.jus-wunt,*a.* Renown-ed.
-wur, -ed, -y; as nam-wur, *a.* Renown-ed, nus'eeb-wur, *a.* Luck-y.

☞ FOR SCHEME OF LETTERS, vide page ii.

ABBREVIATIONS.

f. .... *feminine.*
h. .... *hindu.*
m. .... *moohummudun.*
arab.......... *arabic.*
ben. .... *bengalee.*
duk. .... *dukkunee.*
hin. .... *hindee.*
pers. .... *persian.*
cor. .... *corruption.*
met. .... *metaphorically.*

Of Hindustani Verbs.

d.—de'na (*v. a.* to give, bestow, impart, grant, yield).

h.—ho'na (*v. n.*, to be, exist, become, belong, have, serve, suit, answer, come, do, stand, die).

j.—ja'na, (*v. n.* to go, move, pass, reach, be, continue).

k.—kur'na (*v. a.* to do, act, practise, achieve, execute, transact, perform, make, effect, avail, set, thrust, use).

l.—le'na (*v. a.* to take, accept, obtain, procure, get, hold, pick, receive, win, buy).

r.—rukh'na (*v. a.* to keep, place, have, hold, lay, set, station, leave, own, stop, reserve).

In instances where verbs differ from their nouns or adjectives in the simple addition of the terminations de'na, ho'na, &c. the verb is expressed, by abbreviation, thus—

Absent, *a.* ghyr-ha'zir.—*v. n.* g-h. (i. e. ghyr-ha'zir-ho'na).

Abuse, ga'lee.—*v. a.* g-d. (i. e. ga'lee-de'na).

Aid, dust'gee'ree, mud'ud.—*v. a.* d-k. m-k. (i. e. dust'geer'ee-kurna, mud'ud-kur'na).

Hindustani *feminine* nouns (with the exceptions too obvious to be mistaken, as girl, woman, &c.) are distinguished by the letter *f.*—the rest are *masculine.*

THE DAYS OF THE WEEK—huf'tuh ka din.

Sunday, itw'ar, et'war, rub'i'bar.
Monday, peer, som-bar.
Tuesday, mun'gul, bhoum-bar.
Wednesday, boodh, boodh-bar.
Thursday, joo'mu-rat, *f.* bri'hus'put'i-bar, goo'roo-bar.
Friday, joo'mu, sookr-bar.
Saturday, sun'ee'chur, shum'bu.

☞ The English MONTHS have no hindustani names.

NUMERALS—hin'dus'u.

1 One, ek
2 Two, do
3 Three, teen
4 Four, char
5 Five, panch
6 Six, chhu, *or* chhe
7 Seven, sat
8 Eeight, ath
9 Nine, nou
10 Ten, dus
11 Eleven, ig'a'ruh
12 Twelve, ba'ruh
13 Thirteen, te'ruh
14 Fourteen, chou'duh
15 Fifteen, pund'ruh
16 Sixteen, so'luh
17 Seventeen, sut'ruh
18 Eighteen, ut'ha'ruh
19 Nineteen, oon'ees
20 Twenty, bees. (Score, ko'ree.)
21 Twenty-one, ik'ees
22 Twenty-two, ba'ees
23 Twenty-three, te'ees
24 Twenty-four, chou'bees
25 Twenty-five, puch'ees
26 Twenty-six, chhub'ees
27 Twenty-seven, sut'a'ees
28 Twenty-eight, ut'ha'ees
29 Twenty-nine, oon'tees
30 Thirty, tees
31 Thirty-one, ik'tees
32 Thirty-two, but'tees
33 Thirty-three, ten'tees
34 Thirty-four, choun'tees
35 Thirty-five, pyn'tees
36 Thirty-six, chhut'ees
37 Thirty-seven, syn'tees
38 Thirty-eight, uth'tees
39 Thirty-nine, oon'ta-lees
40 Forty, cha'lees
41 Forty-one, ik'ta'lees
42 Forty-two, be'a'lees
43 Forty-three, ten'ta'lees
44 Forty-four, chou'a'lees, chou'-ta'lees
45 Forty-five, pyn'ta'lees
46 Forty-six, chhe'a'lees
47 Forty-seven, syn'ta'lees
48 Forty-eight, uth'ta'lees
49 Forty-nine, oon'chas
50 Fifty, pu'chas
51 Fifty-one, ik'a'wun
52 Fifty-two, ba'wun
53 Fifty-three, tir'pun
54 Fity-four, chou'wun
55 Fifty-five, puch'pun
56 Fifty-six, chhup'pun
57 Fifty-seven, sut'a'wun
58 Fifty-eight, ut'ha'wun
59 Fifty-nine, oon'suth
60 Sixty, sath
61 Sixty-one, ik'suth
62 Sixty-two, ba'suth
63 Sixty-three, tir'suth
64 Sixty-four, chou'suth
65 Sixty-five, pyn'suth
66 Sixty-six, chhe'a'suth
67 Sixty-seven, sut'suth
68 Sixty-eight, uth'suth, urh'suth
69 Sixty-nine, oon'hut'tur
70 Seventy, sut'tur
71 Seventy-one, ik'hut'tur
72 Seventy-two, bu'hut'tur
73 Seventy-three, ti'hut'tur
74 Seventy-four, chou'hut'tur
75 Seventy-five, puch'hut'tur

76 Seventy-six. chhu'hut'tur
77 Seventy-seven, sut'hut'tur
78 Seventy-eight, uth'hut'tur
79 Seventy-nine, ooná'see
80 Eighty, us'see
81 Eighty-one, iká'see
82 Eighty-two, be'ásee
83 Eighty-three, tirá'see
84 Eighty-four, chou'rásee.
85 Eighty-five, puch'ásee
86 Eighty-six, chhe'ásee
87 Eighty-seven, sut'ásee
88 Eighty-eight, ut'hásee
89 Eighty-nine, nuw'ásee
90 Ninety, nuw'we
91 Ninety-one, ik'an'we
92 Ninety-two, ban'u'we
93 Ninety-three, tir'an'we
94 Ninety-four, chour'an'we
95 Ninety-five, puch'an'we
96 Ninety-six, chhe'an'we
97 Ninety-seven, sut'an'we
98 Ninety-eight, uth'an'we
99 Ninety-nine, nin'an'we

100 One Hundred, sou
125 One hundred and twenty-five, ek sou puch'ees (*or* suw'a sou)
150 One hundred and fifty, ek sou pu'chas (*or* derh sou)
175 One hundred and seventy-five, ek sou puch'hut'tur (*or* poúne do sou)
200 Two hundred, do sou
250 Two hundred and fifty, do sou pu'chas (*or* ur'háeesou)
275 Two hundred and seventy-five, do sou puch'hut'tur (*or* poúne teen sou)
300 Three hundred, teen sou
350 Three hundred and fifty, teen sou pu'chas (*or* sar'he teen sou)
400 Four hundred, char sou
1,000 One Thousand, huz'ar
100,000 One hundred thousand, lakh.
10,000,000 Ten million, kur' *or* (Crore)
1,000,000,000,000 Billion, khurb

Ordinals—Ud'úd-i-wus'fee.

First, puh'la. puh'lee *f.*
Second, doos'ra. doos'ree *f.*
Third, tees'ra. tees'ree *f.*
Fourth, choútha. choúthee *f.*
Fifth, panch'wan. p-ween *f.*
Sixth, chhut'ha. chhut'hee *f.*
Seventh, sat'wan. sat'ween *f.*
Eighth, ath'wan. a-ween *f.*

And so on, adding the final syllable "wan," *or* "ween," according to the gender of the noun which it may qualify.

Fractions and Mixed Numbers.

Quarter, pa'o.
Fourth part, chouth, chout'ha. chout'ha'ee *f.*
Half. adh. ad'ha *f.*
Quarter less (than one of any given number), poun, pou'ne.
Quarter more (than one of any given number), suw'a.
One and a half, derh.
Two and a half, ur'ha'ee.
Half more, (than one of any given number), sar'he.

SCHEME OF LETTERS

ADOPTED IN THE ROMANIZED TAMIL WORDS OF THE FOLLOWING VOCABULARY.

—:o:—

Vowels.

a as in delta.
á as in father.
i as in pin.
í as in pique.
u as oo in good.
ú as oo in food.
e as in mendicant.
é as in grey.
ai as in aisle.
o as in police.
ó as in story.
au as ou in foul.

Consonants.

k as in king.
ṅ as ng in angle.
ch as in church.
ñ as ni in onion.
ḍ as in drum.
ṇ a hard cerebral n.
t as t in Italian.
n as in fancy.
p as in pardon.
m as in demand.
y as in yellow.
r as in burial.
l as in manly.
v as in marvel.
ḻ a mixture of r,l and the French j.
ḷ as in glove.
ṛ as in crack.
n as in fancy.

Sanskrit Letters, &c.

sh as in shake.
s as in sin.
h as in hunger.
ḥ called aitha.

NOTES ON THE ALPHABET.

1. i when followed by ḍ ṇ ṛ ḻ ḷ is sounded something like u. The character of these consonants modifies the sound of the vowel i.

2. í before ḍ ṇ ṛ ḻ ḷ is sounded like the German úh—as víḍu.

3. é before ḍ ṇ ṛ ḻ ḷ sounds like the German oé in Goethe—as méḍu pronounced moédu.

4. k as an initial and when doubled is sounded as k; but when medial in Tamil words it is pronounced like g—as kágam, pakkam.

5. ch,—the power of this letter representing, as it does, several letters in words of Sanskrit origin as well as Tamil words, is sometimes ch, j and s—as chinna, janam, másam. Use will however soon overcome the difficulties incident to the different sounds of this consonant.

6. t is like t in Italian when initial and when doubled—as tan, katti; and when it is medial and final it has the sound of th—as káthu, puthu.

7. p when preceded by m, or n is sounded very much like b—as pámbu, anbu.

8. ṭch—as máṭchimai.

ñj—as pañju.

ṭṭ is similar to the cerebral ṭ—as in trump—as paṭṭaṇam.

ṛ when mute before a consonant, has the sound of the cerebral ṭ—as kaṛpanai; Double ṛṛ is similar in sound to tt in pattern—as paṛṛi; when ṛ is preceded by n it has very nearly its natural power—as kanṛu, panṛi.

N. B. In pronouncing words in which a consonant is doubled great care must be taken to sound both letters, one of course as a mute. Two or three words are given for the purpose of impressing this caution on the mind of the beginner—as palli, illai, kiḷḷai. If care be not taken to pronounce the first syllable clearly the above words might be mistaken for pali, ilai and kiḷai.

The Days of the Week.

Sunday, ñáyiṛṛukkiḻamai.
Monday, tiṅgaḍkiḻamai.
Tuesday, chevváykkiḻamai.
Wednesday, puthankiḻamai.
Thursday, viyáḻakkiḻamai.
Friday, veḷḷikkiḻamai.
Saturday, sanikkiḻamai.

☞ The English Months have no Tamil names.

Numerals.

1 One, onṛu
2 Two, iraṇḍu
3 Three, múnṛu
4 Four, nálu
5 Five, ainthu
6 Six, áṛu
7 Seven, éḻu
8 Eight, eṭṭu
9 Nine, onbathu
10 Ten, pattu
11 Eleven, pathinonṛu
12 Twelve, panniraṇḍu
13 Thirteen, pathimúnṛu
14 Fourteen, pathinálu
15 Fifteen, pathinainthu
16 Sixteen, pathináṛu
17 Seventeen, pathinéḻu
18 Eighteen, pathineṭṭu
19 Nineteen, pattonbathu
20 Twenty, irubathu
21 Twenty-one, irubattonṛu
22 Twenty-two, irubattiraṇḍu
23 Twenty-three, irubattimúnṛu
24 Twenty-four, irubattinálu
25 Twenty-five, irubattainthu
26 Twenty-six, irubattáṛu
27 Twenty-seven, irubattéḻu
28 Twenty-eight, irubatteṭṭu
29 Twenty-nine, irubattonbathu
30 Thirty, muppathu
31 Thirty-one, muppattonṛu
32 Thirty-two, muppattiraṇḍu
33 Thirty-three, muppattimúnṛu
34 Thirty-four, muppattinálu
35 Thirty-five, muppattainthu
36 Thirty-six, muppattáṛu
37 Thirty-seven, muppattéḻu
38 Thirty-eight, muppatteṭṭu
39 Thirty-nine, muppattonbathu
40 Forty, náṛpathu
41 Forty-one, náṛpattonṛu
42 Forty-two, náṛpattiraṇḍu

43 Forty-three, náṟpattimúṇṟu
44 Forty-four, náṟpattinálu
45 Forty-five, náṟpattainthu
46 Forty-six, náṟpattáṟu
47 Forty-seven, náṟpattéḷu
48 Forty-eight, náṟpatteṭṭu
49 Forty-nine, náṟpattonbathu
50 Fifty, aimpathu
51 Fifty-one, aimpattoṇṟu
52 Fifty-two, aimpattiraṇḍu
53 Fifty-three, aimpattimúṇṟu
54 Fifty-four, aimbattinálu
55 Fifty-five, aimpattainthu
56 Fifty-six, aimpattáṟu
57 Fifty-seven, aimpattéḷu
58 Fifty-eight, aimpatteṭṭu
59 Fifty-nine, aimpattonbathu
60 Sixty, aṟupathu
61 Sixty-one, aṟupattoṇṟu
62 Sixty-two, aṟupattiraṇḍu
63 Sixty-three, aṟupattimúṇṟu
64 Sixty-four, aṟupattinálu
65 Sixty-five, aṟupattainthu
66 Sixty-six, aṟupattáṟu
67 Sixty-seven, aṟupattéḷu
68 Sixty-eight, aṟupatteṭṭu
69 Sixty-nine, aṟupattonbathu
70 Seventy, eḷupathu
71 Seventy-one, eḷupattoṇṟu
72 Seventy-two, eḷupattiraṇḍu
73 Seventy-three, eḷupattimúṇṟu
74 Seventy-four, eḷupattinálu
75 Seventy-five, eḷupattainthu
76 Seventy-six, eḷupattáṟu
77 Seventy-seven, eḷupattéḷu
78 Seventy-eight, eḷupatteṭṭu
79 Seventy-nine, eḷupattonbathu
80 Eighty, eṇpathu
81 Eighty-one, eṇpattoṇṟu
82 Eighty-two, eṇpattiraṇḍu
83 Eighty-three, eṇpattimúṇṟu
84 Eighty-four, eṇpattinálu
85 Eighty-five, eṇpattainthu
86 Eighty-six, eṇpattáṟu
87 Eighty-seven, eṇpattéḷu
88 Eighty-eight, eṇpatteṭṭu
89 Eighty-nine, eṇpattonbathu
90 Ninety, toṇṇúṟu
91 Ninety-one, toṇṇúṟṟoṇṟu
92 Ninety-two, toṇṇúṟṟiraṇḍu
93 Ninety-three, toṇṇúṟṟimúṇṟu
94 Ninety-four, toṇṇúṟṟinálu
95 Ninety-five, toṇṇúṟṟainthu
96 Ninety-six, toṇṇúṟṟáṟu
97 Ninety-seven, toṇṇúṟṟéḷu
98 Ninety-eight, toṇṇúṟṟeṭṭu
99 Ninety-nine, toṇṇúṟṟonbathu
100 One Hundred, núṟu
125 One hundred and twenty-five, núṟ-ṟirupattainthu
150 One hundred and fifty, núṟ-ṟaimbathu
175 One hundred and seventy-five, núṟ-ṟeḷupattainthu
200 Two hundred, irunúṟu
225 Two hundred and twenty five, irunúṟ-ṟirupattainthu
250 Two hundred and fifty, irunúṟ-ṟaimbathu
275 Two hundred and seventy-five, irunúṟ-ṟeḷubattainthu
300 Three hundred, munnúṟu
350 Three hundred and fifty, munnúṟ-ṟaimbathu
400 Four hundred, nánúṟu
1,000 One Thousand, áyiram
100,000 One hundred thousand, iladcham *or* laḍcham
10,000,000 Ten million, kóḍi
1,000,000,000,000 Billion, laḍcha-kóḍi *or* núṟáyirakóḍi

ORDINALS.

First, muthalávathu.
Second, iraṇḍávathu.
Third, múṇṟávathu.
Fourth, nálávathu.
Fifth, ainthávathu.
Sixth, áṟávathu.
Seventh, éḷávathu.
Eighth, eṭṭávathu.

And so on, adding the word ávathu to every number.

FRACTIONS.

¼ Quarter, kál.	¾ Three-fourth, mukkál.
½ Half, arai.	1· One onṛu.

English, Burmese, Hindustani & Tamil
VOCABULARY
IN
English Characters.

English.	Burmese.		Hindustani.	Tamil.
A is the first letter of the alphabet. It is the indefinite article, set before nouns of the singular number, as *a man;* before words beginning with a vowel, and *h* mute, it is written *an;* as *an ox, an honor*	တခု။တစ်။တဆိုတခု။ (*a*)	t'koo, tit, t'sóhn-t'koo, (*a*)	ek	oru, onṛu, ór.
	တယောက်။ (*a man*)	t'yowk', (*a man*)	ek jun'a (*or*) ma'noos	oru manithan, *or* manushaṇ.
	တခု။ (*an*)	t'koo, (*an*)	ek	onṛu, oru, ór.
	တကောင်။ (*an ox*)	t'gowng, (*an ox*)	ek byl (*or*) go'roo	oru eruthu.
Aback', *adv.*	နောက်သို့။	nowk-tho	peech'he, peech'hul	pinnáy, pinnaṇiyattil.
Ab'acus, *s.*	တွက်ရန်သင်ပုံး။	twet-yun-thing-bóhn	ilm-i-his'abka nuk'shu	oru kaṇithak-karuvi.
Abaft', *adv.*	ပဲ့ဆီးမှာ။ပဲ့ဆီသို့	peh-see-hmah	peech'hul, peech'he	pinnaṇiyattil, abarattil.
Aban'don, *v. a.*	စွန့်သည်။ပြစ်ထားသည်။	soon-the, pyit-tah-the	chhor-na, ty'ag'na	vilakku, viṭṭuviḍu.
Abásement, *s.*	နှိမ့်ချချင်း။	hnain-chyah-gying	khif'fut, *f.* dub'ao	tál̲ttal, tál̲vaḍaithal, il̲ivu.
Abáte, *v. a.*	လျော့သည်။	shyaw-the	ghut'a'na, ghut'ee	kuṛai, taṇi, oḍuṅgu.
Ab'bey, *s.*	ကျောင်း။	kyoung	da'i'ru, ra'hibka-gir'ja-ghur.	sanniyási-maḍam.
Ab'bot, *s.*	ကျောင်းနေပုဂ္ဂိုလ်။	kyoung-nay-pohk-goh	ra'hib-girja-ghurka surdar.	maḍa-talaivan

English.	Burmese.		Hindustani.	Tamil.
Abbréviate, *v. a.*	တိုစေသည်။အကျဉ်းချုပ်သည်။	toh-say-the	ikh'ti'sar-k, mookh'tus'ur-k.	su-ru-kku, ku-ṛu-kku.
Abdicátion, *s.*	အရာကိုစွန့်ပြစ်ချင်း။	a-yah-go-soon-pyit-chying.	ty'ag, tus'leem, *f.*	rásínámá, amaivu.
Abdómen, *s.*	ဝမ်း။	woon	pe'roo	aḍi-vayiṛu, kíḻ-vayiṛu.
Abed', *adv.*	အိပ်ရာပေါ်မှာ။	ayt-yah-baw-hmah	pul'ung-pur	sayanattil, paḍukkaiyil.
Abet', *v. a.*	အားပေးသည်။	ah-pay-the	mud'ud-k, him'áyut-k	uthavu, túṇḍu, évu.
Abey'ance, *s.*	အခွင့်မရှိသေး။	a-kwing-m'shee-thay	in'tiz'ar, oom'med, *f.*	nambikkai, niṛaivéṛámai.
Abhor', *v. a.*	ရွံသည်။မုန်းသည်။	yoon-the, mohn-the	nuf'rut-k	veṛu, aruvaru, arósi.
Abíde, *v. a.*	နေသည်။စောင့်နေသည်။	nay-the, sowng-nay-the	suh'na, pur'wur'ish	táṅgu, sagi, poṛu.
Abil'ity, *s.*	အစွမ်းသတ္တိ။ဉာဏ်သတ္တိ။	a-swon-thattee, nyan-thattee	dust-rus, li'ya'kut, *f.*	sakti, sámártiyam.
Ab'ject, *a.*	ယုတ်ညံ့သော။	yoot-nyan-thaw	fur'o'ma'yu, ku'mee'nu	nícha, ína, táḻvána.
A'ble, *a.*	တတ်နိုင်သော။	tut-hnuyng-thau	ka'bil, suk'na	vallamai-yuḷḷa,
Ablútion, *s.*	ရေနှင့်ဆေးကြောခြင်း။	yay-hning-say-kyau-gying.	ghoosl, nu'han	snánam, níráṭṭu.
Aboard', *adv.*	သင်္ဘောပေါ်မှာ။	thing-baw-baw-hma	kish'tee-pur	tóniyil, kappal-mél.
Abóde, *s.*	နေချင်။နေရာ။	nay-chyin, nay-yah	muk'an, muk'am	víḍu, vásam.
Abol'ish, *v. a.*	ဖျက်ဆီးသည်။ဖျက်သည်။	pyet-tsee-the, pyet-the	oot'ha-d, mou'koof'k	taḷḷu, níkku, vilakku, aḻi.
Abound', *v. n.*	ပေါများသည်။	paw-myah-thee	bhur'na	migu, mali, tiraḷáyiru.
Abrásion, *s.*	ပွန်းသည်။	poon-thee	ghis'a'o, ghis'a'wut	téytu-viḍugiṛathu.
Abrid'ge, *v. a.*	အကျဉ်းချုပ်သည်။	a-chyin-chyoht-the	ikh'ti'sar-k, mookh'tus'ur-k.	su-ru-kku, ku-ṛu-kku.
Abroad', *adv.*	တချားနိုင်ငံမှာ။	t'chyah-nuyng-ngan-hmah.	ba'hur, pur'des	pradésattil, veḷiyé.
Ab'scess, *s.*	အိုင်နား။	uyng-nah	doom'bul, doom'mul, pho'ra.	silanti, oḍukkuṭṭi.
Ab'sence, *s.*	မရှိချင်း။	m'shee-chyin	ghyr-ha'zir'ee	kúḍayiṛámai, illá-mai.
Ab'sent, *a.*	မရှိ။ (in mind) သတိမရှိ။	m'shee, tha-tee-m'shee	ghyr-ha'zir	illátha, vaṛátha.
Absol've, *v. a.*	အပြစ်လွှတ်သည်။ ဝန်ကင်းစေသည်	apyit-hloot-thee, woon-kin-say-the	moo'bur'ra-k	manni, viḍuthalaiyákku.
Abstáin, *v. n.*	ရှောင်သည်။	shyoung-the	pur'hez-k	vilakku, viḍu, tavir.
Ab'stract, *s.*	နှုတ်ထွက်၍ပေါင်းချုပ်သောစာ။	hnoht-twet-yue-hpoung-chyoht-thaw-tsah	ikh'ti'sar, khoo'la'sa	chu-ru-kkam, aḍakkam.

Abstrúse, *a.* ...	ခက်ခဲနက်သော။ ...	ket-keh-net-thau ...	duk'eek, chhip'a, moosh'kil.	marai-porulána.
Absurd', *a.* ...	မိုက်သော။ ...	muyk-thau ..	be'hoo'du, moo'tu'ghy'yir ...	yuttikku-viróthamána.
Abun'dance, *s.* ...	ပေါများသော။များပြားသော။	pau-myah-thaw, myah-byah-thau ...	fur'a'khee, bu'hoo'tat, if'rat..	tiral, miguthi.
Abúse, *s.* ...	ဆဲရေးချင်း။ ...	tseh-yeh-chyin ...	khur'ab'eekam ...	keduthi, palu-thákku.
Abúse, *v. a.* ...	မကောင်းအောင်သုံးဆောင်သည်	tseh-the, mkoung-oung-thohn-sowng-the ...	ga'lee, bud-zub'an'ee ...	ninthanai, dú-shanai.
Abut', *v. a.* ...	အခြားကိုထိအောင်။အစွန်းထွက်သည်။ ...	a-chyah-goh-tee-ounng, a-swon-twet-the ...	mil'a'na, nuz'deeka'na ...	chár, ellaiyilliru.
Academ'ic, Academ'ical, } *a.* ...	သိပ္ပံအတတ်များကိုသင်ချင်း အမှုနှင့်ဆိုင်သော။	theyp-pun-a-tut-myah-go-thin-chyin-a-hmoo-hning tsuyng-thaw ...	put'salka tul'meez, sha'gird.	sarvvakalá-sabhai-in-máná-kkan, (*or*) sarvva-sástra-palliyai-chárndón.
Accede, *v. n.* ...	ဝန်ခံသည်။ ...	woon-cun-the ...	ra'zee ...	inangu, sammathi.
Accel'erate, *v. a.* ...	မြန်စေသည်။ ...	myun-say-the ...	juldee-k, chul'a'na ...	virai-vi, tíviramákku.
Ac'cent, *s.* ...	ဂရုသံ။ ...	ga-yoo-thun ...	nish'an, dagh, bol'na ...	asai-yúnral, su-ram.
Accent', *v. a.* ...	ဂရုသံပေးသည်။ ...	ga-yoo-thun-pay-the ...	ooch'chur'na, tuluffooz-k ...	eduttuchchari.
Accept', *v. a.* ...	ခံယူသည်။ ...	cun-yoo-the ...	koob'ool-k ...	angikari, oppukkol.
Accep'table, *a.* ...	ခံယူစရာကောင်းသော။ ...	cun-yoo-syah-kowng-thau...	muk'bool, mun'zoor ...	ishtamána.
Ac'cess, *s.* ...	အထံသို့ဝင်ရာသောအခွင့်။ ...	a-tun-thoh-wing-yah-thau-a-kwing ...	zi'ya'du, il'hak ...	chérppu, pravésam.
Acces'sary, *s.* ...	ကူညီသောသူ။ ...	koo-nyee-thau-thoo ...	uf'zood, il'ha'kee, ud'hik ...	udanthaiyáli.
Acces'sion, *s.* ...	နန်းစံချင်း။ ...	nun-sun-chyin ...	bur'ha'o, burh'ta ...	chér-mánam, varattu.
Ac'cident, *s.* ...	အမှတ်တမဲ့ဖြစ်သောအမှု။ ...	a-hmut-tmeh-pyit-thau-a-hmoo ...	ha'di'su, it'if'ak ...	tarcheyal, tattu.
Accliv'ity, *s.* ...	ကုန်းတက်ရာ။ ...	kohn-tut-yah ...	chur'ha'o, dhal, nush'eb ...	érram, cháral, cháyppu.
Accom'modate, *v. a.*	တော်လျော်အောင်ပြုသည်။ ...	tau-lyau-oung-pyoo-the ...	khub'ur-l, soodh-l ...	ubacharanai-pannu.
Accom'modating, *a.*	အသုံးအလိုသို့လိုက်၍ ကျေးဇူးပြုတတ်သော။	a-thohn-aloh-thoh-luyk-yue-kyay-zoo-pyoo dut-the.	khuleek ...	tayaiyulla.

ENGLISH.	BURMESE.		HINDUSTANI.	TAMIL.
Accom'pany, *v. a.*	အတူလိုက်သည်။ပါသည်။	a-too-luyt-the, pah-the	hum'rah	tuṇaipó, kúḍappó, chér.
Accom'plice, *s.*	မကောင်းသောအမှု၌လက်ခံဖော် လက်ခံဖက်။	m'koung-thau-a-hmoo-hnuyt-lekkun-bau, lekkun-	shur'eek, sa'thee	uḍanthaikkáṛan.
Accord', *v. a.*	ညီညာသည်။	nyee-nyah-the, pet,...	fur'man, sun'ud, ut'a	isai, orumanam.
Accost', *v. a.*	နှုတ်ဆက်သည်။	hnoht-set-the	a'mud-a'mud, kuh'na	sandhittupésu.
Accouch'ement, *s.*	သားမွေးဖွားရာတွင်ပြုစုချင်း။	thah-mooay-pwah-yah-twin-pyoo-zoo-chyin	juch'a	prasavikkai.
Accoucheur', *s.*	ဝမ်းဆွဲသမား။	woon-sway-th'mah	juch'a-huk'eem, byd	maruttuvan.
Account', *s.*	အရေအတွက်။ငွေစာရင်း။	ayay-atwet, ngway-sah-yin.	sun'man, gin'tee, nukl	kaṇakku, togai, vivaram.
Account', *v. a.*	တင်မှတ်သည်။	tin-hmut-the	his'ab, uz'eez-jan'na	eṇṇu, kaṇi.
Accoun'tant, *s.*	ရေတွက်ကတ်သောသူ။ ငွေစာရင်းကိုစီရင်သောသူ။	yay-twet-dut-thau-thoo, ngway-sah-yin-goh-see-yin-thau-thoo	moo'ha'sib	kaṇakkan, nisinthá.
Account'-book, *s.*	ငွေစာရင်းအုပ်။စာရင်းအုပ်။	ngway-sah-yin-ohk, sah-yin-ohk	his'ab-kit'ab	kaṇakkupustakam.
Accou'tre, *v. a.*	စစ်တန်ဆာဆင်သည်။	tsit-t'sah-tsin-the	puh'in'na, sur'bur'a'hee-k...	pórkólamaṇi, kólantari.
Accoútrement, *s.*	စစ်တန်ဆာဝတ်ရုံ။	tsit-t'sah-woot-sohn	sin'gar, a'ra'ish	pórkólam, póraṇi.
Accred'it, *v. a.*	ယုံလောက်သောအခွင့်ကိုပေးသည်။	yoon-louk-thau-a-kwing-goh-pay-the	ikh'ti'yar, muk'door	uttaravu, athikáram.
Accrue', *v. n.*	တန်ရှိဖြစ်လာသည်။	tun-yue-hpyit-lah-the	bih'tur'ee, nuf'a	viḷai, chér, uṇḍákku.
Accúmulate, *v. a.*	ဆည်းပူးသည်။စုပေါင်းသည်။	tsee-hpoo-the, soo-poung-the	bur'ha'na, jum'ak	kúṭṭu, chér, tiraḷ.
Ac'curate, *a.*	သေချာသော။	thay-chyah-thau	su'heeh, theek, bur'a'bur	tiruttamána.
Accusation, *s.*	အပြစ်တင်ချင်း။	a-pyit-tin-chyin	it'ti'ham	kuṛṛamcháṛṛu.
Accus'tom, *v. a.*	အကျင့်။	a-chyin	a'dut-k, khodal'na	paḷagu, payilu, paḷakku.
Ache, *v. n.*	ခဲသည်။ကိုက်သည်။	keh-the, kuyt-the	durd, dookh	nó, vali, iḍi, kutthu.
Achieve', *v. a.*	ကြိုးစား၍ပြီးစီးအောင်ပြုသည်။	(kyoh-sah-yue-pyee-zee-	fa'i'du, nuf'a, class-kur'na...	cheythumuḍhi, lábamaḍai.

Ac'id, *s.* ...	ချိသည်။ ...	chyin-the, (oung-pyoo-the,	khut'ta, toorsh ...	ḍrávagam, puḻippu.
Acknowl'edge, *v. a.*	အါမခံသည်။ ဝန်ခံသည် ...	ah-mah-cun-the, (woon-cun-	ka'il, koob'ool-k ...	ottukkol, aṛikkaiyiḍu.
Ac'me, *s.* ...	ထိတ်။အထွတ်။ ...	tait, a-toht, the.) ...	oon'cha'ee ...	uchchi, nuṇi.
Ac'onite, *s.* ...	ဆေးတမျိုး။ ...	say, (tmyoh) ...	bish-nak ...	ónáy-vishappúṇḍu.
A'corn, *s.* ...	ဝက်သစ်ခြသီး။ ...	wet-thit-chyah-thee ...	bul-oot ...	oru-marattin-vittu.
Acous'tic, *a.* ...	သဏ္ဍာရုံခြင်း။ဆိုင်သောအတတ်။	thutta-yohn-chyin-suyng-thau-a-tut ...	shun'eed, *f.* ...	kéṭkai, kannamúlam.
Acquiesce', *v. n.* ...	မငြင်းဘဲနေသည်။ ...	mngying-beh-nay-the ...	it'ti'fak, ra'zee ...	iṇangu, uḍanpaḍu.
Acquire, *v. a.* ...	ရသည်။ ...	yah-the ...	ha'sil-k, py'da-k, pa'na ...	labamaḍai, chér, sambáthi.
Acquit', *v. a.* ...	လွတ်စေသည်။ ...	loht-say-the ...	moo'bur'ra-k, choot'gaiya ...	viḍuthalaiyákku.
Ac'rid, *a.* ...	စပ်ပုသည်။ ...	sut-poo-the ...	tez, tee'ta, toond, tulkh ...	kárppána, káramuḷḷa.
Acrimónious, *a.* ...	စိတ်နာစေတတ်သော။ ...	sayt-nah-say-dut-thau ...	toond, tulkh ...	káṛamána, uṛaippána.
Acer'bity, *s.* ...	စိတ်ဆိုးချင်း။ ...	say-soh-chyin ...	khut'a'ee, toor'shee ...	puḻippu, veḍuveḍuppu.
Across', *pr.* ...	တဖက်မှတဖက်သို့။ ...	tpet-hmah-tpet-thoh ...	a'ra, ben'da ...	kuṛukké.
Act, *s.* ...	အပြုအမူ။ ...	a-pyoó-a-hmoo ...	kam, kriya, chul'a'na ...	cheykai, vinai, karumam.
Act, *v. n.* ...	လှုပ်သည် ...	loht-the ...	nukl-k, chul'un-chul'na ...	naḍa, pali, oḻugu, chey.
Ac'tive, *a.* ...	လှုပ်တတ်သော ...	loht-tut-thau ...	cha'book, cha'lak, phoor'	karma, jakkirathaiyuḷḷa.
Acúte, *a.* ...	ချွန်သည် ...	chyohn-the ...	tez, [tee'la, ...	kúrmaiyána, karukkána.
Ad'age, *s.* ...	စကားကြက် ...	sgah-chyet ...	mus'ul, zurb-ool-mus'ul ...	múthurai, paḻamoḻi.
Ad'amant, *s.* ...	စိန် ...	tsain ...	hee'ra, ul'mas, bujr ...	vairam, vayirakkal.
Add, *v. a.* ...	ပေါင်းသည် ...	poung-the ...	i'za'fa-k, jum'a-k, lug'a'na...	chér, kúṭṭu, éṛṛu.
Ad'der, *s.* ...	မြွေဆို ...	moo-ay-tsoh ...	bis'el'a, *or* bis'ha-samp, *or*	viriyanpámbu.
Addit'ion, *s.* ...	ထပ်၍ပေါင်းသောအရာ	tut-yue-poung-thau.a-yah..	zi'ya'du, il'hak, [sa'pin,...	kúṭṭal, aḍakkam, chérkkai.
Ad'dle, *v. a.* ...	အဆန်ချောင် ...	a-sun-chyoung ...	fa'sid, khurab ...	paḻuthána, úsiya.
Address', *s.* ...	နှုတ်ဆက်၍ပြောခြင်	hnoht-set-yue-pyau-chyin...	sur'na'ma ...	mélvilásam, vakkaṇai.
Ad'equate, *a.* ...	တန်သော ...	tun-thau ...	bur'a'bur, moo'sa'wee ...	pórntha, taguthiyána.
Adhére, *v. n.* ...	စေကတ်သည် ...	say-kut-the ...	chip'uk'na, lug'na ...	paṛṛu, chér, oṭṭu, iṇai.
Adieu', *adv.* ...	ချမ်းသာပါစေ ...	chyun-mah-bah-say! ...	hid'a, wid'a ...	vanthanam, subhamoḻi.

English.	Burmese.		Hindustani.	Tamil.
Ad'jective, *s.* ...	ဝိသေသနာ ...	wee-thay-th'nah ...	ism-i-sif'ut ...	peyarurichchol.
Adjoin'ing, *a.* ...	စပ်လျက်ရှိခြင် ...	tsut-lyet-she-chyin ...	moot'tus'sil ...	arugána, aḍutta.
Adjúdicate, *v. a.* ...	စီရင်ခြက်ချသည် ...	see-yin-chyet-chyah-the ...	thuh'ra'na, uzm-k ...	vicharittutír, tírmáni.
Adjúre, *v. a.* ...	ကြိန်ဆိုစေသည် ...	chain-soh-zay-the ...	ka'sum-khana, hákim ...	áṇaiyiḍu, áṇaiyiṭṭukkél.
Adjust', *v. a.* ...	တော်လျော်အောင်ပြင်သည် ...	tau-lyau-oung-pyin-the ...	door'oost-k, fysul-k ...	sarikkaṭṭu, tiruttu.
Admin'ister, *v. a.* ...	ထုပ်ပေသည် ...	toht-pay-the ...	de'na ...	naḍappi, cheluttu.
Admin'istrator, *s.* ...	လူသေဥစ္စာများကိုစီရင်သောသူ။	loo-thay-ohtsah-myah-goh-see-yin-thau-thoo ...	wus'ee ...	vicháraṇaikáraṇ.
Ad'miral, *s.* ...	တိုက်သင်္ဘောများဗိုလ်ချုပ်ကြီး။	tuyk-thing-baw-myah-boh-chyoht-gyee ...	mun'sub-dar ...	pórkappal-kúṭṭa-talaivan.
Admíre, *v. a.* ...	နှစ်သက်အံ့သြသည်။ ...	hnit-thet-un-au-the ...	taj'joob-k, uj'ub-k ...	meechchu, viya.
Admit', *v. a.* ...	ဝင်ရအခွင့်ပေးသည်။ခံဝန်သည်။	wing-yun-akwing-pay-the.. cun-woon-the ...	a'ne-d, rah-d, man'na ...	iḍaṅkoḍu, ottukkol.
Admon'ish, *v. a.* ...	ဆုမ္မသတိပေးသည်။ ...	sohm-mah-th'dee-pay-the...	mus'lu'hut, mul'a'mut-k ...	echchari, buddhichol.
Ado', *s.* ...	မောပန်းအောင်ပြုသည်။ ...	maw-bun-oung-pyoo-the...	bur'hum'ee, moosh'kil ...	víṇáṭṭam, víṇtollai.
Adoles'cence, *s.* ...	ပျိုသောအရွယ်။ ...	pyoh-thau-a-yueh ...	ju'wan'ee, ju'wan ...	iḷamparuvam.
Adopt', *v. a.* ...	သားအရာနှိမ့်မွေးစားသည်။ ...	thah-a-yah-hnuyt-mooay-sah-the ...	ikh'ti'yar-k, le-pal'na ...	eḍuttukkoḷ, urithákku.
Adóre, *v. a.* (to worship) idolatry,	ကိုးကွယ်သည်။ ...	koh-gweh-the ...	pur'us'tish, pa-boos'ee-k ...	namaskari, vaṇaṅgu, tuti, *idolatry* in (*sans.*) pújá, *or* archchaná.
Adorn', *v. a.* ...	တန်ဆာဆင်သည်။ ...	ta-sah'-tsin-the ...	sin'gar'na, khil'ut ...	chiṛappi, siṅgári.
Adrift', *adv.* ...	အလွှတ်မျောလျက်။ ...	a-loht-myaw-lyet ...	la-char, be-char'u ...	tikkaṛṛu.
Adroit', *a.* skilful...	အလျှင်အမြန်ပြုခြင်းကြီထမြောက်တတ်သည်။	a-lyin-a-myun-pyoo-yue-a-khyun-tah-myouk-tut-the ...	hoo'nur-mund, phoor'tee'la.	keṭṭiyána, chádhuriya.

English	Burmese	Burmese (transliterated)	Hindustani	Tamil
Adulátion, *s.* ...	ချီးမွမ်းချင်း။ ...	chyee-mohn-chyin ...	bun'dug'ee, khoorsh'a'mud...	ichchagam, mu-gastu-thi.
Adult', *s.* ...	လူလားမြောက်သောသူ။ ...	loo-lah-myouk-thau-thoo ...	ba'ligh, ju'wan ...	kumaran, viragarintavan.
Adul'terate, *v. a.* ...	ရောနှော၍ညံ့စေသည်။ ...	yau-hnau-yue-nyun-say-the	khon'-ta-k, mil'ou'nee-k ...	paluthákku.
Adul'tery, *s.* ...	သူ့မယားကိုပြစ်မှားချင်း မြောက်မထားချင်း။	thoo-mayah-go-pyit-hmah-chyin, myouk-mah-tah-chin ...	chhinála-zee, zin'a'ka'ree ...	vipacháram, chórattanam.
Advan'ce, *v. n.* ...	တိုးတက်စေသည်။စရံပေးသည်။	toh-tet-say-the, tsa-yun pay-the ...	a'mud ...	munthu, téṛu, uyar.
Advan'tage, *s.* ...	အကျိုး။ ...	a-kyoh ...	in'tifa, fai'du, nuf'a ...	ilábam, nayam, palan.
Ad'vent, *s.* ...	ကြွလာချင်း။ ...	kyoo-ah-lah'-chyin ...	a'mud, am'dun'ee ...	varugai, tóṛṛam.
Adven'ture, *s.* ...	စွန့်စားချင်းနှင့်ဆိုင်သောအမှု။...	tsohn-tsah-chyin-hnin-suyng-thau-a-hmoo ...	ha'di'su, ma'jur'a ...	tuṇivu, muyarchiyánachey-[gai.
Adven'turous, *a.* ...	ရဲရင့်တတ်သော။ ...	yeh-yin-dut-thau ...	mun'chul'a, bu'ha'doo'ree...	tuṇi-kara-mána.
Ad'versary, *s.* ...	ရန်သူ။ဆန့်ကျင်ဘက်ပြုသောသူ။	yun-thoo, tsun-kyin-bek-pyoo-thau-thoo ...	moo'kha'lif, doosh'mun ...	ethiri, pagai-van.
Adver'sity, *s.* ...	ဘေးအန္တရယ်။ဆင်းရဲချင်း။ ...	bay-undreh, tsin-yeh-chyin.	bud-bukh'tee ...	chiṛumai, tunbam.
Advíce, *s.* ...	အကြံပေးချင်း။တိုင်ပင်ချင်း။ ...	akyun-pay-chyin, tuyng-	mus'lu'hut, sul'ah ...	álóchanai, buddhi.
Advíse, *v. a.* ...	အကြံပေးသည်။ ...	akyun-pay-the, bin-chyin.	sul'ah-d ...	buddhi-chollu, u-padési.
Ad'vocate, *s.* ...	ထောက်မသောသူ။ရှေ့နေ။ ...	towk-mah'thaw-thoo, shay-ney ...	wuk'eel, sha'fi ...	niyáya-váthi, vakkíl.
Adze, or Adz, *s.* ...	ထံစည်း။ ...	t'see ...	bus'oo'la ...	váychchi.
Afar', *adv.* ...	အဝေး။ဝေးရွာ။ဝေးဝေး။ ...	a-way, way-swah, way-way.	door, moo'fa'sil'u ...	dúramáy, agala, etṭa.
Affair', *s.* ...	အမှု။အခင်း။အခွင့်။အရေး။ ...	a-hmoo, a-kin, a-quin, a-yay	bat, kam, kaj, kar ...	káriyam, saṅgathi.
Affec'tion, *s.* ...	စိတ်။မေတ္တာ။ ...	tsayt, myittah ...	pi'yar, prem, ishk, chah ...	paṭcham, nésam, anbu.
Affec'tionate, *a.* ...	မေတ္တာရှိသော။ ...	myittah-shee-thau ...	pi'ya'ra, prem'ee, cha'hee'ta	anbána, nésamána.
Affíance, *s.* ...	ယုံကြည်ချင်း။ ...	yohn-gyee-chyin ...	bhur'o'sa, mang'na-sug'a'ee-[k.	sam-bandham, nambikkai.
Affidávit, *s.* ...	ကြိန်ဆို၍သက်သေခံသောစကား	chyain-tsoh-yué-thet-thay-cun-thau-sgah ...	kasum, saoh'cha'ka'kes ...	sattiyam, sattiya-pattiram.

English.	Burmese.		Hindustani.	Tamil.
Affin'ity, *s.* ...	သဘောခြင်းတူခြင်း။ ...	th'bau-chyin, too-chyin ...	tuk'reer, nis'but ...	uṛavu, inam.
Af'fix, *s.* ...	စကားများ၌ဆက်သောဝိဘတ်။	sgah-myah-hnuyt-tset-	hij'jee, bund ...	vigu-thi, véṛṛumai-urubu.
Affix', *v. a.* ...		thau-wee-bet ...	lug'a'na, sant'na ...	iḍu, chér, púṭṭu.
Afflict', *v. a.* ...	နာစေသည်။ဆင်းရဲစေသည်။ ...	nah-say-the, tsin-yeh-say-the ...	ee'za-d, sut'a'na ...	váthi, tunba-paḍuttu.
Afford', *v. a.* ...	ပေးကမ်းသည်။ ...	pay-kun-the ...	de'na, de'suk'na ...	koḍu, í, tá.
Affray', *s.* ...	ခိုက်ရန်ဖြစ်၍ ရုန်းရင်းခတ်မှုရှိချင်	kuyk-yun-pyit-yue-yohn-yin-cut-hmoo-shee-chyin.	kuz'i'ya, shor, hun'ga'mu...	chaṇḍai, saruvugai. [paṇṇu.
Affright, *v. a.* ...	ထိတ်လန့်စေသည်။ ...	tait-lun-say-the ...	dur'a'na, duh'shut-de'nee...	bhayappaḍuttu, tigaikkap-
Affront', *s.* ...	စိတ်ဆိုးအောင်ပြုချင်း။ ...	sait-tso-owng-pyoo-chyin...	ga'lee, bud-soo'loo'kee ...	nintanai, avamánam.
Afloat', *adv.* ...	ရေပေါ်မှာပေါလော။ ...	yay-bau-hma-pau-law ...	tyr'ta, buh'ta ...	mithanthu, nínti.
Afóre, *adv.* / Afórehand, *adv.*	လွန်ပြီးကာလ။ ...	hlohn-byee-kah-lah	sam'ne, roo'bu'roo, kub'ul	mun, athi-síkkiramáy.
Aforetime, *adv.* ...	အရင်ပြင်ဆင်နှင့်လျက်။ ...	ayin-pyin-tsin-hnin-lyet	a'ge, puh'le, ug'a'ree ...	munnamé, muntha.
Afraid', *a.* ...	ကြောက်သည်။ ...	khyowk-the ...	kha'if, turs'an, dur'ak ...	bhayamána, achchamuḷḷa.
Aft, *adv.* ...	ပဲ့ပီမှာ။ ...	peh-see-hmah ...	peech'hul ...	pinpuṛattil, pinnaṇiyatil.
Af'ter, *pr.* or *adv.*...	နောက်။ ...	nowk ...	peech'he, baud ...	piṛpádu. pinbu.
Afternoon', *s.* ...	မွန်းလွဲအချိန်။ ...	hmohn-lwé-a-chayn ...	sip'uh'ur, sip'uh'ree ...	pin-néram, abaráṇam.
Af'terwards, *adv.*...	နောက်မှာ။ ...	nowk-hmah ...	baud, peech'he ...	pinbu, piṛpádu.
Again', *adv.* ...	တဖန်။နောက်တဖန်။ပြန်။ ...	tpun, nowk-tpun, pyun ...	pher, phir ...	maṛupaḍiyum, mélum.
Against', *pr.* ...	တဘက်၌ဆန့်ကျင်ပက်။ ...	tpet-hnyut-tsun-kyin-bet...	khil'af, moo'ka'bil ...	viróthamáy, ethiriḍaiyáy.
Ag'ate, *s.* ...	သင်္ဘောမဟူရာ။ ...	thingbaw-mahoo-yah ...	yush'ub, yush'um ...	ór-vagai-rattinam.
Age, *s.* ...	အသက်။ ...	a-thet ...	joog, oomr ...	vayasu, práyam, váḻnáḷ.
A'ged, *a.* ...	အသက်ကြီးသော။အိုသော။ ...	a-thet-kyee-thau, oh-thau...	boor'ha, bood'dha ...	vayathu-chenṛa, kiḻa.
A'gency, *s.* ...	ပြုနိုင်သောအခွင့်။ကိုယ်စားလှယ်အရာ။	pyoo-hnuyng-thau-a-kwing, koh-sa-leh-ayah.	goo'mash'tu'gee, wik'a'-lut.	káriyavicháraṇai.

A'gent, *s.* ...	ပြုသောသူ။ကိုယ်စားလှယ်။ ...	pyoo-thau-thoo, koh-sah-leh	goom'ash'tu, (*law*) wuk'eel.	káriyakarttan, karttá.
Agglom'erate, *v. a.*	လိုအောင်ရုန်ထားသည်။ ...	lohn-oung-soo-yueh-tah-the	dher, but'or'na, jum'a ...	tiraṭṭu, kúṭṭu, kuvi.
Ag'grandize, *v. a.*...	ဘုန်းအသရေထိုးစေသည်။ ...	hpohn-a-tharay-toh-say-the	bur'ha'na, oon'cha'na ...	mechchu, pugal̤, éṟṟu.
Ag'gravate, *v. a.*...	သာ၍ဆိုးသည်။ ...	thah-yueh-tsoh-the ...	bud'tur-k, bhub'ka'na ...	bharamákku, athikakéḍákku
Ag'gregate, *s.* ...	အစုအပေါင်း။အနက်။ ...	a-tsoo-a-poung, a-nek ...	jum'a, joomla, kool ...	tiraṭṭu, mottam.
Aghast', *a.* ...	အလွန်ထိတ်လန့်၍ မိန်းမောတွေဝေလျက်နေသည်။	a-hlohn-tait-lun-yueh-mayn maw-tway-way-lyet-nay-the ...	bhuch'uk, hy'but, houl ...	ékkamána, tigaippuḷḷa.
Ag'itate, *v. a,* ...	အနှိုင်အထက်နှိုးဆော်သည်။ ...	a-hnuyng-a-tet-hnoh-tsau-the ...	hil'a'na, hur'uk'ut-d ...	kalakku, kulukku, asai.
Agó, *adv.* ...	လွန်ခဲ့ပြီးသောကာလ။ ...	hlohn-geh-pyee-thau-kah-lah ...	a'ge, a'goo, gooz're, pee'chhe.	kaḍantha, chendṛa, mun.
Ag'ony, *s.* ...	အပြင်းဆုံးသောဝေဒနာကိုခံခြင်း	apyin-tsohn-thau-way-dnah-go-oun-ghyin ...	kusht, jan'kun'dun, si'ya'sut.	tíviravéthanai, kasti.
Agree', *v. n.* ...	သဘောတူသည်။သင့်သည်။ ...	th'bau-too-the, thinn-the...	it'ti'fak, mil'na, lug'na ...	iṇaṅku, orumanappaḍu.
Agree'ment, *s.* ...	သဘောတူချင်း။သင့်ခြင်း။ ...	th'baw-too-chyin, thinn-[chyin,	kur'ar, ik'rar, it'ti'fak ...	uḍanpaḍikkai, poruttam.
Ag'riculture, *s.* ...	လယ်ယာလုပ်ခြင်း။ ...	leh-yah-loht-chyin,	khet'ee-ba'ree, kis'ny ...	véḷáṇmai, payirohcheykai.
Aground, *adv.* ...	မြေပေါ်မှာတင်လျက်။ ...	myay-baw-hmah-tin-lyet...	ut'ka ...	kalattil, nilattil.
A'gue, *s.* Fever, ...	ထုန်ဖျား။ ...	tohn-pyah ...	tup-i-lur'za, joo'ree ...	kuḷir, kuḷir-káychchal.
Ah, *int.* ...	အော်။ ...	aw! ...	ah! ...	á, (*or*) ah! aiyó.
Aha', *int.* ...	အေဟေ။ ...	ay-hay! ...	aha!, uh'a-ha'ha! ...	á á! (*or*) ah ah!, ágá!
Ahead', *adv.* ...	ရှေ့မှာ။ရှေ့သို့။ ...	shay-hmah, shay-thoh ...	a'ge, a'goo ...	munthi, munné.
Aid, *v. a.* ...	ကူညီခြင်း ...	koo-nyee-chyin ...	zor-d, be'ra-par-lug'a'na ...	saháyampaṇṇu, tuṇaichey.
Air, *s.* ...	လေ ...	lay ...	huwa, pu'wun, joom'bish ...	káṟṟu, váyu.
Alarm', *s.* ...	ကြောက်လန့်စေသည် ...	chyouk-lun-say-the ...	dur'a'na duh'shut, houl ...	achcham, ékkam, keḍi.
Alas', *int.* ...	အလိုလေး။ ဖြစ်ရလေခြင်း ...	a-loh-lay! pyit-yah-lay-chyin ...	ha!, ha'e ha'e!, hy!, uf'sos!	aiyó, appá, óhó, achchó.
Al'chemy, *s.* ...	အဂ္ဂိရတ် ...	eg-gee-yut ...	kee'mi'ya-gur'ee, kee'mi'ya.	irasa-vátham,

ENGLISH	BURMESE.		HINDUSTANI.	TAMIL.
Al'cohol, *s.*	အရက်ပြန်	ayet-pyun	koo'hul, shur'ab-i-nab	sáráyatin-sáram.
Alcóve, *s.*	အခန်းငယ်	a-cun-ngeh	bagh, baghchu, phool-war'ee	taniyarai, tóṭṭam.
Al'gebra, *s.*	အက္ခရာသင်္ချာ	ekkayah-thinchya	ub'ikt-gun'it	bíja-kaṇitham.
A'lias, *Lat. adv.*	သို့မဟုတ်	thoh-m'hoht	nu'heen-to	maṛṛapaḍi, maṛunámam.
Alíke, *adv.*	တူသည်	too-the	bur'a'bur, ek'san	sarivara, oppáy.
Al'koran, *s.*	ပသီကျမ်းစာ	bă-thee-kyun-sah	koran, kooran	kuṛán-védam.
All, *a.*	အားလုံး	ah-lohn	sub, sa'ra, kool	ellá, sarvva, samasta.
Al'lah, *s.*	ပသီဘုရားသခင်	payah-th'kin	khoo'da, ul'lah, rub	paráparan, ísuran.
Al'ligator, *s.*	မိကျောင်း	mee-gyoung	ghur'i'yal,koom'heer,magur.	muthalai, vanmín.
Allot', *v. a.*	ခွဲခန့်သည်	kweh-cun-the	bant'na, fur'man, sun'ud	paṅgiḍu, pagir.
Allow', *v. a.*	အခွင့်ပေးသည်	a-kwin-pay-the	ij'a'zut-d, de'na, man'na	iḍaṅkoḍu, ottukkoḷ.
Allúde, *v. n.*	ရည်စောင်းသည်	yee-sowng-the	ish'a'ra, roo'joo-k	chuṭṭippésu, kuṛi.
Allúre, *v. a.*	မြှူသည်	hmyoo-the	fur'eb-d. moh'na	nayaṅkáṭṭu, mayakku.
Al'manac, *s.*	ပြက္ခဒိန်	pyek-ka-dain	put'ra, tuk'weem	pañcháṅgam.
Almíghty, *a.*	အနန္တတန်ခိုးနှင့်ပြည့်စုံသော	anun-dah-t-goh-hnin-pyee-sohn-thaw	ul-ka'dir	sarvva-vallamaiyulla.
Al'mond, *s.*	ဗါတန်သီး	bah-tun-thee	ba'dam	váthumai.
Almóst, *adv.*	လုပြီ	loo-byee	un'kur'eeb, nuz'deek	koñjam-kuṛaiya.
Alms, *s.*	အလှူ	a-hloo	bheekh, zuk'at	pichchai, thánam, koḍai.
Alóne, *a.*	တယောက်ထည်း	t-yowk-tee	tun'ha, uk'e'la	tanittu, taniyé.
Along', *adv.*	ရှေ့သို့လိုက်သည်	shay-thoh-luyt-the	a'ge, lum'ba	neḍuga, néré.
Al'phabet, *s.*	ဗျည်း	byee	ulif'be, ub'jud	aṭchara-vari, varṇamálai.
Alread'y, *adv.*	ယခုဘင်	y'koo-bin	a'ge, ub'hee	itharkumunné, ippoluthé.
Al'so, *adv.*	ငှင် လည်း	l'gowng, lee	our, neez, hum, bhee	kúḍa, aṇṛiyum.
Al'tar, *s.*	ယဇ်ပလ္လင်	yit-pălin	be'dee, koor'ban'gah	píḍam, bali-pídam.
Al'ter, *v. a.*	ပြောင်းလဲသည်	pyowng-leh-the	bud'ul'na, tub'deel-k	máṛṛu, véṛákku.

Although', *conj.* ...	သော်လည်း။ ...	thaw-lee ...	go'ki, hur'chund'ki, ug'ur'chi	álum, um.
Al'titude, *s.* ...	အမြင့်။အထွဋ်ပြား။ ...	a-myin, a-toht-pyah ...	oon'cha'ee, ir'tif'a ...	uyaram, uchcham.
Altogeth'er, *adv.* ...	အတူတကွ။ ...	a-too-t'gwah ...	moot'luk, ek'dust, ek'sur ...	orumikka, muluthum.
Al'um, *s.* ...	ကျောက်ချဉ်။ ...	khyouk-khyín ...	shub, zaj'i'soo'fyd ..	sínakkáram, padikkáram.
Al'ways, *adv.* ...	အစဉ်မပြတ်။ ...	a-tseen-m'pyut ...	hum'esh'u, sud'a ..	enrum, nittamum.
Am, *v. i.* ...	ရှိသည်။ဖြစ်သည်။ ...	shee-the, pyit-the ...	ru'ha'o, ruh'na ...	iru, tangu, tari.
Amal'gam, *s.* ...	ပြဒါးနှင့်ရောနှောသောလော ဟာ။	pyadah'-hnin-yaw-hnaw-thaw-law-hah ...	rus'ka'poor ...	irasapúram.
Aman'uensis, *s.* ...	နှုတ်ထွက်အတိုင်းရေးသောစာ ရေး။	hnoht-twet-gah-atuyng-yay-thaw-tsă-yay ...	mud'ud'nu'wees ...	chollak-kéttaluthuvón.
Am'aranth, *s.* ...	မညှိုးပန်း။ ...	m'nyoh-bun ...	ehou'la'ee ...	váḍá-malligai.
Amass', *v. a.* ...	စုပုံသည်။ ...	tsoo-pohn-the ...	jum'a-k: sum'etna ...	kuvi, tirattu, chér.
Amáze, *v. a.* ...	အံ့ဩသည်။ ...	un-aw-the ...	bhuch'ka'na, hy'ran-k ...	áchchariyappaduttu.
Am'azon, *s.* ...	စစ်တိုက်သောမိန်းမ။ ...	tsit-túyt-thaw-maym-mah..	lur'an'ka'ou'rut ...	chandaikkári, án-mári.
Ambas'sador, *s.* ...	သံတမန်။ ...	thun-da-mun ...	el'chee, suf'eer ...	túthan, samarathi.
Am'ber, *s.* ...	ပုရင်း။ ...	pa-yin ...	kuh'roo'ba ...	ambar, nimilai.
Ambig'uous, *a.* ...	အနက်နှစ်ပါးရှိသော။ ...	a-net-nib-bah-she-thau ...	shuk'kee ...	samusaya-mulla.
Ambit'ion, *s.* ...	လှုံ့ဆော်သောရတ်အားကြီးသော။	hlohn-geh-thau-soht-ah-kyee-thau ...	hou'sil'a, hirs ...	pérásai, periya-chintai.
Ambuscáde, *s.* ...	တတ်သာပုန်းခိုနေချင်း။ ...	tut-thah-pohn-hnuyt-nay-chyin ...	dub'kee, d-mar'na ...	pathividai, olipadai.
Améliorate, *v. a.* ...	သာ၍ကောင်းစေသည်။ ...	thah-yueh-kowng-say-the...	suh'eeh-k, dooroost-k ...	tiruttu, chírppaduttu. [thu.
Amen', *adv.* ...	အာမင်း။မှန်ပါစေ။ ...	ah-men, hmun-bah-say ...	tuh'keek, such, wa'ki'ee ...	áman, appadi-yágakadava-
Amend', *v. a.* ...	ပြင်သည်။ ...	pyin'-the ...	doo'roost-k, suh'eeh-k ...	tiruttu, chírppaduttu.
Aménity, *s.* ...	နေရာသာယာချင်း။ ...	nay-yah-thah-yah-gyin ...	khoo'shee, (*pleasentness*) ...	irammiyam-tarum-tanmai.
Amer'ce, *v. a.* ...	ငွေဒဏ်ခံစေဟုစီရင်သည်။ ...	ngway-dahn-cun-say-hoo-tsee-yin-the ...	dand, dund, (*penalty*) ...	abaráthampódu.
Ameri'can, *a.* ...	အမေရိကံ။ ...	american ...	america'wa'la ...	amerikkáthésattán

ENGLISH.	BURMESE.		HINDUSTANI.	TAMIL.
Am'ethyst, *s.* ...	သီဟိုဠ်နီလာ။ ...	thee-ho-nee-lah ...	lal-i-bud-ukh'shan ...	suganthikkal.
A'miable, *a.* ...	ချစ်ပွယ်သော။ ...	chyit-pweh-thaw ...	hur-dil-uz'eez ...	manathukkiniya.
Am'icable, *a.* ...	သင့်တင့်သော။ ...	thin-tin-thaw ...	mihr-ban, oolfut'ee ...	nésamána, iṇakkamána.
Amid', Amidst', *pr.*	အလယ်မှာ။ ...	a-leh-hmah ...	dur'mi'yan, mudh ...	mattiyil, iḍaiyil, naḍuvil.
Amiss'. *a.* or *adv.*...	အလွဲ။ ...	a-lweh ...	tuk'seerwar ...	tappáy, piḷaiyáy.
Am'ity, *s.* ...	မိတ်ဆွေဖွဲ့ခြင်း။ ...	mait-sway-pweh-gyin ...	dost-dar'ee, dos'tee, mihr ...	nésam, aikkiyam, tóḷamai.
Ammónia, *s.* ...	ဇဝက်သာရေပြန်။ ...	za-wet-thah-yay-byun ...	navau'chaur ...	navachchára m.
Ammunit'ion, *s.* ...	ခဲယမ်းမီးကျောက်။ ...	keh-yun-mee-kyowk ...	sa'man-i-jun'gee ...	yutta-taḷaváḍaṅgaḷ.
Among', Amongst', [*pr.*	အလယ်တွင်။ ...	a-leh-dwing ...	beech, men ...	il, iḍai-il, uḷ.
Am'orous, *a.*	ချစ်ကြိုက်တတ်သော။ ...	chyit-chyuyt-dut-the ...	ishk-un'gez ...	kámamuḷḷa.
Amount', *s.* ...	အရအပေါင်း။ ...	a-suo-a-powng ...	joom'lu, mot, jum'a ...	mottam, ágattugai.
Amphithéatre, *s.* ...	ပွဲခံရန်တိုက်ဝိုင်း။ ...	pweh-cun-yun-tuyk-wing...	nach'ghur ...	naḍanachálai.
Am'putate, *v. a.* ...	ကိုယ်အင်္ဂါကိုဖြတ်သည်။ ...	koh-ingah-goh-pyut-the ...	kat'dal'na ...	aṅga-chéthanam-chey.
Am'ulet, *s.* ...	လက်ဖွဲ့။ ...	let-pooeh ...	ta'weez, totka ...	káppu, iraṭchábanthanam.
Amúse, *v. a.* ...	ပျော်သည်။ ...	pyaw-the ...	buh'la'na, tuf'reeh-d ...	santóshappaḍuttu.
An, *in-art.* ...	တခု။ ...	t'koo ...	ek ...	oru, onṛu, ór.
Anal'ogy, *s.* ...	လက္ခဏာတူသော။ ...	lekka-nah-too-thaw ...	shub'eeh, tush'a'booh ...	tulliyam,sámániyadharmam
Anal'ysis, *s.* ...	ရောနှောလျက်ရှိသော အရာတို့ကို အမျိုးအလိုက် တပါးစီခွဲထားသည်။	yaw-hnaw-lyet-she-thaw-a yah-doh-goh, a-myo-a-luyt t-bah-see-queh-tah-the...	fih'rist ...	paguppu, aṭṭavaṇai.
An'archy, *s.* ...	ပြည်မိုးမင်းမရှိသဖြင့်မငြိမ်မသက်ရှိခြင်း။	pyee-soh-ming-m'shee-th-pyin-mnyain-mthek-she-chyin ...	khul'bul, hul'chul ...	tárumáṛu, úrkkalagam.
An'cestor, *s.* ...	ဘိုးဘေး။ ...	boh-bay ...	jud, bap'da'da, boo'zoorg ...	púrvaprushan, munnón.
An'chor, *s.* ...	ကျောက်ဆူး ...	chyowk-soo ...	lun'gur, nungur ...	naṅgúram.
A'ncient, *a.* ...	ရှေးကာလနှင့်ဆိုင်သော ...	shay-kah-lah-hning-suyng-		

		thaw ...	kooh'na, kud'eem ...	púrva, paḻamaiyána.
And, *conj.* ...	၎င်း။ထိုမှတပါး။နှင့်။ ...	l'goung, to-hmah-t'bah, hnin	o, our, (*or*) owr ...	kúḍa, um, mélum.
Anew', *adv.* ...	အသစ်။အဖန်။ ...	a-thit, a-pun ...	nou, phir, pher ...	navamáy, tirumbavum.
A'ngel, *s.* ...	ကောင်းကင်တမန်။ ...	kowng-gin-t-mun ...	fir'ish'tu, mul'uk ...	dévatúthan, túthan.
An'ger, *s.* ...	စိတ်ဆိုးခြင်း။ဒေါသ။ ...	sayt-tsoh-chyin, daw-thah...	ghoos'sa, be'za'ree ...	sinam, kóbam, múrkkam.
An'gle, *s.* ...	ထောင့်ကျယ်။ ...	doung-chyeh ...	ko'na, za'wi'yu ...	kóṇam, múlai, túṇḍil.
An'glican, *a.* ...	အင်္ဂလိပ်အသင်းတော်နှင့်ဆိုင်သော။	ing-galait-a-thin-dau-hnin-suyng-thaw ...	ung'rez'ee ...	veḷḷaikkáran, aṅgléyan.
An'gry, *a.* ...	စိတ်ဆိုးသည်။ ...	tsayt-soh-the ...	ghoos'sa, khu'fu ...	sinamána, kóbamuḷḷa.
An'guish, *s.* ...	အလွန်နာကြင်ခြင်းဝေဒနာ။ ...	a-hloon-nah-kyin'-gyin-way'da-nah ...	ul'um, uz'ab ...	kavalai, viyákulam.
Animadvert', *v. n.*...	အကြောင်းပြု၍ပြောသည်။ ...	a-kyoung-pyoo-yueh-pyau-the ...	il'zam ...	kaṇḍi, kaḍinthukkoḷ.
An'imal, *s.* ...	အသက်ရှင်သောမြေသတ္တဝါ။ ...	a-thet-shin-thaw-myay-thutta-wah ...	jan'wur, hy'wan ...	práṇi, jenttu, sívan.
An'imate, *v. a.* ...	အသက်ရှင်စေသည်။ ...	a-thet-shin-say-the ...	jil'a'na, zin'du-k ...	uyirppí, évu.
Animos'ity, *s.* ...	မုန်းတားခြင်း။ ...	mōhn-tah-chyin ...	doosh'mun'ee, byr, kee'na...	pagai, pagaimai.
An'kle, *s.* ...	ခြေမျက်စိ။ ...	chyay-myek-see ...	gut'ta, tukh'na ...	kaṇukkál, káṛparaḍu.
Anneal', *v. a.* ...	မီးဖြင့်ဖျင်သည်။ ...	mee-byin-pying-the ...	ta'ona ...	chúṭṭinálé-patha-paḍuttu.
Annex', *v. a.* ...	ဆက်သည်။ ...	set-the ...	jor'na, wusul-k ...	kúṭṭu, oṭṭu.
Annihilátion, *s.* ...	အကြွင်းမဲ့ပျောက်ပျက်ခြင်း ...	a-kyew-in-meh-pyouk-pyet-chyin ...	nest'ee, nas ...	sarvanásam, nirmúlam.
Announ'ce, *v. a.* ...	ကျော်ညာသည်။ ...	kyau-nyah-the ...	khub'ur-d ...	kúṛu, viḷambaramohey.
Announ'cement, *s.*...	ကျော်ညာခြင်း။ ...	kyau-nyah-chyin ...	mun'a'dee, ish'ti'har ...	prachittam, kúṛal.
Annoy', *s.* ...	နှောင့်ရှက်သည်။ ...	hnowng-shet-the ...	tuk'leef, dookh ...	alaṭṭu, iḍaiñjaṛpaṇṇu.
An'nual, *s.* ...	နှစ်စဉ်။ ...	hnit-seen ...	sa'li'ya'nu, hursal ...	varushanthóṛum-varuvathu
Annul', *v. a.* ...	ပပျောက်စေသည်။ ...	pah-pyouk-say-the ...	met'na, mou'koof-k ...	taḷḷu, máṛṛu, oḻiyachey.
An'nular, *a.* ...	အကွင်းပုံရှိသော။ ...	a-kwin-pōhn-she-thaw ...	chum'bur'ee, moo'dou'wur..	vaṭṭavaḍivána.

English.	Burmese.		Hindustani.	Tamil.
Annunciátion, *s.* ...	သိတင်းကြားပြောခြင်း။ ...	th'din-kyah-pyau-chyin ...	num'oo'dar'ee, uf'wah ...	kúṛugai, prasittam.
Anoint', *v. a.* ...	လိမ်းသည်။လူးသည်။ ...	layn-the, loo-the ...	mul'na, choo'pur'na ...	abishégam-paṇṇu.
Anon'ymous, *a.* ...	နာမည်မပါသော။ ...	nah-mee-m'pah-thau ...	be-nam ...	peyaṛillátha.
Anoth'er, *a.* ...	အခြား။ ...	a-chyah ...	dee'gur, our-ek ...	véṛoru, pinnoru.
An'swer, *s.* ...	ထုသည်။ပြေသည်။ ...	htoo-the, pyay-the ...	juw'ab ...	viḍai, maṛumoḻi.
Ant, *s.* ...	ပရွက်ဆိတ်။ ...	pyuet-sayt ...	mor, numl ...	eṛumbu.
Antag'onist, *s.* ...	ဆန့်ကျင်ဘက်ပြုသော။ ...	tsan-kyin-bek-pyoo-thau ...	doosh'mun ...	pakaivan, ethiri.
Antarc'tic, *a.* ...	တောင်ဖုဝန်နှင့်ဆိုင်သော ...	toung-soo-woon-hnin-suyng-thau ...	ju'noob, (*arab*), duk'khun..	teṭchaṇa, ten.
Antecédent, *s.* ...	အရင်ဖြစ်သော။ ...	ah-yin-pyit-thau ...	mookud'dum ...	munmoḻi.
An'telope, *s.* ...	တောဆိတ်။ ...	taw-tsait ...	hur'un, hir'un ...	kaṛuppumán, mán.
An'them, *s.* ...	သီခြင်းတမျိုး။ ...	thee-chyin-t'myo ...	bhuj'un, us'toot ...	ñánakírttanam.
An'tic, *s.* ...	လူပျက်ကဲ့သို့ဖြစ်သော။ ...	loo-byet-geh-tho-pyit-thau	hee'la, nukh'ra ...	kómáḻi, chéshṭaikkáran.
Antic'ipate, *v. a.* ...	ဦးအောင်ပြုသည်။ ...	oo-oung-pyoo-thee ...	pesh'dus'tee-k ...	muntikkoḷ.
An'tidote, *s.* ...	အဆိပ်ကိုနိုင်သောဆေး။ ...	a-tsait-go-hnuyng-thau-[tsay,...	tir'yak-far'ook ...	visha-muṛikkum-marunthu.
An'timony, *s.* ...	ခနောက်စိမ်း။ ...	k-nouk-tsun,	an'jun, un'jun, koohl ...	anjaṇakkal, nimiḷai.
Antip'athy, *s.* ...	အလိုလိုမုန်းရွံ့ရှောင်ချင်သောစိတ်	a-lo-lo-mohn-yueh-shyoung chyin-thau-sait ...	ohir, nuf'rut ...	manaveṛuppu, pakai.
Antiq'uity, *s.* ...	ရှေးကာလ။ ...	shay-kah-lah ...	kud'eem-war, mooddut ...	púrvakálam, paḻamai.
An'tler, *s.* ...	သမင်ဦးချိုအတတ်။ ...	th'min-oo-chyoh-a-tut ...	jhank, seeng ...	mánkombu.
An'vil, *s.* ...	ပေ။ ...	pay ...	ghun, ni'ha'ee ...	aḍaikuṛaḍu, aḍaikkal.
Anxíety, *s.* ...	စိုးရိမ်ခြင်း။ ...	tso-yain-chyin ...	tur'ud'dood, fikr ...	kavalai, ával, áttiram.
Anx'ious, *a.* ...	စိုးရိမ်သော။ ...	tso-yain-thau ...	fikr-mund, fik'ree ...	chintanaiyuḷḷa, ávaluḷḷa.
An'y, *a.* ...	တစုံတခု။ ...	t-sohn-t'koo ...	ko'ee, koochh ...	yáthoru, yáthénum.
Apáce, *adv.* ...	အလျင်အမြန်။ ...	a-lyin-a-myun ...	jul'dee, toort, jhut-put ...	chíkkiramáy, viraiváy.
Apart', *adv.* ...	တခြားစီ။ခွဲခွဲခြမ်းခြမ်း။ ...	t-chyah-see, qweh-qweh-		

		chyun-chyun ...	ul'ug, jood'a ...	tanié, puṛambáy, piṛiváy.
A'part'ment, *s.* ...	အိမ်ခန်း။ ...	ayn-cun ...	koth'ree, kum'ra ...	víṭṭinarai, (*inner*) uḷḷaṛai.
Ap'athy, *s.* ...	ထိုးပေးခြင်း။ ...	toh-pay-chyin ...	soos'tee, ka'hil'ee, as'kut ...	chómbu, támasam.
Ape, *s.* ...	မျောက်။ ...	myowk ...	mur'kut ...	válillák-kuraṅgu.
Ap'erture, *s.* ...	အပေါက်။ ...	a-powk ...	goo'zur, syr-gah ...	tuváram, vaḻi.
A'pex, *s.* ...	အထွဋ်ဖျား။ ...	a-toht-pyah ...	mo'nee, nok, nuk'oo'a, un'ee.	uchchí, munai, kúr.
Aph'orism, *s.* ...	ပညာနှင့်ဆိုင်သော ရသောစကား ချက်။	pinyah-hnin-suyng-thau-yah-thau-sgah-chyet ...	mus'ul, zurb-ool-mus'ul ...	paḻamoḻi, súttiram.
A'piary, *s.* ...	ပျားအိမ်များကိုထားရာအရပ်...	pyah-ayn-myah-goh-tah-yah-a-yut ...	chhut'ta, shan ...	ténîkkúḍu.
Apiéce, *adv.* ...	စီ။ ...	zee ...	ek-ek, hur-ek ...	ov-vonṛukku.
Ap'ologue, *s.* ...	ပုံစကား။ ...	hpohn-sgah ...	hik'a'yut, kis'sa, ku'ha'nee..	uvamai, níthimoḻi, kathai.
Apol'ogy, *s.* ...	အပြစ်ပြေရာစကား။ ...	apyit-pyay-yah-s-gah ...	oozr, it'i'zar ...	niyáyam, mannippu-kéṭkai.
Ap'ophthegm, *s.* ...	မှတ်စရာကောင်းသောစကား ချက်။	hmat-sa-yah-kowng-thaw-sgah-chyet ...	tum'seel, ku'ha'wut ...	paḻamoḻí, níti-moḻí.
Ap'oplexy, *s.* ...	ဝက်ရူးနာ။ ...	wek-shoo-nah ...	pa'rus'sool, suk'tu ...	janní, aṅga-vigirtí.
Apos'tle, *s.* ...	တမန်တော်။ ...	t'mun-daw ...	fir'ish'ta, hu'wa'ree ...	appóstalan.
Apoth'ecary, *s.* ...	ဆေးဝါးကိုဖော်၍ရောင်းသော သူ။	tsay-wah-go-pau-yueh-yowng-thau-thoo ...	du'wa-saz, pun'sa'ree, ut'tar.	aviltham-virpón.
Apotheósis, *s.* ...	ဘုရားအဖြစ်သို့ချီးမြှောက်ခြင်း။	payah-apyit-tho-chyee-myowk-chyin ...	choo'pur'na, mul'na ...	abishé-kam, pratishṭai.
Apparátus, *s.* ...	တန်ဆာပလာ ...	ta-sah-balah ...	us'bab, sa'man, cheez'bust...	karuvi, ubakaraṇam.
Appar'el, *s.* ...	အဝတ် ...	a-woot ...	kup're, puh'na'wa ...	vastiram, áḍai.
Appárent, *a.* ...	ထင်ရှားသော ...	tin-shah-thau ...	ash'kar, noom'a'yan, sur'eeh.	veḷiyána, teḷivána.
Apparit'ion, *s.* ...	ရူပါရုံ၊တစ္ဆေ ...	yoo-pah-yohn, t'say ...	nuz'ur, hoo'zoor, noo'ma'ish.	tharisanai, ávésam.
Appeal', *v. n.* ...	အယူတော်ခံ ...	a-yoo-dau-cun ...	moor'a'fu ...	abayam, maṛu-vijáraṇaikéḷ
Appear', *v. n.* ...	ပေါ်လာသည် ...	pau-hlah-the ...	dikh'la'ee-d, soojh'na ...	tónṛu, káṇappaḍu.
Appease', *v. a.* ...	ငြိမ်းစေသည် ...	nyain-say-the ...	tus'keen-d ...	sánthap-paḍuttu, taṇi.

English.	Burmese.		Hindustani.	Tamil.
Appel'lant, *s.* ...	အယူတော်ခံသူ ...	a-yoo-dau-cun-thoo ...	da'wa-dar, da'wee-dor ...	maṛu-visáṛanai-kéṭppón.
Appel'late, *a.* ...	အယူတော်ခံခြင်းနှင့်ဆိုင်သော...	a-yoo-dau-cun-chyin-hnin-tsuyng-thau ...	urzee, ni'yaz'ee ...	viṇṇappattukkuriya.
Append', *v. a.* ...	ဆွဲရွိထည့်သော ...	tsweh-yueh-tee-the ...	jor'na, lug'a-l, ganth'na ...	toḍu, chér, kúṭṭu.
Appen'dix, *s.* ...	စကားဆက် ...	s-gah-sut ...	tu'tim'mu, zyl ...	anubantham, chérppu.
Appertain', *v. n.* ...	ဆိုင်သည် ...	tsuyng-the ...	dakh'il, ul'a'ka-r ...	chér, urittágu.
Ap'petite, *s.* ...	စားသောက်ချင်ခြင်း ...	sah-thouk-chyin-gyin ...	bhookh, chah ...	pasí, bójana-priyam.
Applause', *s.* ...	ချီးမွမ်း ...	chyee-mohn ...	tuh'seen, afr'een ...	pugaḻchchi, viyappu.
Ap'ple, *s.* ...	သစ်သော်သီး ...	thit-thau-the ...	seb, se'o ...	thappuváp-paḻam.
Ap'plicant, *s.* ...	လုပ်ကိုင်ရာတန်ဆာ ...	loht-kuyng-yah-ta-zah ...	ni'yaz'ee ...	manukéṭppón.
Apply', *v. a.* ...	လျှောက်သည် ...	hlyouk-the, (shouk-the) ...	kuh'na ...	iḍu, kaiyáḻu.
Appoint', *v. a.* ...	ခန့်ထားသည် ...	cun-tah-the ...	moo'kur'rur-k ...	kuṛi, niyami.
Appoint'ment, *s.* ...	ခန့်ထားခြင်း ...	cun-tah-chyin ...	wa'du ...	niyamippu, kuṭṭaḻai.
Appor'tion, *v. a.* ...	တော်လျော်အောင်ဝေငှသည် ...	taw-lyaw-oung-way-hngah-the, ...	dil'a'na, moo'kur'rur-k ...	í, paghiṛ, pangiku.
Ap'posite, *a.* ...	တော်လျော်သော ...	taw-lyaw-thaw, ...	nou'but, door'oost ...	tagunthа, uriya, eṛṛa.
Appraise', *v. a.* ...	အဘိုးဖြတ်သည်။ ...	a-poh-pyut-the ...	ank'na ...	vilaimathi, vilaikuṛi.
Appréciate, *v. a.* ...	ဤမည်သောအဘိုး ထိုက် သည်ဟု စိတ်ထဲမှာထင်မှတ်သည်။	ee-mee-thau-a-poh-tuyk-the-hoo-sayt-teh-hmah-tin-hmut-the ...	kee'mut, kudr ...	mathi, kaṇi, eṇṇu.
Apprehen'sion, *s.* ...	နား လည်ခြင်း။ ထင် မှတ် ခြင်း ဉာဏ်။	nah-lee-chyin, tin-hmut-chyin, nyahn ...	shoob'ha, khul'ish ...	eṇṇam, santékam.
Appren'tice, *s.* ...	လက်သား။ ...	let-thah ...	sha'gird, sikh ...	toḻil-payila-uḍanpaṭṭavan.
Approach', *s.* ...	ချဉ်း ကပ် သည်။ အနီး သို့ လာ သည်။	chyeen-cut-the, anee-thoh-lah-the ...	a'mud-a'mud, a'wa'tee ...	chérukai, kiṭṭugai.
Approbátion, *s.* ...	နှစ်သက်ခြင်း ...	hnit-thet-chyin ...	pus'und, tuh'seen ...	sammathi, piriyam.
Appropriate, *a.* ...	အလှုံတော်လျော်သော။ ...	a-hlohn-taw-lyaw-the ...	dakh'il, moo'kur'rur-k ...	niyami, urittákku.

Approve', *v. a.* ...	နှစ်သက်သည်။ ...	hnit-thet-the ...	pus'und-k, tuh'seen-k ...	pugal, meohchu, angikari.
A'pril, *s.* ...	ပေပြီလ ...	ay-pree-lah ...	april-mu'hee'na (*or*) mas ...	chittirai.
A'pron, *s.* ...	ရှေ့ပုံးခါးစည်းကြိုး။ ...	shay-pohn-cah-see-kyoh ...	dhuk'nee, sur'posh ...	muntángi, dúsitángi.
Apt, *a.* ...	တော်သော။သင့်သော။ ...	taw-thaw, thin-thaw ...	ma'il, tez-fuhm ...	taguntha, erra, takka.
Aq'ueduct, *s.* ...	ရေပြွန်။ ...	yay-pyohn ...	mooh'ree, nabdan ...	sálagam, váykkál.
Ar'abic, *a.* ...	အရပိတ်။ ...	a-ra-bait ...	ur'ub'ee ...	arábi-désattán.
Ar'able, *a.* ...	လယ်လုပ်ရန်ကောင်းသော။ ...	leh-loht-yun-kowng-thau...	jy'yud, joo'ta'ee ...	payircheygaikkána.
Ar'biter, *s.* ...	စပ်ကြားမှာ စီရင် ဆုံးဖြတ်သော သူ။ ...	sut-chyah-hmah-tsee-yin-sohn-pyut-thaw-thoo ...	sa'lis ...	naduvan, dharumakarttan.
Ar'bitrary, *a.* ...	ကိုယ်စိတ်ရှိရာသို့လိုက်သောသူ။	koh-sait-shee-yah-thoh-loht-thaw-thoo ...	moos'tuk'il ...	kodunkónmaiyána.
Ar'bitrate, *v. a.* ...	စပ်ကြားမှာစီရင်ဆုံးဖြတ်သည်။	sut-chyah-hmah-tsee-yin-sohn-pyut-the ...	sa'lis'ee-k, fy'sul-k, uzm-k...	tírmáni, nichchayi, alavaru, [tír.
Ar'bour, *s.* ...	ပန်းနွယ်။သစ်ပင်ရွဲသောတဲအုံ။	pun-nooeh-thit-pen-pweh-thaw-teh-ohn ...	koonj, mund'wa ...	kodipadarntha-pantal.
Arc, *s.* ...	စက်ဝိုင်းတခြမ်း။တပိုင်း။ ...	set-wuyng-t'chyun, t'sait ...	kum'an, goom'buz ...	valaiyam, piraivadivu.
Arch, *s.* ...	ပေါင်းကူး။ ...	powng-koo ...	goom'buz, kum'an ...	vilvalaivu, viruttapágam.
Arch'er, *s.* ...	လေးသမား။ ...	lay-th'-mah ...	teer'un'daz ...	vilkáran.
Ar'chitect, *s.* ...	ပိသုကာ။ ...	pay-tha-kah ...	ban'ee'kar, mi'u'mar ...	sirpáchári sirpan.
Ar'dent, *a.* ...	စိတ်အားကြီးသော ...	sayt-ah-gyee-thaw ...	gurm ...	analána, veppamána.
Ar'duous, *a.* ...	အပန်းတကြီးပြုရသော ...	a-pun-t-gyee-pyoo-yah-thaw ...	doosh'war ...	pirayásamána.
A'rea, *s.* ...	ပိုင်းခြားသောတလင်းပြင် ...	puyng-chyah-thaw-t-lin-pying ...	fuz'a ...	parappu, paravai.
3 Ar'id, *a.* ...	သွေ့ခြောက်သော ...	thway-chyouk-thaw ...	yoo'boos, sokh'tu ...	veppamána, varatchiyána.
Aríght, *adv.* ...	မှန်ကန်စွာ ...	hmun-cun-swah ...	huk ...	tittamága, sariyága.
Aríse, *v. n.* ...	တသည် (as the sun) ထွက်သည် ...	tah-the, twet-the ...	ooth'na ...	uthi, elumbu, tónru.

English.	Burmese.		Hindustani.	Tamil.
Aristoc'racy, *s.*	မှူးမတ်အုပ်စိုးခြင်း	moo-mut-oht-soh-chyin	shur'a'fut, koo'leen'a'ee, *or* shur'uf	pirabhukkaḷin-arasátchi, *or* pirabhugaḷ.
Arith'metic, *s.*	အရိသမိတိတ်	a-yith-ma-tait	ilm-i-his'ab	kaṇakku, kaṇitham.
Ark, *s.*	ရေလုံသောသစ်တာ	yay-lohn-thaw-thit-tah	nooh'a'ka-ju'haz	péḻai, kappal.
Arm, *s.*	လက်မောင်း	let-moung	banh, baz'oo, huth-bandh'na.	puyam, kai, karam.
Ar'mistice, *s.*	စစ်တိုက်ဆုတ်ဆိုင်စာချုပ်	tsit-tuyk-soht-tsuyng-sah-chyoht	moch'lut, tu'hum'mool, *arab.*	pór-niruttivaittal, pórviḍu-gai.
Arm'let, *s.*	လက်ကောက်	let-kowk	ba'zoo-bund	káppu, bájubanthu.
Ar'mour, *s.*	သံချပ်။ သံအင်္ကျီ	thun-chyut, thun-ing-gyee.	zir'u-bukh'tur	yutta-áyuthangaḷ.
Arms, *s.*	လက်နက်များ	let-net-myah	huth'i'yar, si'lah	yutta-áyuthangaḷ.
Ar'my, *s.*	ရဲမက်ဗိုလ်ခြေ။	yeh-met-boh-chyay	fouj, lush'kur	paḍai, iráṇuvam, sénai.
Aróma, *s.*	အနှုန်း	a-hnun	khoosh'bo	parimaḷam, sugandham.
Around', *pr.*	ပတ်လည်။ ပတ်ဝန်းကျင်	put-lee, put-woon-kyin	as'pas, gird'pesh, gher'na	súḻa, churrilum, churri.
Arouse', *v. a.*	နှိုးဆော်သည်	hnoh-saw-the	tur'gheeb-d	évu, túṇḍu.
Ar'rack, *s.*	ဆန်အရက်	tsun-a-yet	ur'uk	sáráyam.
Arraign', *v. a.*	စစ်ကြောရန်ခေါ်ထားသည်	tsit-kyaw-yun-caw-tah-the	il'zam-d	kuṟṟam-cháṟṟu.
Arránge, *v. a.*	စီစဉ်သည်။ ပြင်ဆင်သည်	see-seen-the, pyin-sin-the	suj'a'na, tur'teeb-d	kramapaḍuttu.
Ar'rant, *a.*	အလွန်ဆိုးသော	a-hlohn-soh-thaw	roos'wa, fuz'eeh	koḍiya, durkírttiyuḷḷa.
Arráy, *v. a.*	ခင်းကျင်းသည်။ (to adorn) တန်ဆာဆင်သည်	kin-chyin-the, tsah-sin-the.	a'ras'tu-k, sin'garna	aṇivagu, chiṟappi.
Arréar, *s.*	ကျန်ငွေ	kyun-ngway	bak'i'yat	niluvai, bákki.
Arrest', *s.*	မင်းအခွင့်နှင့်ဖမ်းဆီးသည်။ (to stop) ဆီးတားသည်	min-a-kuin-hnin-pun-see-thee, see-tah-the	kyd, nuz'ur'bun'd'ee	niṟuttu, piḍi, paṟi.
Arríval, *s.*	ရောက်ခြင်း	yowk-chyin	woo'rood, pu'hoonch	varugai, póyohérugai.

Ar'rogant, *a.* ...	တောင်လွှားစော်ကားသော ...	towng-hlwah-saw-kah-thaw	goos'takh, mugh'roor ...	eḍuppána, agantaiyulla.
Ar'row, *s.* ...	မြှား ...	hmyah ...	teer ...	ambu, attiram, páṇam.
Ar'row-root, *s.* ...	အာရောရွတ် ...	arrah-root ...	arrah-root ...	kúvakkilaṅgu.
Ar'senal, *s.* ...	လက်နက်တိုက် ...	leh-net-tuyk ...	mukh'zum ...	rasttuchálai, paḍaiviḍu.
Ar'senic, *s.* ...	စိန် ...	sayn ...	snuk'hi'ya, hur'tal ...	páshánam.
Ar'son, *s.* ...	မနာလိုသေားစိတ်နှင့်သူအိမ်ကိုမီးရှုခြင်း ...	ma-nah-loh-thaw-sayt-hning-thoo-ayn-go-mee-shoo-chyin ...	kha'nu-so'zee ...	víḍuchuḍum-kuṟṟam.
Art, *s.* ...	အတတ်ပညာ တတ်ခြင်း။ လိမ္မာခြင်း ...	a-tut-pin-yah, tut-chyin, laym-mah-chyin ...	hoon'ur, fun ...	kalai, tolil, vittai.
Ar'tery, *s.* ...	နှစ်လုံး ထဲက ထွက်သော သွေးကြော ...	hnit-lohn-deh-gah-twet-thaw-thway-chyaw ...	shir'yan ...	náḍi, narambu.
Art'ful, *a.* ...	လိမ္မာသော ...	laym-mah-thaw ...	nut'khut, sy'a'na ...	súlohcha, kabaḍa.
Ar'ticle, *s.* ...	အချက် a *or* an, and the, ဟူသောစကား ...	a-chyet, (*a* or *an*, and *the*,) hoo-thaw-sgah ...	ba'but, cheez, mu'sul'a ...	pápattu, uru, sáriyai.
Artif'icer, *s.* ...	လက်မှုပညာနှင့်လုပ်သောသူ ...	let-hmoo-pin-nyah-hnin-loht-thaw-thoo ...	dust'kar, ka'reegur ...	kammáḷan, siṟpan.
Artific'ial, *a.* ...	လက်လုပ်သော ...	let-loht-thaw ...	um'ul'ee, mus'noo'ee ...	vichittra, oppána.
Artil'lery, *s.* ...	အမြောက်စု။အမြောက်မှုထမ်းစု ...	a-myouk-soo, a-myouk-hmoo-mut-soo ...	top, gujnal ...	píraṅgi-paṭṭáḷam.
Artisan', *s.* ...	လက်ပညာနှင့်လုပ်တတ်သောသူ ...	let-pin-nyah-hnin-loht-dut-thaw-thoo ...	ka'ree'gur, mis'tree ...	kammáḷan, chitrakáṛan.
Ar'tist, *s.* ...	ပညာ အတတ် တစုံအခုတတ်သောသူ ...	pin-nyah-a-tut-t-sohn-t-koo-tut-thaw-thoo ...	hoo'nur-posh'a, moo'suw'wir	chitrakáran.
As, *conj.* ...	ကဲ့သို့။ အတိုင်း။ အညီအအမျှ။ while, အခါ ...	geh-tho, a-tuyng, a-nyee, a-hmyah, a-cah ...	jon, jy'sa, jis'tur'uh ...	póla, udháraṇamága.
Asafœ'tida, *s.* ...	ရှိန်းခို ...	shayn-goh ...	heeng ...	peruṅkáyam, iṅgu.
Ascend' *v. n.* ...	တက်သည် ...	tet-the ...	churh'na ...	uyar, éṟu.

ENGLISH.	BURMESE.		HINDUSTANI.	TAMIL.
Ascen'sion, *s.* ...	တက်ခြင်း ...	tet-chyin ...	chur'ha'o, oo'rooj, ir'tif'a ...	éṛram, árúḍam.
Ascent', *s.* ...	တက်ခြင်းမြင့်သောအရပ် ...	tet-chyin, myin-thaw-a-yut	chur'ha'ee ...	méḍu, uthayam, uyaram.
Ascertain', *v. a.* ...	သေချာအောင်သိသည် ...	thay-chyah-owng-thee-the..	thuh'ra'na ...	nithâni, nichchayi.
Ascet'ic, *s.* ...	အထီးမြိုးခြိုစွာကြင့်သောသူ ...	a-tee-chyoh-chyin-swah-chyin-thaw-thoo ...	go'shu-geer, go'shunish'een.	tavasi, tuṛavi.
Ascríbe, *v. a.* ...	စပ်ပေးသည် ...	sut-pay-the ...	lug'a'na ...	chumattu, cháṭṭu.
Ashámed, *a.* ...	ရှက်သည် ...	shet-the ...	shur'min'du, khuj'il ...	veḍkamuḷḷa, náṇamuḷḷa.
Ashóre, *adv.* ...	ကမ်းပေါ်မှာ ...	kun-baw-hmah ...	kun'a're-pur ...	karaiyil, karaiyé, karaikku.
Asíde, *adv.* ...	အလွဲ ...	a-lweh ...	ul'ug, ek-tur'uf, jood'a ...	pakkattil, vilagi, puṛattil.
Ask, *v. a.* ...	တောင်းသည်။မေးသည် ...	towng-the, may-the ...	mang'na, poochh'na ...	vichári, kéḷ, vinávu.
Asleep', *adv.* ...	အိပ်ပျော်လျက် ...	ay-pyaw-lyet ...	so'ta ...	nittiraiyáy, timiráy.
As'pect, *s.* ...	မြက်နှာထား ...	myeh-hnah-tah ...	hoo'zoor ...	káṭchi, tóṛṛam.
Asper'se, *v. a.* ...	ဖြန်းသည်။သူအသရေဖျက်အောင်ကဲ့ရဲ့သည်	pyun-the, thoo-atheray-pyet oung-keh-yeh-the ...	ga'lee, bud-zub'an'ee ...	ésu, ninti, tiṭṭu.
Asphalt', *s.* ...	အင်္ဂတေတမျိုး ...	inga-deh-t'myoh ...	nuf'at, nift ...	nilakkíl.
Aspirate, *v. a.* ...	ဟထိုးသံနှင့်ပြောသည် ...	ha-toh-thun-hnin-pyaw-the ...	ooch'char, tul'uf'fooz ...	vallisaikkuṛi.
Aspirátion, *s.* ...	စိတ်နှစ်လုံးထဲမှာဆုတောင်းခြင်း	sayt-hnit-lohn-deh-hmah-soo-towng-chyin ...	ir'a'da, chah, ar'zoo, khwa'hish-mund, ar'zoo'mund...	avá, káthal, náṭṭam, tagá.
Ass, *s.* ...	မြည်း ...	myeh ...	gud'ha, gud'hee ...	kaḻuthai.
Assail', *v. a.* ...	တိုက်သည် ...	tuyk-the ...	hum'la-k, hul'lu-k ...	saruvu, mélviḻu.
Assas'sin, *s.* ...	မထင် မရှားလူ အသက်ကို သတ်သောသူ	m'tin-m'shah-loo-ăthet-goh-thut-thaw-thoo ...	khoon'rez, hut'ti'ya'ra ...	sathikáran.
Assem'ble, *v. a.* ...	စုဝေးသည် ...	soo-way-the ...	jum'a-k ...	kúṭṭu, sér, tiraḷ.
Assent', *v. n.* ...	သဘောတူ၍ဝန်ခံသည် ...	th'baw-too-yu-eh-woon-cun-the ...	ruz'a, it'ti'fak ...	uḍenpaḍu, sammathi.

Assid'uous, *a.* ...	လုံ့လပြုသည် ...	loh-lah-pyoo-the ...	mool'a'zim ...	muyarchchiyulla, úkkamána
Assignee', *s.* ...	အလှူခံသောသူ ...	a-hlu-eh-ahcun-thaw-thoo...	ka'im-muk'am ...	káriyakáran, oppadaiyérpón
Assign, *v. a.* ...	ခွန့်ထားသည် ...	kohn-tah-the ...	dil'a'na, moo'kur'rur-k ...	niyami, kuri, pagir, oppdai.
Assim'ilate, *v. a.* ...	တူစေသည် ...	too-say-the ...	sum'an, ek-san, ik-sar ...	samáni, oppákku, nigarákku
Assist', *v. a.* ...	ကူညီသည် ...	koo-nyee-the ..	mud'ud-k ...	uthavichey, tunainil.
Assíze, *s.* ...	တရားသူကြီးတို့ရဝေးခြင်း ...	tyah-thoo-gyee-tsoo-way-	dur'bar ...	niyáyasangam.
Assóciate, *v.* ...	ပေါင်းပေါ်သည် ...	powng-paw-the, [chyin ...	sat'hee, sat'hin ...	kúttáli, tólan.
Assort', *v. n.* ...	အမျိုးအလိုက်ခွဲခြားထားသည် ...	ahmoo-a-luyt-kweh-yueh-	it ti'fak, bant'na ...	vagu, vagaippaduttu.
Assuáge, *v. a.* ...	ငြိမ်စေသည် ...	nyain-say-the, [tah-the ...	tus'-keen-d ...	tani, sántappaduttu, árru.
Assúme, *v. a.* ...	ယူဆောင်သည် ...	yoo-sowng-the ...	le'na, le'le'na ...	karpi, edu, tuni, sambávi.
Assúrance, *s.* ...	ကြစ်ကြစ်ပြောတားခြင်း ...	kyut-kyut-pyaw-tah-the ..	dil'e'ree, yuk'een ...	nichchayam, uruthi, tunivu.
Assúre, *v. a.* ...	မှန်စေသည် ...	hman-say-the ...	tus'ul'lee-d ..	uruthichol, nichchayi.
Astern', *adv.* ...	ပဲ့ဆီသို့ ...	peh-see-thoh ...	peech'hul ...	pinnanipatil, abarattil.
Asth'ma, *s.* ...	ပန်းနာ ...	pun-nah ...	dum'u, sankh, kas-swas ...	swásakásam, ílai.
Aston'ish, *v. a.* ...	အံ့ဩစေသည် ...	un-aw-say-the ...	tu'aj'joob-k ...	bramippi, tigaippi.
Aston'ishment, *s.* ...	မှိုင်တွေသည် ...	hmuyng-tway-chyin ...	hy'ra'nee, uch'um'bha ...	áchchariyam, bramippu.
Astound', *v. a.* ...	အလွန်မှိုင်တွေစေသည် ...	a-hloon-hmuyng-tway-say the ...	tu'aj'joob-k ...	tigaippi, bramippi, kalakku.
Astrol'oger, *s.* ...	ဟူးရား။ ဗေဒင်အတတ်ကိုတတ်သောသူ ...	hoo-yah, bay-din-a-tut-go-tut-thaw-thoo ...	jo'tish'ee, jo'ti'kee, noo'joo'	sóthidan, jóshiyan, kanitan.
Astron'omer, *s.* ...	နေ လ ကြယ် နက္ခတ် တတ်သော ဗေဒင်ဆရာ ...	nay, lah, kyeh-nekkut-tut-thaw-bay-din-tsay-yah...	hy'ut'dan [mee,...	vánasástiri.
Asun'der, *adv.* ...	တကွဲစီ ...	t'gweh-hsee ...	jood'a, ul'ug ...	pirinthu, vittu, ara.
At, *pr.* ...	တွင်။နှိုက်။မှာ ...	dwin, hnuyt, hmah ...	pas, pur, men ..	il, idattil, ága, andai,
A'theist, *s.* ...	ဘုရားမရှိဟုယူသောသူ ...	pa-yah-m'shee-hoo-yoo-	duh'ri'ya, mool hid, nas'tik..	súnyaváthi, nástikan.
Athirst', *a.* ...	ရေငတ်သော ...	yay-ngut-thaw, [thaw-thoo,	pi'ya'sa, pi'ya'see, tish'nu ...	tavippáy, táhamáy.
Athlet'ic, *a.* ...	လက်ပွေသည် ...	let-pway-the ...	dho'kur, kut'ta ...	sattuvamulla.
Athwart', *pr.* ...	ကန့်လန့် ...	kun-lun ...	a'ra, ben'da ...	úḍé, kurukké, uruva.

English.	Burmese.		Hindustani.	Tamil.
At'mosphere, *s.* ...	လေ ...	lay ...	a'kash, hu'wa ...	váyu, anilam.
A'tom, *s.* ...	အနုမြူ ...	a-nah-myoo ...	ba'reek, ...	paramáṇu, aṇunutpam.
Atóne, *v. n.* ...	ပြေအောင်ပြုသည် ...	pyay-owng-pyoo-the ...	kuf'a'ra-d ...	ídụcheluttu, iṇakku.
Atrócious, *a.* ...	အလွန်ဆိုးသော ...	a-hloon-tsoh-thaw ...	khub'ees ...	kaḍiya kcḍiya.
At'rophy, *s.* ...	ပိန်ချုံးသောအနာ ...	payn-chyohn-thaw-a-nah ...	bee'ma'ree, a'zar, murz ...	kayam kayarógam.
Attach', *v. a.* ...	တွဲကပ်သည် ...	tsweh-cut-the ...	ganth'na, lug'a-l ...	chér, oṭṭu, aṇai, parru, aḍu.
Attack', *v. a.* ...	စတင်၍တိုက်သည် ...	sah-tin-yueh-tuyk-the ...	hum'lu ...	tákku, mélviḻu, jáḍu.
Attain', *v. a.* ...	ရသည် ...	yah-the ...	pu'hoonch, py'da-k ...	peṛu, aḍai, chér.
Attempt', *v. a.* ...	ပြုစမ်းသည် ...	pyoo-sun-the ...	ko'shish, kusd ...	tuṇi, prayattani, muyal.
Attend', *v. a.* ...	လိုက်ပါသည် ...	luyt-pah-the ...	khid'mut-k, ha'zir ...	chevikoḍu, avadháni.
Atten'dance, *s.* ...	ပါရှိအောင်လာခြင်း ...	pah-she-owng-lah-chyin ..	ha'zir-ba'shee, khid'mut ...	pónavargaḷtogai, parijanam.
Atten'tion, *s.* ...	နားထောင်ခြင်း ...	nah-towng-chyin ...	tun'dih'ee ...	karuttu, chintanai.
Atten'tive, *a.* ...	မှတ်သားသော ...	hmut-thah-thaw ...	hosh'yar, mool'a'zim ...	karuttuḷḷa, ninaippuḷḷa.
Attest', *v. a.* ...	သက်သေခံသည် ...	thet-thay-cun-the ...	gu'wah'eede'-na ...	sákshichol.
Attíre, *s.* ...	ဝတ်ဆင်သည် ...	woot-tsin-the ...	po'shak ...	uḍai, vastrabhúshaṇam, aṇi.
At'titude, *s.* ...	အနေအထိုင် ...	a-nay-a-tuyng ...	joom'bish, tuk'an ...	kólam, nilai, abinayam.
Attor'ney, *s.* ...	ရှေ့နေ ...	shay-nay [the,...	wak'eel ...	niyáyaturantaran.
Attract', *v. a.* ...	ကိုယ်ဆီသို့ဆွဲငင်သည် ...	koh-tsee-thoh-tsweh-ngin-	loob ha'na ...	váṅgu, iḻu, vali, ír. karushi.
At'tribute, *s.* ...	ဆိုင်ကြောင်းကိုပြောသည် ...	tsuyng-gyowng-goh-pyaw-	sif'ut ...	kuṇam, iladchaṇam, payani-
Attrit'ion, *s.* ...	ပွတ်၍ပွန်းခြင်း ...	poht-yu-eh-pohn-chyin [the.	ghis'a'o, rug'ur, ma'lish ...	téyppu, uraippu. [lai-
Attúne, *v. a.* ...	သီခြင်းသံညီအောင်ညှိသည် ...	thee-chyin-thun-nyee-oung	a'lapcha'ree, *sans.* toon'too'	isaitiruttu, sutikúṭṭu, (*sans.*)-
Auc'tion, *s.* ...	လေလံ ...	lay-lun, [pyoo-the,...	nee'lam [na'na,...	élam, kúṛiviṛkai. [-a'lap'na.
Auctioneer', *s.* ...	လေလံပြုသောသူ ...	lay-lun-pyit-thaw-thoo ...	nee'lam-wa'la ...	élamnaḍattuvón *or* kúṛuvón.
Audácious, *a.* ...	ရဲရင့်သော ...	yeh-yin-thaw ...	mun'chul'a ...	tuṇikaramána, karuvamuḷḷa.
Audac'ity, *s.* ...	ရဲရင့်ခြင်း ...	yeh-yin-chyin ...	joor'ut ...	tuṇikaram, ahaṅkáram.
Au'dible, *a.* ...	ကြားလောက်သော ...	kyah-lowk-thaw ...	moo'fus'sul, furk ...	teḷiváṇa, kéṭkattakka.

Au'dience, *s.* ...	နားကြားခြင်း ...	nah-kyah-chyin ...	soon'nee-wa'la, sami'a ...	kétpór, sabai, arangam.
Au'dit, *s.* ...	စာရင်းကိုတွက်စစ်သည် ...	tsah-yin-goh-twet-tsit-the..	his'abjanch'na ...	kaṇakkuparisóthanai.
Au'ger, *s.* ...	လွန်ပူကြီး ...	lohn-boo-gyee ...	bur'ma ...	tuṛappaṇam tamrúsi.
Au'gust, *s.* ...	အောဂုတ်လ ...	au-goot-lah ...	august ...	ávaṇi.
Au'gust, *a.* ...	ဘုန်းကြီးသည် ...	bohn-gyee-the ...	jub'eel-ool-kudr ...	máḍchimaiyuḷḷa, magattuva.
Aunt, *s.* ...	မိကြီး။ကြီးတော် ...	mee-gyee, gyee-daw ...	kha'la, phoop'hee, phoo'a ...	periyatáy, attai, chiriyatáy.
Au'ricle, *s.* ...	နားရွက် ...	nah-yu-et ...	kan, gosh ...	chevi, káthu, siravam.
Author'ity, *s.* ...	အာဏာ ...	ah-nah ...	ikh'ti'yar, muk'door ...	athikáram, piramáṇam.
Avaunt', *interj.* ...	သွားတဲ့ ...	thwah, heh ...	hut, chukh'e ...	dúrappó, agal, appuṛam.
Avert', *v. a.* ...	လွှဲသည် ...	hlweh-the ...	duf'a-k, tal'na ...	taḍu, níkku, máṛṛu, tavir.
A'viary, *s.* ...	ငှက်များလှောင်ရာခြုံ ...	hnget-myah-hlowng-yah-chuyng ...	chi'ri'ya-kha'na ...	kuruvikkúḍu, pañcharam.
Avocátion, *s.* ...	ကိုယ်နှင့်ဆိုင်သောအလုပ်။ ...	koh-hnin-tsuyng-thaw-a-lohk ...	kam, kaj, kar ...	aluval, kariyam, toḻil, vélai
Avoid', *v. a.* ...	ရှောင်သည် ...	shyowng-the ...	door-bhag'na ...	níngu, vilakku, níkku, oḻi.
Awáke, *a.* ...	နိုးသည် ...	noh-the ...	jug'ta, be-dar ...	jákkrathaiyána, viḻippána.
Awáre, *a.* ...	သတိရှိသော ...	th-dee-she-thaw ...	hosh'yar, chou'kus, khub'ur'	echcharippuḷḷa, aṛintha.
Away', *adv.* ...	အခြားတပါးသို့ ...	a-chyah-t-bah-thoh ...	door, tuf'a'wut [dar,...	eṭṭa, nínga, dúra, vilagi.
Awe, *s.* ...	ကြောက်ရွံ့ရှိသေးခြင်း ...	chyowk-yohn-she-thay-chyin ...	dur, dur'na ...	achcham, ékkam, bhayam.
Aw'ful, *a.* ...	ကြောက်ရွံ့ဖွယ်ဖြစ်သော ...	chyowk-yohn-bweh-pyit-thaw ...	turs'an, mooheeb ...	bhayankaramána, vimmitha
Awl, *s.* ...	သားရေနယ်ကိုဖေါက်ရန်ရူး ...	tha-yay-neh-goh-powk-[yun-soo,...	ra'pee, soot'a'ree ...	cheruppúsi. sarumánúsi.
Aw'ning, *s.* ...	မိုဃ်းကာ ...	moh-kah, ...	sha'mi'yan'a, num'gee'ra ...	kúḍáram, vithánam.
Axe, *s.* ...	ပုဆိန် ...	powk-sayn ...	kool'ha'ree ...	kóḍari, kuḍáram.
Ax'is, *s.* ...	ဝင်ရိုး။ ...	win-yoh ...	me'roo, mih'wur ...	kóḷattinmaiyam, uruváṇi.
Ay, or Aye, *adv.*...	ဟုပ်ကဲ့ ...	hoht-keh ...	jee, bul'e ...	ám, ámám.
Aye, *adv.* ...	အစဉ်အမြဲ။ ...	a-seen-a-myeh ...	hum'esh'u, sud'a ...	eppoḻuthum.

English.	Burmese.		Hindustani.	Tamil.
Bab'ble, *v. n.*	အကလေးကဲ့သို့ စကားမပြီ မသပြောသည်။	a-klay-geh-thoh-sgah-m'pyee-m'thah-pyaw-the	buk-buk'a'na, buk'na	pitharral, alappu.
Bábe, Baby, *s.*	နို့စို့ကလေး။	noh-zoh-k'lay	buch'cha, ba'la, ba'lak	kulantai, pálakan, savalai.
Bábel, *s.*	ရှုတ်ထွေးခြင်း။	shoht-tway-chyin	khul'bul, hul'chul,	tárumáru, kulappam.
Baboon', *s.*	မျောက်ကြီးတမျိုး။	myowk-gyee-t'myo	my'moon	peruṅkuraṅgu, vánaram.
Bach'elor, *s.*	မယားမနေသေးသောသူ။	m'yah-m'nay-thay-thaw-thoo,	mooj'ur'rud,	viváhamohey-yáthavan.
Back, *s.*	ကျော။အနောက်။	kyaw, ahnowk,	peeth	muthugu, pinpuram.
Back'bite, *v. a.*	ကတိုက်သည်။	ga-tuyk-the	tooh'mut, budgo'ee, booh'tan, lim,	puraṅkúru, puranipésu.
Backgam'mon, *s.*	အန်ကစားခြင်းတမျိုး။	un-ga-'sah-chyin-t'myo	nurd,	vaṭṭáḍal, páchchigai.
Back'ward, *a.*	နောက်ပြန်။	hnowk-pyun	roo'gur'dan	karuttillátha, mantha.
Bad, *a.*	ဆိုးသော။မကောင်း။	soh-thaw, m'kowng	boor'a, bud, khur'ab, mund.	ágátha, iḻappána, keṭṭa.
Badge, *s.*	အမှတ်အလား။	a-hmut-a-lah	nish'an, ul'u'mut	aḍaiyáḷam, kuṛi, muttirai.
Bad'ger *s. v.*	ခွေးတူ။ဝက်တူး။ထွေဝေစေသည်။	kway-too, wet-too-tway-way-say-the,	bee'joo, bij'joo	oru-mirugam, tagasu.
Bag, *s.*	အိတ်။	ait,	thy'la, thy'lee	pai, sákku, kóṇi, jóḷikai.
Bail, *s.*	ခံဝန်သူနှင့်လွှတ်သည်။	cun-woon-thoo-hnin-hloot-the,	za'min'ee	uttaravátham, piṇai, zámin.
Bail'iff, *s.*	မြို့စာရေး။	myo-sah-yay,	moo'hus'sil	kaṭṭaḷaikkáran, muttiraiperṛa-sévagan.
Bait, *s.*	ငါးမျှားစာ။ငှက်တောင်းစာ။	ngah-hmyah-sah-hngeh-towng-sah,	cha'ra	irai, uṇavu, vaḻiyuṇavu.
Bake, *v. a.*	ပေါင်းသည်။	powng-the,	puk'a'na	chuḍu, pori, chúḷaiyirchuḍu
Báker, *s.*	မုန့်သည်။	mohn-the	nan'puz, ro'tee-wa'la	roṭṭikkáran, appakkáran.
Bal'ance, *s.*	ချိန်ခွင်။	chayn-kwin	mee'zan, ba'kee, fa'zil	samam, niluvai, bákki.
Bale, *s.*	ကုန်ထုပ်။	kohn-toht	gut'hur, mot	kaṭṭu, múṭṭai, sippam.
Bale, *v. a.*	အမင်္ဂလာဖြစ်သည်။	ah-mingalah-pyit-the,	oôleech'na	sippamákku, kaṭṭu.
Ball, *s.*	အလုံး။ အမြောက်ဆန်။ ကသောပွဲ။	a-lohn, a-myowk-tsun, kah-thaw-pweh	go'la, ruks, nach	panthu, kuṇḍu, náṭṭiyam.
Bal'lad, *s.*	သီချင်းတမျိုး။	thee-chyin-t'myoh	geet, gan, sur'od	oruvithappáṭṭu.

Bal'sam, *s.* ...	သွက်သောသစ်စေးမွေး။ ...	thwet-thaw-thit-say-	bul'u'san ...	tailam, marappisin, jalébam.
Bamboo', *s.* ...	ဝါး။ ...	wah, [hmooay, ...	bans, buns ...	múṅgil, kaḻai.
Band, *s.* ...	စည်းနှောင်သောကြိုး။ စစ်သူရဲတပ်။ ...	tsee-hnowng-thaw-kyoh, tsit-thoo-yeh-tut ...	bund, *troop.* gur'oh, ta'i'fa...	kaṭṭu, kúṭṭam, váttiyam.
Ban'dage, *s.* ...	ကြိပ်စည်းသောအဝတ်။ ...	chyut-tsee-thaw-a-woot ...	bund, bund'hun, put'tee ...	kaṭṭu, bandam, káyakkaṭṭu.
Ban'dit, *s.* ...	ထားမြ။ဗလက္ကာရပြုသောသူ။...	dah-myah, blek-kayah-pyoo-thaw-thoo ...	loo'te're ...	koḻḻaikkáran.
Bane, *s.* ...	သေစေတတ်သောအဆိပ်။ ...	thay-say-dut-thaw-a-tsait...	bis, ma'hoor, bish, bikh ...	nañju, visham, násam. [tu.
Ban'ish, *v. a.* ...	နှင်ထုတ်သည်။ ...	hnin-toht-the ...	be-wut'un-k ...	puṛatdésattiṛkagaṛṛu, turat-
Bank'rupt, *s.* ...	ကြွေးမြီတင်၍မဆပ်သောသူ။ ...	kyoo-ay-myee-tin-yue-m'sut-thaw-thoo ...	de'wa'li'ya, na-dar ...	kaḍaniṛukkavagaiyilláthav-
Ban'ner, *s.* ...	အောင်လံ။ ...	owng-lun ...	nish'an, jhun'da ...	tugiṛkoḍi, viruthukkoḍi. [an.
Ban'quet, *s.* ...	စားပွဲသောက်ပွဲ။ ...	sah-pweh-thowk-pweh ...	je'o'nar, ziy'a'fut ...	virunthu, uṇḍáṭṭu, paṇḍikai.
Ban'yan, *s.* ...	ညောင်ပင်။ ...	nyowng-bin ...	bur, but ...	ál, álamaram.
Bap'tism, *s.* ...	နှစ်ခြင်း မင်္ဂလာ။ ဗတ္တိဇံ မင်္ဂလာ။ ...	hnit-chyin-mingalah, butteezan-mingalah ...	gho'ta ...	ñánasnánam, niráṭṭu.
Bap'tize, *v. a.* ...	ဗတ္တိဇံမင်္ဂလာကိုပေးသည်။ ...	butteezan-mingalah-goh-pay-the ...	ghota-d ...	ñánasnánaṅkoḍu.
Bar, *s.* ...	သံချောင်း။သစ်ချောင်း။ ...	thun-chyowng, thit-	bil'lee ...	salágai, kuṛunthaṛi.
Barbárian, *s.* ...	လူရိုင်း။ ...	loo-yuyng, [chyoung,...	na-tur'a'shee'du ...	miléchchan, dushṭan pullan.
Bar'barous, *s.* ...	ရိုင်းစိုင်းသော။ ...	yuyng-suyng-thaw ...	kut'hor, nirdy ...	dushṭṭa, koḍiya, kochchai.
Bar'ber, *s.* ...	ဆတ္တာသည်။ ...	suttah-the ...	huj'jam, na'ee, na'pit, oos'ta.	ambaṭṭan, návithan.
Bard, *s.* ...	စာဆို။ ...	tsah-soh ...	sha'ir, nuz'mee ...	kaviráyan, pulavan, kaviññjan
Bare, *a.* ...	ပလာ။ဟင်းလင်း။ ...	p'lah, hin-lin ...	nun'ga, ...	niruváṇa, veṛu, tanitta.
Bar'gain, *s.* ...	ရောင်းဝယ်သောအရာ။ ...	yowng-weh-thaw-a-yah ...	chook'tee, shurt ...	oppantam, uḍanpaḍikkai.
Barge, *s.* ...	သံဗန်ကြီးတမျိုး။ ...	thun-bun-gyee-t'myoh ...	kut'o'ra, put'e'la ...	salaṅgu, paḍagu.
Bark, *s.* ...	သစ်ခေါက်။ ...	thit-kowk, [tun-ayn,...	chhil'ka ...	marapaṭṭai.
Bar'rack, *s.* ...	စစ်သူရဲတို့နေရာတန်းအိမ်။ ...	tsit.thoo-yeh-doh-nay-yah-	chhou'nee ...	póṛchchéyakarvásam.

ENGLISH.	BURMESE.		HINDUSTANI.	TAMIL.
Bar'rel, *s.* ...	စည်၊မြောင်း။ ...	see, myowng ...	pee'pa, nal ...	píppá, kuḷal, kuḷáy.
Bar'ren, *a.* ...	မြုံသော၊ဖိုသော။ ...	myohn-thaw, poh-thaw ...	banjh, ran'da, bebur ...	páḷána, payanpaḍátha.
Barricáde, *s.* ...	ရန်သူတို့ကိုကာဆီးသောအရာ။ ..	yun-thoo-doh-goh-kah-see-thaw-a-yah ...	sud, ut'ka'o, rok'un ...	aḍaippu, taḍai, vaḷiyaḍaippu.
Bar'rier, *s.* ...	အကာ၊အဆီးအကာ။ ...	a-kah, a-tsee-a-kah ...	rok, ut'uk ...	araṇ, ellaikkuṛi, taḍai.
Bar'rister, *s.* ...	ဝတ်လုံရသောရှေ့နေ။ ...	woot-lohn-yaw-thaw, shay-	wuk'eel ...	niyáyaváthi, vakkíl.
Bar'ter, *s.* ...	လဲသည်၊တပ်သည်။ ...	leh-the, tut-the, [nay, ...	de'wa'le'yse ...	paṇḍamáṛṛu, viyápáram.
Base, *s.* ...	ယုတ်သော။ ...	yoht-thaw ...	ka'i'du, bin'a, ny'o ...	aḍi, astiváram.
Bash'ful, *a.* ...	ရှက်တတ်သော။ ...	shet-dut-thaw ...	shur'min'du ...	kúchchamuḷḷa, náṇamuḷḷa.
Básin, *s.* ...	ဇလုံ၊အင်တုံ။ ...	za-lohn, ing-dohn ...	ba'sun, zurf ...	kiṇṇam, kalasam, kuḷam.
Básis, *s.* ...	အမြစ်။ ...	a-myit ...	ny'o, bin'a, jur ...	astiváram, átharavu, nilai.
Bask, *v. n.* ...	နေစာလှုံသည်။ ...	nay-sah-hlohn-the ...	ghum'a'na ...	kuḷirkáy, veyiliṛkiḍa.
Bas'ket, *s.* ...	တောင်း။ ...	towng ...	tok'ra, tok'ree ...	kúḍai, petty.
Bass, *s.* ...	အောက်သံ။ ...	owk-thun ...	bum ...	mantaram, gambírasubdam.
Bat, *s.* ...	လင်းနို့၊လင်းဆွဲ။ ...	lin-noh, lin-sweh ...	ba'door, chum'gee'dur ...	vauvál, turiñjil, vával.
Batch, *s.* ...	အစုအပေါင်း။ ...	a-tsoo, a-powng ...	jum, bheer, umboh ...	oru-kúṭṭam.
Bathe, *v. a.* ...	ရေချိုးသည်။ ...	yay-chyoh-the ...	ghoosl-d, nuh'la'na ...	níráṭṭu, snánam, kuḷi.
Bat'ten, *v. a.* ...	တံခါးပေါင်။ ...	t'kah-powng ...	mo'ta ...	pushṭiyákku, cheḷuppi.
Bat'ter, *v. a.* ...	ရောနှောသောစားစရာတမျိုး ...	yaw-hnaw-thaw-sah-sayah-t'myoh ...	mil'a'o mil'a'na ...	kalakku, kúṭṭu, iḍi, tákku.
Bat'tery, *s.* ...	အမြောက်တင်ရန်မြေကတုတ် ...	a-myowk-tin-yun-myay-	mor'chu, hum'la, hul'lu ...	iḍittal, pírañginirai.
Bat'tle, *s.* ...	စစ်တိုက်ခြင်း။ ...	tait-tuyk-chyin, [ga-tote, ...	lur'a'ee, run, jung ...	chaṇḍai, pór, yuttam.
Bawl, *v. n.* ...	အော်သည်။ ...	aw-the ...	ḷul'kar, poo'kar ...	kúvu, kúkkuraliḍu.
Bay, *s.* ...	ပင်လယ်အောင်ကွေ့။ ...	pin-leh-towng-kway ...	kol ...	kuḍákkaḍal.
Bay'onet, *s.* ...	သေနတ်စွပ်လှံ။ ...	the-nut-soht-hlun ...	khun'jur, kut'ar ...	saniyan.
Bazaar', *s.* ...	ဈေး။ ...	zay ...	doo'kan, bazaar ...	kaḍai, santai, ávaṇam.

English	Burmese	Burmese in English characters	Hindustani	Tamil
Be, *v. n.*	ဖြစ်သည်။	pyit-the	ho'na	iru.
Beach, *s.*	ကမ်းမြေသောင်ပြင်။	kun-myay-thowng-pyin	kin'a'ra, kun'a'ra	kadarkarai, kadalóram.
Bead, *s.*	ပုတီး။	pa-dee	mun'ka, pot	mani, manipólattirandathu.
Beak, *s.*	ငှက်နှုတ်သီး။	hngek-hnoht-thee	nok, chonch	paravaimúkku.
Beam, *s.*	တုင်။	toht	kur'ee, shuh'teer	uttiram, túlam.
Bear, *s.*	ဝက်ဝံ။	weh-woon	bhal, bha'loo, reech	karadi.
Bear, *v. a.*	ယူတင်သည်။	yoo-tin-the	dho'na	kondupó, chuma, edu.
Beard, *s.*	မုဆိတ်။	moh-sayt	dar hee, reesh	mísai, tádi.
Beast, *s.*	တိရစ္ဆာန်။	te-ray-sun	hy'wan, pus'oo, jan'wur	nárkálmirugam, vilangu.
Beat, *v. a.*	ရိုက်ပုတ်သည်။	yuyk-poht-the	mar'na, peet'na	kottu, adi, móthu, kuttu.
Beatific, *a.*	ကောင်းကင် ချမ်း သာ နှင့် ဆိုင် သော။	kowng-gin-chyun-thah-hning-suyng-thaw	jun'nut, sa'a'dut-i-da'im'ee	périnbamulla.
Beaútiful, *a.*	လှသော။	hlah-thaw	khoob-soo'rut, soon'dur	sundara, chiranta, alakiya.
Beauty, *s.*	လှသောသူသည်။	hlah-thaw-thoo-the	khoob-soort'ee, soon'dra'ee	saundariyam, alagu.
Because, *conj.*	သော့ကြောင့်။ကြောင့်။	thaw-kyowng, kyowng	ki, ky'oon'kur	ákaiyál, nimittam, padiyál.
Bec'kon, *v. n.*	အမှတ်ပေးသည်။	a-hmut-pay-the	ish'a'ra-k	saigaikáttu.
Behínd, *pr.*	နောက်။	nowk	peech'he	piragé, pin, pírpurattil.
Behóld, *v. a.*	ကြည့်သည်။	kyee-the	yih! dekh!	kán, darisi, pár, nókku.
Belch, *v. a.*	လေတတ်သည်။	lay-tut-the	a'rogh, duk'ar, duk'ar'na	éppamidu, kakku.
Beléaguer, *v. a.*	ဝိုင်းရံသည်။	wuyng-yun-the	moo'ha'sur'u-k, gher'a-dal'na	murrugaichey, valai.
Beliéf, *s.*	ယုံကြည်ချက်။	yohn-gyee-chyet	ba'wur, e'ti'kad, put'i'ya'ra	visuvásam, nambikkai.
Beliéve, *v. a.*	ယုံကြည်သည်။	yohn-gyee-the	e'ti'kad-k, put'i'ya'ra-k	visuvási, nambu, ninai.
Bell, *s.*	ခေါင်းလောင်း။	kowng-lowng	ghun'ta	mani chalangai.
Bellows, *s.*	ဖို။	bpoh	dhounk'nee, dounkee, dum'a	ulaitturutti, úthunturutti.
Belly, *s.*	ဝမ်း။	woon	pet, shik'um	vayiru, utharam.
Belong', *v. n.*	ဆိုင်သည်။	tsuyng-the	dakh'il, lug'na, ul'a'ka-r	chár, urittágu, udaiyathágu
Belov'ed, *a.*	ချစ်သော။	chyit-thaw	jan, cha'hee'ta, muh'boob, pi'[yar'a	anbána, prítiyána, ithamána
Belt, *s.*	ခါးပတ်။	kah-but	bund, pur'tul'a, dab,	araikkachchu, pattigai.

English.	Burmese.		Hindustani.	Tamil.
Bench, *s.* ...	ခုံရှည်။ ...	kohn-shay ...	tukht, tukht'a ...	ásanam, píḍam.
Beneath', *adv.* ...	အောက်။ ...	owk ...	nee'che, tul'e ...	kíḻé, táḻa, paṇiya.
Benedic'tion, *s.* ...	မေတ္တာပို့ခြင်း။ ...	myittah-poh-chyin, kowng-gyee-mingalah-pay-chyin.	doo'a, us'ees ...	ásírvátham, váḻttu, palláṇḍu
Benefac'tor, *s.* ...	ကျေးဇူးရှင်။ ...	kyay-zoo-shin ...	moon'im, da'ta ...	dharmasáli, upakári.
Benef'icent, *a.* ...	ကျေးဇူးပြုတတ်သော။ ...	kyay-zoo-pyoo-dut-thaw ...	mihr'ban, moosh'fik ...	ígaiyuḷḷa, nanmaicheygira.
Ben'efit, *s.* ...	ကျေးဇူးအကျိုး။ ...	kyay-zoo-a-kyoh ...	fa'i'du, ha'sil, nuf'a, labh ...	upakáram, prayójanam.
Benev'olent, *a.* ...	ကြည်ညိုသောသဘော။ ...	kyee-nyoh-thaw-th-baw ...	a'tir, bhul'a, mihr'ban ...	kirupaiyuḷḷa, karuṇaiyána.
Benígn, *a.* ...	ကျေးဇူးပြုချင်သော။ ...	kyay-zoo-pyoo-chyin-thaw.	mihr'ban, moosh'fik ...	káruṇya, subha, saháya.
Benig'nity, *s.* ...	ကြည်ညိုခြင်း။ ...	kyee-nyoh-chyin ...	mihr'banee, kur'um ...	kaḍáksham, aruḷ.
Bent, *s.* ...	အကောက်။အကွေ့။ ...	a-kowk, a-kway ...	ter'ha, ir'a'da, ir'a'dut ...	kúniya, vaḷainta, kóṇaláṇa.
Bequeath', *v. a.* ...	အမွေကိုပေးသည်။ ...	a-moo-ay-goh-pay-the ...	hib'u-k, wu'si'yut-k ...	maraṇasáthanameḻuthik-
Bereave', *v. a.* ...	(တစုံတခု)မဲ့ဖြစ်အောင်ပြုသည်။ .	meh-pyit-owng-pyoo-the ...	le'le'na, chheenle'na ...	abakari, kavar, paṛi. [koḍu.
Bergamot', *s.* ...	နံ့သာတမျိုး။ ...	nun-thah-t'myoh ...	khoosh'bo, utr, soo'gundh...	kantam, maṇam, parimaḷam
Beséech, *v. a.* ...	တောင်းပန်သည်။ ...	towng-bun-the ...	dur'khwast-k ...	iṛanthukéḷ, véṇḍuthalchey.
Besmear', *v. a.* ...	လူးသည်။ ...	loo-the ...	les'na, lep'na, pot'na ...	taḍavu, púsu.
Bésom, *s.* ...	တံမြက်စည်း။ ...	tu*n*-byet-see ...	jha'roo, boo'ha'ree ...	tuḍaippam, viḷakkumáṛu.
Besot'ted, *a.* ...	အရူးကဲ့သို့ဖြစ်စေသည်။ ...	a-yoo-geh-tho-pyit-say-the.	be-hosh ...	mathimaruṇḍa, veṛiyána.
Bespeak', *v. a.* ...	အရင်တင်၍ပြောသည်။ ...	ah-yin-tin-yue-pyaw-the ...	kuh-rukh'na ...	munpésu, munkuṛi.
Best, *a.* ...	အကောင်းဆုံး။ ...	a-kowng-sohn ...	bhi'tur-een, khoobtur'een ...	uttama, uchita.
Bes'tial, *a.* ...	တိရစ္ဆာန်နှင့်ဆိုင်သော။ ...	te-ray-sun-hnin-suyng-[thaw,	hy'wan'ee, wuh'shee ...	mirugatanamána.
Bestir', *v. a.* ...	နိုးဆော်သည်။ ...	hnoh-saw-the, ...	dha'na, juldee-k, chul'a'na...	aruṭṭu, urchcháhappaḍuttu.
Bestow', *v. a.* ...	ပေးကမ်းသည်။ ...	pay-cun-the ...	de'na, uta-k ...	í, aruḷ, koḍu, aḍukku.
Bet, *s.* ...	လောင်းသည်။ ...	lowng-the ...	shurt, ba'zee ...	óṭṭam, panthayam.
Be'tel-leaf, *s.* ...	ကွမ်းရွက်။ ...	kohn-yu-et ...	pan ...	veṛṛilai, támbúlam.
Be'tel-nut, *s.* ...	ကွမ်းသီး။ ...	kohn-thee ...	soop'a'ree, soo'pi'yar'ee ...	pákku.

English	Burmese	Burmese pronunciation	Hindustani	Tamil
Betray′, *v. a.* ...	မရိယာယ်အားဖြင့် ရန်သူလက်သို့ အပ်နှံသည်။ ...	pa-ree-yeh-ah-pyin-yun-thoo-let-tho-ut-hnun-the.	dugh-a-k ...	irandakampannu.
Betróth, *v. a* ...	ထိမ်းမြန်းသည်။ ...	tayn-hmun-the ...	mang′na-sug′a′ee-k ...	viváhapporuttampannu.
Between, *pr.* or *adv.*	စပ်ကြားမှာ။ ...	tsut-kyah-hmah ...	dur′mi′yan ...	idaiyil, ullé, údé, naduvil.
Bev′erag′e, *s.* ...	သောက်ဖွယ်ရန်။ ...	towk-pweh-yun ...	pun′na, shoorb ...	pánam, kudippana.
Bewail′, *v. a.* ...	ညည်းတွားသည်။ ...	nyee-twah-the ...	uf′sos-k ...	alu, alaru, pulambu.
Bewail′ing, *s.* ...	ညည်းတွားခြင်း။ ...	nyee-twah-chyin ...	ghum, ma′tum, ghum-geen′ [ee,...	oppári, pulambal.
Beware, *v. n.* ...	သတိပြုသည်။ ...	th-dee-pyoo-the ...	zeen′har ...	echcharikkaiyáyiru.
Bewil′der, *v. a.* ...	မှိုင်တွေစေသည်။ ...	hmuyng-tway-say-the ...	bhut′ka′na, bhoo′la′na, goom′ [rah-k,...	mayakku, tigaippi, kalakku.
Bewitch′, *v. a.* ...	ပြုစားသည်။ ...	pyoo-sah-the ..	tot′ka	súnyañchey, maruttu.
Beyond′, *pr.* ...	အလွန်။ရှေ့အရပ်မှာ။ ...	a-lohn, shay-a-yut-hmah...	a′ge ...	appál, appuram, ettákkaiyil.
Bíble, *s.* ...	သမ္မာကျမ်းတော်။ ...	thum-mah-kyun-daw ...	kitab-moo′kuddus, tou′ret...	vétha-pustakam, vétham.
Bid, *v. a.* ...	ဖိတ်သည်။မိန့်တော်မူသည်။ ...	pait-the, mayn-daw-moo-the	ir′shad-k, kuh′na, boo′la′na.	kattalaiyidu, évu, karpi, alai
Big, *a.* ...	ကြီးသော။ ...	kyee-thaw ...	bur′a, bha′ree, mo′ta ...	parumanána, periya, parutta
Big′ot, *s.* ...	ကိုယ်အယူ ကိုသာ စွဲလမ်းသော [သူ။...	koh-a-yoo-goh-thah-ts weh-thee-chyay, [lun-thaw-thoo.	moo′tu′us′sib ...	vínbaktan, kuruttuppattan.
Bile, *s.* ...	သည်းခြေ။		pit, suf′ra ...	pittam, pittu.
Bilk, *v. a.* ...	လှည့်စားသည်။ ...	hlee-sah-the ...	dugh′a, fur′eb ...	mósappaduttu, tattividu, éy.
Bill, *s.* ...	နှုတ်သီး။စာရင်း။ ...	hnoht-thee-sah-yin ...	chonch, min′kar ...	chíttu, undi, alagu.
Bil′lion, ...	ရာကုဋေ။ ...	yah-koo-day ...	khurb ...	núráyirakódi, lachchakódi.
Bil′low, *s.* ...	လှိုင်း။ ...	hluyng ...	mauj, dhe′oo, hilko′ra ...	alai, tirai, tarangam.
Biog′raphy, *s.* ...	လူ၏ အကြောင်းအရာ အထုပ္ပတ္တိ ကိုစီရင်ရေးထားသောစာ ...	loo-ee-a-kyoung-a-yah-a-toh-puttee-go-sah-yin-yay-tah-thaw-sah ...	tuz′ki′ru ...	oruvanudaiya-charittiram.
Bíped, *s.* ...	ခြေနှစ်ချောင်းရှိသောသတ္တဝါ။ .	chye-hnit-chyoung-she-	do′pa′ya ...	irukáli, irukárpiráni.
Bird, *s.* ...	ငှက်။ ...	hnget, [thaw-thuttawah,.	chir′i′ya, punch′hee, pur′ind	kuruvi, paravai, padchi.
Birth, *s.* ...	မွေးခြင်း။ ...	mooay-chyin ...	jun′um, py′da′ish, by′ant ...	jananam, piravi.
Birth′-day, *s.* ...	ဖွားနေ့။ ...	pwah-nay ...	jun′um-din, sal′gir′ih ...	janana-nál, piranthanál.
Birth′-right, *s.* ...	အရိပ်အရာ။ ...	a-yait-a-yah ...	huk-i-wi′la′dut ...	janmasutantaram.

ENGLISH.	BURMESE.		HINDUSTANI.	TAMIL.
Birth'-place, *s.*	မွေးဖွားရာအရပ်။	moo-ay-pwah-yah-a-yut	mou'lud, wut'un	janmabhúmi, piranthaiḍam.
Bis'cuit, *s.*	ဂျုံမုန့်ပြား။	jōn-mohn-pyah	kak, koo'lee'cha	oruvagaikkóthumaiyappam.
Bish'op, *s.*	ဂိုဏ်းအုပ်၊သာသနာပိုင်။	guyng-oht,thah-thah-nah-[buyng,	kis'sees, im'am	kaṅkáṇi, attiyaḍchaguru.
Bitch, *s.*	ခွေးမ။	kway-mah,	koo'ti'ya, koot'tee	peṇṇáy, muḍuval.
Bite, *v. a.*	ကိုက်သည်။	kuyt-the	kat'na	kaḍi, kavvu, tíṇḍu.
Bit'ter, *a.*	ခါးသည်။	kah-the	kur'wa, tulkh, tee'ta	kasappána, kaippána.
Bitúmen, *s.*	ကျောက်ပွဲလျက်။	kyowk-pweh-lyet	nu'fat, nift, nuft	silájattu, nilakkíl.
Black, *a.*	နက်သည်။	net-the	ka'la, si'yah	karuppu, kariya, iruṭṭána.
Black'ing, *s.*	သုတ်ရန်ဆေးနက်။	thoht-yun-say-net	ka'lik	karuppu-mai.
Black'smith, *s.*	ပန်းပဲ။	ba-beh	lo'har, a'hungur	karumán, kollan.
Blad'der, *s.*	ကျင်ငယ်အိမ်။	kyin-ngeh-ain	phook'na	úṟṟámpetti, salappai.
Blame, *v. a.*	အပြစ်တင်သည်။	a-pyit-tin-the	dos, mul'am-k, mul'amut-k.	kuṟṟam-cháṟṟu, kuraichollu.
Blank, *s.*	ဖြူသော၊လွတ်လပ်သော။	pyoo-thaw, loht-lut-thaw	kha'lee, soo'nan	verumai, veḷi.
Blan'ket, *s.*	သက္ကလပ်စောင်။	thekkalut-sowng	kum'bul, kum'mul	kambaḷam, veḷḷaikkambaḷi.
Blasphéme, *v. a.&n.*	ဘုရားကို ပြစ်မှားသည်။	pa-yah-go-pyit-hmah-the	koofr-kuh'na	dévadúshaṇampaṇṇu, dúshi.
Blaze, *s.*	မီးတောက်သည်။	mee-towk-the	anch, bhur'uk'na	suválai, oḷi, koḷunthu.
Bleach, *v. a.*	ဖြူစေသည်။	pyoo-say-the	nikh'ar'na, suf'ed-k	veḷu, salavaipaṇṇu, viḷakku.
Bleed, *v. a.*	သွေးယိုသည်။	thway-yoh-the	fusd-k, f-kho'lna, lo'hoo-le'[na,	irattam-kutti-váṅku.
Blem'ish, *s.*	အဆင်းပျက်သောအရာ။	a-tsin-pyet-thaw-a-yah	bud-shukl'ee	ínam, kuṟṟam, paḻutu.
Blend, *v. a.*	ရောနှောသည်။	yaw-hnaw-the	mil'a'na	kala, kúṭṭu, chér.
Bless, *v. a.*	ကောင်းကြီးပေးသည်။	kown-gyee-pay-the	doo'a-d, bur'kut-d	ásírvathi, stóttiri, tuthi.
Blind, *a.*	မျက်စိကန်းသော။	myet-see-cun-thaw	na-bee'na, und'ha	kuruḍána, maṟaivu.
Bliss, *s.*	ချမ်းသာ။	chyun-thah	sa'a'dut-i-da'im'ee	périnbam, móḍchánandam.
Blis'ter *s.*	အပေါင်း၊လောင်မီး။	a-powng, lowng-mee	phup'ho'la, chha'la, a'bi'la	kárachílai, koppuḷam.
Blockáde, *s.*	ဝန်းရံသည်။	wun-yun-the	moo'ha'sur'a	muṟṟukai, aranvaḷaippu.
Block'head, *s.*	လူမိုက်။	loo-muyt	be-woo'koof, bhud'da	maḍayan, múḍan, maṭṭi.

Blood, *s.* ...	သွေး။ ...	thooay ...	khoon, lo'hoo ...	irattam, uthiram.
Bloom, *s.* ...	အပွင့်။ ...	a-pwing ...	phool, pooshp ...	pushpam, malarchchi.
Blow, *s.* ...	ရိုက်ပုတ်သည်။ ...	yuyk-poht-the ...	mar, sud'ma ...	aḍi, aṛai, tákku, iḍi.
Blow, *v. a.* ...	မှုတ်သည်။ ...	hmoht-the ...	phoonk'na ...	úthu, vísu, káṛṛuvísu.
Blue, *a.* ...	ပြာသော။ ...	pyah-thaw ...	nee'la, lee'la ...	nílam, veṇṇílam.
Blun'der, *s.* ...	အယောင်ယောင်အမှားမှား။ ...	a-yowng-yowng-a-hmah-[hmat, ...	chook, khut'a ...	piḻai, tappitham, pisagu.
Blunt, *a.* ...	တုံးသော မထက်။ ...	tohn-thaw, m'tet, ...	bhon'tha, koond ...	maḻukkána, moṭṭai.
Boar, *s.* ...	ဝက်ထီး။ ...	wet-tee ...	ba'rah ...	áṇpanṛi.
Boat, *s.* ...	လှေ သံဘန်။ ...	hlay, thunbun ...	dou'na, do'nee, kish'tee ...	óḍam, tóṇi, paḍagu.
Boat'man, *s.* ...	လှေသား။ ...	hlay-thah ...	dand'ee, mul'lah ...	óḍakkáran, tóṇikkáran.
Boatswain, *s.* ...	ကိုထိန်းသော။ ...	koh-tain-thaw ...	sur'hung ...	kappalsaráṅgu.
Bod'y, *s.* ...	ကိုယ်ခန္ဓာ။ ...	koh-oun-dah ...	ang, bud'un ...	saríram, uḍambu, uḍal.
Boil, *s.* ...	ဆူသည် ပြုတ်သည်။ ...	soo-the, pyoht-the ...	kho'la'na, oo'sun'na ...	avi, vey, kothippi.
Bold, *a.* ...	ရဲသော။ ...	yeh-thaw ...	mun'chul'a ...	tíramuḷḷa, tuṇivána.
Bólt, *s.* ...	မြား မိုး ကြိုး သွား သော ကျင်။ ...	hmyah, moh-gyoh-thwah-[thaw-kyin, ...	bil'lee, koofl ...	tálppál, púṭṭinná, vilaṅgu.
Bone, *s.* ...	အရိုး။ ...	a'yoh, ...	hud'dee, har, uzm ...	elumbu, (*of a fish*) mínmuḷ.
Book, *s.* ...	စာအုပ်။ ...	sah-ohk ...	kit'ab. pot'hee ...	puttakam, pustakam.
Book'-binder, *s.* ...	စာအုပ်ချုပ်သောသူ။ ...	sah-ohk-chy-oht-thaw-thoo.	jild'gur, suh'haf ...	pustakaṅkaṭṭuvón.
Book'-keeping *s.* ...	ကုန်စာရင်း။ ...	kohn-sa-yin ...	his'ab-kit'ab ...	kaṇakkeḻuthivaikkumuṛai.
Book'-seller, *s.* ...	စာအုပ်ရောင်းသောသူ။ ...	sah-ohk-yowng-thaw-thoo..	kit'ab-fur'osh ...	pustakaviyápári.
Bórax, *s.* ...	လက်ကြား။ ...	let-chyah ...	boo'ruk, so'ha'ga ...	veṅkaram, velikáram.
Bor'row, *v. a.* ...	ချေးသည်။ ...	chyee-the ...	kurz-l, a'ri'yut-l ...	kaḍanváṅgu, iravalváṅgu.
Box, *s.* ...	သစ်တာ။ ...	thit-tah ...	sun'dook, sun'dook'chu ..	peṭṭi, peṭṭagam, chimiḻ.
Boy, *s.* ...	လူကလေး။ ...	loo-ga-lay ...	lur'ka, chhok'ra ...	áṇpiḷḷai, iḷaiñan, pálakan.
Brah'min, *s.* ...	ပုဏ္ဏား။ ...	pohn-nah ...	brah'mun ...	birámaṇan, párppán.
Brain, *s.* ...	ဦးနှောက်။ ...	oh-hnowng ...	bhej'a, mughz ...	múḷai, uṇarvu, buddhi.
Bran, *s.* ...	ဖွဲနု။ ...	pweh-noo ...	bhoo'see, chokur ...	taviḍu.
Branch, *s.* ...	အကိုင်း။ ...	a-kuyng ...	dal, dy'na, shakh ...	kombu, kóḍu, kiḷai, jagai.

English.	Burmese.		Hindustani.	Tamil.
Brass, *s.*	ကြေးဝါ။	kyee-wah	pee'tul, bir'inj	pittaḷai.
Brave, *a.*	ရဲရင့်သော။	yeh-yin-thaw	dil-chul'a, dil-a'wur, jur'rar.	víramána, dhairya.
Bread, *s.*	မုန့်	mohn	nan, ro'tee,	roṭṭi, appam, ágáram.
Break'fast, *s.*	နံနက်စာ။	m'net-sah	chasht, haz'ree, nash'ta	kalaippósanam.
Breast, *s.*	ရင်ပတ်။	yin-butt	chha'tee, see'na	neñju, márpu, mulai.
Breath, *s.*	အသက်ရှူခြင်း။	a-thet-shoo-chyin	dum, sans	múchchu, ávi, suvásam.
Bribe, *s.*	တံစိုးထိုးသည်။	ta-soh-toh-the	rish'wut	lañjam, kaikúli, paridánam.
Brick, *s.*	အုတ်။	oht	eent, eenta, khisht	cheṅkal.
Brick'-kiln, *s.*	အုတ်ဖို။	oht-poh	puz'a'wa	cheṅkarchúḷai, káḷaváy.
Brick'layer, *s.*	ပန်းရန်သမား။	pa-yun-thum-mah [tha-mee.	raj, thu'wy	kollattukkáran, karsippan.
Bride, *s.*	မင်္ဂလာဆောင်သတို့သမီး။	ming-glah-sowng-tha-doh-	dool'hun, ur'oos	maṇaváṭṭi, maṇaváli.
Brídegroom, *s.*	မင်္ဂလာဆောင်သတို့သား။	ming-glah-sowng-tha-doh-	dool'ha	maṇaváḷan, máppiḷḷai.
Bridge, *s.*	တံတား။	ta-dah, [thah,...	pool	pálam, várávathi.
Brídle, *s.*	ဇက်ကြိုး။	zet-kyoh	lug'am	kaḍiváḷam, kalinam.
Brief, *a.*	တိုသော။	toh-thaw, [thaw,...	ko'tuh, mookh'tus'ur	churukkamána, poḷippána.
Bright, *a.*	ပြောင်သော။ထွန်းလင်းသော	pyowng-thaw, tohn-lin-	tab'an, rou'shun	tulakkamána, pirakásamána
Bril'liant, *a.*	အရောင်ဖိတ်ဖိတ်တောက်သော	a-yowng-payt-payt-towk-	rou'nuk-dar	paḷapaḷappána, kántiyuḷḷa.
Brim'stone, *s.*	ကန့်။	kun, [thaw,...	gund'huk	kantagam.
Bring, *v. a.*	ယူခဲ့သည်။	yoo-geh-the	la'na, le'a'na	konḍuvá, aḻaittuvá.
Brinjal, *s.*	ချဉ်ရံသီး။	chyun-yun-thee	by'gun, byn'gun	kattarikkáy.
Broad, *a.*	ကျယ်သော။	chyeh-thaw	chou'ra	agalamána, visála.
Bróker, *s.*	ပွဲစား။	pweh-sah	dul'lal	taravan, taravukáran.
Brókerage, *s.*	ပွဲခ။	pweh-kah	dul'lal'ee	taravu, taravukkúli.
Broom, *s.*	တံမြက်စည်း။	ta-byet-see, [pyoht-yay,...	jha'roo, boo'ha'ree	tuḍaippam, viḷakkumáṛu.
Broth, *s.*	အမဲသား။ကြက်သားပြုတ်ရည်။	a-meh-thah,kyet-thah-[ayn,	yukh'nee, shor'ba	áṇam, sáṛu, kuḷambu.
Brothel, *s.*	ပြည်တန်ဆာများနေသောအိမ်	pyee-t'sah-myah-nay-thaw-	kus'bee-kha'na	vésiviḍu.

Broth'er, *s.* ...	အစ်ကို ညီ။ ...	it-koh, nyee ...	bha'ee, bir'a'dur ...	sahótharan, tambi, tamaiyan
Brow, *s.* ...	ပြက်ခုံး၊တောင်စောင်း၊နဖူး ...	pyet-kohn, towng-sowng,	pesh'a'nee ...	puruvam, neṟṟi.
Brown, *a.* ...	ညိုသော။ ...	nyoh-thaw, [napoo,...	bhoo'ra, oo'da ...	úḍániṟamána, kabila.
Buc'ket, *s.* ...	ရေပုံး။ ...	yay-bohn ...	dol, dol'chee. bal'dee ...	éṟṟachchál, iṟaichál.
Bud, *s.* ...	အဖူး၊အငုံ။ ...	a-poo, a-hnun ...	phoon'gee, kub'ee, moul'na.	arumbu tuḷir.
Buf'falo, *s.* ...	ကျွဲ။ ...	kyoo-eh ...	bhyn'sa, bhyns ...	erumai, méthi.
Buffoon', *s.* ...	လူပြက်။ ...	loo-byet ...	mus'khur'uh ...	vigaḍakavi, pariyásappaṭṭan
Bug, *s.* ...	ကြမ်းပိုး။ ...	chyub-boh ...	khut'mul, khut-geer, nin'a'-	múṭṭuppúchchi, mugaḍu.
Build, *v. a.* ...	ဆောက်သည်။ ...	tsowk-the ...	bun'a'na, ta'meer-k, [ya,...	kaṭṭu, samai.
Bull, *s.* ...	နွားထီး။ ...	noh-ah-dee ...	an'doo-byl, sand, nurga'o...	iḍabam, eruthu, rishabham.
Bul'lock, *s.* ...	နွားဖိုက်။ ...	noh-ah-wuyk ...	bud'hi'ya ...	eruthu.
Bunch, *s.* ...	အဖူး (of fruit) အပြွတ်။ ...	a-poo, a-pyoht ...	kho'sha, gooch'chha ...	kulai, kottu muḍichchu.
Bun'dle, *s.* ...	အထုပ်။ ...	a-toht ...	guth'ree ...	chumai.
Bur'den, *s.* ...	ဝန်။ ...	woon ...	bojh, bar ...	báram múṭṭai, chumai.
Bur'ial, *s.* ...	သင်းချုပ်ခြင်း။ ...	thin-chyoht-chyin ...	kuf'un-duf'un, tujheez ...	aḍakkam, puthaippu.
Bur'ial-ground, *s.*...	သင်းချိုင်း။ ...	thin-chyuyng ...	go'ris'tan, kub'ur'is'tan ...	savakkálai, mayánastánam.
Burn, *s.* ...	မီးလောင်သည်။ ...	mee-lowng-the ...	jul'a'na, jul'na ...	chuḍu, eri.
Bur'nish, *v. a.* ...	မှတ်တင်သည်။အရောင်တင်သည်။	hmut-tin-the, a-yowng-tin-	chik'na'na, ghot'na ...	merugiḍu, minukku.
Bur'y, *v. a.* ...	သင်ချုပ်သည်။ ...	thin-chyoht-the, [the,...	gar'na, duf'un-k ...	puthai, aḍakkampaṇṇu.
Bus'iness, *s.* ...	အလုပ်အကိုင်။အမှု။ ...	a-loht-a-kuyng, a-hmoo ...	kam, kaj, kar ...	vélai, toḻil, udyógam.
But, *conj. pr. adv.*...	မူကား။သို့ရာတွင်။သို့သော်လည်း။	moo-gah, thoh-yah-dwin, tho-thaw-lee ...	bul'ki, le'kin, um'ma, pur...	ánálum, tavira, oḻiya.
But'cher, *s.* ...	နွားသတ်သမား ...	noh-ah-thut-thum-mah ...	kus'a'ee, kus'sab ...	iṟaichchikkáran, kasáí.
But'ler, *s.* ...	စားပွဲထိန်း။ ...	sah-bweh-tayn ...	khan'sa'man ...	víṭṭin-muthal-vélaikkáran.
But'ter, *s.* ...	ထောပတ်။ ...	tawbut ...	muk'khun ...	veṇṇai.
But'ter-fly, *s.* ...	လိပ်ပြာ။ ...	layt-pyah ...	teet'ree, titlee, pur'wa'nu ...	vaṇṇáttippúchchi.
But'termilk, *s.* ...	နို့ကြက်။ ...	noh-jyeh ...	ghol, mut'tha ...	mór.
But'ton, *s.* ...	အင်္ကျီသီး။ ...	ingyee-thee ...	ghoon'dee, took'ma ...	kumiḻ, pottán.

English.	Burmese.		Hindustani.	Tamil.
Buy, *v. a.* ...	ဝယ်သည်။ ...	weh-the ...	mol-le'na, khur'eed'na ...	koḷ, vilaikkuváṅgu.
By, *pr.* ...	အားဖြင့်။ ...	ah-pyin ...	pas, se, sen ...	ál, il, aruhil, koṇḍu.
Cab'bage, *s.* ...	သင်္ဘောမုန်လာ။ ...	thing-baw-mohn-lah ...	ko'bee, kur'um'kul'la ...	oru-vagaikkírai.
Cab'in, *s.* ...	သင်္ဘောအခန်း။ ...	thing-baw-a-cun ...	dub'oo'sa ...	sirrarai, kappalinuḷḷarai.
Cac'kle, *s.* ...	ကြက်ကဲ့သို့မြည်သည်။ ...	khyet-geh-thoh-myee-thee.	koor'koor'a'na ...	kokkarippu, pitharru, kattu.
Cage, ...	လှောင်အိမ်။ ...	hlowng-ain ...	pinj'ra, khan'cha, kufus ...	kúḍu, pañcharam, karappu.
Cal'culate, *v. a.* ...	တွက်သည်။ ...	twet-the ...	gin'na, his'ab-k, jor'na ...	kaṇi, eṇṇu, kaṇakkiḍu.
Cal'endar, *s.* ...	နှစ်၊လ၊နေ့ရက်မှတ်စာရင်း။ ...	hnit, lah, nay-yet-hmut-sa-[yin,...	tuk'weem, put'ra ...	pañcháṅgam.
Calf, *s.* ...	နွားကလေး။ ...	no-ah-galay ...	buchh'ra, buchh'roo ...	kanṛu, pasukkanṛu.
Call, *v. a.* ...	ခေါ်သည်။ ...	caw-the ...	poo'kar'na, kuh'na, bool'a'na	kúppiḍu, aḻai, kuṛi.
Cam'el, *s.* ...	ကုလားအုတ်။ ...	ka-lah-ohk ...	juml, jum'ul, oont, oont'nee.	oṭṭagam, oṭṭai.
Cam'phor, *s.* ...	ပရုပ်။ ...	pa-yoht ...	ka'foor, kup'oor ...	karppúram, pálugam.
Can, *v. n.* ...	နိုင်သည်။ ...	hnuyng-the ...	suk'na ...	kúḍum, élum, ám.
Can'dle, *s.* ...	ဖယောင်းတိုင်။ ...	pa-yowng-duyng ...	but'tee, shu'mu ...	meḻugutiri.
Cane, *s.* ...	ကြိမ်လုံး။ ...	chyain-lohn ...	bed, ny ...	pirambu, kaikól.
Can'non, *s.* ...	အမြောက်။ ...	a-myowk ...	top, *large* gujnal, *small* rhu-chha'o'nee, [kul'a...	píraṅgi.
Canton'ment, *s.* ...	တပ်စွဲနေရာအရပ်။ ...	tut-sweh-nay-yah-a-yut ...		iráṇuvastalam.
Cap, *s.* ...	ဦးထုပ်။ ...	oh-toh ...	top, to'pa, to'pee ...	toppi, kulláy.
Cap'ital, *s.* ...	မြို့တော်။ ...	myo-daw ...	dar-ool-moolk, dar-ool-sul'[tun'ut,...	talaippaṭṭaṇam, táynagar.
Cap'ture, *v. a.* ...	လက်ရလူ။ ...	let-yah-loo ...	gir'if'tug'ee,	piḍi, chiṛaippaḍuttu.
Car'damon, *s.* ...	ပါလာစေ့။ ...	pah-lah-say ...	il'a'chee, ka'kool'á ...	élam *seed* élarisi *fruit* élakkáy
Cáreful, *a.* ...	စိုးရိမ်တတ်သော။ ...	soh-yayn-dut-thaw ...	hosh'yar, khubur'dar ...	eṇṇamuḷḷa, vicháramána.
Cáreless, *a.* ...	သတိလစ်သော။ ...	th'dee-lit-thaw ...	be-hosh'yar, bekhub'ur ...	ajákkrathaiyána, eṇṇátha.
Car,go, *s.* ...	လှေ၊သင်္ဘော၌တင်သောဝန်။ ...	hlay, thing-baw-hnuyt-tin-[thaw-woon,...	bhur'tee, khep ...	éṛṛumathi, kapparsarakku.
Car'penter, *s.* ...	လက်သမား။ ...	let-th'mah,	bur'hy, nuj'jar, soot'ar ...	tachchan.
Car'pet, *s.* ...	ကော်စော။ ...	kaw-saw ...	fursh, shut'run'jee, gha'lee'	kambaḷam, samukkáḷam.

Cash, *s.*	ကြေးငွေ။	kyee-ngway	nukd, rok, [chu,	kásu.
Cash'ier', *s.*	ငွေထိန်း။	ngway-dain	fo'tu'dar, khuz'anchee	saráppu, pokkasakkáran.
Cask, *s.*	စည်။	tsee	pee'pa	píppá, pélai, pattal.
Caste, *s.*	ဇာတ်။အမျိုး။	zut, a-myo	koum, zat	játi, varuṇam, kulam.
Cat, *s.*	ကြောင်။	kyowng	bil'la, bil'lee	púnai, iṛpuli, púñai.
Cat'alogue, *s.*	စာရင်း။	tsă-yin	fih'rist	jápithá, peyarédu.
Catch, *v. a.*	ဖမ်းဆီးသည်။	pun-see-the	puk'ur'na	piḍi, kavar, paṛru.
Cat'tle, *s.*	နွားတို့။	noh-ah-doh	du'wab, dhor	áḍu, máḍu. muthaliyavai.
Cause, *s.*	အကြောင်းဖြစ်စေသော။	ă-kyowng-pyit-say-thaw	sub'ub, sub'ub-ee'yut	káraṇam, mukántharam.
Cav'alry, *s.*	မြင်းတပ်။	myin-dut	ris'a'lu, su'warkar'ee	kuthiraivírar, rávuttar.
Cave, *s.*	ကူ။	koo	ghar, goo'pha, kun'dur'a	kugai, kebi, páli, mulaiñju.
Cent, *s.*	၁၀၀။ကြေးနီဒင်္ဂါး။	t'-yah, kyay-din-gah	sou, sud, senka'ra	núru, satham, órnáṇayam.
Cen'tre, *s.*	အလယ်ချက်။	ă-leh-chyet	beech, mur'kuz	naḍu, maiyam, maddhi.
Cen'tury, *s.*	အနှစ်တရာ။	ă-hnit-t'yah	sou-bur'us, sud'ee	núṛuvaruḍam, núṛáṇḍu.
Cer'emony, *s.*	ကျင်းပမြဲနည်းဖြင်း။	kin-see-mun-chyin	chul'un, tuk'ul'loof	kriyai, saḍaṅgu, karmam.
Cer'tain, *a.*	ဟုတ်သော။အမှန်။	hoht-thaw, ă-hmun	moo'kur'rur, yuk'een, ba'ze.	nija, uṛuthiyána.
Certif'icate, *s.*	သက်သေခံလက်မှတ်။	thet-thay-cun-let-hmut	dust-a'wez, sun'ud	yógiyadápattiram.
Chain, *s.*	ကြိုး။	chyoh	zun'jeer, san'kul, san'kur	saṅgili, saraḍu, toḍar, taḷai.
Chair, *s.*	ကုလားထိုင်။	kul-lah-tuyng	chou'kee, koor'see	nárkáli, ásanam, píḍam.
Chámber, *s.*	အခန်း။	ă-tet-cun	kumra	maṇḍapam, máḍam, aṛai.
Chance, *s.*	အမှတ်တမဲ့ဖြစ်သည်။ကံ။	ă-hmut-t'meh-pyit-the, cun.	it'ti'fak, it'ti'fa'kee	athishṭam, samayam.
Change, *v. a.*	လဲသည်။	leh-the	too'ra'na, khoor'da-k	máṛṛu, vérupaḍuttu, máṛu.
Chan'nel, *s.*	ရေမြောင်း။ရေကြောင်း။	yay-yoh, yay-gyowng	wa'dee	váykkál, kálváy, nírkkál.
Chap'el, *s.*	သုဓမ္မာဇရပ်။	thoo-dum-mah-za-yut	gir'ja-ghur, ib'a'dutkha'na.	jepálayam, chiṛukóvil.
Chap'ter, *s.*	အခန်းကြီး။	a-cahn-gyee	bab, is'kundh	athikáram, paḍalam.
Charge, *s.*	စာရင်းနှင့်မှတ်ခြင်း။	tsă-yin-hnuyt-hmut-chyin.	huw'a'lu, soo'poord, khurch.	chelavu, vilai.
Charge, *v. a.*	ခဲယမ်းထိုးသည်။	keh-yun-toh-the	soo'poord-k, huw'a'lu-k	chumattu.
Cheap, *a.*	အဘိုးချိုသော။	a-poh-chyoh-thaw	mun'da, sus'ta	maliváná, nayamána.

English.	Burmese.		Hindustani.	Tamil.
Cheat, *v. a.* ...	လိမ်လည်သည်။ ...	layn-lee-thaw ...	dugh'a, fur'eb, thug'a'ee ...	vañji, éy, ettu, émárṛu.
Cheque, *s.* ...	ငွေစာ။ ...	ngway-sah ...	bur'at, hoon'dee ...	uṇḍichchíṭṭu.
Chest, *s.* ...	သစ်တာ။ ...	thit-tah ...	pet'ee ...	peṭṭagam.
Chic'ken, *s.* ...	ကြက်ကလေး။ ...	khyet-gă-lay ...	ching'nee, choo'zu ...	kóḷikkuñchu.
Chief, *s.* ...	အကြီး။ ...	ă-gyee ...	sur'dar, moo'kud'dum ...	sréshṭan, talaivan, prathâni.
Child, *s.* ...	သား၊ သမီး။ ...	thah, thă-mee ...	buch'cha, ba'luk ...	piḷḷai, kuḻantai.
Childbearing, *s.* ...	သားဖွားမြင်ခြင်း။ ...	thah-pwah-myin-chyin ...	nuf'as, juch'kee ...	piḷḷaippéṛu, prasavam.
Chin, *s.* ...	မေးစေ့။ ...	may-say ...	thood'dee, thor'hee ...	móváy, mugakkaṭṭai.
Chis'el, *s.* ...	ဆောက်။ ...	sowk ...	rook'ha'nee, tan'kee ..	uḷi, taṛigai.
Chol'era, *s.* ...	အော့နာဝမ်းကျ။ ...	aw-nah-woon-chyah ...	hy'za, ola'oot'thee ...	vánthibhédi, vishabhédi.
Christ, *s.* ...	ခရစ်တော်၊ ဘုရား။ ...	kă-rit-daw-pă-yah ...	mus'eeh, mus'eeh'a ...	abishékampaṇṇapaṭṭavar.
Chris'tian, *s.* ...	ခရစ်ယာန်ဘာသာကိုယုံသောသူ။	kă-rit-yan-bah-thah-goh-yoo-thaw-thoo ...	ee'sa'ee, ee'suw'ee ...	kṛistumárkkattán, kṛistiyan
Christ'mas-day, *s.* ...	သခင်ယေရှုခရစ်မွေးသောပွဲတော်နေ့။	th-kin-yay-shoo-ka-rit-mway-thaw-pweh-daw-nay.	mus'eeh, kee'py'da'ish'ka'din	kṛistujananatirunál.
Church, *s.* ...	သုဓမ္မာဇရပ်ကြီး၊ အသင်းတော်။	thoo-dum-mah-ză-yat-gyee, a-thin-daw ...	gir'ja-ghur, kul'ee'su ...	dévâlayam, kóyil.
Cir'cle, *s.* ...	အဝိုင်း၊ စက်ဝိုင်း။ ...	ă-wuyng, tset-wuyng ...	da'i'ru, hul'ka, chum'bur ...	vaṭṭam, sakkaram, churṛu.
Cir'cular, *s.* ...	အရပ်ရပ်သို့ပေးလိုက်သောစာ။	a-yut-yut-thoh-pay-luyt-thaw-sah ...	moo'dou'wur, chum'bur'ee...	churṛuviḷambaram.
Cir'culate, *v. a.* ...	လှည့်ပတ်သည်။ ...	hlee-put-the	phir'na ...	prasittappaḍuttu.
Cit'y, *s.* ...	မြို့။ ...	myo ...	nug'ur, shuhr, poor, poo'ree.	paṭṭaṇam, nagari, puram.
Class, *s.* ...	ရတ် ...	a-tahn ...	fir'ka, tub'ku ...	kúṭṭam, vaguppu, inam.
Clay, *s.* ...	မြေစေး။ ...	myay-tsay ...	chik'nee-mit'tee ...	kaḷiman.
Clean, *a.* ...	စင်သော။ ...	tsin-thaw ...	saf, pak, pa'kee'za, pak'saf...	túya, suddha, tuppuraváṇa.
Clear, *a.* ...	ကြည်သော။ ...	kyee-thaw ,,	ash'kar, u'yan, saf ...	tulakkamáṇa, teḷiváṇa.
Cler'gyman, *s.* ...	ဓမ္မဆရာကြီး။ ...	dum-mah-say-yah-gyee ...	pad'ree ...	guru.

Clerk, *s.* ...	စာရေး။ ...	tsah-yay ...	likh'ne-wa'la, likh'nee-das..	kumástá, kaṇakkan.
Clev'er, *a.* ...	လိမ္မာသော။ ...	laym-mah-thaw ...	hoon'nur-mund ...	keṭṭiyána, samarttuḷḷa.
Clock, *s.* ...	နာရီ။ ...	nah-yee ...	ghun'ta, ghur'ee ...	kaḍiyáram.
Clock-maker, *v. a.*...	နာရီလုပ်သောသူ။ ...	nah-yee-loht-thaw-thoo ...	ghur'ee-saz, ghur'ee-wala...	kaḍikárayánthrigan.
Cloth, *s.* ...	အဝတ်။ ...	a-woot ...	kup'ra, par'chu ...	chílai, vastram, puḍaivai.
Cloud, *s.* ...	တိမ်။ ...	tayn ...	ba'dul, megh, ubr ...	mégham.
Coach, *s.* ...	ရထား။ ...	yittah ...	sej-gar'ee, ruth ...	iratham, náluruḷaibaṇḍi.
Coach'man, *s.* ...	ရထားထိန်း။ ...	yittah-tayn ...	coach-wan ...	irathasárathi, térppágan.
Coast, *s.* ...	ပင်လယ်ကမ်း။ ...	pin-leh-kun ...	lub-i-dur'ya, kin'a'ra ...	kaḍalóram, kaḍarkarai, tisai
Cock, *s.* ...	ကြက်ဖ။ ...	chyek-pah ...	moorgh, khan'gee-moorgh.	chéval.
Cock, *v. a.* ...	မှိုင်ပေါင်။ ...	suyng-powng ...	gho'ra, to'ta, gho'ra-chur'ha	tuppákkikkuthirai.
Cock'roach, *s.* ...	ပိုးဟပ်။ ...	poh-hut ...	til'chut'ta, [na,...	kakkaláttu.
Cócoa-nut, *s.* ...	အုန်းသီး။ ...	ohn-thee ...	nar'jeel, na'ri'yul, *unripe* dab,	téṅkáy, *unripe* iḷanírkáy.
Cof'fee, *s.* ...	ကာဖီ။ ...	kah-pee ...	boon, kuh'wa,[*ripe* jhoo'na.	káppikkoṭṭai, káppittaṇṇír.
Cof'fin, *s.* ...	တလား။ ...	tă-lah ...	kuf'un, to'boot ...	savappeṭṭi, préthátháram.
Coin, *s.* ...	ဒင်္ဂါး။ ...	din-gah ...	sik'ka ...	náṇayam.
Collect', *v. a.* ...	ရုသည်။ ...	tsoo-the ...	jum'a-k, but'or'na ...	kúṭṭu, chér, tiraṭṭu.
Col'lege, *s.* ...	ပညာရှိတို့အပေါင်းအသင်း။ ...	pin-yah-she-doh-a-powng-	mud'rus'sa, path'sha'la ...	vittiyáchálai, kalvichchálai.
Col'our, *s.* ...	အရောင်။အဆင်း။ ...	a-yowng, a-sin, [a-thin,...	rung, loun ...	niṛam, varṇam, cháyam.
Comb, *s.* ...	ဘီး။ဖြီး။ ...	bee, pyee ...	kung'hee ...	chíppu.
Come, *v. n.* ...	လာသည်။ ...	lah-the ...	a'na, a'ja'na, wa'rid ...	vá, chér, sambhavi, tóṇṛu.
Com'et, *s.* ...	ကြယ်တံခွန်။ ...	kyeh-t'gohn ...	sit'a'ru-i-doom'dar ...	válnakshattiṛam, válmín.
Command', *s.* ...	မိန့်တော်မူသည်။ ...	mayn-daw-moo-thee ...	fur'man, hookm, ir'shad ...	kaṭṭaḷai, kaṛpanai, éval, vithi
Commen'ce, *v. a.* ...	စသည်။ ...	tsah-the ...	shoo'roo-k ...	toḍaṅku, tuvakku, árambi.
Com'merce, *s.* ...	ကုန်သွယ်ခြင်း။ ...	kohn-thweh-chyin ...	sou'da'gur'ee, be'o'par ...	varttakam, váṇigam.
Commis'sion, *v. a.*...	ကိုယ်စားလှယ်ခံ။ပွဲခ။ ...	koh-sah-leh, pweh-gah ...	dus'toor'ee, bur'at ...	taragu, athikáraṅkoḍu.
Commis'sioner, *s* ...	အရေးပိုင်။ ...	a-yay-buyng,[thaw-loo-soo,	um'een ...	vichárаṇaikkáran.
Commit'tee, *s.* ...	အမှုကိုဆောင်ရသောလူစု။ ...	a-hmoo-goh-sowng-yah-	muj'lis, punch'a'yut ...	káriyavicháraṇai-chabaiyár.

ENGLISH.	BURMESE.		HINDUSTANI.	TAMIL.
Com'pany, *s.* ...	အရ။အပေါင်း။ ...	a-tsoo, a-powng ...	muj'lis, sooh'but ...	kúṭṭam, saṅgam, tóḻamai.
Com'pass, *v.* ...	ပတ်သည်။ ...	put-the ...	da'i'ru, chum'bur, hul'ka ...	vaḷai, churṟu, cúhḷ.
Com'pass, *s.* ...	အိမ်မြှောင်။ ...	ayn-myowng ...	kootbnoo'ma, kib'la-noo'ma	maṭṭu, aḷavu.
Compas'sion, *s.* ...	ကရုဏာ။မေတ္တာ။ ...	g'yoo-nah, myit-tah ...	durd-mun'dee ...	irakkam, urukkam, anbu.
Complain', *v. n.* ...	မြည်တွန်သည်။ ...	myee-tohn-the ...	fur'i'yad-k, na'lish-k ...	muṛaiyiḍu, kuṛaichollu.
Compléte, *v. a.* ...	ပြည့်စုံသော။ ...	pyee-sohn-thaw ...	poo'ra-k, ty'ar-k, tum'am-k.	púraṇamákku, muṟṟuvi.
Com'pliment, *s.* ...	လော ကဝတ် စကား။ ချီးမွမ်း [ခြင်း။ ...	law-ga-woot-sgah, chyee-soo-powng-the, [mohn-chyin	bun'dug'ee ...	upacharaṇai, vantanam.
Compóse, *v. a.* ...	ရပေါင်းသည်။ ...	soo-powng-the, ...	tus'neef-k ...	kúṭṭu, vásagaṅkaṭṭu, aḍukku
Composit'ion, *s.* ...	စီသောစာ။ ...	see-thaw-sah ...	tus'neef ...	vásagakaṭṭu, tiraṭṭu, kúṭṭu.
Com'promise, *s.* ...	လျှော့ရှုပြေမီသည်။ ...	lyaw-yue-pyoo-me-the ...	moo'sa'lu'hu ...	iṇakku, samádhánappaḍal.
Concéive, *v.* ...	ထင်မှတ်သည်။ ...	tin-hmut-the ...	khi'yal ...	eṇṇu, ninai, karuthu.
Conclúde, *v. a.* ...	ဆုံးဖြတ်သည်။ ...	tsohn-pyut-the ...	a'khir-k tum'am-k ...	muḍi, tír.
Conclúsion, *s.* ...	အဆုံး။ ...	a-tsohn ...	tum'a'mee, a'khir, un'jam...	muḍivu, tírppu.
Condit'ion, *s.* ...	အကြောင်း။အရာ။ ...	a-kyowng, a-yah ...	hal, ky'fee'yut ...	tanmai, nilaimai, antastu.
Con'duct, *s.* ...	ကြင့်ဆောင်သော။အပြုအမူ။ ...	kyin-tsowng-thaw, a-pyoo-[a-hmoo, ...	chul'un ...	naḍakkai, oḻukkam.
Confec'tion, *s.* ...	ယို။ ...	yoh ...	mit'ha'ee ...	inittapaṇḍam, miṭṭáy.
Confess', *v. a.* ...	ဝန်ခံသည်။ ...	woon-eun-the ...	ik'rar-k, kub'ool-k ...	aṛivi, aṛikkai-iḍu, ottukkoḷ.
Confes'sion, *s.* ...	ဝန်ခံခြင်း။ ...	woon-eun-chyin ...	ik'rar, tuk'reer ...	páva-aṛikkai, vikyápanam.
Confirm', *v. a.* ...	မြဲမြံစေသည်။ ...	myeh-myun-say-the ...	sa'bit-k, tik'nar'na ...	tiḍappaḍuttu, balappi.
Confirmation, *s.* ...	လက်ထပ်မင်္ဂလာ။ ...	let-tin-min-glah ..	is'bat, is'tikh'dam, soo'boot.	tiḍappaḍuttal, stiram.
Con'fúsion, *s.* ...	ရုံးရင်းခတ်မှုပြခြင်း။ ...	yohn-yin-cut-hmyah-pyoo-[chyin, ...	khult ...	kuḻappam, kalakkam.
Congregátion, *s.* ...	ပရိသတ်။ ...	pă-ray-thut, ...	jum'a'ut, sub'ha ...	janakkúṭṭam, sabhai, saṅgam
Con'quer, *v. a.* ...	နိုင်သည်။ ...	nuyng-the ...	fut'ih-k, jeet'na ...	vel, veṟṟikoḷ, jeyi, keli.
Conqueror, *s.* ...	အောင်သူ။ ...	owng-thoo ...	gha'zee, zuf'ur'yab, moo'zuf	veṟṟiyáḷan, venṟón, vijayan.
Con'quest, *s.* ...	နိုင်ခြင်း။အောင်ခြင်း။ ...	nuyng-chyin, owng-chyin.	fut'ih, zuf'ur, [fur, ...	veṟṟi, jayam, vijayam.
Conscience, *s.* ...	အတွင်းစိတ်။ ...	a-twin-sait ...	di'ya'nut, ee man ...	manasákshi, jívasákshi.

Con'sequence, *s.* ...	အကျိုးအကြောင်း။ ...	ă-kyoh-ă-khyowng, [yoh,...	nut'ee'ju ...	viḷaivu, káriyam, palan.
Con'serve, *s.* ...	လိုဖြေအောင်ထားသည်။ယို ...	lohn-gyohn-owng-tah-the,	moo'rub'ba, gool-kund, gool-	tittippuppaṇḍam, kulkanthu
Consolátion, *s.* ...	နှစ်သိမ့်ခြင်း။ [ခြင်း။...	hnit-thayn-chyin ...	dil'a'sa, tus'ul'lee, [shuk'ur...	áruthal, téṛṛaravu.
Conspir'acy, *s.* ...	မကြောက်သောအကြံနှင့် သင်းဖွဲ့	m'kowng-thaw-a-kyun-hnin-thin-pweh-chyin ...	gosht, sa'zish, it'ti'fak ...	rájadróham, durálóchanai.
Conspir'ator, *s.* ...	ပုန်ကန်မည်အကြံအစီရှိသောသူ။ .	pohn-cun-mee-a-kyun, a-see-she-thaw ...	sa'zish'ee, hum'raz ...	rájadróhi, sathiyósanaikáran
Con'stable, *s.* ...	ရာဇဝတ်။ ...	yah-ză-woot ...	dhu'lyt, sar'jun ...	úrkkávarkáran.
Consult', *v. a.* ...	တိုင်ပင်သည်။ ...	tuyng-bin-the ...	mus lu'hut-k ...	álóchi, yósanaikéḷ.
Consúme, *v. a.* ...	ကျွမ်းစေသည်။ ...	kyoo-un-zay-the ...	tu'luf-k ...	aḷi, násappaḍuttu, tin.
Contain', *v. a.* ...	ဆံ့သည်။ပါဝင်သည်။ ...	tsun-the, pah-win-the ...	moosh'tum'il-k ...	aḍakku, piḍi, amai.
Contaminátion, *s.* ...	ညစ်ညူးခြင်း။ ...	nyit-nyoo-chyin ...	a'loo'du'gee, chhoot ...	asusi, másu, kaṛai.
Content *v. a.* ...	ဝန်ခံခြင်း။ ...	woon-cun-chyin ...	ra'zee-k ...	manarammiyap-paḍuttu.
Conten'tion, *s.* ...	အထိုက်သည်။ ...	ă-tuyk-the ...	lur'a'ee ...	tarkkam, chaṇḍai, piṇakku.
Con'test, *s.* ...	ငြင်းခုံသည်။ ...	ngyin-kohn-the ...	tuk'rar ...	chaṇḍai, tarkkam, vivátham
Con'tract, *s.* ...	စာချုပ်။ ...	sah-chyoht ...	kur'ar, koul-kur'ar, uhd ...	kuttagai, uḍanpaḍikkai.
Contrac'tor, *s.* ...	စာချုပ်ခံသောသူ။ ...	sah-chyoht-cun-thaw-thoo..	moos'ta'jir, thee'ke'dar ...	kuttagaikkáran.
Convert', *v. a.* ...	ပြောင်းသည်။ ...	pyowng-the ...	moond'na, pul'ta'na ...	máṛṛu, guṇappaḍuttu.
Convey, *v. a.* ...	ယူဆောင်သည်။ ...	yoo-sowng-the, [gyee,...	le'chul'na, le'ja'na ...	cheluttu, tá, koṇḍupó.
Cook, *v.* & *s.* ...	ချက်ပြုတ်သည်။အိုးသူကြီး။ ...	chyet-pyoht-the, *s.* oh-thoo	puk'a'na, ba'wur'chee ...	samai, samayaṛkáran.
Cook'ery, *s.* ...	ချက်ပြုတ်သောအတတ်။ ...	chyet-pyoht-thaw-a-tut ...	ba'wur'chee-gur'ee ...	samaiyalvélai, pákasástiram
Cool, *s.* ...	အေးသော။ ...	ay-thaw ...	thun'da ...	kuḷirchchi, sítam.
Cool'y, *s.* ...	အလုပ်သမား။ ...	a-loht-th'mah ...	koo lee ...	kúli.
Co-op'erate, *v. n.* ...	ဆုံရှိပြုလုပ်သည်။ ...	sohn-yoo-eh-pyoo-loht-the.	moot'tuf ik ...	kúḍichchey.
Cop'per, *s.* ...	ကြေးနီ။ ...	kyee-nee ...	tam'ba ...	chembu, támbiram.
Cop'peras, *s.* ...	ဓာတ်စိမ်း။ပါလာဓာတ်။ ...	doht-tah-sayn-pah-lah-	zaj ...	annabhédi, mayiṛruttam.
Cop'y, *s.* ...	ကူးရေးသော။ ...	koo-yay-thaw, [doht-tah,...	chhap, nukl, [ab,...	pratirúbam, pratichchíṭṭu.
Cop'y-book, *s.* ...	လက်ရေးစာ။ ...	let-yay-sah ...	chhap ka-kit'ab, nukl ka-kit	urup-peḷuttup-pustakam.

English.	Burmese.		Hindustani.	Tamil.
Corian'der, *s.* ...	နံနံစေ့။ ...	nun-nun-seh ...	dhun'i'ya, koth'meer ...	kottamalli, taṇigam.
Cork, *s.* ...	ဘူးဆို့။ ...	paw, boo-soh ...	thek'a, thep'ee, dut'ta ...	takkai.
Cork'screw, *s.* ...	ဝက်အူ။ ...	wet-oo ...	pech'kush ...	takkai-eḍukkum-áyutham.
Cor'morant, *s.* ...	တင်ကျီး။ ...	tin-gyee ...	choo'he-mar, chhoo-mar ...	nírkkágam.
Corn, *s.* ...	စပါး။ ...	să-bah ...	un'aj, naj, bhoot'ta ...	chóḷam, annam, dhányam.
Cor'ner, *s.* ...	ထောင့်။ ...	downg ...	ko'na, kon, go'shu ...	múlai, kóṇam, kóḍi, kuḍá.
Corps, *s. Fr.* ...	စစ်သူရဲအစု။ ...	tsit-thoo-yeh-a-tsoo ...	pul'tun, ghol ...	aṇi, paḍaivaguppu.
Corpse, *s.* ...	အလောင်းကောင်။ ...	ă-lowng-gowng ...	moor'du, lash, loth ...	savam, piṇam, prétham.
Correct', *a.* ...	ပြင်သည်။ပြောင့်စေသည်။ ...	pyin-the, pyowng-say-the...	theek, doo'-roost, soodh ...	tiruttamána, sariyána.
Correspond', *v. n.*...	အချင်းချင်းစာပေးသည်။ ...	a-chyin-chyin-sah-pay-the.	bur'u'bur, moo'ta'bik ...	iṇaṅku, isai, ottiru.
Correspond, *s.* ...	ညီညာသည်။ ...	nyee-nyah-the ...	khut-kit'a'butrukh'na ...	kákithameḷuthu.
Cos'tive *a.* ...	ဝမ်းချုပ်သော။ ...	woon-chyoht-the ...	pet-bund ...	malavaraṭchiyána.
Cot, or Couch, *s.* ...	ခုတင်။ ...	kă-din ...	khat, khut, khut'i'ya ...	mañjam, kaṭṭil.
Cot'tage, *s.* ...	အိမ်ကလေး။ ...	ayn-gălay ...	jhomp'ra, jhomp'ree ...	kuḍisai, chiṟṟil, kuḍil.
Cotton, *s.* ...	ဝါ။ ...	wah ...	kootu, poom'bu, ban'ga ...	pañju, parutti.
Cough, *s.* ...	ချောင်းဆိုးသည်။ ...	chyowng-soh-the ...	khan'see ...	irumal, kásam.
Coun'oil, *s.* ...	တိုင်ပင်သောလူစု။ ...	tuyng-bin-thaw-loo-zoo ...	punch, puncha'a'yut ...	saṅgam, álóchanaisaṅgattár
Coun'sel, *s.* ...	သတိပေးသည်။ ...	th'-dee-pay-the ...	mus'lu'hut, nus'ee'hut ...	abhiprâyam, yósanai.
Coun'tenance, *s.* ...	မျက်နှာ။ ...	myet-hnah ...	chih'ru, soo'rut ...	cháyal, mukham.
Coun'try, *s.* ...	ပြည်။ ...	pyee ...	des, moolk ...	désam, náḍu, úr, símai.
Coun'tryman, *s.* ...	ပြည်သား။ ...	pyee-thah ...	gaon-wa'la ...	náṭṭán, úrán, désattán.
Courage, *s.* ...	ရဲရင့်ခြင်း။ ...	yeh-yin-gyin ...	dil-a'wur'ee, bu'ha'doo'ree...	víram, áṇmai, manóṛchágam
Court, *s.* ...	တရားရုံး။ ...	tă-yah-yohn ...	dur'bar, ud'a'lut ...	nyáyastalam, aramanai.
Cous'in, *s.* ...	ညီအစ်ကိုယ်မောင်နှမတော်။ ...	nyee-it-koh-mowng-hnit-	chuch'e'ra-bha'ee ...	táy-tantaiyar-sahótaraṅ-
Cow, *s.* ...	နွားမ။ ...	no-ah-mah, [mah-daw,...	ga'e, g'roo, gao ...	pasu, kó, á. [kaḷinmaga.
Cowárd, *s.* ...	ကြောက်တတ်သောသူ။ ...	khyowk-dut-thaw-thoo ...	dur-pok'na, booz-dil ...	iḷaneñjan, athairiyaván.

Cow'-pox, *s.* ...	နွားကျောက်။ ...	no-ah-chyowk ...	go'thun-seet'la ...	kóvaisúri, kómári.
Crab, *s.* ...	ဂဏန်း။ ...	gă-nun ...	kek'ra ...	naṇḍu.
Create, *v. a.* ...	ဖန်ဆင်းတော်မူသည်။ ...	pun-zin-daw-moo-the ...	py'da-k, khil'kut-k ...	uṇḍákku, paḍai, ákku.
Creat'ure *s.* ...	သတ္တဝါ ...	thut-tă-wah ...	af'ree'du ...	jívapráṇi, sirushṭi.
Cred'it, *s.* ...	ယုံသည်။ ...	yohn-the ...	it'i'bar, it'i'mad, ba'wur ...	nambikkai, náṇayam.
Cred'itor, *s.* ...	ကြွေးရှင်။ ...	kyoo-ay-shin ...	kurz-khwah ...	kaḍankoḍuttavan.
Creed, *s.* ...	ယုံချက်။ ...	yohn-chyet ...	kul'i'ma ...	visuvásap-pramáṇam.
Crime, *s.* ...	ပြစ်မှားခြင်း။ ...	pyit-hmah-chyin ...	goo'nu, tuk'seer ...	kuṟṟam, paḻi, tavaṟu.
Criminal, *a.* ...	အပြစ်ရှိသော။ ...	a-pyit-she-thaw ...	mooj'rim ...	kuṟṟamuḷḷa, dushkrittiya.
Croc'kery, *s.* ...	ပုကန်အမျိုးမျိုး။ ...	pă-gun-ă-myo-myo ...	mit'tee-ya-chee'nee-ke-bur'	maṭpáṇḍam, kuyakkalam.
Croc'odile, *s.* ...	မိကျောင်း။ ...	mee-gyowng ...	koom'heer, mug'ur, [tun,...	muthalai.
Crook'ed, *a.* ...	ကောက်သော။ ...	kowk-thaw ...	ben'da, khum, tir'chha ...	kúnalána, kóṇaláná.
Cross, *a.* ...	ကန့်လန့်နေသော။ ...	kun-lun-nay-thaw ...	a'ra, tir'chha ...	kuṟukkána, muranḍána.
Cross, *s.* ...	လက်ဝကတိုင်။ ...	leh-wah-kah-tuyng ...	chul'ee'pa, sul'eeb ...	chiluvai, puḷḷaḍi, varuttam.
Crow, *s.* ...	ကျီးကန်း။ ...	kyee-gun ...	kou'wa, kak, kul'agh ...	kákkai, kágam, kákkáy.
Crow'bar, *s.* ...	သံတူးရွင်း။ ...	thun-too-yoo-in ...	kud'ee'ma ...	kaḍappárai.
Crowd, *s.* ...	လူအစုအဝေး။ ...	loo-ă-soo-ă-way ...	bheer, um'boh, jum ...	kumbu, kúṭṭam, tiraṭchi.
Crown, *s.* ...	သရဖူ။ ...	thă-ră-poo ...	taj, moo'koot, chan'dee ...	maguḍam, muḍi, kríḍam.
Crúel, *a.* ...	ရက်စက်သော။ ...	yet-set-thaw ...	kut'hor, nirdy ...	kurúra, irakkamillátha.
Cry, *s.* ...	ငိုသည်။ ...	ngoh-the ...	ro'na, too'suk'na ...	aḻugai, pulambal.
Cub, *s.* ...	ဝက်ဝံသငယ်။မြေခွေးကလေး။ ...	weh-woon-th-ngeh, myay-	buch'a, pil'la ...	karaḍikkuṭṭi, kuṭṭi.
Cubit, *s.* ...	တောင်။ ...	downg, [gway-gälay,...	hath, dust, hust ...	muḻam, muḻakkól.
Cuc'koo, *s.* ...	ဥဩ။ ...	oo-aw ...	ko'hil, pik, sy'am ...	kukkuṟuván, kukkiṟpaḍchi.
Cul'tivate, *v. a.* ...	လယ်လုပ်သည်။ ...	leh-loht-the ...	a'bad-k, khet'ee-k, oop'ja'na.	chírppaḍuttu, krushipaṇṇu.
6 Cul'tivator, *s.* ...	လယ်လုပ်သမား။ ...	leh-loht-th'mah ...	kis'an, khet'ee'hur, kisht-kar	uḻavan, krushigan.
Cum'in, *s.* ...	ဇီးယာ။ ...	zee-yah ...	jee'ra, zee'ra, kum'moon ...	chíragam.
Cun'ning, *a.* ...	လိမ္မာသော။ ...	laym-mah-thaw ...	sy'ya'na, chut'oor, sy'yan ...	chúthána, tantramána.
Cup, *s.* ...	ခွက်။ ...	kwet ...	pi'ya'lu, kas, ka'sa, jam ...	kiṇṇam, páttiram, kóppai.

ENGLISH.	BURMESE.		HINDUSTANI.	TAMIL.
Cure, *s.* ...	ကုသည်။ပျောက်သည်။ ...	koo-the, pyowk-the ...	il'aj, uch'chha-k ...	sugam, sostam.
Cúrious, *a.* ...	ထူးဆန်းသော။ ...	too-zun-thaw ...	shoukeen, ragh'ib ...	kóraṇiyána, núthana.
Curl, *v. s.* ...	လိပ်သည်။ကောက်။ ...	layt-the, kowk ...	ka'kool, zoolf ...	churuḷ, chuḷi, muṛukku.
Cur'rent, *a.* ...	ရေစီး။စီးသောရေ။ ...	yay-see, see-thaw-yay ...	ja'ree, *f.* dha'ra ...	óḍugiṛa, chellugiṛa, páygiṛa.
Cur'rier, *s.* ...	သားရေလုပ်သမား။ ...	thah-yay-loht-th'mah ...	chum'ar, dub-gur ...	tólpathamiḍuvón.
Cur'ry, *s.* ...	ဟင်း။ ...	hin ...	sal'un, kul'i'ya ...	kaṛi, pathárttam.
Cur'ry-comb, *s.* ...	သံဘီး။ ...	thun-bee ...	khu're'ra, khur'uh'ra ...	kurappam.
Cur'ry-stuff, *s.* ...	ဟင်းနှင့်အတူးချက်ပြုတ်သောအ [ရာ။ ...	hin-hnin-a-too-chyet-poht-[thaw-a-yah.	sal'un-ka-mus'a'le ...	karimasálai, kúṭṭu.
Curse, *s.* ...	ကျိန်ဆဲသည်။	chyain-seh-the ...	phit'kar, la'nut ...	sápam, tímoḷi, tiṭṭu.
Cur'tain, *s.* ...	ချင်တောင်။ ...	chyin-downg ...	pur'du ...	tiraichchílai.
Cus'tom, *s.* ...	ထုံးစံ။ဓလေ့။ ...	tohn-zun, d'lay ...	dus'toor, ru'waj ...	vaḷakkam, mámúl.
Cus'tom, *s. dues* ...	အကောက်။ ...	ă-kowk ...	muh'sool, kur ...	tírvai, áyam.
Cus'tom-house, *s.* ...	အကောက်တိုက်။ ...	a-kowk-tuyk ...	pur'mit-ghur, chub'oo'tur'u..	áyatturai, révu.
Cus'tomer, *s.* ...	ဖေါက်သည်။ ...	powk-the ...	khur'eed'ar ...	vaḷakkamá-yorukaḍaiyiṛ-sarakku-váṅguvón.
Cut, *s.* ...	ဖြတ်သည်။ ...	pyut-the ...	kat, zukhm ...	veṭṭu, taḻumbu, kíṛṛu.
Cut'ler, *s.* ...	ထားရောင်းသောသူ။ ...	dah-yowng-thaw-thoo ...	suk'kak ...	veṭṭu-karuvi-cheyvón.
Cyl'inder, *s.* ...	စည်ပုံ။ ...	zee-bohn ...	sit'oon-i-gird ...	tambam, tiranḍavaḍivu.
Cym'bal, *s.* ...	ရကွင်း။ ...	yă-gwin ...	jhanjh ...	kiṇkiṇi, kaittáḷam.
Dag'ger, *s.* ...	တိုသောသန်လျက်။ ...	toh-thaw-thun-lee-et ...	khun'jur, kut'ar ...	kuttuváḷ.
Dáily, *a.* ...	နေ့တိုင်း။ ...	nay-duyng ...	you'mi'ya, roz-roz, hur-ro'za.	anudinamum, nitham.
Dam, *s.* ...	တိရစ္ဆာန်တို့တွင်အမိ။ ...	te-ray-sun-do-dwin-ămee...	ma, *bank* hubs, mend ...	táymirugam, aṇai.
Dam'age, *s.* ...	လျော်ပြစ်။ ...	hlee-aw-pyit ...	nook'san, khur'ab'ee ...	aḻivu, keḍuthi, nashṭi.
Damp, *a.* ...	ထိုင်းသော။ ...	tuyng-thaw ...	mur'toob, num, surd ...	íramána, talarchchiyána.
Dam'sel, *s.* ...	အပျို။ ...	ă-pyōh ...	ju'wan ...	iḷampeṇ, kumari.
Dance, *s.* ...	က။ ...	kah ...	nach, ruks ...	kúttu, náṭṭiyam.

Dan'cing-girl, *s.* ...	ကသောမိန်းမလေး။ ...	kah-thaw-mayn-gă-lay ...	ba'ee, kun'chun'ee, ram'jun	náttiyapen, nadanamáthu.
Dán-ger, *s.* ...	ဘေး။ ...	bay ...	khut'ra, khut'ur-nak'ee,[ee,.	apáyam, ábattu.
Dark, *a.* ...	မှောင်မိုက်သော။ ...	moung-muyk-thaw ...	un'dhe'ra, dyjoor ...	iruḷ, andhakáram.
Date, *fruit s.* ...	စွန်ပလွံသီး။ ...	sohn-bă-lohn-thee ...	khoor'ma, khuj'oor ...	péríchchampaḻam.
Date, *s.* ...	သက္ကရာဇ်။ ...	thek-ka-rit ...	ta'reekh ...	téthi, tithi.
Daugh'ter, *s.* ...	သမီး။ ...	thă-mee ...	be'tee, dookh'tur ...	magaḷ, puthalvi, putri.
Daugh'ter-in-law, *s.*	ချွေးမ။ ...	choo-ay-mah ...	bu'hoo, put'oh ...	maganmanaivi, marumagaḷ
Day, *s.* ...	နေ့။ ...	nay, [thaw-sah-yin-sah-ohk.	din, roz ...	náḷ, dinam, pagal.
Day'-book, *s.* ...	နေ့တိုင်မှတ်ရသောစာရင်းစာ	nay-duyng-hmut-yah-	roz-nam'chu, roz'na'ma ...	dinakkaṇakkup-pustakam.
Dead, *a.* ...	သေသော။ [အုပ်။...	thay-thaw ...	fou'tee, moo'a ...	uyirarra, kálañchenra.
Deaf, *a.* ...	နားပင်းသော။ ...	nah-pin-thaw ...	byh'ra, seom, kur ...	chevidána.
Deal'er, *s.* ...	ကုန်သည်။ ...	kohn-thay, [thaw,..	kar'ba'ree ...	viyápári, varttakam.
Dear, *a.* ...	ချစ်သော။ အဘိုးကြီးသော ...	chyit-thaw, a-poh-gyee-	jan, jan'ee, *price* muh'un'ga.	priyam, naṇban, kuṛaich-
Death, *s.* ...	သေချင်း။ ...	thay-chyin ...	fout, kal, mout ...	maraṇam, sávu. [chalána.
Debáse, *v. a.* ...	ယုတ်ညံ့စေသည်။ ...	yoht-nya-say-the ...	zul'eel-k ...	tálttu iḻivupaduttu.
Debáte, *v. a.* ...	ဆွေးနွေးငြင်းခုံသည်။ ...	sway-nway-hnyin-kohn-the	bu'hus'na ...	váthádu, tarkki.
Debt, *s.* ...	ကြွေး။ ...	kyoo-ay ...	dyne, kurz ...	kaḍan, iruṇam.
Debt'or, *s.* ...	ကြွေးရှင်။ ...	kyoo-ay-shin ...	kurz-dar, dyn'dar ...	kaḍanáḷi, kaḍankáran.
Deceit'ful, *a.* ...	လှည့်စားတတ်သော။ ...	hlee-sah-dut-thaw ...	dugh'a-baz, mukr'ha'ee ...	kapaḍamána, vañjaga.
Deceive', *v. a.* ...	လှည့်စားသည်။ ...	hlee-sah-the ...	dugh'a-dena ...	vañji, émáṛṛu, ettu.
Décent, *a.* ...	လျောက်ပတ်သော။ ...	lseowk-put-thaw ...	la'ik ...	oḻukkamána, yókkiyamána.
Deck, *s.* ...	ကုန်းပတ်။ ...	kohn-put ...	too'tuk ...	kappalin-méṛṛalam.
Deck, *v. a.* ...	ဝတ်ဆင်သည်။ ...	woot-sin-the ...	sin'gar'na, sun'war'na ...	alaṅkari, jóḍi.
Decoc'tion, *s.* ...	ပြုတ်ခြင်း။ ...	pyoht-chin ...	josh'an'du, kar'ha ...	kasháyam, kuḍinír.
Dec'orate, *v. a.* ...	တန်ဆာဆင်သည်။ ...	t'sah-sin-the ...	a'ras'tu-k, sin'gar'na ...	alaṅkari, jóḍi, siṅgári.
Decrease', *v. a.* ...	လျော့သည်။ ...	shaw-the ...	ghut'a'na, kum-k ...	kuṛai, kammi.
Decree', *s.* ...	စီရင်ဆုံးဖြတ်သည်။ ...	tsee-yin-sohn-pyut-the ...	hookm, fy'sul'a ...	tírppu, tírmánam.
Deduct', *v. a.* ...	နုတ်ယူသည်။ ...	hnoht-yoo-the ...	min'ha-k, kat'koot-k ...	kaḻi, kuṛai, níkku.

English.	Burmese.		Hindustani.	Tamil.
Deep, *a.* ...	နက်သော။ ...	net-thaw ...	guh'ra ...	álamána, áḻiya.
Deer, *s.* ..	သမင်။ ဒရယ်။ ဆတ်။ ...	thă-min, dă-yeh, sut ...	hur'un, koo'rung, mirg ...	mán, piṇai.
Defeat', *s.* ...	ပျက်သည်။ ...	pyet-the ...	huz'ee'mut, bhug'el ...	ṭólvi, abajayam.
Defec'tive, *a.* ..	မစုံမလင်။ ...	m-sohn-m'lin ...	ka'sir, na'kis ...	únamána, kuṟaivuḷḷa.
Defen'dant, *s.* ...	တရားခံ။ ...	ta-rah-cun ...	mood'da'leh, us'a'mee ...	prativáthi, ethiri.
Definit'ion, *s.* ...	အနက်ကိုဖေါ်ပြသည်။ ...	a-nek-go-paw-pyah-the ...	buk'han ...	arttam, viyákkiyánam.
Defraud', *v. a.* ...	ဥစ္စာကိုလိမ်လည်၍ယူသည်။ ...	oht-sah-go-layn-lee-yu-eh-	fur'eb-d ...	vañji, abakari, kavar.
Déity, *s.* ...	ဘုရားသခင်။ ...	pa-yah-thă-kin, [yoo-the,...	dev'ta, *m.* a'dit'yu ...	deyvíkam, deyvattuvam.
Delay', *s.* ...	ဆိုင်းသည်။ ...	suyng-the ...	der'ee, dir'ung ...	támatham, iḻukku.
Del'icate, *a.* ...	အရသာကောင်းသော။ ...	a-yah-thah-kowng-thaw ...	na'zook ...	teḷintha, chiṟantha.
Deliv'er, *v. a.* ...	လွှတ်သည်။ ...	hloot-the ...	a'zad-k, choo'ra'na ...	ṭappuvi, míḷ, viṭṭuviḍu.
Demand', *s.* ...	တောင်းသည်။ ...	towng-the ...	tulub ...	kéḷvi, athikárattuḍankéṭṭal.
Démon, *s.* ...	နတ်ဆိုး။ ...	nut-tsoh ...	bhoot, deo ...	pisásu, péy, véthálam.
Deny', *v. a.* ...	ငြင်းခုံသည်။ ...	ngyin-kohn-the ...	in'kar-k, moo'kur'na, nut'na	maṟu, maṟuthali.
Depart', *v. n.* ...	ထွက်သွားသည်။ ...	twet-thwah-the ...	ni'kul'ja'na, sid'har'na ...	puṟappaḍu, níṅgu, pó, agalu
Depart'ment, *s.* ...	အခန်းအတာ။ ...	a-cun-a-tah ...	kha'nu, muh'al ...	paguthi, kúṟu, tóḻil.
Depen'dent, *s.* ...	မှီခိုနေသော။ ...	hmee-yoo-eh-nay-thaw ...	moo'tu'wus'sil ...	chárnthavan.
Depos'it, *s.* ...	ချထားသည်။ သိုထားသည်။ ...	chyah-tah-the ...	um'a'nut ...	vaippu, oppaḍaipporuḷ.
Depth, *s.* ...	အနက်။ ...	ă-net ...	guh'ra'ya, gyh'ra'o ...	áḻam, táḻvu.
Dep'uty, *s.* [sioner,..	ကိုယ်စားလှယ်။ ...	koh-sah-leh ...	na'ib, moo'tu'uy'yin ...	prathiyáḷ, prathistan.
Dep'uty-Commis-	အရေးပိုင်။ ...	a-yay-buyng ...	naib-um'een ...	prathi-viohárapaikkáran.
Descend', *v. a.* ...	ဆင်းသည်။ ...	tain-the, [pyay-the,...	oo'tar'na ...	iṟaṅgu, táḻ, paṇi.
Des'ert, *s.* ...	သဲကန္တာရ။ ထွက်ပြေးသည်။ ...	theh-gun-da-yah, twet-	suh'ra ...	pálaivanam, vanántaram.
Desígn, *s.* ...	ကြံစည်သည်။ ...	kyun-seen-the ...	ir'a'da, ir'a'dut ...	eṇṇu, karuthu, uttési.
Desíre, *s.* ...	အလိုရှိသည်။ ...	a-loh-she-the ...	ar'zoo, chah, ir'a'da, kam...	ásai, ichchai, viruppam.
Despatch', *v.* ...	စေလွှတ်သည်။ ...	say-hloot-the ...	is'ti'uf'al ...	sikkiram, tíviram, churu-

Dessert', *s.* ...	အနောက်မှာစားသောအစာ။ ...	a-nowk-hmah-sah-thaw-a-	nookl ...	tímpaṇḍam. [churuppu.
Destroy', *v. a.* ...	ဖျက်ဆီးသည်။ ...	pyet-see-the, [sah,...	gha'rut-k, mar'na, bur'bad-k	aḻi, keḍu, saṅgari.
Detect', *v. a.* ...	ဖေါ်ပြသည်။ ...	paw-pyah-the ...	dur'i'yaft-k ...	kaṇḍupiḍi, piḻaipiḍi.
Deter'mine, *v. a.* ...	စိတ်ချသည်။ ...	sayt-chyah-the ...	thuh'ra'na, uzm-k ...	tírmáni, nichchayi, kuṛi.
Dev'il, *s.* ...	မာန်နတ်။ ...	mahn-nut, [cut-the,...	ib'lees, shy'tan ...	péy, pisásu, paisásam.
Devóte, *v. a.* ...	သစ္စာပြု၍ဆက်ကပ်သည်။ ...	thiss-sah-pyoo-yoo-eh-set-	mukh'soos-k, ni'yaz-k ...	nér, niyami, pirathishṭai-
Devotee', *s.* ...	ဘုရားမှူ။ ...	pă-yah-hmoo ...	bhug'ut, a'bid ...	dásan, toṇḍan, pattan. [chey.
Devour', *v. a.* ...	ဖြိုဝါးသည်။ ...	pyohn-wah-the ...	bhukh'na, bhuk'os'na ...	paṭchi, uṇ, viḻuṅgu.
Dew, *s.* ...	နှင်း။ ...	hnin ...	os, shub'num, sis'ir ...	pani, ímam.
Dex'terous, *a.* ...	စိတ်ကူးလျင်သော။ ...	sayt-koo-le-in-thaw ...	goon'ee, cha'lak ...	samarttuḷḷa, sádhuriyamána
Díal, *s.* ...	နာရီ။ [ပြောသည်။ ...	nah-ee, [s'gah-pyaw-the,...	juntr ...	súriyakaḍiyáram.
Díalogue, *s.* ...	နှစ်ယောက် အချင်းချင်း စကား	hnit-yowk-a-chyin-chyin-	gooft'goo, bat-cheet ...	sambháshaṇai, sallápam.
Diam'eter, *s.* ...	အချင်း။ ...	ă-chyin ...	koot'oor ...	viṭṭam, kuṛukkaḷavu.
Díamond, *s.* ...	စိန်။ ကြောက်။ ...	sayn (khyowk) ...	hee'ra, ul'mas, bujr ...	vairam, vajram.
Diarrhœ'a *s.* ...	ဝမ်းကျနာ။ ...	woon-chyah-nah ...	is'hal, ut'i'sar ...	sítabéthi.
Díary, *s.* ...	နေ့စဉ်မှတ်စာ။ ...	nay-seen-hmut-sah ...	roz-nam'chu, roz-na'ma ...	dinavarttamánam.
Dice, *s.* ...	အန်စာများ ...	un-zah-myah ...	kim'ar, pa'se, joos ...	páchchigai.
Dic'tionary, *s.* ...	အဘိဓါန်။ ...	ă-bee-dun ...	fur'hung, loo'ghut ...	agaráthi.
Did, *s.* ...	ပြုပြီးသည်။ ...	pyoo-bee-the ...	kee'ya ...	siddhi, ágina.
Die, *v. n.* ...	သေသည်။ ...	thay-the ...	murja'na, mur'na ...	chá, iṛa, maraṇi, mari.
Díet, *s.* ...	အစားအသောက်။ ...	a-sah-a-thowk ...	khoo'rak, ghiz'a ...	uṇavu, sáppáḍu.
Dif'ference, *s.* ...	ခြားနားခြင်း။ ...	chyah-nah-chyin ...	furk, tuf'a'woot, [kil,...	vittiyásam, bhédam.
Dif'ficult, *a.* ...	ခက်ခဲသော။ ...	kek-keh-thaw ...	doosh'war, duk'eek, moosh'	maṛaiváṇa, prayásamána.
Dig, *v. a.* ...	တူးသည်။ ...	too-the ...	khod'na, goo'ra'na, gor'na...	kiṇḍu, tóṇḍu.
Dig'nity, *s.* ...	မြင့်မြတ်ခြင်း။ ...	myin-myut-chyin ...	mun'sub, mur'tub'u, [ee,...	ménmai, mahatuvam.
Dil'igence, *s.* ...	လုံ့လဝီရိယရှိခြင်း။ ...	lohn-lah-we-ree-yah-she-	dhoon, tun'dih'ee, sur'gurm'	muyaṛchi, jákkrathai.
Dilúte, *v. a.* ...	ပေါ့စေသည်။ ...	paw-zay-the, [chyin,...	put'la-k, ruk'eek-k ...	nírákku, karai.
Dim, *a.* ...	မှိန်သော။ ...	hmohn-thaw ...	dhoondh'la ...	kammalána, mantha.

ENGLISH.	BURMESE.		HINDUSTANI.	TAMIL.
Dimin'ish, *v.* ...	ငယ်သည်။ ...	ngeh-the ...	ghut'ee, kum ...	kuṛai, tani, surukku.
Dine, *v. n.* ...	ညစာကိုစားသည်။ ...	nyah-zah-go-sah-the ...	kha'na-kha'na ...	tin, prathánabhójanamchey.
Din'ner, *s.* ...	ညစာ။ ...	nyah-sah ...	kha'na ...	tín, prathána-bhójanam.
Dip, *s.* ...	နှစ်သည်။ ...	hnit-the ...	doob, doob'kee, gho'tu ...	amilttu, tóy.
Dipper, *s.* ...	ရေမှုတ်။ ...	yay-hmoht ...	chum'chu, gho'tu-khor ...	agappai, *wood* karaṇḍi, *brass.*
Direct', *a.* ...	ဖြောင့်သော။ ...	pyowng-thaw ...	moos'tuv'ee ...	néṛiya, tírkkamána.
Direc'tion, *s.* ...	မှာစာလိပ်။ ...	hmah-sah-layt ...	put'a ...	mélvilásam, nithánam.
Direct'ly, *adv.* ...	ချက်ချင်း။ ...	chyet-chyin ...	seed'ha'ee-se ...	néré, kaiyóḍé, uḍané.
Direc'tor, *s.* ...	စီရင်ပိုင်ဖြင်သောသူ။ ...	tsee-yin-peh-pyin-thaw-[thoo, ...	ha'dee, sur'kob ...	káriyaturantaran.
Dirt, *s.* ...	အညစ်အကြေး။ ...	a-nyit-a-chyeh, ...	myl, keech, kee'chur ...	maṇ, aḷukku, malam.
Dir'ty, *a.* ...	ညစ်သော။ ...	nyit-thaw ...	my'la, nuj'is ...	aḷukkuḷḷa, iḷiváua.
Disagree', *v. n.* ...	သဘောမတူ။ ...	th'-baw-mă-too ...	na'moo'wa'fik ...	iraṇḍupaḍu, pisagu.
Disappoint', *v. a.* ...	အကြံဖျက်သည်။ ...	a-chyun-pyet-the ...	bich'ka'na ...	nambikkaikeḍu, éy.
Discharge, *v. a.* ...	တိုးလိုက်သည်။ သေနတ်ပြစ်သည်။	toh-luyt-the, thay-nut-pyit-[the, ...	bur'tur'uf-k, chhoo'ra na ...	taḷḷu, viḍuthalai.
Discíple, *s.* ...	တပည့်။ ...	tă-byee, ...	sha'gird ...	síshan, máṇákkan.
Dis'count, *s.* ...	လျှော့ပေးသည်။ ...	shaw-pay-the ...	but'ta, cho'ta ...	kaḷivu, taḷḷupaḍi.
Discov'er, *v. a.* ...	ပေါ်ပြသည်။ ...	paw-pyah-the ...	py da-k, dur'yaft-k ...	kaṇḍupiḍi, veḷiyákku.
Disease', *s.* ...	အနာရောဂါ။ ...	a-nah-yaw-gah ...	bee'ma'ree, a'zar, murz ...	viyáthi, nóy, piṇi.
Disgráce, *s.* ...	အသရေပျက်သည်။ ...	ă-the-ray-pyet-the ...	roos'wa'ee ...	avakírtti, avamánam.
Disgust', *s.* ...	ရွံသည်။ ...	yohn-the ...	ghin, nuf'rut ...	veṛuppu, asaṅgiyam.
Dish, *s.* ...	ပုကန်ပြားကြီး။ ...	pă-gun-byah-gyee ...	rik'ab, rik'ab'ee, rik eb ee ...	taṭṭu, páttiram.
Dishon'est, *a.* ...	မရိုးမဖြောင့်သော။ ...	m'yoh-m'pyowng-thaw ...	na-rast, ...	náṇayaṅgkeṭṭa.
Dishon'our, *v. a.* ...	မရိုသေသော။ ...	m'yoh-thay-thaw ...	be-hoor'mut-k, ab'roo-oo'[tar'na, ...	avamánappaḍuttu, táḷttu.
Dislíke, *v. a.* ...	မနှစ်သက်။ ...	m'hnit-thet ...	nuf'rut-k ...	veṛuppu, priyavínam.
Dis'locate, *v. a.* ...	အလွဲထားသည်။ ...	a-lweh-tah-the ...	oo'khar'na ...	kaḷaṛṛu, peyar.
Dismount', *v. a.* ...	မြင်းပေါ်ကဆင်းသည်။ ...	myin-baw-gah-sin-the ...	oo'tar'na ...	iṛakku, iraṅgu, taḷḷu.

Disobédience, *s.* ...	နားမထောင်ချင်။ ...	nah-m'towng-chyin ...	sur'kush'ee, na-fur'man'ee...	kíḻppaḍiyámai, amaiyámai.
Dispen'sary, *s.* ...	ဆေးဝါးကိုဝေပေးသောအရပ်။	tsay-wah-goh-way-pay- thaw-a-yut ...	du'wa-kha'nu ...	aviḻthachálai.
Displéase, *v. a.* ...	စိတ်ဆိုးစေသည်။ ...	sayt-soh-say-the ...	na'khoosh-k ...	kópamúṭṭu, veṛuppunḍákku
Disprove', *v. a.* ...	မဟုတ်ကြောင်းကိုပြသည်။ ...	m'hoht-gyowng-goh-pyah-	rud-k, jhoo'tal'na ...	allaveṇrurúbi.
Dispúte, *s*, ...	ငြင်းခုံခြင်း။ ...	ngyin-kohn-gyin, [the,...	buhs, tuk'rar ...	viyáchchiyam, tarkkam.
Disrespect', *s.* ...	မထီမဲ့မြင်ပြုသော။ ...	m'tee-meh-myin-pyoo-thaw.	be-ud'ub'ee, turk-i-ud'-ub...	avamathippu, achaṭṭai.
Dissimulátion, *s.*...	လျှို့ဝှက်ခြင်း။ ...	shoh-wet-chyin ...	mukr, ri'ya ...	iranḍagam, kaḻḻakkaruttu.
Dis'solute, *a.* ...	ကာမဂုဏ်သွန်းသော ...	kah-m-gohn-thohn-thaw ...	ou'bash'a'nu ...	tunmárkkamána.
Dissol've, *v. a.* ...	အရည်ဖြစ်သည်။ ...	a-yee-pyit-the ...	gul'a'na ...	karai, pri, vilakku, tavir.
Dis'tance, *s.* ...	အကွာအဝေး။ ...	a-kwah-a-way ...	door, moo'fa'ail'u, mus'a'fut.	dúram, tolai. [pón.
Distil'ler, *s.* ...	အရက်ကိုချက်သောသူ။ ...	a-yet-go-chyet-thaw-thoo...	ab'kar, soon'ree ...	iṛakkuvón, káychchivaḍip-
Distinct', *a.* ...	ခြားနားသော။ ...	chyah-nah-thaw ...	moo'fus'sul ...	tírkkamuḻḻa, tiruttamána.
Distress', *s.* ...	နာစေသည်။ ...	nah-say-the ...	hy'ran'ee, pur'e'shan'ee ...	tuyaram, tunbam,varuttam.
Distrib'ute, *v. a.*...	ဝေငှသည်။ ...	way-hngah-the ...	bant'na ...	pakunthukoḍu, pańgiḍu.
Dis'trict, *s.* ...	နယ်။အရပ်။ ...	neh, a-yut ...	zil'a, pur'gun'u ...	náḍu, úr, désam, mákánam.
Disturb'. *v. a.* ...	မွှေသည်။ ...	hmway-the ...	hun'ga'mu-k ...	alaṭṭuppannu, alai, kalakku.
Ditch, *s.* ...	မြောင်း။ ...	myowng ...	kha'ee, khun'duk ...	agal, agali, chákkáḍai.
Diver'se, *a.* ...	ကွဲပြားသော။ ...	kweh-pyah-thaw ...	un'wa ...	palavitha, nánávitha.
Divíde, *v. a.* ...	ကွဲသည်။ ...	kweh-the ...	bant'na ...	pri, pańgiḍu, pagu.
Div'idend, *s.* ...	အစုသင့်။ ...	a-tsoo-thin ...	da'ma'sa'hee, his'su. [ee,...	págam, páchchiyam.
Divíne, *a.* ...	ဘုရားနှင့်ဆိုင်သော။ ...	pă-yah-hnin-suyng-thaw ...	rub'ba'nee, il'a'hee, khoo'da	deyvíka, parama, ñána.
Divin'ity, *s.* ...	ဘုရားသခင်ဇါဇာတိအဖြစ်။ ...	pa-yah-th'kin-ee-zah-dee-	khoo'da'ee, il'a'hee'yut ...	kaḍavuḷ, deyvam, déyvattu-
Divis'ion, *s.* ...	ကွဲခြင်း။ ...	kweh-chyin, [a-pyit,...	his'su, *town* muh'ul'lu ...	pirivu, pańgu, págam.[vam.
Divis'ion, *s.* ...	စားခြင်း။ ...	tsah-chyin ...	tuk'seem ...	vaguttal. [vilakku.
Divor'ce, *s.* ...	လင်မယားကွာသည်။ ...	lin-mă-yah-kwah-the ...	tul'ak ...	taḻḻuthal, vivágasambantha-
Do, *v. a.* ...	ပြုသည်။ ...	pyoo-the, [khyin,...	bun'a'na, kur'na ...	olugu, naḍa, chey.
Dock'-yard, *s*, ...	သင်္ဘောသွင်းထားရန်ကျင်း။ ..	thin-baw-thwin-tah-yun-	kar-kha'na, kha'ree ...	kappalcheppaniḍunturai.

English.	Burmese.		Hindustani.	Tamil.
Doc'tor, *s.* ...	ဆေးသမား။ ...	tsay-thum-mah ...	byd, huk'eem ...	vaittiyan, paṇḍithan.
Doc'trine, *s.* ...	ပြသခြင်း။ ...	pyah-thah-chyin ...	sich'chha ...	pótham, upadésam, matham
Doc'ument, *s.* ...	စာရင်း၊လက်မှတ်။ ...	sah-yin, let-hmut ...	dus'ta-wez, sun'ud ...	pattiram, dastávéju.
Doe, *s.* ...	ဒရယ်မ။ ...	dă-yeh-mah ...	hur'nee, hir'nee ...	peṇmán, piṇaimán.
Dog, *s.* ...	ခွေး ...	kway ...	koot'ta, koo'ti'ya, *f.* ...	náy, *common* ánnáy, *m.*
Doll, *s.* ...	ယဉ်မင်း၊ရုပ်။ ...	yeh-min, yoht ...	goo'ri'ya, poot'lee ...	pommai, pávai.
Dol'phin, *s.* ...	ငါးကြီးတမျိုး။ ...	ngah-gyee-t'myo ...	dool'fin, dool'feen ...	kaḍarpanṛi,órmín.[iṛkuriya.
Domes'tic, *a.* ...	အိမ်တွင်းအမှု။ ...	ayn-dwin-a-hmoo ...	bhee'tur'hi'ya, khan'gee ...	víṭṭuvélaikáṛan, kuḍumbat-t
Domin'ion, *s.* ...	အာဏာ။ ...	ah-nah ...	hoo'koo'mut, raj, sul'tun'ut-	iráchchiyam, rájarikam.
Donátion, *s.* ...	ဒါန။ ...	dah-nah ...	bukh'shish, dan ...	ívu, íkai, dánam.
Dónor, *s.* ...	ပေးကမ်းသောသူ။ ...	pay-cun-thaw-thoo ...	da'ta, da'ee, da'ik ...	íkaiyáḷan, dátá.
Door, *s.* ...	တံခါး။ ...	t'gah ...	dur, dur'wa'zu, dwar ...	kathavu.
Dor'mitory, *s.* ...	အိပ်ခန်း။ ...	ayt-cun ...	khwab-gah ...	paḷḷiyaṛai,sayaṇamaṇḍapam
Dose, *s.* ...	ဆေးတကျိုက်။ ...	t'say-t'chuyk ...	pur'im'an, khoo'rak ...	orutharam-koḍukkumarun-
Dot, *s.* ...	ဗိန္ဒု။ ...	bayn-doo ...	boon'da, soon'na, nook'tu ...	puḷḷi, poṭṭu. [thu.
Doub'le, *a.* ...	နှစ်ဘက်ရှိသော။ ...	hnit-pet-shee-thaw ...	doh'ra, do-bur ...	iraṭṭaiyána, irumaḍaṅgána.
Doubt, *s.* ...	ယုံမှားသည်။ ...	yohn-hmah-the ...	shuk, dhok'ha ...	sandékam, samusayam.
Dove, *s.* ...	ချိုး။ ...	jyoh ...	fakh'tu, koo'koo ...	puṛá, kapótham.
Dow'er, Dow'ry, } *s.*	{ လက်ထပ်ရာတွင် မိန်းမ မိဘ ပေး သောလက်ဖွဲ့ငွေ။ ...	let-tut-yah-dwin-maym-mah-mee-bah-pay-thaw-let-	} muhr, ka'been, ju'hez ...	síthanam, stritanam.
Down, *s.* ...	မွေးနု။ ...	mway-noo, [pweh-oht-sah.	ro'en ...	melliṛagu.
Down'ward, *adv.* ...	အောက်သို့။ ...	owk-thoh ...	nee'che ...	kíḷé.
Draft, *v. write roughly*	စာစီကုံးသည်။ ...	tsah-see-kohn-the ...	kha'ka ...	chaṭṭam, nagal.
Draft, *s. money* ...	ငွေလွှဲလက်မှတ်။ ...	ngway-hlew-ah-let-hmut ...	bur'at, hoon'dee ...	uṇḍichchíṭṭu.
Drain, *s.* ...	ရေမြောင်း။ ...	yay-myoung ...	bud'ur'rou, mooh'ree ...	kálváy, chálakam.
Dram'a, *s.* ...	ဇာတ်။ဇာတ်ပွဲ။ ...	zaht, zaht-pweh ...	nukl ...	náḍakam, parathasástiram.

Draw, *v. a.*	ဆွဲသည်။	tsweh-the	khynch'na	iḻu, váñgu, vali.
Draw'ing, *s.*	ရေးသောရုပ်ပုံ။	yay-thaw-yoht-pohn	nuk'shu	chitrappaḍam, eḻuttu.
Dream, *s.*	အိမ်မက်။	aym-met	khwab, sup'na	kanavu, soppanam.
Dregs, *s. pl.*	အနှစ်။	a-hnit	doord, tul'chhut	manḍi, kúlam, vanḍal.
Dress, *s.*	အဝတ်	a-woot	po'shak	uḍai, uḍuppu, áḍai.
Drink, *s.*	သောက်သည်။	thowk-the	nosh, pee'na, shoorb	pánam, mathu, pániyam.
Driver, *s.*	မောင်းသောသူ။	mowng-thaw-thoo	ga'ree'ban	óttugiravan, págan.
Drop, *v. n.*	အစက်။	ă-set	tup'uk'na	tuḻi, oḻuku.
Drop'sy, *s.*	ရေဖျဉ်းနာ။	yay-pyee-nah	is'tis'ka, jul'un'dur	víkkam, nírámayam. [rakku.
Drug, *s.*	ဘယဆေး။	bah-yah-tsay	dur'mun, ou'shudh	aviltham, marunthuchcha-
Drug'gist, *s.*	ဘယဆေးရောင်းသောသူ။	bah-yah-tsay-yowng-thaw-	pun'sa'ree, ut'tar	marunthu-charakku-viyáb-
Drum, *s.*	ဘုံ။စည်။	bohn, see, [thoo,...	ta'sa, dhol, mri'dung	mélam, mattaḷam, paṛai. [ári.
Drunk, *a.*	ယစ်မူးသော။	yit-moo-thaw	mut, mut-wa'la	veṛimayakkamána.
Drunk'ard, *s.*	ယစ်ထုပ်။	yit-toht	nush'a-khor, shur'ab'ee	kuḍiyan, veṛiyan.
Dry, *a.*	သွေ့ခြောက်သော။	thoo-ay-chyowk-thaw	shook'ha, khooshk	káyntha, varantha, ularntha.
Duck, *s.*	ဝမ်းဘဲ။	woom-beh	but'uk	pentárá, pettai-tárá.
Dumb, *a.*	အသော။	ah-thaw	goong, goon'ga	úmaiyána, péchcharra.
Dúplicate, *s.*	အဖက်။လက်ခွံ။	ă-pet, let-oun	moo'sun'na	prathi, nakal, anuprathi.
Dust, *s.*	အမှုန်။	ă-hmohn	dhool, gurd, khak	túl, túsi, puḻuthi.
Dúty, *s.*	ဝတ်ပြုသော။	woot-pyoo-thaw	furz	kaḍamai, urimai, toḻil.
Dúty, *s. tax,*	အကောက်။	a-kowk	muh'sool	tírvai, áyam.
Dwel'ling, *s.*	နေရာ။	nay-yah	muk'an, muk'am, mus'kun.	vásam, iruppiḍam.
Dye, *s.*	ဆေး။ဆေးဆိုးသည်။	tsay, tsay-soh-the	rung	cháyam, varṇam.
Dy'er, *s.*	အထည်ဆိုးသမား။	ă-tee-soh-thă-mah	rung'rez, run'gee	cháyakkáran, varṇakkáran.
7 Dys'entery, *s.*	သွေးပါဝမ်းကျနာ။	thoo-ay-pah-woon-chyah-	is'hal-i-khoon, ut'i'sar	irattakkaḻichchal.
Each, *pron.*	တိုင်း။စီ။	tuyng, see [nah,...	hur'ek	ovvoru, antantha.
Ea'ger, *a.*	စိတ်အားကြီးသော။	sayt-ah-kyee-thaw	sur'gurm	ávaluḷḷa, pérásaiyuḷḷa.
Ear, *s.*	နား။	nah	kan	káthu, chevi,

English.	Burmese.		Hindsutani.	Tamil.
Earl'y, *a.* ...	စောစော။ ...	saw-zaw ...	sub'er ...	kálamé, athikála.
Earth, *s.* ...	မြေ၊မြေကြီး။ ...	myay, myay-gyee ...	zum'een ...	bhúmi, bhúlókam, maṇ.
East, *s.* ...	အရှေ့။ ...	a-shay ...	poo'rub, shurk ...	kiḻakku, kíḻttisai.
Eas'y, *a.* ...	လွယ်သော။ ...	loo-eh-thaw ...	suhl, sul'ees, a'san ...	eḷitháṇa, chuḷuváṇa.
Eat, *v. n.* ...	စားသည်။ ...	tsah-the ...	kha'na, bhuchh'na ...	sáppiḍu, tin, pusi, uṇ.
Ebb, *s.* ...	ရေကျသည်။ ...	yay-chyah-the ...	bhat'ha, juzr ...	nírvaṛṛam, kuṛai.
Eb'ony, *s.* ...	သစ်တာနက်။ ...	thit-tah-net ...	ab'noos ...	karuṅkáli, kathiram.
Eclip'se, *s.* ...	ကြတ်သည်။ ...	khyut-the ...	gru'hin, gu'hin ...	grahaṇam.
Ed'dy, *s.* ...	ဝဲဆန်။ ...	weh-sun ...	bhun'wur ...	níróṭṭam, nírchuḻi.
Edge, *s.* ...	အသွား။ ...	ă-thwah ...	kin'a'ra, bar, kor ...	óram, tíram. [ṭam.
E'dict, *s.* ...	အမိန့်တော်။ ...	a-mayn-daw ...	fur'man, sa'sun ...	pramáṇam, kaṭṭaḷaichchaṭ-
Edit'ion, *s.* ...	တခါတဦးပုံနှိပ်သောစာမောင်း။	tă-kah-dee-pohn-hnait-thaw-sah-mowng ...	chha'pa, chhap'a'ee ...	puttakappathippu.
Ed'ucate, *v. a.* ...	တတ်အောင်ဆုံးမသွန်သင်သည်။	tut-owng-sohm-mah-thohn-thin-the ...	tur'bi'yut-d ...	karpi, paḻakku. [dhi.
Effect', *s.* ...	အကျိုးအကြောင်း။ ...	a-kyoh, ă-khyowng ...	ta'seer, us'ur ...	siddhi, palippu, káriyasid-
Effem'inacy, *s.* ...	မိမ္မကဲ့သို့နုးညံ့သော။ ...	maym-mah-geh-thoh-noo- ...	zun'a'nu-pun ...	peṇmai, péthaimai, náṇam.
Ef'fort, *s.* ...	ကြိုးစားခြင်း။ ...	kyoh-sah-chyin, [nyun-thaw	ko'shish, su'ee ...	uṛchágam, muyaṛchi, úkkam.
Egg, *s.* ...	ဥ။ ...	oo ...	un'da, by'zu ...	muṭṭai, aṇḍam.
Eject', *v. a.* ...	ထုတ်ပြစ်သည်။ ...	toht-pyit-the ...	ni'kal-d, ni'kal'na ...	eṛi, viḍu, umiḻ, níkku.
Elap'se, *v. n.* ...	လွန်သည်။ ...	lohn-the ...	goo'zur'na, goo'zur-ja'na ...	vaḻuvu. pó, saṛukku,
El'bow, *s.* ...	တံတောင်။ ...	t-downg ...	koh'nee, mir'fuk ...	muḻaṅkai.
El'der, *s.* ...	အသက်ကြီးသော။ ...	ă-thet-kyee-thaw ...	bur'a, jet'ha, kul'an ...	mútta, jéshṭa.
El'ephant, *s.* ...	ဆင်။ ...	tsin ...	hat'hee, *m.* huth'nee, *f.* ...	yánai, ánai.
El'evate, *v. a.* ...	ချီးပင့်သည်။ ...	chyee-pin-the ...	oon'cha'na ...	uyarttu, éṛṛu, méḍu.
Else, *adv.* ...	အခြားတပါး။ ...	ă-chyah-t'bah ...	wur'nu, nu'heen'to, our ...	allathu, allávittál.

Else'where, *adv.* ...	အခြားတပါးမှာ။ ...	a-chyah-t'bah-hmah ...	our-ku'heen ...	véreṅgum, maṛṛeṅgéyágu-thal.
Emac'iate, *v. a.* ...	ပိန်သည်။ ...	payn-the ...	sook'ha'na, sookh'na ...	meli, oḍuṅgu, ular.
Em'bers, *s. pl.* ...	မီးမှုန်။ ...	mee-hmohn ...	bhoo'bhul, ung'a'ra ...	talal, taṇal.
Em'erald, *s.* ...	မြ။ ...	myah ...	pun'na, zum'oor'rud ...	pachchaikkal, marakatha-maṇi.
Em'inent, *a.* ...	မြင့်သော။ ...	myin-thaw, ...	a'lee, sur-bul'und ..	chiṛanta, ménmaiyána.
Em'issary, *s.* ...	ရှိုဝှက်၍စေလွှတ်သောသူ။ ...	sho-wet-yu-eh-tsay-hloot-thaw-thoo, ...	ja'soos, bhe'dee, bhe'di'ya ...	túthan, oṛṛan.
Employ'ment, *s.* ...	အလုပ်အကိုင်။ ...	a-loht-a-kuyng ...	kam, shooghl ...	vélai, udyógam, toḻil.
Emp'ty, *a.* ...	လစ်သော။ ...	lut-thaw ...	kha'lee. soo'nan ...	veṛumaiyána, veṛu, veṛṛu.
Encour'age, *v. a.* ...	အားပေးသည်။ ...	ah-pay-the ...	dil'a'se-d ...	tiḍappaḍuttu, téṛṛu, évu.
End, *s.* ...	အဆုံး။ ...	a-sohn ...	a'khir, in'ti'ha, unt ...	muḍivu, nuṇi, munai.
Endeav'our, *s.* ...	ကြိုးစားသည်။ ...	kyoh-sah-the ...	ko'shish ...	muyaṛchchi, uṛchágam.
En'emy, *s.* ...	ရန်သူ။ ...	yun-thoo ...	by'ree, doosh'mun ...	bagaiñan, ethiri, satturu.
En'gine, *s.* ...	စက်။ ...	set ...	kul, sun'ut ...	yanthiram, súttiram.
Engráve, *v. a.* ...	ထုံသည်။ ...	too-the ...	kun'da-k, nuksh-k ...	kottu, chitramveṭṭu.
Enig'ma, *s.* ...	နက်နဲခက်ခဲသောစကား။ ...	net-neh-ket-keh-thaw-să-gah, ...	moo'um'ma, puh'el'ee ...	viḍukathai, maraichol.
Enjoy', *v. a.* ...	ပျော်မွေ့သည်။ ...	pyaw-moo-ay-the, ...	bi'hur'na, kkoosh'ee-k ...	sukhamanubhavi.
Enough', *a.* ...	လောက်သော။ ...	lowk-thaw ...	bus, ka'fee ...	póthumána, tirptikaramána.
Enslávе, *v. a.* ...	ကျွန်ခံစေသည်။ ...	kyoon-cun-say-the ...	ghoo'lam-k ...	chiṛaipiḍi, chiṛaippaḍuttu.
En'ter, *v. a.* ...	ဝင်သည်။ ...	win-the ...	pyth'na, dakh'il-k ...	peyareḻuthu, pravési.
Entíce, *v. a.* ...	သွေးဆောင်သည်။ ...	thoo-ay-sowng-the ...	phoos'la'na ...	iḻu, éy, mayakku.
Entíre, *a.* ...	အကုံအစင်။ ...	ă-kohn-ă-sin ...	poo'ra, sa'boot, tum'am ...	púraṇamána, muḻu, muṛṛána.
En'trance, *s.* ...	ဝင်ခြင်း။ အဝင်။ ...	win-gin, a-win ...	dukhl, pu'hoonch, pyth ...	utpravésam, váyil.
Ep'ilepsy, *s.* ..	ဝက်ရူးနာတမျိုး။ ...	wet-yoo-nah ...	mir'gee, sur'u, up'us'mar ...	kákkáyvali, kóraṇi.
E'qual, *a.* ...	ညီမျှသော။ ...	nyee-hmyah-thaw ...	bur'a'bur, moo'sa'wee ...	oppána, samánamuḻḻa.
Eq'uity, *s.* ...	ဖြောင့်မှတ်သောတရား။ ...	pyowng-hmut-thaw-ta-yah.	in'saf, huk, udl ...	naḍuniyáyam, dharumam.
Eráse, *v. a.* ...	ချေဖျက်သည်။ ...	chyay-pyet-the ...	muhv-k, met'na ...	tuḍai, kiṛukku, kíṛu.
Ere, *adv.* ...	အရင်။ အထက်။ ...	ă-yin, a-tet ...	a'ge, pesh'tur ...	mun, munné, munnam.
Erect', *a.* ...	မတ်သော။ တည့်သော။ ...	mut-thaw, tee-thaw ...	khur'a ...	nimirttu, niṛuttu, náṭṭu.

English.	Burmese.		Hindustani.	Tamil.
Err, *v. n.* ...	မှားသည်။လွဲသည်။ ...	hmah-the, lweh-the ...	bhool'na ...	tavaṛu, tappu, pisagu.
Er'ror, *s.* ...	အမှား။ ...	ă-hmah ...	bhool, khut'a, ghul'ut'ee ...	piḻai, kuṛṛam, tappitham.
Estab'lish, *v. a.* ...	တည်ဆောက်သည်။ ...	tee-sowk-the ...	thuh'ra'na ...	stápi, érpaḍuttu.
Estáte, *s.* ...	ပိုင်နက်။ဥစ္စာ။ ...	puyng-net, oht-sah ...	sur'kar ...	stiti, bhústiti, tanmai.
Es'timate, *s.* ...	ခြင့်တွက်သည်။ ...	chyin-twet-the ...	un'daz, bur'a'woord ...	mathippu, uddésam.
Eúnuch, *s.* ...	မိမ္မစိုး။ ...	maym-mah-soh ...	kho'ja, khwa'ja-sur'a ...	áṇmaiyilláthavan, péḍan,
Ev'ening, *s.* ...	ညဦး။ ...	nyah-oo ...	sham, sanjh ...	sáyṅkálam, málai, [ivu.
Event', *s.* ...	အဖြစ်။အဖျက်။ ...	ă-pyit, a-pyet ...	ma'jur'a, sur'goo-zusht ...	varttamánam, tírppu, muḍ-
Ev'er, *adv.* ...	တရံသောအခါ။ ...	tă-yun-thaw-ă-kah ...	hum'e'shu, hur'giz, kub'hoo.	eppoḻuthum, enṛaikkáyinum
Everlas'ting, *a.* ...	အစဉ်အမြဲတည်သော။ ...	a-seen-a-myeh-tee-thaw ...	ub'in'a'see, uk'huy, uk'shuy.	enṛumuḷḷa, muḍivaṛṛa.
Ev'ery, *a.* ...	တိုင်း။လူတိုင်း။ ...	tuyng, loo-duyng ...	hur, sub ...	ovvoru, sagala, ellá.
Ev'ery-day, *a.* ...	နေ့တိုင်း။ ...	nay-duyng ...	hur-roz, din-din ...	dinamdinam, náḷthóṛum.
Ev'ery-where, *adv.* ..	နေရာတိုင်း။ ...	nay-yah-duyng ...	hur'ja, hurku'heen ...	eṅgum, aṅgaṅgé.
Ev'idence, *s.* ...	သက်သေခံချက်။ ...	thet-thay-cun-chyet ...	gu'wa'hee, izhar, shu'ha'dut.	sáṭchi, vákkumúlam.
E'vil, *s.* ...	ဆိုးသော။မကောင်းသော။ ...	tsoh-thaw, m'kwonwg-thaw	bud'ee, boo'ra'ee, khur'ab'ee.	tímai, tunmárkkam.
Ewe, *s.* ...	သိုးမ။ ...	thoh-mah ...	bher, bher'ee ...	chemmaṛi, chemmaṛi-áḍu.
Exact', *a.* ...	သေချာသော။ ...	thay-chyah-thaw ...	bur'a'bur, theek ...	sariyána, tiṭṭamána.
Exam'ine, *v. a.* ...	စစ်ဆေးသည်။ ...	tsit-tsay-tho ...	janch'na, pur'ukh'na ...	paríṭchi, sóthi, áráy.
Exam'ple, *s.* ...	ပုံသက်သေ။ ...	pohn-thet-thay ...	num'oo'nu, mus'ul'un ...	máthiri, uthárаṇam.
Exceed', *v. a. & n.* ...	သာသည်။ ...	thah-the ...	zi'ya'du, toj'a'wooz-k ...	kathi, talaippaḍu, mérpaḍu.
Exchánge, *s.* ...	လဲသည်။ ...	leh-the ...	bud'ul, udl-budl ...	baṭhil, kaimáṛu, uṇḍi.
Ex'crement, *s.* ...	အချေး။မစင်။ ...	ă-chyee, mă-sin ...	bish'tha ...	malam, kashṭam, naragal.
Excúse, *v. a.* ...	အပြစ်မှလွှတ်သည်။ ...	apyit-hmah-hloot-the ...	bu'ha'na-k ...	piḻaiporu, manni.
Exhort', *v. a.* ...	နှိုးဆော်သည်။ ...	hnoh-saw-the ...	nus'ee'hut-k ...	póthi, echchari.
Exist', *v. n.* ...	ဖြစ်သည်။ ...	pyit-the ...	ho'na, ruh'na, [rukh'na, ...	iru, jívi, nilaittiru.
Expect', *v. a.* ...	မျှော်လင့်သည်။ ...	hmyaw-lin-the ...	in'tiz'ar-k, oom'med-	nambu, káttiru.

Expel', *v. a.*	နှင်ထုတ်သည်။	hnin-toht-the	ni'kal'na	ót̤t̤u, níkku, turattu.
Expense', *s.*	စရိတ်။	sah-yait	khurch, khurj	chelavu, chenṛachelavu.
Expen'sive, *a.*	စရိတ်များသော။	sah-yait-myah-thaw	khur'choo	miguchelavul̤l̤a, athikavilai-yul̤l̤a.
Explain', *v. a.*	အနက်အဓိပ္ပာယ်ကိုဖော်ပြသည်။	ă-net-ă-deg-beh-goh-paw-pyah-the,	but'a'na, but'la'na, sum'jha'na	vistari, terivi.
Ex'tract, *s.*	နှုတ်သည်။	hnoht-the,	choom'buk	sañgraham, eḍukkappat̤t̤a-thu.
Eye, *s.*	မျက်စိ။	myet-see	ankh, nyn, chushm	kaṉ, vil̤i, néttiram.
Eye'brow, *s.*	မျက်ခုံးမွေး။	myet-kohn-moo-ay	ub'roo, bhoun	neṟṟippuruvam.
Fáble, *s.*	ဒဏ္ဍာရီ။	dun-da-ree	hik'a'yut, kis'sa, ku'ha'nee	kat̤t̤ukathai, poykkathai.
Face, *s.*	မျက်နှာ။	myet-hnah	moonh, chih'ru, mookh	mukam, *or* mugam, cháyal.
Facil'ity, *s.*	လွယ်ချင်း။	loo-eh-chyin	a'sa'nee, a'san'i'yut	sulabham, tuṇai.
Fact, *s.*	ဟုတ်မှန်ချင်း။	hoht-hmun-chyin	huk'ee'kut	uṇmai, yathárttam.
Fade, *v. n.*	ညှိုးနွမ်းသည်။	nyoh-hno-un-the	jhoor'na, koom'la'na	vathañgu, váḍu, chór.
Fair, *a.*	လှသော။	hlah-thaw	saf, soon'dur	al̤akul̤l̤a, tel̤ivána.
Faith, *s.*	ယုံကြည်ခြင်း၊သဒ္ဓါ။	yohn-chyee-chyin, this-sah	ee'man, tu'wuk'kool	visuvásam, baktti, ñánam.
Fall, *s.*	ကျသည်။	kyah-the	put'kun	vil̤vu, iṟakkam.
False, *a.*	မဟုတ်သော၊မမှန်သော။	m'hoht-thaw, m'hmun-thaw	jhoo'ta, ka'zib	poyyána, abatta.
Fame, *s.*	ကျော်စောကိတ္တိ။	kyaw-saw-kait-tee	jus, shooh'ra, nek'nam'ee	kírtti, pugal̤, pugal̤chchi.
Fam'ily, *s.*	အိမ်သူအိမ်သားအစု။	ayn-thoo, ayn-thah, ă-soo	ghur'bar, ghur'a'na, koo'toom,	samusáram, kuḍumbam.
Fan, *s.*	ယပ်တောင်။	yut-towng	punk'ha,	visiṟi.
Fan'cy, *s.*	စိတ်အထင်။	sayt-ă-tin	khi'yal	eṇṇam, viruppam.
Far, *a.*	ဝေးသော။	way-thaw,	door	dúramána, et̤t̤átha.
Fare, *s.*	ကုတ္တိခ၊စား ဘွယ်သောက် ဘွယ်။	koo-to-kah, sah-bweh-thowk-bweh,	bha'ra, kir'a'ya, uj'oo'ra	naḍaikkúli, kákkúli,
Farewell', *s.*	သွားသောအခါ နှုတ်ဆက်သော စကား။	thwah-thaw-a-kah-hnoht-set-thaw-s'gah	bid'a, wid'a	vanthanam, subhamol̤i.
Fash'ion, *s.*	ပုံလုပ်သည်။	pohn-loht-the	doul, oos'loob	máthiri, vitham.
Fast, *s.*	အစားရှောင်ချင်း။	ă-sah-shyowng-chyin	ro'za, oo'pas	upavásam, nónbu.
Fast, *a.*	လျှင်မြန်စွာ။	hlyin-myun-swah	juld' tez-gam	sikkiramána, turithamána.
Fat, *s.*	ဆူသော၊ဝသော။	soo-thaw, wah-thaw	chur'bee	kol̤uppu, únam.

English.	Burmese.		Hindustani.	Tamil.
Fath'er, *s.* ...	အဘ။ ...	ă-pah ...	bap, ba'ba, wa'lid ...	pithá, appan, tagappan.
Fath'er-in-law, *s.* ...	ယောက္ခမယောကျ်ားသူ။ ...	yowk'mah-yowk-yah-thoo ..	sus'oor, khoo'sur, khoosr ...	peṇkoḍuttamáman.
Fath'om, *s.* ...	အလံ။ ...	ă-lun ...	bam ...	áḻam, bágam.
Fault, *s.* ...	အပြစ်။ ...	ă-pyit ...	khut'a, tuk'seer ...	kuṟṟam piḻai.
Fávour, *s.* ...	ကြည်ညိုသည်။ ...	kyee-nyoh-the ...	mihr'ba'nee, kur'um ...	dayai, aruḷ, príthi. [naḍai.
Fawn, *s.* ...	ဒရယ်သငယ်။ ...	dă-yeh-th'ngeh ...	ghuz'al, ghuz'a'lu, a'hoo-	mánkanṟu, ichchagamána-
Fear, *v. a. & n.* ...	ကြောက်သည်။ ...	khyowk-the ...	dur, [bur'u,...	bhayam, achcham, ékkam.
Feast, *s.* ...	စားပွဲသောက်ပွဲ။ ...	sah-bweh, thowk-bweh ...	je'o'nar, ziy'a'fut ...	virunthu, paṇḍigai.
Feath'er, *s.* ...	ငှက်မွေး။ ...	hnget-moo-ay ...	pur, punkh ...	iṟagu, chiṟagu.
Fel'low, *s.* ...	အပေါင်းအဖော်။ ...	ă-powng-ă-paw ...	hum-chushm, humjo'lce, jot.	iṇai, tólan, kúttáli. [kuriya.
Fémale, *a.* ...	အမ။ ...	ă-mah ...	ma'du, ma'deen, zun'a'nu...	pengaḷukkaḍutta, penbáluk-
Fes'tival, *s.* ...	ပွဲလမ်းသဘင်။ ...	pweh-lun-th'pin ...	purb, pur'ub, eed ...	paṇḍikai, tiruviḻá.
Fetch, *v. a.* ...	သွား၍ယူခဲ့သည်။ ...	thwah-yoo-eh-yoo-geh-the..	la'na, le-a'na ...	koṇḍuvá, eḍuttukkoṇḍuvá.
Féver, *s.* ...	အဖျားအနာ။ ...	a-pyah, a-nah ...	tup, tub ...	juram, káychchal.
Fig, *s.* ...	တည်သီး။ ...	tee-thee ...	unjeer ...	atti, *fruit* attippaḻam.
File, *s.* ...	တံစဉ်းတိုက်သည်။ ...	tă-sin-tuyk-the ...	re'tee, so'han, so'hun ...	aram.
Filth, *s.* ...	အညစ်အကြေး။ ...	ă-nyit-a-chyay ...	myl, [da-k,...	aḻukku, úttai, malam.
Find, *v. a.* ...	တွေ့သည်။ ...	tway-the ...	pana, luh'na, mil'a'na, py'	kaṇḍupiḍi, peṟu, aḍai.
Fin'ger, *s.* ...	လက်ချောင်း။ ...	let-chyowng ...	oong'lee, oon'gul, un'goosht.	kaiviral.
Fin'ish, *s.* ...	ပြီးစေသည်။ ...	pyee-say-the ...	tum'am'ee, sar'na ...	muḍivu, sampúraṇam.
Fire, *s.* ...	မီး။ ...	mee ...	ag, a'tush, ug'ni ...	neruppu, akkini, tí.
Fíre-fly, *s.* ...	ပိုးစုန်းကြူး။ ...	poh-sohn-pyoo ...	joog'noo, bhug-joog'noo ...	minmini, kachchótham.
First, *a.* ...	ပဌမ။ ...	put-tă-mah ...	puh'la, puh'lee ...	muthal, áthiyána, jéshṭa.
Fish, *s.* ...	ငါး။ ...	ngah ...	muchh, muchh'lee, ma'hee..	mín, machcham, pulál.
Fish'ery, *s.* ...	ငါးဖမ်းခြင်းအမှု။ ...	ngah-pun-chyin-a-hmoo ...	ma'hee-shik'ar, ma'hee-gah.	mínpiḍi, mínpiḍituṟai.
Fish'er-man, *s.* ...	တငါ ...	t'ngah ...	jul'i'ya, ma'hee'geer, dhee'	sembhaḍavan.

Flag, *s.* ...	အလံ။ ...	ă-lun ...	jhun'da, nish'an, dhuj'a [wur,	tugiṛkoḍi, viruthu.
Flag'-staff, *s.* ...	အလံတိုင်။ ...	ă-lun-duyng ...	chhur ...	koḍimaram.
Flat, *s.* ...	ပြားသော။ ...	pyah-thaw ...	bur'a'bur, chou'put ...	taṭṭai.
Flea, *s. a small insect*	မွှား။ ...	hmwah ...	kyk, pis'soo, shub'guz ...	teḷḷupúchchi.
Flee, *v. n.* ...	ပြေးသည်။ ...	pyee-the ...	bhag'na, bich'uk'na ...	viraiváyóḍu.
Flesh, *s.* ...	အသား။ ...	a-thah ...	gosht, luhm, mans ...	mámsam, iṛaichchi.
Flock, *s.* ...	သိုးစု။ ...	thoh-soo ...	lend'ha, gul'lu ...	manthai.
Flock, *v. n.* ...	လူအစုံ။ ...	loo-a-sohn ...	jum'a-h ...	kúṭṭam, tiraḷ.
Flow'er, *s.* ...	ပန်း။ပန်းပွင့်။ ...	pun, pun-bwin ...	gool, phool, pooshp ...	pú, pushpam, puḍpam.
Flute, *s.* ...	ပလွေ။ ...	pă-loo-ay ...	ban'see, bun'see ...	pulláṅkuḷal, véyṅkuḷal.
Fly, *s.* & *v. n.* ...	ယင်ကောင်။ ပျံသည်။ ...	yin-gowng, *v. n.* pyun-the...	muk'hee, mug'us, *v.* oor'na...	í, kosugu, *s.* paṛa, páy, óḍu, *v. n*
Food, *s.* ...	အစာ။ ...	a-tsah ...	kha'na ...	bhójanam, ágáram.
Fool, *v. a.* ...	လူရူး။မိုက်။ ...	loo-yoo, muyt ...	be-woo'koof, pa'gul ...	mathikéḍan, múḍan.
Foot, *s.* ...	ခြေးဘဝါး။ ...	chyee-pa-wah ...	pa, pa'on, pyr ...	pátham, aḍi, kál, táḷ.
Forbid', *v. a.* ...	မြစ်တားသည်။ ...	myit-tah-the, see-tah-the...	mun'a-k, rok'na ...	vilakku, taḍu, tavir, maṛi.
For'est, *s.* ...	တော။ ...	taw ...	bun, jun'gul ...	káḍu, vanam, kánagam.
Forget', *v. a.* ...	မေ့လျော့သည်။ မေ့သည်။ ...	may-lyaw-the, may-the ...	bhool'na, bis'ar'na ...	maṛa, ayar.
Forgive', *v. a.* ...	အပြစ်လွှတ်သည်။ ...	a-pyit-pyay-hloot-the ...	moo'af-k, bukhsh'na ...	manni, kuṛṛamporu. [yuḷḷa.
For'mal, *a.* ...	ပြုမြဲထုံးစံရှိသည်အတိုင်း။ ...	pyoo-meh-tohn-zun-she-	tuk'ul'loof-miz'aj ...	vaḷakkamána, puṛakkiriyai-
For'mer, *a.* ...	အရင်။ ...	ah-yin, [the-a-tuyng,...	kud'eem, sabik ...	púrva, munthina, cheṇṛa.
Fort, *s.* ...	မြို့။ရဲတိုက်။ ...	myo-yoh, yeh-tuyk ...	gurh, kil'a ...	kóṭṭai, araṇ.
Fowl, *s.* ...	ငှက်။ကြက်။ ...	hnget, kyet ...	moorgh, moorgh'ee ...	kóḷi, peṭṭai.
Fox, *s.* ...	မြေခွေး။ ...	myay-kway ...	lom'ree, lum'bur, ro'ba ...	kuḷinari, kuḷḷanari.
Fréquent, *a.* ...	ခဏခဏဖြစ်သော။ ...	ka-nah-ka-nah-pyit-thaw,...	uk'sur ...	aḍikkaḍiyána.
Friend, *s.* ...	အဆွေခင်ပွန်း။မိတ်ဆွေ။ ...	ă-tsway-kin-bohn, mait-	dost, mitr, dost-dar ...	snéhan, nésan, uṛavan.
Fright, *s.* ...	ကြောက်လန့်ခြင်း။ ...	kyowk-lun-chyin, [sway,...	hy'but, duh'shut ...	bhayam, thikil, ékkam.
Frog, *s.* ...	ဖား။ ...	pah ...	beng, men'duk, bhek ...	tavaḷai, manḍúgam.
Fruit, *s.* ...	အသီး။ ...	a-thee ...	phul, bur, mewu, sum'ur ...	paḷam, kani, *unripe* káy.

English.	Burmese.		Hindustani.	Tamil.
Fulfil′, v. a.	ဖြည့်စုံစေသည်။	pyee-sohn-say-the	ud′a-k, poo′ra-k	niṛaivéṛṛu, tír, sáthi.
Fúture s.	ဖြစ်လတ္တံ့သော။	pyit-lă-tun-thaw	moos′tuk′bil	ethirkálam, varuṅkálam.
Gag, s.	ပစပ်ကိုဆို့ပိတ်သည်။	pă-sut-go-payt-the	moonh-bund	váyaḍai, váykaṭṭu.
Gain, s.	နှင်ရသည်။	hnuyng-yah-the	fa′i′du, nuf a	átháyam, ilábam.
Gale, s.	လေပြင်း။	lay-pyin	an′dhee, too′fan	kaḍuṅkáṛṛu, puyal.
Gal′lant, a.	ရဲရင့်သော	yeh-yin-thaw	shah′zor	víramuḷḷa.
Gal′lop, s.	ခါးဆုံပြေးသည်။	kah-t′sohn-pyay-the	bug′chhoot, dup′ut	óṭṭam páchchal.
Game, s.	ကစားသည်။	kah-sah-the	khel, bazee, ba′zee′chu	áṭṭam, viḷaiyáṭṭu, kelippu.
Gang, s.	လူစု။	loo-zoo	jut′ha, ghol	kúṭṭam, saṅgam.
Gaol, s.	ထောင်။	towng	kyd-kha′nu, bun′deekha′nu.	kávarkúḍam, chiṛaichálai.
Gape, v. n.	သမ်းသည်။	thun-the	jum′ha′ee-le′na, jum′ha′na...	koṭṭáviviḍu.
Gar′den, s.	ဥယျာဉ်။	oo-yin	bagh, baghchu	tóṭṭam, kollai.
Gar′lic, s.	ကြက်သွန်ဖြူ။	khyet-thohn-byoo	luh′sun, seer	veḷḷaipúṇḍu, uḷḷi.
Gas, s.	ဓါတ်။	dut	nus′um-i-na′foos′oor′dun′ce.	váyu, káṛṛu, ávi.
Gath′er, v. a.	ရုံးသည်။	soo-yohn-the	but′or′na	kúṭṭu, chér.
Gay, a.	ရွှင်လန်းသော။	shwin-lun-thaw	khoosh, mug′un	magiḷchchiyána, kaḷippána.
Gem, s.	ကျောက်မျက်။	kyowk-myek	rut′un, ju′wa′hir	irattinam.
Gen′eral, s. & a.	အချုပ်။ အကြီး။ အများ။	ă-chyoht, ă-gyee, s. a-myah, a	sa′lar, s. oo′moom, um′eem, a.	sénápathi, s. sátháraṇa, a.
Gen′erally, adv.	အများအားဖြင့်။	ă-myah-ah-pyin	oo′moom′un	pothuváy, sátháraṇamáy.
Generátion, s.	အမျိုးအနွယ်။	a-myoh-a-hnweh	py′da′ish, oot′put	talaimuṛai, santhathi, janippippu.
Gen′tle, a.	နူးညံ့သိမ်မွေ့သော။	noo-nyun-thain-mooay-thaw,	dhee′ma, mool′a′im, mun′da.	sáthuvána.
Gen′tleman, s.	သခင်။	th′kin,	bhul′a-ad mee, sa′hib	thurai-magan, ghanaván.
Ger′man, s.	ဇာမနီအမျိုး။	zah-ma-nee-a-myoh	ul′a′man	jermániyá-thésattán.
Get, v. a.	ရသည်။	yah-the	pa′na, ha′sil-k	sambháthi, váṅgu.
Ghost, s.	နံဝိညာဉ်။	nun-wing-ngin	pret, pul′eet, rooh	ávi, áttumá, uyir.
Gift, s.	လက်ဆောင်။	let-sowng	bukh′shish, dan, hib′u	koḍai, ívu, vegumathi.

Gin'ger, *s.* ...	ချင်းစိမ်း။ ...	gyin-sayn ...	a'da, ud'ruk, *dried* sonth ...	iñji, *dried* sukku.
Give, *v. a.* ...	ပေးသည်။ ...	pay-the ...	de'na, bukhsh'na, buksh-d...	koḍu, tá, iḍu, í, aḷi. [yuḻḻa.
Glad, *a.* ...	ဝမ်းသာသော။ ...	woon-thah-thaw ...	koosh, khoosh-hal ...	santhóshamána, magiḻchchi-
Glare, *s.* ...	ထင်ရှားသော။ ...	tin-shah-thaw ...	jhul'uk, jhum'kee ...	kánti, jóthi.
Glass, *s.* ...	ဖန်။မှန်။ ...	pun, hmun ...	shee'shu, bil'lour ...	kaṇṇáḍi.
Globe, *s.* ...	အလုံး။ပထဝီမြေကြီးလုံး။ ...	a-lohn, bud-da-wee, myay-chyee-mohn-the[gyee-lohn.	koo'ru-i-urz, chum'bur ...	púkóḷam, uṇḍai.
Glórify, *v. a.* ...	ချီးမွမ်းသည်။ ...		humd-k ...	kírttanampaṇṇu, váḻttu.
Glóry, *s.* ...	ဘုန်းတံခိုး။ ...	pohn-tă-goh ...	jul'al, pur'um'gut'i, tej ...	mahimai, máṭchimai.
Glue, *s.* ...	ကျွဲကော် ...	kyoo-eh-kaw ...	sur'esh, uh'ar ...	vachchirappasai, pasai.
Gnash, *v. a.* ...	အံသွားခဲကြိတ်သည်။ ...	a-thwah-keh-chayt-the ...	pees'na, kir'kir'a'na ...	pallai-naṛumu; paṛkaṛi.
Go, *v. n.* ...	သွားသည်။ ...	thwah-the ...	ja'na, ja'no, chul'na ...	pó, égu, chellu, naḍa.
Goat, *s.* ...	ဆိတ်။ ...	sayt ...	buk'ra, buk'ree, *f.* ...	veḷḷáḍu.
Gob'let, *s.* ...	ဖလားကြီး။ ...	pa-lah-gyee ...	ab'khoor'u, jam, mee'na ...	kiṇṇi, kiṇṇam.
God, *s.* ...	ဘုရားသခင်။ ...	pa-yah-th-kin ...	khoo'da, ul'lah, rub ...	paráparan, kaḍavuḷ, ḍévan.
God'-child, *s.* ...	ခေါင်းကိုင်ကလေး။ ...	gowng-kuyng-ka-lay ...	dhurm-buch'cha *or* ba'luk...	ñánappiḷḷai.
God'daughter, *s.* ...	ခေါင်းကိုင်သမီး။ ...	gowng-kuyng-tha-mee ...	dhurm-bet'ee ...	ñánamagaḷ.
God'father, *s.* ...	ခေါင်းကိုင်အဘ။ ...	gowng-kuyng-ă-pay ...	dhurm-bap ...	ñánattagappan.
God'head, *s.* ...	ဘုရားသခင်၏ဇာတိအဖြစ်တော်။	pa-yah-th'kin-ee-zah-dee-a-pyit-daw ...	khoo'da'ee ...	parattuvam, deyvattuvam.
God'liness, *s.* } ...	ဘုရားဝတ်၌မွေ့လျော်သော ...	{ pa-yah-woot-hnuyt-	{ khoo'da-pur'ust'ee ...	} bhaktiyuḷḷanaḍai, tiru.
God'ly, *a.* }		moo-ay-lee-aw-thaw.	rub'ba'nee, khoo'da-pur'ust.	} dévabhakti, deyvíga.
God'mother, *s.* ...	ခေါင်းကိုင်အမေ။ ...	gowng-kuyng-a-may ...	dhurm-ma, *or* um'ma ...	ñánattáy.
God'son, *s.* ...	ခေါင်းကိုင်သား။ ...	gowng-kuyng-thah ...	dhurm-be'ta ...	ñánamagan.
Gold, *s.* ...	ရွှေ။ ...	shway ...	so'na, til'a, zur ...	pon, tañgam.
8 Góld-leaf, *s.* ...	ရွှေမျက်ပါး။ ...	shway-myet-pah ...	tab'uk ...	tañgarékku.
Góldsmith, *s.* ...	ပန်းတိမ်သမား။ ...	pă-dayn-thum-mah ...	soon'ar, zur-gur ...	taṭṭán, poṛkollan.
Gone, *p. p. of* Go,...	လွန်ပြီးသော။ ...	loon-byee-thaw ...	gu'ya, ruf'tu ...	póna, póyviṭṭathu.
Good, *s.* ...	ကောင်းသော။ ...	kowng-thaw ...	uch'chha bhul'a'ee ...	nanmai, nal, uttama.

English.	Burmese.		Hindustani.	Tamil.
Good'ness, *s.* ...	ကောင်းခြင်း။ ...	kowng-chyin ...	ne'kee, nik'o'ee, *f.* ...	uttamam, nanmai.
Goods, *s.* ...	ကုန်စည်။ ဥစ္စာပစ္စည်း။ ...	kohn-see, oht-tsah, pyit-see.	mal, us'bab ...	sámán sarakku.
Gos'pel, *s.* ...	ဝမ်းမြောက်စရာသိတင်းတော်...	wun-myowk-să-yah-the-	kit'ab-i-in'jeel ...	suvisésham.
Gov'ern, *v. a.* ...	အုပ်ချုပ်သည်။ ...	oht-chyoht-the [din-daw,...	hoo'koo'mut-k, sa'hib'ee-k...	álu, álukaichey, aḍakku.
Gov'ernment, *s.* ...	အစိုးရ။ ...	a-soh-yah ...	hoo'koo'mut ...	rájarikam, sarkkár.
Gov'ernor, *s.* ...	အုပ်စိုးသောမင်း။ ...	oht-soh-thaw-min ...	a'mil, na'zim, soo'ba ...	arasan, désáthipathi.
Grace, *s.* ...	ကျေးဇူး။ ...	kyay-zoo ...	fuzl ...	kirubai, aruḷ, dayavu.
Grácious, *a.* ...	ကျေးဇူးပြုတတ်သော။ ...	kyay-zoo-pyoo-dut-thaw ...	dy'al, kur'eem ...	káruṇiya, kirubaiyuḷḷa.
Grad'ually, *adv.* ...	တရွေ့ရွေ့ဖြစ်သော။ ...	t-yu-ay-yu-ay-pyit-thaw ...	ruf'tu-ruf'tu ...	varavara, paḍippaḍiyáy.
Grain, *s.* ...	စပါး။ ...	sa-bah ...	da'nu, ghul'lu, naj, un'aj...	tháṇiyam.
Gram'mar, *s.* ...	သဒ္ဒါ။ ...	tha-dah ...	by'a'kur'un, dus'toor-i-zub'	ilakkaṇam, ilakkaṇanúl.
Grammárian, *s.* ...	သဒ္ဒါကိုနားလည်သောသူ။ ...	tha-dah-goh-nah-leh-thaw-	by'a'kur'un'ee, [an,...	ilakkaṇavittuván, ilakkaṇi.
Grand, *a.* ...	ကြီးကျယ်သော။ ...	kyee-kyeh-thaw, [thoo,...	uz'eem, ul'ee, oom'da ...	ménmaiyuḷḷa, mahá, pira-
Grand'child, *s.* ...	မြေး။ ...	myee ...	pis'ur-za'du, sibt ...	pérappiḷḷai. [tháṇa.
Grand'daughter, *s.* ..	မြေးမိန်းမ။ ...	myee-maym-mah ...	na'tin, nut'nee, nuw'a'su ...	pétti, pértti.
Grand'father, *s.* ...	အဘိုး။ ...	ă-poh ...	jud, a'ja, da'da, na'na ...	páṭṭan, mútáthai.
Grand'mother, *s.*...	အဘွား။ ...	ă-pwah ...	da'dee, *maternal* na'nee ...	páṭṭi, mútáy.
Grant, *v. a.* ...	ပေးကမ်းသည်။ ...	pay-cun-the ...	de'na, ut'a-k ...	koḍu, ígai, aruḷ.
Grape, *s.* ...	စပျစ်သီး။ ...	să-byit-thee ...	ung'oor, in'ub, ruz ...	dráḍchappaḻam.
Grass, *s.* ...	မြက်။ မြက်ပင်။ ...	myet, myet-bin ...	gee'ah, ghas, trin ...	pul, kórai.
Grass'hopper, *s.* ...	နှံကောင်။ ...	hnun-gowng ...	phun'ga, *brown* tid'ila ...	veṭṭukkiḷi, kilippúchchi.
Gráteful, *a.* ...	ကျေးဇူးကိုသိသော။ ...	kyay-zoo-go-thee-thaw ...	num'uk-hul-'al, sha'kir ...	nanṛiyaṛivuḷḷa, nanṛiyuḷḷa.
Grátis, *adv. Lat.* ...	အဘိုးမပေးရဘဲ။ ...	a-poh-m'pay-yah-beh ...	mooft, mooft-men ...	ilavasamána.
Grat'itude, *s.* ...	ကျေးဇူးတင်ခြင်း။ ...	kyay-zoo-tin-chyin ...	num'uk-hul'al'ee ...	nanṛi, nanṛiyaṛivu.
Grave, *s.* ...	သင်းချိုင်း။ ...	thin-chuyng, [rit,...	gor, kubr, muz'ar ...	préthakkuḻi, samáthi.
Grav'el, *s.* ...	သေးနုပ်သောကျောက်စရစ်။ ...	thay-noht-thaw-kyowk-sah-	kun'kur'ee, puth'ree ...	kúḻáṅkal, parukkaikkal.

Grávy, *s.* ...	အသားကို ကင်၍ ထွက်သောဆီ [ရည်။ ...	a-thah-goh-kin-yu-eh-twet-[thaw-a-yee...	ab-i-ghost, ab'josh ...	únam, tasainír, niṇam.
Gray, *s.* ...	ဖောင်းဝတ်။	powng-woot,	kub'ra, ush'hub ...	veṇṇiṛamána, naraitta.
Grease, *s.* ...	ဆီဥ။ ...	tsee-oo ...	chur'bee, rou'ghun ...	koḻuppu, neypparru.
Great, *a.* ...	ကြီးသော။ ...	kyee-thaw ...	bur'a, boo'zoorg, ju'leel ...	parumaiyána, mahattána.
Green, *s.* ...	စိမ်းသော။ ...	sayn-thaw ...	subz, hur'a ...	pasumai, pachchai.
Greet, *v. a.* ...	နှုတ်ဆက်သည်။ ...	hnoht-set-the ...	sul'am-k ...	vállttu, ácháramparnu.
Grief, *s.* ...	ဝမ်းနည်းခြင်း။ ...	woon-nee-chyin ...	ghum, dookh ...	tukkam, tuyaram, kavalai.
Grin, *s.* ...	ပြုံးခြင်း။ ...	pyohn-chyin ...	khees, moos'kan ...	iḷippu, nagaippu.
Grind, *v. a.* ...	ကြိတ်သည်။ ...	chyait-the ...	pees'na, dul'na ...	arai, tíṭṭu, cháṇaipiḍi.
Gross, *s.* ...	၁၄၄။ ...	t'yah-lay-zay-lay ...	ek-sou'chou'a'lees ...	núṛṛu-nárpattunálu.
Gross, *a.* ...	ထုပ်ထုပ်ဝဝရှိသော။ ...	toht-toht-wah-wah-she-[thaw,...	mo'ta ...	parumam, mottam.
Ground, *s.* ...	မြေကြီး။ ...	myay-gyee,	zum'een, bhoon ...	nilam, bhúmi, káṇi.
Grow, *v. a.* ...	ပေါက်သည်။ကြီးပွါးသည်။ ...	powk-the, kyee-pwah-the...	oo'ga'na ...	viḷaivi, payirchey.
Grum'ble, *v. n* ...	မြည်တမ်းသည်။ ...	myee-tun-the ...	tur'ra'na ...	uṛumu, muṛugu.
Guan'a, *s.* ...	ဖွတ်။ ...	poht ...	goh, ghor-phor ...	uḍumbhu, malaióṇán.
Guarantee', *s.* ...	အာမခံသည်။ ...	ah-mah-cun-the ...	banh, *f.* za'min ...	uttaravátthi.
Guard, *s.* ...	စောင့်နေသည်။ ...	sowng-nay-the ...	puh'ra, pas'ban, ni'gu'ban...	kával, iraṭchippu.
Guess, *s.* ...	ယမ်းဆသည်။ ...	yun-sah-the ...	ki'yas, ut'kul ...	uddésam, anumánam.
Guilt, *s.* ...	အပြစ်။ ...	ă-pyit ...	goo'na, pap ...	pávam, dósham.
Guilt'less, *a.* ...	အပြစ်ကင်းသော။ ...	a-pyit-kin-thaw ...	be-goo'na ...	kuṛṛamaṛṛa, suddha.
Guil'ty, *a.* ...	အပြစ်ရှိသော။ ...	a-pyit-shee-thaw ...	goo'na'gar, tuk'seer'war ...	kuṛṛamuḷḷa, dóshamuḷḷa.
Gulf, *s.* ...	ပင်လယ်ထောင့်ကွေ့။ ...	pin-leh-downg-gweh ...	khul'eej, buhr, kol ...	kuḍákkaḍal, áḻi.
Gum, *v. a.* ...	သစ်စေး။ ...	thit-see ...	gond, sumgh ...	pisin, *lac* arakku.
Gun, *s.* ...	သေနတ်။ ...	thay-nut ...	bun'dook ...	tuppákki.
Guzzle, *v. a.* ...	ဖွတ်ဖိုသောက်သည်။ ...	soht-soh-thowk-the ...	ghoot'na ...	ávaláy-uṇ.
Ha, ! *int.* ...	ဟာ။ ...	hah, ...	wah ! ...	ágá, óhó.
Hab'erdasher, *s.* ...	ကုန်ထိုစည်စကိုရောင်းသောသူ။	kohn-doh-see-sah-goh-yowng-thaw-thoo, ...	bis'a'tee ...	pattu-paruttinúrpuḍavai-muthaliya-viṛkum-viyápári

English.	Burmese.		Hindustani.	Tamil.
Haft, *s.*	လက်နက်ရိုး။	let-net-yoh	dun'dee, *f.*	piḍi, kaippiḍi.
Hail, *v. s.*	မိုးသီး။	moh-thee	o'la, *small* bin'ou'lee, *f.*	áli, álánkaṭṭi.
Hail, *interj.*	ချမ်းသာပါစေ။	chyun-thah-bah-zay	mur'hub'a, moo'ba'ruk, !	váḻi, váḻga, subhamangala-[moḻi.
Hair, *s.*	အမွေး၊ ဆံခြည်။	a-moo-ay, tsun-gyin	bal, bar, moo, *of the head* kes, *of the animal* pushm.	mayir, urómam, késam.
Half, *s.*	တဝက်။	t'wet	adh, ud, adh'a, neem, nisf.	arai, araivási, onṟupáthi.
Hall, *s.*	ခန်းမ။	cun-mah	da'lan, *of audience* dur'bar	manḍapam, nyáyastalam.
Ham'mer, *s.*	သံတူ။	thun-too	hut'hou'ree, mar'tol	sutti, chammaṭṭi.
Hand, *s.*	လက်။	let	hath, dust, pun'ja	kai, karam.
Hand'kerchief, *s.*	လက်ကိုင်ပဝါ။	let-kuyng-pă-wah	roo'mal	kaikkuṭṭai, lénju.
Hap'py, *a.*	ပျော်မွေ့သော။	pyaw-moo-ay-thaw	khoosh, moo'ba'ruk	santóshamána.
Har'bour, *s.*	သင်္ဘောဆိုက်သောအရပ်။	thing-baw-suyk-thaw-a-yut	bun'dur	tuṟaimukham, kaḍaṟkuḍá.
Hard, *a.*	မာသော။	mah-thaw	sukht	kaḍinamána, keṭṭiyána.
Hare, *s.*	ယုန်။	yohn	khur'gosh, khur'ha, sus'a	muyal, musal.
Har'lot, *s.*	မိမ္မရွှင်။	maym-mah-shwin	kus'bee, ves'ya, chhin'al	vési, pothuppeṇ.
Harm, *s.*	အပြစ်ပြုသည်။	a-pyit-pyoo-the	nook'san, zur'ur	tíngu, tímai, nashṭam.
Harm'less, *a.*	အပြစ်မရှိသော။	a-pyit-m'shee-thaw	bho'la, bho'ra	kuṟṟamillátha, kapaḍillátha.
Har'ness, *s.*	ပွဲကြိုးတန်ဆာစုံ။	pweh-kyoh-ta-sah-sohn	saz, saj	kuthirai-uḍuppu, *or* jíni.
Harp, *s.*	စောင်း။	tsowng	bur'but, chung, ka'noon, ood.	suramanḍalam, víṇai.
Hart, *s.*	သမင်ဒရယ်အဖို။	th'min-da-yeh-a-poh	hur'in, hur'un	kalaimán.
Haste, *s.*	လျှင်မြန်အောင်ကြိုးစားသည်။	hlin-myun-owng-kyoh-sah-[the,	juld-baz'ee, juld'ee	síkkiram, turitham.
Hat, *s.*	အုပ်ထုပ်။	oht-toht,	top, to'pa, to'pee, *f.*	toppi, kullá.
Hate, *s.*	မုန်းသည်။	mohn-the	doosh'mun ee, byr, kee'na	pagai, virótham.
Have, *v. a.*	ရှိသည်။	she-the	dhal'na, rukh'na	vaittiru, aḍainthiru, peṟu.
He, *pron.*	သူ။	thoo	wo, wooh, oos'ne	avan, ivan, uvan.
Head, *s.*	ခေါင်း။	gowng	sir, sur, sees, moond	talai, sirasu.

Head, *a.*	အကြီးအကဲ။	a-kyee-a-keh	sur'dar, mookud'dum	talaimaiyána, prathána.
Head'ache, *s.*	ခေါင်းကိုက်။	gowng-kuyt	durd-sur, sir-ka-durd	talainó, talaivali.
Health, *s.*	ကျန်းမာခြင်း။	chyum-mah-chyin	sih'hut, tus'leem, tun'door'	sugam, sostam, árókkiyam.
Hear, *v. a.*	ကြားသည်။	kyah-the	soon'na, kan-d,[oos-tee, *f.*	kél, chevikoḍu.
Heart, *s.*	နှစ်လုံး။	hnit-lohn	dil, kha'tir, kulb, chit	iruthayam, ithayam.
Heat, *s.*	အပူ။	ă-poo	gur'ma, gur'mee	chúḍu, káṅgai, veppam.
Heav'en, *s.*	မိုဃ်းကောင်းကင်။	moh-kowng-gin	as'man, churkh, mee'na	vánam, viṇ, paramaṇḍalam.
Heav'y, *a.*	လေးသော။	lay-thaw	bha'ree, gur'an	bháramána, ghanamána.
Hedge, *s.*	စည်းစောင့်ရန်။	see-sowng-yun	dhan, tut'ree	véli, aḍaippu, paḍal.
Height, *s.*	အမြင့်။	a-myin	oon'cha'ee	uyaram, uchcham, méḍu.
Hell, *s.*	ငရဲ။	ngă-yeh	do'zukh, nar, nur'uk, suk'ur.	narakam, páthálam.
Help, *s.*	ကူသည်။	koo-the	mud'ud	uthavi, ottásai, tuṇai.
Help'less, *a.*	ကူခြင်းမရှိ။	koo-chyin-m'she	be-char'u, la-char	tuṇaiyaṟṟa, dikkaṟṟa.
Hen, *s.*	ကြက်မ။	khyet-mah	moorgh'ee, mak'i'yan, kook'[ree,	kóḷippéḍu, peḍai.
Her, *pron.*	သူ။	thoo	oos'ka, oos'ko,	avaḷai, avaḷuḍaiya.
Her'ald, *s.*	သံတော်ဆင့်။	thun-daw-zin	moo'na'dee	túthan, kaṭṭiyakkáran.
Herb, *s.*	ဟင်းသီးဟင်းရွက်။	hin-tnee-hin-yu-eh	ou'shudh	púṇḍu, payir, kírai.
Here, *adv.*	သည်မှာ။	thee-hmah, (dee-mah)	ee'dhur, id'hur, is'jug'u	iṅgé, ivviḍam.
Hereaf'ter, *adv.*	နောက်မှ။	nowk-hmah	min-bad, is'ke-bad	ini, inimél, pinné
Héro, *s.*	ရဲရင့်သောသူ။	yeh-yin-thaw-thoo	bu'ha'door, beer	víraván, súran, sauriyaván.
Hey, ! *int.*	ဟေ။	hay !	sha'bash !	á á, óhó !.
Hide, *v. a.*	ပုန်းသည်။	pohn-the	chhip'a'na, chhoo'pa'na	maṛai, oḷi, puthai, ká.
High, *a.*	မြင့်သော။	myin-thaw	oon'cha	uyaramána, unnatha.
Hill, *s.*	ကုန်း။	kohn	pu'har'ee, koh, gi'ri	méḍu, kuṇṛu, malai.
Him, *pron.*	သူကို။	thoo-goh	oos'ko, oo'se, is'ko, i'se	avanai, avaṛai.
Hint, *s.*	အရိပ်ပေးသည်။	a-yait-pay-the	ish'a'ra	kuṛippu, saigai, jáḍai.
Hire, *s.*	ငှါးသည်။	ngah-the	kir'a'yu, bha'ra, uj'oo'ra	kúli, paridánam.
His, *poss. pron.*	သူ၏။	thoo-ee	is'ka, oos'ka	avanuḍaiya, avaruḍaiya.

English.	Burmese.		Hindustani.	Tamil.
His'tory, *s.* ...	ရာဇဝင်။ ...	yah-zah-wing ...	ilm-ool-ta'reekh ...	charitram, varaláṟu.
Hog, *s.* ...	ဝက်။ ...	wet ...	soo'ur, soo'kur, ba'rah ...	panṟi, áṇpanṟi.
Hoist, *v. a.* ...	အထက်သို့ဆွဲယူသည်။ ...	ă-tet-thoh-tsweh-yoo-the ...	oo'tha'na ...	uyarttu, éṟṟu, túkku.
Hole, *s.* ...	အပေါက်။ ...	a-powk ...	bil, bil'a, chhed, gur'ha ...	dwáram, kuḻi, pottal.
Hóly, *a.* ...	သန့်ရှင်းသော။ ...	thun-shin-thaw ...	pak, pak-saf ...	parisuddhamána, tiru, túya.
Hól'iday, *s.* ...	အလုပ်မရှိသောနေ့။ ...	a-loht-m'shee-thaw-nay ...	pur'ub, te'o'har ...	tirunáḷ, viḍumuṟai.
Holy-Ghost, ...	သန့်ရှင်းသောဝိညာဉ်တော်။ ...	thun-shin-thaw-win-ngin-	rooh-ool-koods ...	parisuttávi.
Hom'age, *s.* ...	ဦးညွှတ်ခြင်း။ ...	oo-hnyoht-chyin, [daw,...	tus'leem ...	vaṇakkam, vantanam.
Home, *s.* ...	အိမ်။ ...	ayn ...	ghur, muk'am ...	víḍu, il, illam.
Hon'est, *a.* ...	ရိုးသားသော။ ...	yoh-thah-thaw ...	khur'a, di'ya'nutdar ...	yógyamána, yathárttamána.
Hon'ey, *s.* ...	ပျားရည်။ ...	pyah-yeh ...	shuhd, mud'hoo, mou, us'ul.	tén, mathu, naṟavu.
Hon'ey-comb, *s.* ...	ပျားလပို့။ ...	pyah-la-boh ...	chhut'ta, shan ...	ténkúḍu, ténvathai.
Hon'our, *s.* ...	ဂုဏ်အသရေ။ ...	gohn-ă-thă-ray ...	ab'roo, man, wukr, iz'zut ...	ghanam, mánam, kírtti.
Hon'ourable, *a.* ...	ဂုဏ်အသရေရှိသော။ ...	gohn-ă-thă-ray-she-thaw ...	sha'yus'ta ...	ghanamuḷḷa, saṅgaiyuḷḷa.
Hope, *s.* ...	မျှော်လင့်သည်။ ...	hmyaw-lin-the ...	as, as'a, oom'med, bhur'o'sa.	nambikkai, ásai.
Hópeless, *a.* ...	မျှော်လင့်ခြင်းမရှိ။ ...	hmyaw-lin-chyin-m'she ...	na-oom'med ...	nambikkaiyaṟṟa.
Horn, *s.* ...	ဦးချို။ ...	oo-chyoh ...	seeng, shakh, sring ...	kombu, kóḍu.
Horse, *s.* ...	မြင်း။ ...	myin ...	gho'ra, ghoor, ba'jee, ush'wu.	kuthirai, asuvam, pari.
Hot, *a.* ...	ပူသော။ ...	poo-thaw ...	gurm, [ghur,...	veppamána, káṅgaiyána.
Hotel', *s.* ...	ထမင်းဆိုင်ကြီး။ ...	t'min-suyng-gyee ...	sur'a'e-un'grez'ee, punch-	chattiram, taṅgumaḍam.
House, *s.* ...	အိမ်။ ...	ayn ...	ghur, hu'wel'ee, muk'an ...	víḍu, manai, illiḍam.
How, *adv.* ...	ဘယ်သို့။ ...	beh-thoh ...	kistur'u, ky'sa ...	eppaḍi, evváṟu, evvaṇṇam.
Húman, *a.* ...	လူမျိုးနှင့်ဆိုင်သော။ ...	loo-myoh-hnin-suyng-thaw	in'sa'nee ...	manushatanmaiyána, máni-
Hum'ble, *a.* ...	နှိမ့်ချသော။ ...	hnayn-chyah-thaw ...	ghur'eeb, ud'heen ...	kíḻmaiyána, táḻmaiyuḷḷa. [ḍa
Hun'ger, *s.* ...	ဆာငတ်ခြင်း။ ...	tsah-ngut-chyin ...	bhookh, ish'ti'ha, [ee,...	pasi, paṭṭini.
Hur'ry, *s.* ...	မြန်သော။ ...	myun-thaw ...	juld'ee, juld-baz'ee, hur'bur'	turitham, churuchuruppu.

Hurt, *s.* ...	နာစေသည်။ ...	nah-say-the ...	chot, ee'za, zi'yan ...	tíñgu, úṛu, taḻumbu.
Hyéna, *s.* ...	သားရဲတမျိုး။ ...	thah-yeh-t'myoh ...	gir'ir, kuf'tar, luk'ra ...	kaḻuthaippuli, kaḍuváy.
Hymn, *s.* ...	သီခြင်း။ ...	thee-chyin ...	bhuj'un, us'toot, stoo'ti ...	ñánapáṭṭu, gítham.
Hyp'ocrite, *s.* ...	ရှိုဝှက်သောသူ။ ...	shyoh-wet-thaw-thoo ...	ri'ya'ee, ri'ya'kar ...	véshathári, vañjagan, kabaḍi
I, *pron.* ...	ငါ။ကျွန်ုပ်။ ...	ngah- kyoon-hnoht ...	myn, mun ...	nán, yán.
Ice, *s.* ...	ရေခဲ။ ...	yay-geh ...	burf, too'khar, too'sar, yukh	uṛainír, nírkkaṭṭi, panikaṭṭi.
Ichneu'mon, *s.* ...	မြွေကျောင်းဥကိုဖောက်စားတတ်သောမြွေပါမျိုး။	me-gyowng-oo-goh-powk-sah-tut-thaw-moo-ay-pah-myoh ...		
Idéa, *s.* ...	စိတ်အထင်အမှတ်။ ...	sayt-a-tin-a-hmut ...	bee'jee, moon'goos ...	kírippiḻlai, nagulam.
Iden'tical, *a.* ...	တူသော။ ...	too-thaw ...	khi'yal, wuhm ...	eṇṇam, karuttu, abhiprâyam
Iden'tity, *s.* ...	အတူတူဖြစ်ခြင်း။ ...	a-too-doo-pyit-chyin ...	ek-san, yuk-san ...	suyamána, suya.
Id'iom, *s.* ...	စကားမျိုး။ ...	s'gah-myoh ...	ek-san'ee, yuk-san'ee ...	orétanmai, suyambu.
Id'iot, *s.* ...	အရူး။ ...	a-yoo ...	moo'ha'wir'u, is'til'a ...	páshaippókku, páshainaḍai.
Id'le, *a.* ...	ပျင်းရိသော။ ...	pyin-yee-thaw ...	ga'o'dee, gee'dee, pa'gul ...	múḍan, maṭṭi.
I'dol, *s.* ...	ရုပ်တု။ဆင်းတု။ ...	yoh-too-sin-doo ...	a'ram'ee, a'rus'ee ...	chómbána, víṇáṇa.
Idol'ater, *s.* ...	ရုပ်တု။ဆင်းတုကိုးကွယ်သောသူ။	yoh-too-sin-doo-koh-gweh-[thaw-thoo, ...	boot, moo'rut ...	silai, surúbham, vigraham.
If, *conj.* ...	လျှင်။ ..	hlin, (yin), ...	boot-pur'ust ...	vigrahabaktikkáran.
Igni'te, *v. a.* & *n.* ...	ညှိသည်။ ...	nyoh-the ...	ug'ur, gur, ur, jo ...	il, ál, él, ánál, ákil.
Ignóble, *a.* ...	အမျိုးယုတ်သော။ ...	ă-myoh-yoht-thaw ...	jul'a'na, jul'na ...	koḻuttu, eri, suḍu.
Ignomin'ious, *a.* ...	အသရေပျက်သော။ ...	a-thă-ray-pyet-thaw ...	kum'ee'na, sif'la ...	iḻiváua, kíḻmaiyána, ína.
Ignorámus, *s.* ...	ဝါဝင်သောလူမိုက်။ ...	wah-win-thaw-loo-muyk ...	roos'wa ...	iḻivána, nintaiyána.
Ig'norance, *s.* ...	မိုက်မဲခြင်း။ ...	muyk-meh-chyin ...	moo'rukh ...	múḍan, péthai, aññan.
Ig'norant, *a.* ...	မိုက်မဲသော။ ...	muyk-thaw ...	na'da'nee ...	péthaimai, kallámai.
Ill, *s.* ...	ဆိုးသော။နာသော။ ...	tsoh-thaw, nah-thaw ...	na'dan, un'jan ...	péthaimaiyána, kallátha.
Illégal, *a.* ...	မတရားသော။ ...	mă-tă-yah-thaw, [thaw, ...	bul'a, khur'ab'ee, bee'mar...	ína, keṭṭa, asaukkiya.
Illegit'imate, *a.* ...	မဟုတ်မမှန်အဲဖြစ်သော။ ...	m'hoht-m'hmun-beh-pyit-	hur'am ...	aníthamána, níthikkéḍána.
			hur'am-za'du, chup'et'a ...	vambiléprantha, vésittana-mána.

English.	Burmese.		Hindustani.	Tamil.
Illib'eral, *a.* ...	စေးနှဲသော။ ...	say-neh-thaw ...	be-fyz ...	ulóbamána,kaiyiṛukkamána
Illic'it, *a.* ...	မတရားသော။ ...	m'tă-yah-thaw ...	hur'am ...	oḷuṅgaṛṛa, muṛaipiṛaḷvána.
Illit'erate, *a.* ...	စာမတတ်သော။ ...	sah-m'tut-thaw ...	na-khwan'da ...	kallátha, paḍiyátha.
Ill'ness, *s.* ...	နာခြင်း။ ...	nah-chyin ...	bee'ma'ree, a'zar ...	viyáthi, róham, tímai.
Illuminátion, *s.* ...	လင်းစေသောအရာ။ ...	lin-say-thaw-a-yah ...	rosh'nee ...	oḷi, tulakkam, pirakásam.
Illúsion, *s.* ...	လိမ်လည်ခြင်း။ ...	layn-lee-chyin ...	dhok'ha ...	mayakkam, jálam.
Il'lustrate, *v. a.* ...	ထွန်းလင်းစေသည်။ ...	tohn-lin-say-the ...	but'a'na, but'la'na, sum'jha'	oppanaikáṭṭu.
Illus'trious, *a.* ...	ဂုဏ်အသရေထင်သော။ ...	gohn-a-tha-ray-tin-shah-	jul'eel, [na,...	kírttiyuḷḷa, chiṛappána.
Im'age, *s.* ...	ရုပ်ပုံ။ ...	yoht-pohn, [thaw,...	boot, moo'rut ...	vigraham, piratirúbham.
Imag'inary, *a.* ...	စိတ်ထင်ရုံသာရှိသော။ ...	sayt-tin-yohn-thah-she-	khi'yal'ee ...	víṇtóṛṛamána.
Imaginátion, *s.* ...	စိတ်ကူးခြင်း။ ...	sayt-koo-chyin, [thaw,...	khi'yal ...	pávigam, manakkaṛpanai.
Imag'ine, *v.a.* & *n.*...	ထင်မှတ်သည်။ ...	tin-hmut-the ...	khi'yal-k ...	eṇṇu, pávi, karuthu.
Imbíbe, *v. a.* ...	စုပ်သည်။ ...	soht-the ...	juzb-k ...	kuḍi, uriñju, uṇṇu.
Im'itate, *v. a.* ...	နည်းကိုလိုက်သည်။ ...	nee-go-luyk-the ...	nukl-k ...	pávi, cháyalpiḍi.
Immac'ulate, *a.* ...	အစွန်းအကွက်မရှိသော။ ...	ă-sohn, a-twet-m'shee-thaw	pak ...	másaṛṛa, túya.
Immatúre, *a.* ...	မမှည့်သေးသော။ ...	m'hmeh-thay-thaw ...	kham ...	muthirátha, kaniyátha.
Immédiately, *adv.*...	ရုပ်ခနဲ။ ...	yoht-kă-neh ...	bil'fi'ul, fil'hal, toort ...	uḍané, támathaminṛi.
Immemórial, *a.* ...	ကာလရှည်ကြာ၍မမှတ်နိုင်ဘွယ်ဖြစ်သော။	kah-lah-she-kyah-yoo-eh-m'hmut-hnuyng-bweh-pyit-thaw ...	yad-se-ba'hur ...	ñápagattiṛkeṭṭátha.
Immen'se, *a.* ...	အလွန်ကြီးကျယ်သော။ ...	ă-hloon-kyee-kyeh-thaw ...	kub'eer ...	aḷavaṛṛa, maṭṭillátha.
Immer'se, *a.* ...	နှစ်သည်။ ...	hnit-the ...	doo'bo na, gho'tu-d ...	táḻttu, amiḻttu, puthai.
Immer'sion, *s.* ...	နှစ်ခြင်း။ ...	hnit-chyin ...	doob'kee, gho'tu ...	táḻvu, amiḻchchi. [ta.
Immod'est, *a.* ...	အရှက်မရှိသော။ ...	ă-shet-m'she-thaw ...	be-shurm, nahy'a ...	mariyáthaiyaṛṛa, veṭkaṅket-
Im'molate, *v. a.* ...	ယဇ်ပူဇော်သည်။ ...	yit-poo-zaw-the ...	zubh-k ...	baliyiḍu, balicheluttu. [na.
Immor'al, *a.* ...	ဆိုးယုတ်သော။ ...	tsoh-yoht-thaw ...	bud-kir'dar ...	tunmárkkamuḷḷa, nítitappá-

English	Burmese	Burmese (romanized)	Hindustani	Tamil
Immov'able, *a.*	နေရာမှမရွှေ့နိုင်သော။	nay-yah-hmah-m'yoo-ay-hnuying-thaw	uch'ul, ut'ul	asaivarra, nilaipérána.
Imp, *s.*	နတ်သားသီး။	nut-thah-tha-mee	bhoot'na	kuttichcháttán, kural, péy.
Impart', *v. a.*	ဝေငှပေးကမ်းသည်။	way-hngah-pay-cun-the	de'na, bol'na, by'an-k	kodu, pagu, tá, arivi. [la.
Impar'tial, *a.*	သာနာညီမျှဖြစ်သော။	thah-nah-nyee-hmya-pyit-	be-ghur'uz	párapatchamillátha, nítiyul-
Impas'sable, *a.*	မကူနိုင်သော။	m-koo-hnuyng-thaw [thaw.	ou'bhut, ug'um	chellakkúdátha.
Impátience, *s.*	သည်းမခံတတ်သော။	thee-m'cun-dut-thaw	na-sub'ree, *f.*	porámai, avá.
Imped'iment, *s.*	အဆီးအတားခြင်း။	ă-tsee-ă-tah-chyin	rok, ut'ka'o	tadai, vikkinam, idaru.
Impel', *v. a.*	ရှေ့သို့တွန်းသည်။	shay-thoh-tohn-the	chul'a'na, dou'ra'na	cheluttu, tallu, túndu.
Impen'etrable, *a.*	မဖောက်နိုင်သော။	m'powk-hnuyng-thaw	be-dukhl	utchellakkúdátha.
Impen'itent, *a.*	နောင်တမရသော။	nowng-dah-m'yah-thaw	ghyr-nud'a'mut	visanamarra.
Imper'fect, *a.*	မစုံလင်သော။	m'sohn-lin-thaw	na-tum'am	niraivarra, apúrana.
Impérial, *a.*	အစိုးရခြင်းနှင့်ဆိုင်သော။	a-tsoh-yah-chyin-hnin-tsuyng-thaw	bad-sha'hee	rájariga, rájáṅgattirkuriya.
Imper'tinent, *a.*	မဆိုင်သော။	m'tsuyng-thaw	goos'takh	adátha, ovvátha.
Impetuos'ity, *s.*	အဟုန်ပြင်းသော။	ă-hohn-pyin-thaw	juld'ee, *f.* tez'ee, *f.*	végam, kadumai, ugram.
Impet'uous, *a.*	နှင်သောအား။	nuyng-thaw-ah	juld, tez	ugramána, végamána.
Impíety, *s.*	ဘုရားကိုမရိုသေသော။	păyah'-goh-m'yoh-thay-	be-deen'ee, *f.*	avapatti, dévanintai.
Implóre, *v. a.*	တောင်းပန်သည်။	towng-bun-the, [thaw	doo'a-k, min'nut-k	manrádu, véndu, kenchu.
Import', *v. a.* & *n.*	သွင်းသောကုန်။	thwin-thaw-kohn	am'du'nee, *f.* muk'sud	irakkumathipannu, karuthu.
Impos'sible, *a.*	မဖြစ်နိုင်။	m'pyit-hnuyng	na-moom'kin	kúdátha, élátha, arumaiyána
Im'post, *s.*	အကောက်တော်။	a-kowk-daw	muh'sool	tírvai, vari, paguthi.
Impos'tor, *s.*	လိမ်လည်သောသူ။	layn-lee-thaw-thoo	dugh'a'baz	chúthan, ettan, vanjagan.
Imprecátion, *s.*	ကျိန်သန်။	chyain-thun	bud-doo'a, *f.*	tittu, sápam, sapatham.
9 Impreg'nable, *a.*	တိုက်၍မရနိုင်သော။	tuyk-yoo-eh-m'yah-hnuyng-thaw	kulb, mun'ee'u	vellakkúdátha.
Impress', *v. a.*	ပုံနှိပ်သည်။	pohn-hnayt-the, [tah-the	chhap'na, nukah-k	pathi, aluttu, uruttu.
Impris'on, *v. a.*	ထောင်ထဲမှာလှောင်ထားသည်။	towng-deh-hmah-hlowng-	kyd-k	kávarpannu, kávalilvai.

English.	Burmese.		Hindustani.	Tamil.
Improb'able, *a.* ...	ဖြစ်မည်လက္ခဏာမရှိသော။ ...	pyit-mee-lek-ka-nah-m'shee-thaw ...	khil'af-i-ki'yas ...	samusayamána.
Improp'er, *a.* ...	မတော်မသင့်သော။ ...	m'taw-m'thin-thaw ...	na-moo'na'sib ...	tagátha, nyáyavirótbamána
Improve', *v. a.* ...	တိုးပွါးသည်။ ...	toh-pwah-the, [thaw...	bih'tur-k ...	athikari, uyar, téṛu.
Imprúdence, *s.* ...	သတိနှင့်မဆင်ခြင်သော။ ...	th'dee-hnin-m'tsin-gyin-	be-hosh'yar'ee, *f.* ...	avivékam, árávyinmai.
Impúre, *a.* ...	မစင်ကြယ်သော။ ...	m'tsin-gyeh-thaw ...	pul'eed, na-pak ...	suddhamillátha, asusiyána.
Impúte, *v. a.* ...	အပြစ်တင်သည်။ ...	ă-pyit-tin-the ...	lug'a'na ...	poṛuppi, cháṭṭu, chumattu.
In, *pr.* ...	အတွင်း။ နှိုက်။ ...	a-twin, hnuyt ...	un'dur, *adv.* beech, men ...	il, kaṇ, uḷ, uḷi.
Inabil'ity, *s.* ...	မတတ်နိုင်ခြင်း။ ...	m'tut-hnuyng-chyin ...	na-kab'li'yut, *f.* ...	iyalámai, tiráṇiyinmai.
Inacces'sible, *a.* ...	မရောက်နိုင်အောင် အဆီး အတားရှိသော။ ...	m'yowk-hnuyng-owng-ă-tsee-ă-tah-she-thaw ...	mun'ee'u ...	eṭṭátha, váyátha.
Inac'curacy, *s.* ...	မဖြောင့်မမှန်သော။ ...	m-pyowng-m-hmun-thaw...	bhool, *f.* chook *f.* ...	tavaṛu, piḻai, tappu.
Inac'tive, *a.* ...	မလှုပ်တတ်သော။ ...	m'hloht-dut-thaw ...	soost ...	támathamána, chómbulla.
Inan'imate, *a.* ...	အသက်မရှိသော။ ...	ă-thet-m'she-thaw ...	be-jan ...	uyirillátha, jívanillátha.
Inatten'tion, *s.* ...	မမှတ်ဘဲနေသော။ ...	m'hmut-beh-nay-thaw ...	gha'fil'ee, *f.* ...	kavalaiyinmai, parákku.
Incantátion, *s.* ...	မန္တရား။ ...	mun-ta-yah ...	ja'doo, lut'ka ...	mantram, japam, jepam.
Incápable, *a.* ...	မတတ်နိုင်သော။ ...	m'tut-hnuyng-thaw ...	na-ka'bil ...	kúḍátha, tagátha.
Inch, *s.* ...	တလက်မ။ ...	t'let-mah ...	tus'soo ...	aṅgulam, viralidai.
Incíte, *v. a.* ...	နှိုးဆော်သည်။ ...	hnoh-saw'-the ...	tur'gheeb-d ...	évu, eḻuppu, múṭṭu, túṇḍu.
Inclinátion, *s.* ...	နှစ်သက်ခြင်း။ ...	hnit-thet-chyin ...	ir'a'da, ir'a'dut, *f.* ...	cháyvu, chárbu, sarivu, ásai.
Inclúde, *v. a.* ...	စုသည်။အုံသည်။ ...	sohn-the, oun-the ...	sha'mil-k dakh'il-k ...	aḍakku, utpaḍuttu.
In'come, *s.* ...	ဝင်ငွေ။ ...	win-ngway ...	am'du'nee, *f.* ...	varumánam, péṛu, varavu.
Incom'parable, *a.* ...	အတုမရှိသော။ ...	ă'too'm'shee-thaw ...	ud'eem-ool-mis'al ...	oppillátha, nigaraṛṛa.
Incompléte, *a.* ...	မစုံလင်သော။ ...	m'sohn-lin-thaw ..	na-tum'am ...	kuṛaivána, apúraṇamána.
Incorrect', *a.* ...	မမှန်သော။ ...	m'hmun-thaw ...	ghnl'ut ...	piḻaiyána, tappána.
In'crease, *s.* ...	တိုးပွါးသည်။ ...	toh-pwah-the ...	bur'ha'o, burh'ta, burh'tee...	vaḷarchchi, virtti, perukkam

Incred'ible, *a.* ...	မယုံဖွယ်ဖြစ်သော။ ...	m'yohn-bweh-pyit-thaw ...	be-it'i bar ...	nambappadakkúdátha.
Indécency, *s.* ...	မလျောက်ပတ်ခြင်း။ ...	m'lyouk-put-chyin ...	na-sha'yis'tu'gee, *f.* ...	chéshtai, avamariyáthai.
Indeed', *adv.* ...	အကယ်စင်စစ်။ ...	ă-keh-sin-sit ...	fil'wa'ki, such, nl'but'tu ...	meyyága, unmaiyága.
Indem'nity, *s.* ...	ရှုံးပါးသည်အတွက်ပြန်ပေးခြင်း။	yohn-pah-thee-ă-twet-pyun-pay-chyin ...	buch'a'o ...	uttaraváthampannugai, ídu.
Indent', *v. a.* ...	ခွေးသွားစိတ်စိတ်။ ...	kway-thwah-sayt-sayt ...	chup'ka'na, *dukh.* ...	oppanthamurikodu,pathivu.
Indepen'dent, *s.* ...	မှီခိုခြင်းမရှိသော။ ...	hmee-koh-gyin-m'shee-thaw	mookh'tar ...	tannishtamána, suyambána,
In'dex, *s.* ...	ပြညွှန်သောအရာ။ ...	pyah-hnyoon-thaw-a-yah...	fih'rist, *f.* ...	kuri, attavanai.
In'dicate, *v. a.* ...	ပြညွှန်သည်။ ...	pyah-hnyoon-the ...	but'a'na, dul'a'lut-k ...	káttu, velippaduttu.
Indif'ferent, *a.* ...	လျစ်လျူသော။ ...	lyit-lyoo-thaw ...	be-pur'wa ...	samanilaiyána, ubétchai-
Indiges'tion, *s.* ...	မကြေနိုင်သော။ ...	m'khyay-hnuyng-thaw ...	bud-huz'mee, *f.* sikl ...	mantham, ajíranam. [yána.
Individ'ual, *s.* ...	တဦးတည်း။ ...	t'oo-dee ...	ad'mee, *m. f.* shukhs, moof'	ál, oruvan, orutti, onru.
In'dolence, *s.* ...	ပျင်းရိခြင်း။ ...	pyin-yee-chyin ...	soos'tee, *f.* [rud, *a.*...	achattai, chómbhu,
Indus'trious, *a.* ...	လုံ့လပြုသော။ ...	lohn-lah-pyoo-thaw ...	mih'nut'ee ...	churuchruppulla.
In'fant, *s.* ...	ငယ်ရွယ်သောသူ။ ...	ngeh-yoo-eh-thaw-thoo ...	buch'cha ...	kulanthai, kulavi, pálan.
Inform', *v. a.* ...	ကြားပြောသည်။ ...	kyah-pyaw-the ...	khub'ur-d, jut'a'na ...	arivi, terivi.
Inhab'itant, *s.* ...	နေမြဲနေသောသူ။ ...	nay-myeh-nay-thaw-thoo..	ba'see, ruh'newa'la, sa'kin...	kudiyánavan, kudi, prajai.
In'jury, *s.* ...	နာစေသည်။ ...	nah-say-the ...	nook'san, khul'ul ...	úrupádu, paluthu, kurram.
Ink, *s.* ...	မှင်။ ...	hmin ...	roush'na'ee,mus'ee,*f.*si'a'hee.	mai, masi.
In'nocence, *s.* ...	အပြစ်မပြုတတ်သော။ ...	a-pyit-m'pyoo-tut-thaw ...	ma'soom'i'yut, *f.* ...	kurraminmai, suddham.
Inquest, *s.* ...	စစ်ဆေးခြင်း။ ...	tsit-say-chyin ...	punch'a'yut, *f.* ...	vilakkam, maranavichárana
Inscribe, *v. a.* ...	အက္ခရာတင်သည်။ ...	ek-ka-yah-tin-the ...	subt-k ...	eluthu, mélvilásampódu.
In'sect, *s.* ...	ပိုးကောင်။ ...	poh-gowng ...	kee'ra, keet ...	púchchi, pulu, vandu.
Insert', *v. a.* ...	သွင်းသည်။ ...	thwin-the ...	dakh'il-k ...	ullépáychohu, idaiyirohér.
Inside, *s.* ...	အထဲ။အတွင်း။ ...	ă-teh, a-twin ...	bat'in ...	utpuram, ul, agam.
Insol'vent, *s. or a.*...	အကြွေးမပေးနိုင်သောသူ။ ...	a-kyoo-ay-m'pay-hnuyng-thaw-thoo ...	dee'wa'li'ya, na'dar ...	kadanirukkach-chaktiyarra.
Inspect', *v. a.* ...	ကြည့်ရှုသည်။ ...	kyee-shoo-the ...	dekh'na, pur'ukh'na ...	vichári, áráy, sóthi.

English.	Burmese.		Hindustani.	Tamil.
Instal'ment, *s.* ...	ချိန်းချက်သော အချိန်ရောက်မှ ပေးသောငွေ	chyain-chyet-thaw-a-chyain-yowk-hmah-pay-thaw-	kist, *f. parts.* uk'sat ...	paṭṭábishégam, kantháyam.
In'stance, *s.* ...	ပုံသက်သေ ...	pohn-thet-thay, [ngway,...	muz'eer, *m.* ...	tirshtántham, nitarisanam.
In'stant, *s.* ...	အခြားမဲ့ဖြစ်သော ...	a-chyah-meh-pyit-thaw ...	til, chhin, bi'pul, kas'ta ...	taruváy,samayam,tarcham-
Instruc'tion, *s.* ...	သွန်သင်ခြင်း ...	thohn-thin-chyin ...	oos'ta'dee, sikha'ee,ta'leem,*f.*	paḍippu,kalvi,arivu.[ayam.
In'strument, *s.* ...	တန်ဆာ ...	tun-sah ...	a'lut, *f.* ud'at, juntr ...	karuvi, taḷapáḍam, áyutham
Inten'tion, *s.* ...	အကြံအစည် ...	a-kyun-a-see ...	ir'a'da, ir'a'dut, *f.* kusd ...	karuttu, chintai, yósanai.
Inter', *v. a.* ...	သင်းဂြိုဟ်သည် ...	thin-gyoh-the ...	dufn-k. gar'na ...	aḍakkampaṇṇu.
In'terest, *s.* ...	အတိုး ...	a-htoh ...	sood,mu'ha'jun'ee,*f.*nuf'a ...	vaṭṭi, nayam, paṭcham.
Interjec'tion, *s.* ...	ကျူးရေကြော်သောစကား ...	kyoo-ay, kyaw-thaw-s'gah.	hurf-i-nid'a, sout, *f.* ...	taniyidaichchol.
Inter'pret, *v. a.* ...	စကားပြန်သည် ...	s'gah-pyun-the ...	tur'jum'a-k ...	viyákkiyánañchey.
In'to, *pr.* ...	အတွင်းသို့ ...	a-twin-thoh ...	dur, fee, ni ...	il, uḷ, ága, ku, taram.
Invade, *v. a.* ...	ပြည်နယ်ကိုဝင်၍တိုက်သည် ...	pyee-neh-go-win-yoo-eh-tuyk-the ...	takht-k, yoo'rish-k ...	mélvilu, saruvu.
Invariable, *a.* ...	ပြောင်းလဲခြင်းမရှိသော ...	pyowng-leh-chyin-m'she-thaw ...	nit ...	márátha, márṛakkúḍátha.
Inves'tigate, *v. a.* ...	စစ်ဆေးမေးမြန်းသည် ...	tsit-say-may-myun-the ...	tuj'weez-k ...	áráy,vichárаṇaichey,vichári
Invis'ible, *a.* ...	မထင်ရှားသော ...	m'tin-shah-thaw ...	gha'ib, gha'ib'ee ...	tóṛṛátha, adarisanamána.
Invitation, *s.* ...	ဖိတ်သောစာ ...	payt-thaw-tsah ...	da'wut,*f.* ne'o'ta ...	aḻaippu.
Invite, *v. a.* ...	ဖိတ်သည် ...	payt-the ...	da'wut-k, ne'o'ta'na ...	aḻai, varavaḻai, kúppiḍu.
Invocation, *s.* ...	ဆုတောင်းခြင်း ...	soo-towng-chyin ...	doo'a, *f.* doo'a'i'yu ...	véṇḍugai, kaḍavuḷváḻttu.
In'voice, *s.* ...	ဥစ္စာပစ္စည်းကို မှတ်သားသော စရင်း	oht-sah-pyit-see-hmut-thaw-sah-yin ...	bee'juk ...	várnámá, iṭáppu, kaichchá-
In'ward, *a.* ...	အတွင်းနှိုက်ရှိသော ...	a-twin-hnuyt-she-thaw ...	bhee'tur, bheet'ree ...	uḷḷána, uṭpuṛamána. [ttu.
I'ron, *s.* ...	သံ ...	thun, [m'nyee-thaw,...	lo'ha, a'hun, hud'eed ...	irumbu, karumpon.
Irreg'ular, *a.* ...	နည်းဥပဒေနှင့်မညီသော ...	nee-oo-pă-day-hnin-	na-hum'war ...	oḻungaṛṛa, muṛaikéḍána.

Ir'rigate, *v. a.*	ရေနှင့်ရိုစွတ်အောင်ပြုသည်။	yay-hnin-soh-swot-owng-pyoo-the	seench'na, put'a'na, pat'na...	nírpáchchu, taṇṇíriṛai.
Is, *v.*	ရှိသည်။ဖြစ်သည်။	shee-the, pyit-the	hy'ga	irukkiṛathu.
I'sland, Isle, *s.*	ကျွန်း။	kyoon	juz'ee'ru, ta'poo	tívu, tiṭṭu.
Is'sue, *s.*	ထွက်သည်။	twet-the	nut'ee'ju	kaḷivu, muḍivu, chelavu.
It, *pr.*	ထိုဟာ။ထိုအရာ။	toh-hah, toh-a-yah	wo, wooh, wuh	athu, ithu, athai, ithai, tán.
Itch, *s.*	ယားသည်။	yah-the	khooj'lee, khaj, khar'ish, *f.*	chirangu, tinavu, choṛi.
I'tem, *s.* & *adv.*	အချက်။	a-chyet	ba'but, *f. adv.* uy'zun	káriyam, vishayam, togai.
Itself', *pr.*	ထိုအရာပင်။	toh-a-yah-bin	yi'hee, yu'hee	athuvé, athaiyé, táné, tan-yánaikombu, tantham[naiyé
I'vory, *s.*	ဆင်စွယ်။	tsin-zweh	hat'hee-dant, feel-dun'dan.	
I'vy *s.*	နွယ်ပင်တမျိုး။	noo-eh-bin-t'myoh	ba'boo'nu	órpaḍarkoḍi.
Jack'al, *s.*	ခွေးအ။	kway-ah	gee'dur, si'yal, jum'boo	nari, óri, *m.* sambhugam.
Jack'et, *s.*	အင်္ကျီခါးတို။	ing-gyee-ga-toh	kub'a, mir'za'ee, kun-choo...	chaṭṭai, márchchaṭṭai.
Jack'fruit, *s.*	ပိန္နဲသီး။	payn-neh-thee	ko'ee, *f.*	paláppaḷam.
Jail, *s.*	ထောင်။	towng	kyd-kha'nu, zin'dan	kávaṛkúḍam, chiṛaichchálai
Jam, *s.*	ယို။	yoh	moo'rub'ba	inippukkuḷambhu.
Jar, *s.*	စဉ့်အိုး။	sin-oh	ja'la, gol, sub'oo	jáḍi, sál, tarkkam, ovvámai.
Jas'min, *s.*	စပယ်ပင်။	să-beh-bin	yas'min, *m. f.* yas'meen *m. f.*	malligai, málathi.
Jas'per, *s.*	ကျောက်စိမ်း။	khyowk-sayn	zub'ur'jud	ravákkal, súriyakántham.
Jaw, *s.*	ပါးရိုး။	pah-yoh	jub'ha, jubh'ra, thop'ra,	alagu, táḍai, kanu.
Jeal'ous, *s.*	မနာလိုသော။	m'-nah-loh-thaw	rushk-khor, ghy'rut-mund.	erichchaluḷḷa, poṛámaiyuḷḷa.
Jeer, *s.*	သရော်သည်။	th'yaw-the	pu'ri'has, kin'a'yu	kuṛaḷai, kéli, sarasam.
Jel'ly, *s.*	ကြိုချက်သောအစာ။	chyo-chyet-thaw-a-tsah	roob	kuḷambhu, kaḷi, páṇi.
Jeop'ardy, *s.*	ဘေး။	bay	khut'ur	mósam, apáyam, mósanilai.
Jerk, *s.*	တုပ်သည်။	toht-the	jhut'uk, *f.*	tákku, chunḍugai, teṛippu.
Jest, *s.*	ပျက်ရယ်ပြုသည်။	pyeh-yeh-pyoo-the	thut'tha, khil'lee *f.*	sarasam, kéli, parihásam.
Jes'ter, *s.*	လူပျက်။	loo-byet	thut'hol, thut'eh-baz	sarasakkáran, kélikkáran.
Jesus,	သခင်ယေရှု။	th'kin-y-ay-shoo	ee'sa	ésu, kaḍavuḷ, yehóvá.

ENGLISH.	BURMESE.		HINDUSTANI.	TAMIL.
Jew, *s.*	ယုဒလူ။	yoo-dah-loo	yu'hoo'dee	yúthan.
Jew'el, *s.*	ကျောက်မျက်။	khyowk-myet	jou'hir *m. f.* rutun	nagai, bhúshaṇam uḍamai.
Job'work, *s.*	ပုတ်ပုတ်လုပ်ရသည်။	poht-poht-loht-yah-the	tu'hul, *f.* t-tuk'or, *f.*	vélai, kuttagaivélai.
Joc'key, *s.*	မြင်းပြိုင်ရာစီးသောသူ။	myin-pyuyng-yah-see-say-sut-the, [thaw-thoo,	cha'buk-su'war, su'war-kar	kuthiraiviyápári.
Join, *v. a.* & *n.*	ဆေ့စပ်သည်။		jor'na, mil'a'na	isai, kúṭṭu, iṇai, piṇai, aṇai.
Joist, *s.*	ဆင့်။	tsin	ja iz	kuṛukkuviṭṭam.
Joke, *s.*	ပျက်ရယ်ပြုသည်။	pyeh-yeh-pyoo-the	thut'tha, khil'lee, *f.*	kéli, sarasam, naḷinam.
Jol'lity, *s.*	ပျော်ရွှင်သော။	pyaw-shwin-thaw	choo'hul, *f.* chu'hulpu'hul *f.*	koṇḍáṭṭam, líai, viḷaiyáṭṭu.
Jol'ly, *a.*	ဝသော။	wah-thaw	bho'gee, hunsmookh	kaḷippána, kaḷiyáṭṭuḷḷa.
Jolt, *s.*	ဆောင့်သည်။	sowng-the	huch'ka, dhuk'ka	kulukku, kuluṅgu.
Jot, *s.*	အိတ်စိကလေး။	tsait-see-ga-lay, [oht	zur'ru	puḷḷi, kuṛṛu, aṇu. [nam
Jour'nal, *s.*	နေ့စည်မှတ်သောစာအုပ်။	nay-seen-hmut-thaw-sah-	roz-na'mu, roz-nam'chu	náḷágamam, dinavarttamá-
Jour'ney, *s.*	ခရီးသွားသည်။	ka-yee-thwah-the	suf'ur, moo'sa'fur'ut *f.*	yáttirai, payaṇam.
Jour'neyman, *s.*	အခစားသောသူ။	a-kah-tsah-thaw-thoo	kum'er'a, ro'zee'nu-dar	kúlikkuttoḻilcheyvón.
Jóvial, *a.*	ပျော်ရွှင်သော။	pyaw-shwin-thaw	bho'gee, hunsmookh	kaḷippána, magiḻchchiyána.
Joy, *s.*	ဝမ်းမြောက်ခြင်း။	woon-myowk-chyin	khoosh'ee, *f.* sha'dee *f.*	santhósham, magiḻchchi.
Joy'ful, *a.*	ရွှင်လန်းသည်။	shwin-lun-the	khoosh	santhóshamuḷḷa. [vam.
Júbilee, *s.*	ယုဘိလပွဲ။	yoo-bee-lah-pooey	oot'sou.—*v. Festival.*	aimbathám-varushórcha-
Judge, *s.*	တရားမသူကြီး။	ta-rah-ma-thoo-gyee	ka'zee, moon'sif, mou'la	níthipathi, nyáyáthipathi.
Judg'ment, *s.*	တရားစီရင်ဆုံးဖြတ်ချက်။	ta-yah-tsee-yin, tsohn-pyut-chyet	bich'ar, tuj'weez, kuz'a, in'saf.	naḍuttírvai, nyáyatírppu.
Judic'ious, *a.*	သတိပညာရှိသော။	th-dee-pin-yah-she-thaw	ba-tum'eez	vivékamuḷḷa, buddhiyána.
Jug, *s.*	အိုးဝကျဉ်း။	oh-wah-khyin	koom-koom'a, ab'tab'u	kaḻuttoḍu ghiyapáttiram.
Jug'gle, *v. n.*	မျက်လှည့်ပြသည်။	myeh-hlee-pyah-the	kul'a-baz'ee-k	éyppu, kárúḍa (*or*) jála-vittai.
Juice, *s.*	အစေး။အရည်။အဆီ။	a-say, a-yee, a-see	rus, roob, ma, shee'ru	sáru, sáram, pál, ún.
Jum'ble, *s.*	ရောနှောသည်။	yaw-hnaw-the	dur'hum'ee, *f.*	kuḷappu, kalakku, mayakku

Jump, *s.* ...	ခုန်သည်။ ...	kohn-the ...	kood, *f. v. n.* kood'na ...	kuthi, páychchal, tuḷḷu.
Júnior, *s. Lat.* ...	အသက်ငယ်သော။ ...	a-thet-ngeh-thaw ...	looh'ra, *a.* chho'ta ...	iḷaiyavan, iḷaiñan.
Jurisdic'tion, *s.* ...	စီရင်စု။ ...	tsee-yin-soo ...	kuz'a, *f.* ...	duraittanam,nyáyáthikkam
Jurisprúdence, *s* ...	ဓမ္မသတ်နှင့် ဆိုင်သောအတတ် ပညာ။	dum-mah-thut-hnin-tsuyng thaw-a-tut-pin-yah ...	fikh, *f.* ...	rájaníti, rájadharumam.
Júry, *s.* ...	တရားသူကြီးနှင့် ထိုင်ပင်သော လူကြီးတကျိပ်နှစ်ယောက်	t-yah-thoo-gyee-hnin-tuyng-bin-thaw-loo-gyee-t'chayt-hnit-yowk ...	punch'a'yut, *f.* ...	pañjáyat,mattiyastarsabhai.
Just, *a.* ...	ဖြောင့်မတ်သော။ ...	pyowng-mut-thaw ...	huk, rast, ud'eel, su'heeh ...	níthiyuḷḷa, nyáyamána.
Just, *adv.* ...	ကာမျှ။ ...	kah-hmyah ...	theek'um-theek ...	uḍané, sarru, yathárttamáy.
Just'ly, *adv.* ...	မှန်ကြောင်းကိုပြသည်။ ...	hmun-kyowng-go-pyah-the	theek'um-theek ...	nyáyappaḍi, nítiyáy.
Júvenile, *a.* ...	ငယ်ရွယ်သောသူနှင့်ဆိုင်သော။..	ngeh-yoo-eh-thaw-thoo-hnin-suyng-thaw ...	joo'ba, ju'wan ...	iḷaiya,báliya,yauvanamána.
Keel, *s.* ...	ဧရာ။ ...	ay-yah ...	e'rab, e'raf ...	óḍakkaṭṭai, érákkaṭṭai.
Keen, *a.* ...	ထက်မြက်သော။ ...	tet-myet-thaw ...	tez ...	kúrmaiyána.
Keep, *s.* ...	ထိမ်းသည်။ ...	tain-the ...	rukh'na ...	ká, vaittiru, ásari.
Ker'nel, *s.* ...	အဆန်။ ...	a-sun ...	goo'da, mughz ...	koṭṭai, paruppu, arisi, vittu.
Ket'tle, *s.* ...	ရေနွေးအိုး။ ...	yay-nway-oh ...	tut' uh'ra, ket'lee ...	kopparai, kaḍáram.
Key, *s.* ...	သော့။ ...	thaw ...	cha'bee, *f.* ta'lee, *f.* koon'jee, *f.*	tiṛappu, tiṛavukól.
Kick, *s.* ...	ကန်သည်။ ...	kun-the ...	lat, luk'ud, doo'lut'tee *f.* ...	uthai, káleṛi, káluthai.
Kid, *s.* ...	ဆိတ်ကလေး။ ...	sayt-gă-lay ...	hul'wan, pant'ha, mem na...	veḷḷáṭṭukkuṭṭi.
Kid'ney, *s.* ...	ကျောက်ကပ်။ ...	khyowk-cut ...	goor'du ...	pirukkam, kiḍṇi.
Kill, *v. a.* ...	သတ်သည်။ ...	thut-the ...	mar-dal'na, kutl-k ...	kollu, kolaichey, vathai, aḍi.
Kiln, *s.* ...	မီးဖို။ ...	mee-boh ...	bhak'see, *f* bhut *f.* bhut'tha	chúḷai, káḷaváy.
Kin, *s.* ...	အဆွေအမျိုး။ ...	a-tsway-a-myo ...	na'ta, rish'tu ...	urrár, uṛavu, irattakkalappu
Kind, *s.* ...	အမျိုး။ ...	a-myoh ...	jins, kism, *f.* ruk'um ...	vitham, inam, taram, játhi.
Kind, *a.* ...	ကျေးဇူးပြုခြင်သော။ ...	kyay-zoo-pyoo-chyin-thaw.	mihr'ban, moosh'fik ...	dayaiyuḷḷa, paṭchamuḷḷa.
King, *s.* ...	ရှင်ဘုရင်။ ...	shin-boo-yin ...	bad-shah, pad-shah, shah...	rájá, arasan, vénthan.

ENGLISH.	BURMESE.		HINDUSTANI.	TAMIL.
King'dom, *s.* ...	နိုင်ငံ။ ...	nuyng-ngun ...	pad'sha'hut ...	rájyam, arasu.
King'fisher, *s.* ...	ပိန်ညင်း။ ...	payn-nyin ...	much'rung'a ...	mínkoṭṭippuḷ, siral.
Kiss, *s.* ...	နမ်းသည်။ပါးစုတ်သည်။ ...	nun-the ...	bo'suh, choo'ma ...	muttam, mutti.
Kitch'en, *s.* ...	ချက်ပြုတ်သောအခန်း။ ...	chyet-pyoht-thaw-a-cun ...	ba'wur'chee-kha'nu ...	samaiyalvíḍu, pákasálai.
Kite, *s.* ...	စွန်။ ...	sohn ...	put'ung, good'dee, *f.* ...	kárráḍi, paṭṭam.
Kit'ten, *s.* ...	ကြောင်ကလေး။ ...	kyowng-ga-lay ...	bil'leeka-buch'a ...	púnaikkuṭṭi, púnaipparaḷ.
Knap'sack, *s.* ...	စစ်သည် အဝတ်တန်ဆာထည့်သောအိတ်။	tsit-they-a-woot-ta-zah-tee-thaw-ait ...	jho'la jhool, *f.* ...	aḍaippam, pórchchévagan-pothi.
Knave, *s.* ...	ဆိုးညစ်ယိန်လည်သောသူ။ ...	tso-nyit-layn-lee-thaw-thoo.	dugh'a-baz ...	vañjagan, kaḷḷan, chuḷiyan.
Knee, *s.* ...	ဒူး။ဒူးဆစ်။ ...	doo, doo-sit ...	ghoot'na, the'o'na ...	mulaṅkál, mulanthál.
Kneel, *v. n.* ...	ဒူးထောက်သည်။ ...	doo-towk-the ...	do-za'noo-byth'na ...	mulanthátpaḍiyiḍu.
Knife, *s.* ...	ဓား။ ...	dah ...	chhoor'a, chhoor'ee,*f.* ...	katti, karttani.
Knight, *s.* ...	မှူးမတ်။ ...	moo-hmut ...	bu'ha'door ...	orupaṭṭappeyar.
Knock, *s.* ...	ခေါက်သည်။ ...	kowk-the ...	tho'kur, *f.* thes *f,* ...	arai, taṭṭu, aḍi.
Knot, *s.* ...	အထုံး။အမြက်။ ...	a-tohn, a-myet ...	ganth, gir'ih, *f.* ...	muḍichchu, kaṇu.
Know, *v. a.* & *n.* ...	နားလည်သည်။သိသည်။ ...	nah-lee-the, thee-the ...	jan'na,jan'noun, sum'ujh'na.	ari, uṇar, tér, teri.
Knowl'edge, *s.* ...	အတတ်။ ...	a-tut ...	da'nish, *f.* ilm ...	arivu, uṇarvu, buddhi.
Knuc'kle, *s.* ...	လက်ခေါက်။ ...	let-kowk ...	bund, *m.f.* gir'ih, *f.* ...	viralmuḷi, virarkaṇu.
Kóran, *s.* ...	ပသီကျမ်း။ ...	bă-thee-kyun ...	koo'ran ...	kuránvétham.
La'bel, *s.* ...	လိပ်စာ။ ...	layt-sah ...	put'a ...	námavilásam.
Lábour, *s.* ...	အလုပ်။ ...	a-loht ...	mih'nut, muz'doo'ree, *f.* ...	vélai, aluval, prayásam.
Lábourer, *s.* ...	အလုပ်လုပ်သောသူ။ ...	a-loht-loht-thaw-thoo ...	koo'lee, muz'door ...	vélaikkáran, paṇṇaiyáḷ.
Lac, *s.* ...	တသိမ်။ ...	t'thain ...	lakh, *or* luk ...	núṛáyiram, laṭcham.
Lace, *s.* ...	ပေါက်ကြိုး။ဇာ။ ...	powk-kyoh, zah ...	kin'a'ree, bun'ut, *f.* ...	sarigai, keṇḍai, pinnal.
Lad, *s.* ...	လူကလေး။ ...	loo-ga-lay ...	chhok'ra, lur'ka ...	válipan, chiṛuvan, iḷaiñan.
Lad'der, *s.* ...	လှေကား။ ...	hlay-gah ...	seer'hee, *f.* mir'aj, pa'yul ...	éṇi.

Lády, *s.*	ကတော်။သခင်မ။	kă-daw, th'kin-mah	bee'bee, be'gum	duraimagaḷ, perumáṭṭi.
Lake, *s.*	အင်းအိုင်။	ing, uyng	jheel, *f.* jula	éri, vávi, junai.
Lamb, *s.*	သိုးကလေး။	ṭhoh-ga-lay	bur'uh, hul'wan, lel'a	chemmariyáṭṭukkuṭṭi.
Lame, *a.*	ခြေမစွမ်းသော။	chyay-m'swan-thaw	lung'ra	muḍamána, nonḍiyána.
Lament', *s.*	မြည်တမ်းသည်။	myee-tun-the	uf'sos	pulambu, tukki, pralábi.
Lamp, *s.*	မီးခွက်။	me-kwet	chir'agh, *f.* di'ya, sir'aj	viḷakku, dípam.
Land, *s.*	ကုန်း။မြေ။	kohn, myay	zum'een, urz, *f.*	nilam, tarai, bhúmi, désam.
Land'tax, *s.*	မြေသီး။မြေခွန်။	myay-thee, myay-kohn	zum'een-khir'aj	nilavari.
Lane, *s.*	လမ်းကြား။	lun-chyah	gu'lee, *f.* koo'cha	teru, santhu, víthi.
Lang'uage, *s.*	ဘာသာစကား။	bah-thah-s'gah	zub'an, bo'lee, ban'ee, *f.*	páshai, péchchu, moḻi.
Lan'tern, *s.*	မီးအိမ်။	mee-ayn	fa'noos, pha'noos, *f.*	dípakkúḍu, lánthar.
Large, *a.*	ကြီးသော။	kyee-thaw	bur'a, wus'ee, kul'an	parumaiyuḷḷa, parutta.
Lark, *s.*	ငှက်တမျိုး။	hnget-t'myo	bhud'ra, chuk'a'wuk, ug'in...	vánampáḍi, méghappuḷ.
Lascar', *s.*	ခလာသီ။	klah-sea	lush'kur'ee	kalásukkáran.
Lass, *s.*	အပျို။	a-pyo	chhok'ree, lur'kee	kanni, kumari, iḷampiḍi.
Las'situde, *s.*	ပင်ပန်းခြင်း။	pin-pun-chyin	man'du'gee, *f.*	áyásam, melivu, chómbu.
Last, *a.*	နောက်ဆုံး။	nowk-tsohn	ukh'eer, a'khir, peech'he ...	kaḍaisiyána, íṛána, chenṛa.
Latch, *s.*	မောင်းတံခါးကျင်။	mowng-t'gah-khyin	phir'kee, *f.*	tál, tálppál, koḷuvi. [ra.
Late, *a.*	နောက်ကျသော။	nowk-khyah-thaw	pichh'la, der	chenṛa, pinthina, kálañchen-
Lat'itude, *s.*	အကျယ်အဝန်း။	a-kyeh-a-woon	urz, urz-i-bul'ud	vistáram, visálam, virivu.
Lat'ter, *a.*	သာ၍နောက်ကျသော။	thah-yoo-eh-nowk-kyah-	pichh'la	pinthina, pinchollappaṭṭa.
Lat'tice, *s.*	ရာဇမတ်။	yah-za-mut, [thaw,...	jhunjh'ree, *f.* ja'lee, tab'dan.	kiráthi.
Laugh, *s.*	ရယ်သည်။	yee-the	hun'sa, huns'na, hun'see, *f.*...	chirippu, nagaippu, muruval.
Law, *s.*	ဥပဒေ။တရား။	oo-pă-day, ta-yah'	a'een, ud'a lut, dad, *f.*	kaṭṭaḷai, pramáṇam, oḻungu.
Law'suit, *s.*	တရားမှု။	ta-yah-hmoo	da'wa, da'wee, *f.* bi'bad	vaḻakku. viyájyam, práthu.
Law'yer	ရှေ့နေ။	shay-nay	wuk'eel	nyáyavátbi, dharumasástiri.
Lázy, *a.*	ပြင်းရိ။	pyin-yee	soost, ka'hil, dhee'la	chómbaláṇa.
Léader, *s.*	ခေါင်းတည်သောသူ။	gowng-tee-thaw-thoo	sa'lar, sur'dar, sur'gur'oh ...	talaivan, muthaláḷi, vaḻikáṭṭi

English.	Burmese.		Hindustani.	Tamil.
Leaf, *s.* ...	အရွက်။ ...	a-yoo-et ...	burg, dul, pat, put'ta ...	ilai, aḍai, taḻai, éḍu, ithaḻ.
Learn, *v. a.* & *n.* ...	သင်သည်။ ...	thin'the ...	seekh'na, sadh'na ...	paḍi, kal, óthu, paḻagu.
Learn'ed, *a.* ...	စာတတ်သော။ ...	sah'dut-thaw ...	a'lim, fa'zil ...	karra, paḍitta, kalaipayinra.
Lease, *s.* ...	အိမ်မြေလယ်ယာကိုအခနှင့်ငှါး	ayn-myay-leh-yah-a-kah-	kir'a'ya-k, put'ta ...	kuttagai, váḍakai.
Least, *a.* ...	အငယ်ဆုံး။ [သည်။ ...	a-ngeh-sohn [hnin-ngah-the	kun'tur ...	arpa, athichiriya.
Leath'er, *s.* ...	သားရေ။ ...	tha-yay ...	chum'ra, cham ...	pathamittatól.
Leave, *s.* ...	အခွင့်။ ...	a-kwing ...	ij'a'zut, ruz'a, *f.* ...	uttaravu, viḍai, viḍuthalai.
Leave, *v. a.* ...	ထွက်သွားသည်။ ...	twet-thwah-the ...	ty'ag'na, turk-k ...	viḍu, níkku, niruttu.
Ledg'er, *s.* ...	စာရင်းချုပ်။ ...	tsah-yin-chyoht ...	bu'hee, *f.* ...	kaṇakku-puttakam, togai-attai, salúgai. [yéḍu.
Leech, *s.* ...	မျှော့။ ...	hmyaw ...	jonk, *f.* jok, jul'ou'ka ...	
Left, *a.* ...	လက်ဝဲဘက်။ ...	leh-weh-let ...	ba'yan, chup ...	iḍa, iḍappakkamána.
Left, *p. t.* & *p. p.* of	ထွက်သွားပြီး။ ...	twet-thwah-byee ...	ba'kee ...	viḍappatta, kaiviḍappatta.
Leg, *s.* [Leave, ...	ခြေထောက်။ ...	chyee-dowk ...	tang, tang'ree, *f.* pa'on ...	kál tál, pátham.
Lem'on, *s.* ...	ရှောက်ချဉ်သီး။ ...	showk-chyin-thee ...	nee'boo, le'boo ...	elumichchai, sampíram.
Lend, *v. a.* ...	ချေးသည်။ ...	chyee-the ...	joo'ga'na, kurz-d, mung'nee-d	iravalkoḍu, kaḍanáykkoḍu.
Length, *s.* ...	အလျား။ ...	a-lee-ah ...	dur'az'ee, lum'ba'ee, *f.* ...	nílam, neḍumai.
Lep'rosy, *s.* ...	နူ။ ...	noo ...	chur'uk pes, bur'us ...	kushṭam, kushṭaróham.
Less, *a.* ...	သာ၍ငယ်သော။ ...	thah-you-eh-ngeh-thaw ...	kum, tho'ra ...	kuraintha, chiriya.
Les'son, *s.* ...	သင်ရန်အခန်း။ ...	thin-yun-a-cun ...	durs, seekh, *f.* sub'uk ...	páḍam, echcharippu.
Let, *v. a.* ...	ငှါးထားသည်။ ...	hngah-tah-the ...	de'na, bha'ra-d, kir'a'ya-d ...	viḍu, váḍakaikuviḍu.
Let'ter, *s.* ...	မှာစာ။မေတ္တာစာ။ ...	hmah-sah, myittah-tsah ...	chit'thee, *f.* khut, na'm'u ...	kaḍitham, pattiram.
Lev'el, *a.* ...	ညီညာသော။ ...	nyee-nyah-thaw ...	bur'a'bur, chou'rus ...	samamána, otta, mattamána
Líar, *s.* ...	မုသားစကားသုံးသောသူ။ ...	moo-thaw-s'gah-thohn-	jhoo'ta, jhoot'ha, ka'zib ...	poyyan, purattan.
Líbrary, *s.* ...	စာအုပ်ရုံ။ ...	tsah-ohk-tsoo, [thaw-thoo ...	kitab-kha'nu ...	puttakasálai.
Lícense, *s.* ...	ပြုရသောအခွင့်။ ...	pyoo-yah-thaw-a-kwin ...	rookh'sut, hookm ...	uttaravu, chuváthínam.
Lie, *s.* ...	မုသားစကား။ ...	moo-thah-s'gah ...	jhoot, jooth, dur'ogh ...	poy, puḻugu, tapparai.

Life, *s.* ...	အသက်။ ...	a-thet ...	dum, jan, jee, hy'at ...	jívan, práṇaṇ, uyir.
Light, *s.* ...	အလင်း။ ...	ă-lin ...	roush'nee, *f.* oo'ja'la, rou'shun.	oḷi, viḷakku, dípam, jóti.
Líghtning, *s.* ...	လျှပ်စစ်။ ...	hleeut-sit [the,...	bij'lee, *f.* koun'dha ...	minnal, min, oḷi.
Like, *s.* ...	ကဲ့သို့။တူသော။ကြိုက်သည်။ ...	geh-tho, too-thaw, kyuyk-	moo'sha'bih, misal, *f.* ..	otta, nigar, cháyal, máthiri.
Lim'it, *s.* ...	ပိုင်းခြားကန့်။ဆီးသောအမှတ်။ .	puyng-chyah-kohn, tsee-thaw-a-hmut ...	hud, see'ma, *f.* ...	ellai, maṭṭu, aḷavu, attu, varai.
Line, *s.* ...	အတန်း။ကြိုးမြင့်။ ...	atun', kyoh-myin ...	dhar, dha'ree, *f.* ...	vari, irégai, kíṛu, kóḍu.
Lin'guist, *s.* ...	ဘာသာစကားအမျိုးမျိုးကိုတတ်သောဆရာ။	bah-thah-s'gah-a-myoh-myoh-tut-thaw-sa-yah ...	zub'an-dan ...	palapáshaikaṛṛón.
Link, *s.* ...	ကွင်းချင်းဆက်သောကြိုးကွင်းတကွင်း။	goo-in-chyin-set-thaw-kyoh-dwin-t'dwin ...	kur'ee, koo'la'ba ...	kaṭṭu, sangilivaḷaiyam.
Lin'seed, *s.* ...	ပိုက်ဆံစေ့။ ...	puyt-sun-say ...	tee'see, ul'see, *f.* mus'ee'na...	chiṛusaṇalvithai.
Líon, *s.* ...	ချင်သေ့။ ...	chyin-thay ...	singh, mrig-raj, kes'ur'ee ...	singam, áṇsingam, miruga-
Líoness, *s.* ...	ချင်သေ့မ။ ...	chyin-thay-mah ...	singh'nee, sher'nee, *f.* ...	pensingam. [rájan.
Lip, *s.* ...	နှုတ်ခမ်း။ ...	hnoht-cun ...	honth, onth, lub ...	uthaḍu. ithal, viḷimbu.
List, *s.* ...	အစည်။ ...	a-tsee ...	fih'rist, furd, ism-nu'wees'ee, *f*	aṭṭavaṇai, iḍáppu.
Lis'ten, *v. n.* ...	နားထောင်သည်။ ...	nah-towng-the ...	soon'na, kan-d ...	uṛṛukkéḷ, chevikoḍu.
Litigátion, *s.* ...	တရားတွေ့ခြင်း။ ...	ta-yah-tway-chyin ...	kuz'i'ya, tun'ta ...	vivátham, vaḷakkuppésal.
Lit'tle, *a.* ...	ငယ်သော။ ...	ngeh-thaw ...	zur'ru, zurree, *f.* chho'ta ...	koñjam, aṛpam, choṛpam.
Live, *v. n.* ...	နေသည်။ ...	nay-the ...	jee'na, jeew'na ...	iru, vásampaṇṇu, uyiróḍiru.
Liz'ard, *s.* ...	အိမ်မြှောင်။ ...	ayn-hmyowng ...	gir'git, ghir'goot ...	musali, musalivarkkam.
Lo, *interj.* ...	ကြည့်ပါ။ ...	kyee-bah ...	niga'h, nuz'ur ...	pár, ithó, athó, kéḷ.
Load, *s.* ...	ဝန်။ဝန်တင်သည်။ ...	woon, woon-tin-the ...	bojh, bar, bhar, moth[thur...	chumaṭ, bháram, pothi.
Load'stone, *s.* ...	သံလိုက်ကျောက်။ ...	thun-luyt-khyowk ...	choom'uk *or* choom'buk-put'-	kánthakkal.
Loaf, *s.* ...	မုန့်လုံး။ ...	mohn-lohn ...	pa'on-ro'tee ...	roṭṭi, appam.
Loan, *s.* ...	ချေးသောအရာ။ ...	chyee-thaw-a-yah ...	mung'nee, *f.* *of money* kurz.	iraval, kaḍan. [tha.
Loath, *a.* ...	ငြိုငြင်းသော။ ...	pyoo-byin-thaw ...	na-raz ...	viruppamaṛṛa, manamillá-
Lócal, *a.* ...	အရပ်နှင့်ဆိုင်သော။ ...	a-yut-hnin-suyng-thaw ...	muk'an'ee ...	úrukkuriya, iḍattukkuriya.

English.	Burmese.		Hindustani.	Tamil.
Lock, *s.* ...	သော့အိမ်။ ...	thaw-ayn ...	koofl, ta'la ...	púṭṭu,poṛi,piḍippu: aḍaippu.
Lodge, *s.* ...	နေသည်။ ...	nay-the ...	jhomp'ra, muk'an ...	kuḍisai, taṅgumiḍam.
Loft, *s.* ...	အပေါ်ဆင့်။ ...	apaw-tsin ...	bam ...	méṛkaṭṭu, ménilai.
Lofty, *a.* ...	မြင့်သော။ ...	myin-thaw ...	oon'cha ...	uyarntha, unnathamána.
Log'ic, *s.* ...	လောဇိတ်သော အတတ်ပညာ...	law-zayt-thaw-a-tut-pin-	mun'tik, *f.* turk ...	nyáyavilakkaṇam.
Long, *a.* ...	ရှည်သော။ ...	shay-thaw [yah...	tu'weel, lum'ba ...	níḷamána, níṇḍa, neḍu.
Lon'gitude, *s.* ...	အရှည်အလျား။ ...	a-shay-a-lee-ah ...	tool-i-bul'ud ...	tírkkarékai, désántaram.
Look, *s.* ...	ကြည့်သည်။ ...	kyee-thee ...	nig'ah, nuz'ur, *f.* ...	párvai, tóṛṛam, nókkam.
Look'ing-glass, *s.*...	မှန်။ ...	hmun, ...	a'ee'nu ...	mugakkaṇṇáḍi.
Loose, *a.* ...	ဖြေသည်။ ...	pyay-the ...	dhee'la ...	iḷakkamána, toyntha.
Lord, *s.* ...	အရှင်။သခင်။ ...	a-shin, th'kin ...	khoo'da-wund, kha'wind ...	karttá, náthan, talaivan.
Loss, *s.* ...	ပျောက်ဆုံးခြင်း။ ...	pyowk-sohn-gyin ...	nook'san, han ...	nashṭam, chétham, kéḍu.
Lot'tery, *s.* ...	စာရေးတံ ချခြင်း။ ထိ ကောက်	sah-yay-dun-chyah-chyin..	shur'tee, *f.* ...	dáyam, panthayam, chíṭṭu.
Loud, *a.* ...	အသံကျယ်သော။ [ခြင်း။...	a-thun-khyeh-thaw ...	oon'cha, bha'ree, boo'lund...	urattasattamuḷḷa.
Love, *s.* ...	ချစ်သည်။ ...	chyit-the ...	pi'yar, *m. f.* preet, prem ...	anbu, nésam, natpu, snéham.
Lov'er, *s.* ...	ချစ်သောသူ။ရည်းစား။ ...	chyit-thaw-thoo ...	pi'ya, a'shik, prem'ee ...	anban, nanban, náyagan.
Low, *a.* ...	နိမ့်သော။ ...	hnayn-thaw ...	nee'cha; nush'eb ...	kíḷána, táḷntha, níchamána.
Loy'al, *a.* ..	ရှင်ဘုရင်၏ သစ္စာ စောင့် ထိမ်း	shin-bu-yin-ee-this-sah-	num'uk-hul'al ...	rájapakshamuḷḷa.
Luck, *s.* ...	ကံ။ [သောသူ။...	cun, [sowng-tayn-thaw-thoo	nus'eeb, kis'mut, *f.* ...	athirshṭam, yógam.
Lúnatic, *s.* ...	အရူး။ ...	a-yoo ...	khup'tee, pa'gul ...	paittiyakáran. [ram.
Lust, *s.* ...	ကိလေသာစိတ်ရှိသည်။ ...	kee-lay-thah-sayt-she-the...	kam, mus'tee, *f.* ...	durásai, móham, kámaviká-
Lute, *s.* ...	စောင်း။ ...	tsowng ...	bur'but, ka'noon, *f.* ood ...	kiṇṇáram, víṇai, yáḷ.
Lyre, *s.* Harp, ...	စောင်းတမျိုး။ ...	tsowng-t'myo ...	ka'noon, *f.* bur'but ...	víṇai, yáḷ,
Macaróni, *s.* ...	မုန့်ချိုတမျိုး။ ...	mohn-chyo ...	se'wyn, *f.* boogh'ra ...	kóthumaiyinárcheythapala-
Machine', *s.* ...	စက်။ ...	set ...	kul, *f.* juntr ...	yanthiram, enthiram [gáram
Mad, *a.* ...	ရူးသော။ ...	yoo-thaw, [mah,...	dee'wa'nu, pug'la, soud'a'ee.	paittiyam, unmatta.

Mad'am, *s.* ...	မမ၊မယ်ရှင်၊သခင်မ။ ...	mum-mah,meh-shin,th'kin-	jee, joo, la'la ...	esamáṭṭi, srímáṭṭi.
Mad'-house, *s.* ...	အရူးထားသောအိမ်။ ...	a-yoo-tah-thaw-ayn ...	pa'gal-kha'nu ...	unmattarvásam.
Mad'man, *s.* ...	အရူး။ ...	a-yoo ...	pa'gul, khep'a ...	pittan, paittiyakáran.
Magazine', *s.* ...	ဘဏ္ဍာတိုက်။ ...	bun-dah-tuyk ...	mukh'zum ...	paḍaivíḍu, áyuthasálai, ka-
Mag'got, *s.* ...	လောက်။ ...	lowk ...	kee'ra, krim, pil'loo ...	puḻu, kirumi. [laṅjiyam.
Mag'ic, *s.* ...	မှော်၊မြက်လှည့်။ ...	hmaw, myek-hleh ...	ja'doo' ja'doo-gur'ee, *f.* ...	máyájálam, mántrikan.
Magic'ian, *s.* ...	မှော်ဝင်သောသူ။ ...	hmaw-win-thaw-thoo ...	ja'doo'gur ...	máyávi, mantraváthi.
Mag'istrate, *s.* ...	မြို့ဝန်။ ...	myo-woon ...	fouj'dar ...	nyáyáthipathi, athikári
Mag'net, *s.* ...	သံလိုက်။ ...	thun-luyt ...	choom'buk-put'thur ...	kántham, kánthakkal.
Magnif'icence, *s.* ...	မြင့်မြတ်ခြင်း။ ...	myin-myut-chyin ...	uz'mut, *f.* ...	mahattuvam, chirappu.
Maid, Maid'en, *s.* ...	အပျို၊မိန်းမပျို။ ...	ă-pyo, maym-mah-pyo ...	do-shee'zu, koo'ar'ee, kun'	kannippen, vélaikári, válai.
Main, *a.* ...	ကြီးကျယ်သော။ ...	kyee-kyeh-thaw ...	sudr, [ni'ya,...	talaimaiyána, prathána.
Maj'esty, *s.* ...	မြင့်မြတ်သော။ ...	myin-myut-thaw ...	jul'al, dub'dub'u ...	mahattuvam, máḍchimai.
Make, *v. a.* ...	လုပ်သည်၊ဖန်ဆင်းသည်။ ...	loht-the, pun-sin-the ...	bun'a'na, kur'na ...	paḍai, unḍákku, chey.
Male, *s.* ...	အထီးအဖို။ ...	a-htee-a-hpo ...	murd, *n.* & *a.* nur, nur'ee'nu.	áṇ, púmán.
Mal'ice, *s.* ...	ရန်ငြိုးဖွဲ့။ ...	yun-ngyoh-bweh ...	ghoo'na-pun, kee'na ...	vanmam, erivu, pagai.
Mamma', *s.* ...	အမိ၊မိခင်။ ...	a-may, mee-gin ...	ma, um'ma, [dur...	ammá, áyi, táy, máthá.
Man, *s.* ...	လူ၊လူယောက်ျား။ ...	loo, loo-yow-kyah ...	jun, jun'a, ma'noos ...	manushan, naran, áḍavan.
Man'age, *v. a.* ...	စီရင်သည်။ ...	tsee-yin-the ...	chul'a'na ...	naḍappi, kaiyáḷu, chey.
Mane, *s.* ...	လည်ဆံ။ ...	lee-sun ...	uy'al, yal, *f.* ...	piḍarmayir, uḷai.
Mánger, *s.* ...	စားကျင်းစားခွက်။ ...	sah-gyin-sah-kwet ...	kar'ba'ree ...	munnaṇai, máṭṭutoṭṭi.
Man'go, *s.* ...	သရက်သီး။ ...	thă-yet-thee ...	am, amb, umb ...	má, mámaram, máṅkáy.
Man'ner, *s.* ...	နည်း၊ထုံး။ ...	nee, tohn ...	doul, dus'toor, ruk'um ...	vitham, máthiri, prakáram.
Man'ual, *a.* ...	လက်လုပ်သော။ ...	leh-loht-thaw ...	dust'ee ...	kaivélaikkaḍutta, kaippá-
Manufac'tory, *s.* ...	လက်မှုပညာသည်ရုံ။ ...	let-hmoo-pin-nyah-the-yohn	kar-kha'nu ...	kaittoḻilcheyyiḍam. [ḍuḷḷa.
Manufac'ture, *s.* ...	လက်နှင့်လုပ်သော။ ...	let-hnin-loht-thaw ...	ka'ree-gur'ee, *f.* ...	kaivinai, kaittoḻil.
Manufac'turer, *s.* ...	လက်နှင့်လုပ်သောသူ။ ...	let-hnin-loht-thaw-thoo ...	ka'ree-gur ...	kaivinaiyáḷan, kárukan.
Manúre, *s.* ...	အချေး။ ...	a-chyay ...	pans, sar, khad, khat, *f.* ...	eru, uram, kuppai.

English.	Burmese.		Hindustani.	Tamil.
Man'uscript, *s.* ...	လက်နှင့်ရေးသောစာ။ ...	let-hnin-yay-thaw-sah ...	dust-khut ...	kaiyeluttuppratbi.
Man'y, *a.* ...	များသော။ ...	myah-thaw ...	bu'hoot, uk'sur ..	pala, anéka, vegu, náná.
Map, *s.* ...	မြေပုံ။ ...	myay-bohn ...	nuk'shu ...	désapadam, chitrappadam.
Mar'ble, *a.* ...	ကျောက်ဖြူ။ ...	chyowk-pyoo ...	mur'mur, kun'kur'a ...	palavarnamána.
March, *v. a.* ...	တတ်ချီသွားသည်။ ...	tut-chyee-thwah-the ...	suf'ur, moo'sa'fur'ut, *f.* ...	padaipéyarchchi, prayánam.
Mare, *s.* ...	မြင်းမ။ ...	myin-mah ...	gho'ree, mad'wan ..	máthuván, pettaikkuthirai.
Mar'gin, *s.* ...	အစွန်။အနား။ ...	ă-sohn, ă-nah ...	kin'a'ra, ha'shi'ya ...	óram, vilimbu, karai.
Mark, *s.* ...	အမှတ်။တံဆိပ်။ ...	ă-hmut, t'sayt ...	dagh, nish'an, us'ur ...	kuri, adaiyálam, pulli.
Mar'ket, *s.* ...	ဈေး။ ...	zay ...	ba'zar, hat, gunj, good'ree..	kadai, santai, ávanam.
Market-price, *s.* ...	ဈေးပေါက်။ ...	zay-bowk ...	ba'zar-ka-bha'o ...	kadaivilai.
Mar'riage, *s.* ...	လက်ထပ်မင်္ဂလာ။ ...	let-tut-ming-gă-lah ...	bi'ya, sha'dee, *f.* ni'ka'h ...	kaliyánam, viváham.
Mar'ry, *v. a.* ...	လက်ထပ်သည်။ ...	let-tut-the ...	bi'yah-k, sha'dee-k ...	viváhañchey.
Marsh, *s.* ...	စိမ့်မြေ။ ...	sayn-myay ...	sho'ra, tur'a'ee, dul'dul ...	sathuppunilam, chérrunilam
Mar'tial, *a.* ...	စစ်မှုနှင့်ဆိုင်သော။ ...	sit-hmoo-ning-suyng-thaw..	jun'gee ...	yuttattukkadutta.
Mar'tyr, *s.* ...	ခွဲလမ်းသော အယူဝါဒကြောင့် အသေခံရသောသူ။	tsweh-lun-thaw-a-yoo-wah-dah-gyowng-a-thay-cun-[yah-thaw-thoo.	shu'heed ...	irattasátchchi, irattasákshi.
Marvel, *s.* ...	အံ့ဩသည်။ ...	un-aw-the	uj'ub, ij'az, ub'bas ..	áchchariyam, athisayam.
Mas'culine, *a.* ...	အထီး။အဖိုဖြစ်သော။ ...	a-tee, ă-hpo-pyit-thaw ...	mooz'uk'kur, nur, poo'ling..	áṇmaiyulla, áṇava.
Máson, *s.* ...	ပန်းရန်သမား။ ...	pă-yun-th-mah ...	mim'ar ...	korran, sirpan.
Másonary, *s.* ...	ပန်းရန်အတတ်။ ...	pă-yun-a-tut ...	mim'a'ree, *f.* ...	sirpasástiram, kattuvélai.
Mas'sacre, *s.* ...	ရက်စက်စွာသတ်ဖြတ်သည်။ ...	yet-set-swah-thut-pyut-the.	kutl ...	vegujanasaṅkáram, kolai.
Mast, *s.* ...	ရွက်တိုင်။ ...	yuet-tuying ...	dol, mus'tool ...	páymaram, kúmbú.
Mas'ter, *s.* ...	အရှင်။သခင်။ဆရာ။ ...	a-shin, th'kin, tsay-yah ...	ma'lik, sa'hib, oos'tad ...	esamán, samarttan, vátti.
Mat, *s.* ...	ဖျာ။ ...	hpyah ...	chu'ta'ee, *f.* ...	páy.
Mate, *s.* ...	မာလိန်။ ...	mah-layn ...	jot, jooft ...	iṇai, tólan, kúttáli.
Mátron, *s.* ...	မိမ္မကြီး။ ...	may'mah-gyee ...	ma'ma, peer'zun ...	srímátti, avvai, talaivi.

Mat'ter, *s.* ...	အကြောင်းအရာ။ ...	a-kyowng, a-yah ...	kam, hal, ba'but ...	káriyam, saṅgathi.
Mat'ter, *s.* ..	ရုပ်။ ...	yoht ...	jism ...	síl, síḻkkaṭṭu. [thiya.
Matúre, *a.* ...	မှည့်သော။ ...	hmeh-thaw ...	rus,ee'da, pookh'tu ...	pakkuvamána, téṛina, mu-
Maund, *s.* ...	အခွက်နှစ်ဆယ်ကျော်။ ...	a-kwet-hnit-seh-gyaw ...	mun ...	maṇaṅgu, maḍaṅgu.
Max'im, *s.* ...	ဧကရစ်စကား။ ...	ay-ga-woot-sa'gah ...	muk'ool'u ...	paḻamoḻi, matham, níthi.
May, *aux. v.* ...	မေလ။ဖြစ်နိုင်သည်။ ...	may-lah, pyit-hnuyng-the..	sh'ayud, bad ...	ám, kaḍavathu, kúḍum, iyal-
Me, *pron.* ...	ကျွန်ုပ်ကို။ ...	kyoon-hnoht-goh ...	moojh, mooj'he ...	ennai. [vathu.
Meal, *s.* ...	အစား။တနပ်။ ...	a-tsah, t'nut ...	kha'na ...	uṇḍi, tíni, noy, má.
Mean, *a.* ...	အမျိုးမမြတ်သော။ ...	a-myoh-m'myut-thaw ...	kum'ee'nu, pa'jee, riz'al ...	nícha, ína, maddhyam.
Mean, *v. a.* ...	အကျိုးအကြောင်း။ ...	a-kyoh-a-kyowng ...	ir'a'da-rukhna ...	aruttaṅkoḻḻu, karuthu.
Meas'ure, *s.* ...	အတိုင်းအထွာ။ ...	a-tuyng-a-twah ...	map, nap, un'daz ...	ellai, parimáṇam, paḍi.
Meat, *s.* ...	စားရန်အသား။ ...	tsah-yun-ă-thah ...	kha'na, gosht, mans ...	iṛaichchi, mámisam, ágáram.
Mechan'ic, *s.* ...	စစ်မှုပညာတတ်သောသူ။ ...	tset-hmoo-pin-myah-tut-thaw-thoo ...	mis'tree, uhl-i-hir'fu ...	kammáḻan, siṛpakáran.
Med'al, *s.* ...	ပုံတံဆိပ်။ ...	pohn-t'sayt ...	tugh'mu, mood'ra ...	kírttimuttirai.
Médiator, *s.* ...	စပ်ကြားကဝင်သောသူ။ ...	tsut-kyah-gah-win-thaw-	dur'mi'yan'ee ...	maddyastan, naḍuvan.
Med'icine, *s.* ...	ဆေး။ ...	tsay [thoo...	du'wa, *f.* tib ...	aviḻtham, aushatham.
Med'itate, *v. a.* ...	ဆင်ခြင်ခြင်း။ ...	tsin-gyin-gyin ...	soch'na, dhi'ya'na ...	dyáni, chintanaipaṇṇu.
Meed, *s.* ...	ဆု။ ...	tsoo ...	juz'a, *f.* ...	vegumathi, upakáram.
Meek, *a.* ...	စိတ်နူးညံ့သိမ်မွေ့သော။ ...	sayt-noo-nyun-thain-moo-	ghur'eeb, sul'eem ...	táḻmaiyuḻḻa, methuvána.
Meet, *v. a.* ...	တွေ့သည်။ ...	tway-the [ay-thaw...	mil'a'na, mil'na, moo'la'	ethirkoḻḻu, santhi. kúḍu.
Meet'ing, *s.* ...	အစုအဝေး။ ...	a-tsoo-a-way ...	moo'la'kat, *f.* bhet, *f.* [kee-h	sabhai. saṅgam.
Mem'ber, *s.* ...	အင်္ဂါ။ ...	ing-gah ...	oo'zo, ub'yub ...	avayavam. uṛuppu, aṅgam.
Mem'brane, *s.* ...	အမြှေး။ ...	a-hmyay ...	khul'ree, *f* ...	méthai, chavvu, tól
Memoran'dum, *s.*...	မှတ်သောအချက်။ ...	hmut-thaw-a-chyet ...	yad-dasht, *f.* ...	ñápagapattiram.
Mem'ory, *s.* ...	မှတ်မိတတ်သောစိတ်။ ...	hmut-mee-tut-thaw-sayt ...	yad, hifz, chet, soodh, *f.* ...	ñápagam, ninaippu.
Mend, *v. a.* & *n.* ...	ဖျင်သည်။ ...	pyin-the ...	mur'um'mut'k, bun'a'na ...	puthuppi. tirunthu.
Men'dicant, *s.* & *a.*..	သူတောင်းစား။ ...	thoo-downg-sah ...	fu'keer, bhik'ha'ree ...	pichchaikkáran, áṇḍi.

ENGLISH.	BURMESE.		HINDUSTANI.	TAMIL.
Men'ses, *s.* ...	မီးရပ်ဥတု။ရာသီပန်း။ ...	mee-yut-oo-doo, yah-thee-bun ...	hyz, ruj, nu'he'nee, *f.* ...	súthagam, máthatíṭṭu.
Men'tal, *a.* ...	စိတ်နှလုံးနှင့်ဆိုင်သော။ ...	sayt-hnit-lohn-hnin-suyng-	uk'lee ...	manathukkuriya.
Men'tion, *s.* ...	ပြောသည်။ ...	pyaw-the, [thaw...	chur'cha, zikr ...	moḻi, kuṛippu, chollu.
Mer'chandise, *s.* ...	ကုန်စည်။ ...	kohn-see ...	sou'da,sou'da-gur'ee, by'par.	varttakam, váṇigam.
Mer'chant, *s.* ...	ကုန်သည်။ ...	kohn-theh ...	sou'da'gur, by'par'ee ...	varttakan, viyápári.
Mer'ciful, *a.* ...	သနားတတ်သော။ ...	th-nah-dut-thaw ...	shufeek, dy'al ...	irakkamuḷḷa, dayaiyuḷḷa.
Mer'cury, *s.* ...	ပြဒါး။ဗုဒ္ဓဟူးဂြိုဟ်။ ...	pă-dah, bohd-hoo-gyoh ...	para, seem-ab, rus ...	irasam, pátharasam.
Mer'cy, *s.* ...	ကရုဏာ။ ...	gă-yoo-nah ...	ruhm, dy'a, *f.* ...	irakkam, manaurukkam.
Mérely, *adv.* ...	သာ။ ...	thah ...	sirf, fuk'ut ...	suddhamáy, máttiram.
Mer'it, *s.* ...	ကုသိုလ်။ ...	koo-the ...	li'ya'kut, *f.* goon ...	yókkiyam, taguthi, péṛu.
Mer'ry, *a.* ...	ပျော်မြူးသည်။ ...	pyaw-myoo-the ...	khoosh ...	kaḷippána, magiḻchchiyuḷḷa.
Mess, *s.* ...	စစ်ဗိုလ်စု။ ...	tsit-boh-tsoo ...	kha'na, seed'ha, bho'jun ...	bhójanam, uṇavu.
Mes'sage, *s.* ...	စေလွှတ်လိုက်သော။ ...	say-hloht-luyt-thaw ...	py'am, py'gham ...	cheythi, túthu, saṅgathi.
Mes'senger, *s.* ...	စေလွှတ်သောသူ။ ...	say-hloht-thaw-thoo ...	py'am-bur, py'gham-bur ...	túthan, oṟṟan.
MESSI'AH, *s.* ...	ခရစ်တော်။ ...	Ka-rit-daw ...	mus'eeh'a, mus'eeh ...	abishékamperṟavar, mésiyá.
Met'al, *s.* ...	သတ္တု။ ...	thut-too ...	dhat, filiz, bhurt ...	táthu, déyajam.
Metho'd, *s.* ...	အစီအစဉ်။နည်း။ ...	ă-tsee, a-tsin ...	turteeb, *f.* ...	vitham, pramáṇam, vagai.
Metrop'olis, *s.* ...	မြို့တော်။ ...	myo-daw ...	tukhtgah, *f.* raj-dha'nee ...	rájathání, samastánam.
Mid'-day, *s.* ...	မွန်းတည့်။ ...	mohn-teh ...	do-pu'hur ...	uchchi, maddhyánam.
Mid'dle, *s.* ...	အလယ်။ ...	a-leh ...	beech, dur'mi'yan, ou'sut...	naḍu, iḍai, maiyam.
Mid'night, *s.* ...	သန်းခေါင်။ ...	th'gowng ...	ad'hee-rat, dopu'hur-rat ...	naḍuráttiri, sámam.
Mid'wife, *s.* ...	ဝမ်းဆွဲမိန်းမ။ ...	woon-sweh-maym-mah ...	da'ee'jun'a'ee, *f.* kab'il'a ...	maruttuvichchi.
Might, *s.* ...	ခွန်အား။အစွမ်းသတ္တိ။ ...	kohn-ah, a-swan-thut-tee...	mik'nut, *f.* ta'kut, *f.* ...	vallamai, palam, valimai.
Migrátion, *s.* ...	တပြည်မှတပြည်သို့ ပြောင်းသည်။	t-pyee-hmah-t'pyee-thoh-pyoung-the ...	in'tik'al,tub'deel-i-muk'an,*f.*	kuḍiyeḻuchchi, kuḍipóthal.

Milch-cow, *a.*	နို့ထွက်သောနွားမ။	noh-twet-thaw-no-ah-mah.	dhen'oo. *f.*	párpasu, karavaipasu.
Mild, *a.*	နူးညံ့သော။	noo-nyun-thaw	moo'la'im	sánthamulla, miruthuvána.
Mile, *s.*	တတိုင်။	t'duyng	meel, kos, kur'oh	mukkál-náligaivalittúram.
Mil'itary, *s. & a.*	စစ်မှုနှင့်ဆိုင်သော။	tait-hmoo-hnin-suyng-thaw.	lush'kur, us'kur, sip'ah,pul'-	ránuvam, padai, ránuvat-
Milk, *s.*	နို့။	noh	doodh, sheer, chheer,[tun,...	pál, amutham. [tukkuriya.
Milk'man, *s.*	နို့သမား။	noh-thum-mah	go'a'la, gho'see, do'see	párkáran, idaiyan.
Mim'ic, *s.*	အတုလုပ်တတ်သော။	a-too-loht-dut-thaw	nuk'kal, nuk'kalin, *f.*	kélikkáran, sarasakkáran.
Mind, *s.*	စိတ်။	sayt	dil, jee, mun	manam, ullam, priyam.
Mine, *s.*	တွင်း။	twin	kan, khan, nukb, *f.* soo'rung.	ulógamvilainilam, kani.
Mine, *poss. pron.*	ကျွန်ုပ်၏။	kyoon-hnoht-ee	mer'a, up'na, (up'nee, *f.*)	en, ennudaiya, enathu.
Min'eral, *s.*	ဓါတ်။	dut	dhat	táthu, nirasavastu.
Min'gle, *v. a. & n.*	ရောနှောသည်။	yaw-hnaw-the	mil'a'na, mil'a'o'	tóy, pisaru, pisai, kala.
Min'ister, *s.*	မှူးမတ်။	hmoo-mut	dee'wan, wuz'eer	mantiri, sévakan.
Min'ister, *s.*	ဓမ္မဆရာ။	dum-mah-tsay-yah	brahmun, im'an	guru, áchàriyan.
Mint, *s.*	ဒင်္ဂါးခတ်သည့်တိုက်။	ding-gah-cut-thee-tuyk	tuk'sal, *f.*	tangasálai.
Min'ute, *s.*	လိတ္တာ။မိနစ်။	layt-tah, mee-nit	ur'a'ee-pul	nimisham, kalai, vinádi.
Mir'acle, *s.*	ထူးဆန်းသောအမှု။	too-zun-thaw-a-hmoo	kur'a'mut, *f.* moo'jiz'u, ij'az.	arputham.
Mir'ror, *s.*	မှန်။	hmun	a'ee'nu, ab-gee'nu, dur'pun.	kannádi, nilaikkannádi.
Mirth'ful, *a.*	ရွှင်လန်းမြူးတူးသော။	shoo-in-lun-myoo-too-thaw.	tun'naz	magilchchiyána.
Mis'chief, *s.*	အကျိုးဖျက်ခြင်း။	a-kyoh-pyet-chyin	shokh'ee, *f.*	kurram, tíngu, kurumbu.
Misdeed', *s.*	မကောင်းသောအမှု။	m'kowng-thaw-a-hmoo	bud-kir'dar'ee, *f.*	tappu, kurram, tappitham.
Mis'erable, *a.*	ဆင်းရဲသော။	tsin-yeh-thaw	pur'e'shan, [bukh'tee, *f.*)...	nirbantha, ilivána.
Misfor'tune, *s.*	ကံမကောင်းခြင်း။	m'kowng-chyin	bud-(tee'ru-*or* si ya-*or* kum-	idaiyúru, ábattu, tattu.
Miss, *s.*	မိန္မကလေး။	maym-mah-ga-lay	lur'kee, ba'luk, bee'bee	duraimagal, ilampen.
Miss, *v.*	လွဲသည်။	lweh-the	bhool, *f.* chook, *f.*	tavaru, pilai, tappu, valuvu.
Mis'sionary, *s.*	သာသနာပြုဆရာ။	thah-th'nah-pyoo-say-yah..	fir'ish'ta	anuppappattavan.
Mistáke, *s.*	မှားခြင်း။	hmah-chyin, [mah,...	bhool, chook, *f.*	tappu, pilai, tappitham.
Mis'tress, *s.*	အစိုးရသောမိန္မ။	a-tsoh-yah-thaw-maym-	jee, sa'hib-za'dee, be'gum...	esamátti, talaivi, ammál.

English.	Burmese.		Hindustani.	Tamil.
Mist'y, *a.* ...	နှင်းဝေသော။ ...	hnin-way-thaw, ...	dhoondh'la ...	mantháramána.
Misunderstand', *v.a.*	အလွဲယူသည်။ ...	a-lweh-yoo-the ...	hooch'na, khil'af-sum'ujh'na	tappáyaṛi, pisagáyuṇar.
Mitigátion, *s.* ...	ပေါ့စေသည်။ ...	paw-say-the ...	tukh'feef, *f.* ...	taṇivu, áṛuthal.
Mítre, *s.* ...	ဂိုဏ်းအုပ်ဆောင်းသောပေါင်း။	guyng-oht-sowng-thaw-	chou-tur'ka ...	muḍi, talaipágai, gríḍam.
Mix, *v. n.* ...	ရောနှောသည်။ ...	yaw-hnaw-the, [bowng...	mil'a'na, mil'na ...	kalakku, kala.
Mock, *a.* ...	ပြောင်သည်။ ...	pyowng-the ...	tuk'lee'dee ...	parihásam, sarasam. [mai.
Mode, *s.* ...	နည်း။ ...	nee ...	doul, dhub, tour ...	máthiri, vitham, naḍai, tan-
Mod'erate, *a.* ...	မလွန်ကျူးသော။ ...	m'hloon-chyew-thaw ...	kul'eel, mi'ya'nu, moo'tu'dil.	maṭṭána, mithamána.
Moist, *a.* ...	ရေစွတ်သော။ ...	yay-soht-thaw ...	a'bee, gee'la, num, tur ...	nanaintha, framána.
Mon'arch, *s.* ...	ရှင်ဘုရင်။ ...	shin-boo-yin ...	bad-shah, shah, ra'ja ...	égáthipathi, sakkaravartti.
Mon'day, *s.* ...	တနင်းလာနေ့။ ...	tă-ning-lah-nay ...	peer, som-war, do-shum'bu.	tiṅgal, sómaváram.
Mon'ey, *s.* ...	ကျေးငွေ။ ...	kyay-n'gway ...	nukd, zur, roo'py ...	paṇam, kásu, náṇayam.
Monk, *s.* ...	ရဟန်း။ ...	yă-hun ...	ra'hib ...	muni, sanniyási, tuṛavi.
Mon'key, *s.* ...	မျောက်။ ...	myowk ...	bun'dur,(bund'ree,*f*)boz'nu.	kuraṅgu, vánaram.
Monop'oly, *s.* ...	တဦးတည်း ချုပ်၍ ရောင်းဝယ် သောအခွင့်။ ...	tă-oo-dee-chyoht-yoo-eh-yowng-weh-thaw-a-	ij'a'ru ...	suthanthara-varttagam.
Month, *s.* ...	လ။ ...	lah, [kwin...	mas, mu'hee'na ...	mátham, másam, tiṅgal.
Moon, *s.* ...	လ။ ...	lah ...	chand, chundur ...	nilá, chandran, tiṅgaḷ mathi.
Moon'light, *s.* ...	လရောင်။ ...	lah-yowng ...	chand'nee, chund-ri'ka, *f.*	niláveḷichcham, nilavu.
Moonshine, *s.* ...	လအရောင်အဝါ။ ...	lah-a-yowng-a-wah ...		chandra-(kánthi, *or* jóthi.)
Mor'als, *s. pl.* ...	ကျင့်ဝတ်တရား။ ...	kyin-woot-ta-yah ...	neet-shas'tur, ukh'lak ...	nítinaḍai, nallaṛivu.
Morass', *s.* ...	စိမ့်မြေ။ ...	sayn-myay ...	jha'bur, gur'un, *f.* ...	sathuppunilam.
More, *a.* ...	သာ၍။ ...	thah-yoo-eh ...	our, zi'a'du ...	miguntha, athigamána.
Moreóver, *adv.* ...	၎င်းပြင်။ ...	lĕ-gowng-pyin ...	ul'a'wu ...	innum, aṇṛiyum.
Morn, Morn'ing, *s.* ...	နံနက်။ ...	nun-net, [pyaw-the,...	fuj'ur, soobh, *f.* ...	kálai, viḍiyal, athikálam.
Moróse, *a.* ...	မျက်နှာထားနှင့် စကားပြောသည်။	myeh-hnah-tah-hnin-s'gah-	toorsh'roo ...	suḍumúñchi, erichchalulla.

Mor'row, *s.*	နက်ဖန်။	nep-pun	kul	nálai, marunál.
Mort'gage, *v. a.*	ပေါင်သည်။	powng-the	gir'wee-r	aḍaguvai, íḍuvai.
Mosque, *s.*	ဗလီ။	bă-lee	musjid, *f.* dur'gah, suj'jada.	paḷḷivásal, masúthi.
Mosquit'o, *s.*	ခြင်။	chyin	much'chhur	kosugu, masagam.
Most, *a.*	အများဆုံးသော။	a-myah-sohn-thaw	uk'sur, besh'tur, [rung,	méláṇa, miguntha.
Moth, *s.*	ပလံ။	pă-lun	put'ung, pur'wa'nu, ooch'	puḷu, púchchí.
Moth'er, *s.*	အမိ။အမေ။	a-mee, a-may	ma, ma'ee, ma'ta, um'ma	máthá, táy, annai, ammá.
Moth'er-in-law, *s.*	ယောက္ခမမိမ္မသူ။	yowk-ka-mah-maym-mah-	sas, sas'oo, khosh-da'mun	mámi, mámiyár.
Moth'erless, *a.*	အမိမရှိ။	a-may-m'shee, [thoo,	be-ma'dur	táyillátha, táyarṛa.
Mótion, *s.*	လှုပ်ရှားခြင်း။	hloot-shah-chyin	joom'bish, hur'uk'ut, *f.*	asaivu, áṭṭam.
Mould, *s.*	မြေနု။မှို။	myay-noo, hmoh	see'ghu, purg'hut'ee, *f.* kalib	achchu, karu, púñchu.
Mount, *s. v.*	တောင်။တက်သည်။	towng, tet-the	tee'la, pu'har'ee, *f.*	malai, kunṛam, uyarttu, éṛṛu.
Moun'tain, *s.*	တောင်။	towng	pu'har, kooh, gi'ri, pur'but	paruvatham, malai.
Mourn, *v. a.*	ညည်းတွားမြည်တန်သည်။	nyee-twah-myee-tun-the	ghum-k, ma'tum-k	tukkappaḍu, pulambhu.
Mouse, *s.*	ကြွက်။	kyoo-et	moo'sa, moos'ree, choo'hee, *f.*	chuṇḍeli, chuṇḍan.
Mouth, *s.*	ပစပ်။အဝ။	pa-sut, a-wah	moonh, *of river &c.*, moo'ha'na	váy, dwáram, váyil.
Move, *v. a.*	ရွေ့သည်။	yoo-ay-the	hil'a'na, sur'ka'na	áṭṭu, kulukku, évu.
Much, *s.*	များသော။	myah-thaw	bu'hoot, dher, uk'sur	tiraḷ, miguthí.
Múcus, *s. Lat.*	သလိပ်။တံတွေး။	th'layt, t'tway	chit'ka, loo'ab	chaḷi, kóḷai.
Mud, *s.*	ရွံ့။	shohn	chih'la, kee'chur *f.*	chéṛu, uḷai.
Mule, *s.*	လား။	lah	khuch'chur, *m. f.* us'tur	kóvérukaḷuthai.
Multiplicátion, *s.*	မြှောက်ခြင်း။	hmyowk-chyin	zurb, *f.*	perukkal, virutti.
Mul'titude, *s.*	အစုအရုံး။	a'tsoo-a-yohn	bheer, *f.*	janam, kúṭṭam, kumbu.
Mur'der, *s.*	လူအသက်ကိုသတ်သည်။	loo-a-thet-goh-thut-the	khoon, kutl, hutti'ya	kolai, vathai, kátham.
Mur'mur, *s. & v. n.*	မြည်တန်သည်။	myee-tun-the [hmoht-chyin,	chhul'chhul'a'hut	muṛumuṛuppu, muṛumuṛu.
Músic, *s.*	သီခြင်းဆိုခြင်း။တီးမှုတ်ခြင်း။	thee-chyin-soh-chyin, tee-	moo'suk'ee, *f.* sun'geet, rag.	nátham, váttiyam, isai.
Musk, *s.*	ကတိုးသဲခါ။မ။သဲခါးမွေး။	ka-doh, th'kwah-mah, th'kwah-hmway	kus'too'ree, *f.* mirg-mund	kastúri, punugu.

ENGLISH.	BURMESE.		HINDUSTANI.	TAMIL.
Mus'ket, *s.* ...	သေနတ်တမျိုး။ ...	thay-nut-t'myo ...	bun'dook, *f.* ...	tuppákki.
Must, *aux. v.* ...	ရမည်။ ...	yah-mee ...	la'zim-h, zur'oor-h ...	véṇḍum.
Mustache', *s.* ...	နှုတ်ခမ်းမွေး။ ...	hnoht-cun-moo-ay ...	moonchh, *f.* boo'root, *f.* ...	mísai.
Mus'ter, *s.* ...	ရုံးသည်။ ...	t'soo-yohn-the ...	jum'a'ut, (*pattern* num'oo'nu)	tiral, kúṭṭam, (máthiri).
Mus'ty, *a.* ...	အောက်သော။ ...	owk-thaw ...	sur'a, goom'sa ...	púsaṇam-piḍitta.
Mute, *a.* ...	အသော။ ...	ah-thaw ...	goong ...	pésátha, thoniyátha, úmai.
Mútiny, *s.* ...	ပုန်ကန်သည်။ ...	pohn-cun-the ...	dun'ga, fus'ad, sur'kush'ee, *f.*	paḍaichohévagar-kalagam.
Mut'ton, *s.* ...	သိုးသား။ ...	thoh-thah ...	bher-ka-gosht ...	áṭṭiṛaichi, áṭṭukkaṛi.
My, *poss. pron.* ...	ငါ၏။ ...	ngah-ee ...	me'ra, me'ro, mi'ra, me'ree, *f.*	en, enathu, ennuḍaiya.
Myrrh, *s.* ...	မရန်းဆေး။ ...	ma-yun-say ...	moor, bol ...	veḷḷaippóḷam, kantarasam.
Myself', *pron.* ...	ငါကိုယ်တိုင်။ ...	ngah-ko-duyng ...	myn-ap, myn'khood ...	nántán, náné, ennaiyé.
Mys'tery, *s.* ...	လက်မှုပညာ။ ...	leh-hmoo-pin-nyah ...	bhed, rumz, *f.* sirr ...	iragasiyam, maṛaivu. [gam.
Mythol'ogy, *s.* ...	နတ်ဘုရားပညာ။ ...	nut-pa-yah-pin-yah ...	tuw'a'reekh-jinn, *f.* ...	puráṇéthikásam, pauráṇi-
Na'bob, *s.* ...	အရာရှိ။ ...	a-yah-shee ...	nou'wab, *pl.* nu'wab ...	nabáppu, désáthipathi.
Nag, *s.* ...	မြင်းကလေး ...	myin-ga-lay ...	tut'too, gho'ra ...	maṭṭakkuthirai.
Nail, *s. of the hand.*	လက်သည်း။ ...	let-thee ...	na'khoon ...	nagam.
Nail, *s.* ...	သံ။ ...	thun ...	preg, mekh, *small* keel ...	áṇi.
Nákedness, *s.* ...	အချည်းစည်း။ ...	a-chyee-see ...	nung'a'ee, bur'uh'nu'gee, *f.* ...	tanimai, nirváṇam.
Name, *s.* ...	အမည်။ နာမ။ ...	ă-mee, nah-mah ...	nam, ism ...	peyar, námam, kírtti.
Námely, *adv.* ...	ဟူသော။ ...	hoo-thaw ...	ya'neh, ya'nee ...	athávathu, ennavenil.
Nap'kin, *s.* ...	လက်သုတ်ပဝါ။ ...	let-thoht-pă-wah ...	soof'ra ...	kaikkuṭṭai, oṛṛáḍai.
Nar'row, *a.* ...	ကျဉ်းသော။ ...	chyin-thaw, [thaw, ...	tung, suk'ra ...	oḍukkamána, agalamaṛṛa.
Násal, *a.* ...	နှာခေါင်းနှင့်ဆိုင်သော။ ...	hnă-kowng-hnin-tsuyng-	ghoon'nuh ...	násiyaippaṛṛiya.
Nas'tiness, *s.* Nas'ty, *a*	ညစ်ပတ်သော။ ...	nyit-put-thaw ...	nuj'a'sut, *f.* nuj'is ...	úḷal, kasumálam, úsina.
Nátion, *s.* ...	လူမျိုး။ ...	loo-myoh ...	koum, *f.* tub'ar ...	kulam, játhi, kóttiram.
Nátive, *s.* ...	မွေးဖွားသောနေရာ။ ...	moo-ay-pwah-thaw-nay-	wut'un'ee, des'ee ...	suthési, agathési.

Náture, *s.* ...	ကနာ္တတန်ဆာ။ ...	kub-bah-tă-sah, [yah, ...	khus'lut, *f.* zat, *f.* ...	iyarkai, subhávam, tattuvam
Nau'sea, *s.* ...	ပျို့တို့ထိုရှိခြင်း။ ...	pyoh-toh-doh-she-chyin ...	ghin, ur'oo'chi, *f.* ...	arukkalippu, uvattu. [na.
Nau'seous, *a.* ...	စက်ဆုပ်ရွံရှာဖွယ်ဖြစ်သော။ ...	set-soht-yohn-shah-bweh-pyit-thaw ...	ghin'ghin'a ...	arukkalippána, aruvaruppá-
Nau'tical, *a.* ...	ပင်လယ်နှင့်ဆိုင်သော။ ...	pin-leh-hnin-suyng-thaw ...	ju'haz'ee, buh'ree ...	marakkalattirkuriya.
Nável, *s.* ...	ချက်။ချက်မ။ချက်ကြိုး။ ...	chyet, chyet-mah, chyet-kyoh ...	naf, nabh, boom bee, *f.* ...	unthi, nábi.
Navigátion, *s.* ...	သင်္ဘောနှင့်ပင်လယ်လမ်းကိုကူးတတ်သောအတတ်။ ...	thin-baw-hnin-pin-leh-lun-goh'-koo-tut-thaw-a-tut ...	ju'haz-ra'nee, na'khoo'da'ee, *f.*	málumisástiram.
Nav'igator, *s.* ...	သင်္ဘောနှင့်ကူးတတ်သောသူ။ ...	thin-baw-hnin-koo-tut-thaw-thoo ...	kish'tee-ban ...	kappalótti, málumi. [tam-
Návy, *s.* ...	တိုက်သင်္ဘောစု။ ...	tuyk-thin-baw-soo ...	bu'hur ...	kapparsénai, pórkapparkút-
Nay, *adv.* ...	မဟုတ်။ ...	mă-hoht ...	na, na'heen ...	anri, alla, appadiyalla.
Near, *a.* ...	နီးသော။အနီး။ ...	nee-thaw, ă-nee ...	nuz'deek, nuzd ...	kittina, adutta.
Neat, *s.* ...	နွား။ ...	no-ah ...	ga'e, *f.* go'roo, *f.* byl, *m.* ...	pasu, pasukkúttam.
Neat, *a.* ...	စင်ကြယ်သော။ ...	tsin-kyeh-thaw ...	saf, pak, sooth'ra ...	nérttiyána, chirappána.
Nec'essary, *a.* ...	မချွတ်မလွဲဖြစ်ရသော။ ...	m'chyoht-m'loo-eh-pyit-yah-thaw ...	la'zim'ee ...	ávasiyakamána, véndiya.
Neces'sity, *s. poverty.*	အလှုံနှန်ဆင်းရဲခြင်း။ ...	ă-hlohn-tsin-yeh-chyin ...	if'las, ha'jut, zur'oo'rut, *f.* ...	tévai, ávasiyakam, varumai.
Neck, *s.* ...	လည်ပင်း။ ...	leh-bin ...	gul, gul'a, gur'dun *f.* ...	kaluttu, kandam.
Nec'tar, *s.* ...	ချိုသောသောက်ရည်။ ...	chyoh-thaw-thowk-yee ...	um'rit, um'ee, *f.* sood'ha ...	amirtham, tén, mathu.
Need, *s.* ...	အသုံးလိုသည်။ ...	a-thohn-loh-the ...	ha'jut, ih'ti'yaj, *f.* ...	véndiyathu, tévaiyánathu.
Nee'dle, *s.* ...	အပ်။ ...	ut [thaw, ...	soo'ee, sozun, *f.* ...	úsi, súsi.
Need'y, *a.* ...	သုံးဆောင်ရန်မရှိသော။ ...	thoh-sowng-yun-m'shee-	ha'jut-mund ...	tévaiyána, varumaiyulla.
Negátion, *s.* ...	မဟုတ်ဟုပြောထားခြင်း။ ...	m'hoht-hoc-pyaw-tah-chyin	in'kar, nut'un, *f.* ...	inmai, ethirmarai.
Neg'ative, *a.* ...	မှုကျမဖြစ်။ ...	mohk-chyah-ma-pyit ...	mun'fee ...	ethirmaraiyána, inmaiyána.
Neglect', *s.* ...	မပြုဘဲလွှတ်ထားသော။ ...	m'pyoo-beh-hlut-tah-thaw ...	gha'fil'ee, ghuf'lut, *f.* ...	achattai, parámukam.
Neigh, *s.* ...	ဟီသည်။ ...	hee-the ...	shee'hu ...	kanaippu, anumánitham.

English.	Burmese.		Hindustani.	Tamil.
Neigh'bour, *s.* ...	အိမ်နီးချင်း ...	ayn-nee-chyin ...	pur'o'see,pur'o'sin, *f.* ...	ayalán, piṛan, aḍuttavan.
Neigh'bourhood,*s.*...	ပတ်ဝန်းကျင် ...	put-woon-khyin ...	pur'os ...	ayal, samípam, arugámai.
Nei'ther, *conj.* ...	နှစ်ခုတွင်တခုမျှမဟုတ်သော ...	hnit-koo-dwin-t koo-	nu, na, nu'hin ..	alla, anṛu, iraṇḍumallátha.
Neph'ew, *s.* ...	တူ ...	too, [hmyah-ma-hoht-thaw.	bhut'ee'ja, bir'a'dur-za'du ...	marumakan.
Nerve, *s.* ...	အာရုံကြော ...	ah-yohn-kyaw ...	us'ub, rug, nus, *f.* ...	narambhu, táthu.
Nest, *s.* ...	အသိုက် ...	ă-thuyk ...	mus'kun, muk'an ...	kúḍu, uṛaiyiḍam.
Net, *s.* ...	ကွန် ...	kohn [m'hoht,...	jal, ja'la ...	valai, kaṇṇi, chikku.[millai.
Nev'er, *adv.* ...	အဘယ်ကာလမျှမဟုတ် ...	a-beh-kah-lah-hmyah-	kub'hoo-nu'heen, hur'giz ...	orukkálumillai, orupóthu-
Nevertheless', *adv.*..	သို့သော်လည်း ...	thoh-thaw-lee ...	tud'bhee, tis'pur, tou'bhee...	ánálum, áyinum, enṛálum.
New, *a.* ...	သစ်သော ...	thit-thaw ...	ny'a, nou ...	puthiya, nava, núthana.
News, *s.* ...	သိတင်းစကား ...	th'din-să-gah ...	khub'ur, *f.* sum'a'char ...	cheythi, saṅgathi, varttamá-
News'paper, *s.* ...	သိတင်းစာ ...	th'din-sah ...	khub'ur-ka'ghuz, ukh'bar ..	varttamánapattirikai.[nam.
Next, *a.* ...	အနားမှာရှိသော ...	ă-nah-hmah-she-thaw ...	nuz'deek'ka ...	aḍutta, ayaláṇa, maṛṛa.
Nib'ble, *v. a.* & *n.*...	တိကနဲ့ကိုက်သည် ...	tee-kă-neh-kuyt-the ...	toong'na, khoo'tuk'na ...	ari, kóthu, koṛi.
Nice, *a.* ...	ချောသော ...	chyaw-thaw ...	na'zook ...	nérttiyána, chiṛappána.
Niche, *s.* ...	လှိုင်ခေါင်း ...	hluyng-kowng ...	tak, tak-chu ...	kuḷáy, kuḍá. kugai, máḍam.
Nick'name, *s.* ...	ကြီစယ်၍ပေးသောနာမည် ...	kyee-seh-yu-eh-pay-thaw-	bud-luk'ub ...	vasai, vakkaṇai, ninthaippe-
Niece, *s.* ...	တူမ ...	too-mah, [nah-mee...	bhut'ee'jee ...	uḍanpiṛanthárputtari. [yar.
Nig'gard, *s.* ...	လူစေးနှဲ ...	loo-say-hneh ...	bu'kheel, kun'joos ...	ulóbi, pisunan, iḍukki.
Nigh, *a.* & *pr. adv.*...	နီးသော ...	nee-thaw ...	nuz'deek,(kur'eeb *adv.*) ...	kiṭṭa, aḍukka, ayaláy.
Night, *s.* ...	ည။ညည် ...	nyah, nyee ...	rat, rat'ree, shub, lyl, *f.* ...	iravu, irá, al.
Nim'ble, *a.* ...	ပေါ့ပါးလျှင်မြန်သော ...	paw-pah-lee-in-myun-thaw	cha'lak, cha'la [boor...	churukkáṇa, viraivuḷḷa.
Nip'pers, *s. pl.* ...	ညှပ် ...	hnyut ...	mooch'na, moo'chee'na, zum	iḍukki, chiṛukuṛaḍu.
Nip'ple, *s.* ...	နို့သီး ...	noh-thee ...	bhit'nee, choo'chee, *f.* ...	mulaikkaṇ, mulaikkámbu.
Nítre, *s.* ...	ဟင်းစိမ်း ...	hun-sayn ...	sho'ra, ju'wa-khar ...	veḍiyuppu, poṭṭiluppu.
No, *a.* or *adv.* ...	မဟုတ် ...	m'hoht ...	ne, na'hee, na'heen ...	illai,alla,anṛu,onṛumallátha.

Nobil'ity, *s.* ...	မြင့်မြတ်ခြင်း ...	myin-myut-chyin ...	shur'a'fut, shur'uf, *f.* ...	uyarkulam, mahattuvam.
Nóble, *a.* ...	မြင့်မြတ်သော ...	myin-myut-thaw ...	nuj'eeb, koo'leen oom'da ...	ménmaiyána, mémbáḍána.
Nobleman, *s.* ...	မှူးမတ် ...	moo-mut ...	um'eer, ush'ruf, oom'da ...	prabhu, perumán.
Nóbody, *s.* ...	အဘယ်သူမျှ ...	ă-beh-thoo-hmyah ...	ko'ee-nu'heen ...	oruvarumillai.
Nod, *s.* ...	ခေါင်းညိတ်သည် ...	gowng-nyait-the ...	jhoo ka'wut, sun'kar, *f.* ...	talaiyasaippu, sirakkambam
Noise, *s.* ...	အသံ ...	ă-thun ...	ghool, shor, kul'la ...	iraichchal, kúkkural.
Nois'y, *a.* ...	ညံသော ...	nyun-thaw [nah-mee-soo...	kul'la-kar ...	iraichchalána, amalaiyána.
Nómenclature, *s.* ...	ခေါ်ဝေါ်သမုတ်သောနာမည်စု	caw-waw-th'hmoht-thaw-	loo'ghut, *f.* ...	peyarvaliyagaráthi, nigaṇḍu
Nominátion, *s.* ...	သမုတ်ခြင်း ...	th'hmoht-chyin ...	tus'mee'yu ...	kuṛippu, peyarkkuṛippu.
Nom'inative, *s.* ...	ကတ္တား ...	kut-tah ...	fa'il, kur'ta ...	eḻuváy, peyarvéṛṛumai.
Nónage, *s.* ...	တရားမဝင်ရသေးသောအသက်အရွယ် ...	tă-yah-ma-win-yah-thay-thaw-a-thet-a-yoo-eh ...	na-ba'ligh'ee, *f.* ...	iḷavayasu, ilamparuvam.
None, *a.* ...	တခုမျှမရှိသော ...	t'koo-hmyah-m'shee-thaw...	khooch-nu'heen ...	oruvarumillátha onṛumillátha.
Non'sense, *s.* ...	အပြင်စကား ...	a-pyin-săgah ...	be-hoo'du'gee, *f.* ...	vínchol, viyarttam.
Noo'dle, *s.* ...	လူမိုက် ...	loo-muyt ...	sa'da-dil, un'ar'ee ...	múḍan, múrkkan.
Nook, *s.* ...	ထောင့်ကြား ...	downg-khyah ...	ko'na, kon, go'shu ...	múlai, kuḍá, iḍukku.
Noon, **Noon'day**, *s.*	မွန်းတည့် ...	moon-teh ...	do-pu'hur, do-puhur-din ...	maddhyánam, urumam.
Nor, *conj.* ...	လည်း ...	lee ...	nu ...	illai, alla.
North, *s.* ...	မြောက် ...	myowk ...	oot'tur, shim'al ...	vaḍakku, uttaram, vaḍa.
North-east', *s.* ...	အရှေ့မြောက် ...	a-shay-myowk ...	ee'san-kon ...	vaḍakiḻakku, ísánamúlai.
North'ward, *a.* ...	မြောက်မျက်နှာသို့ ...	myowk-myek-hnah-thoh ...	oot'tur-dig ...	vaḍakkáy, vaḍakké.
North-west', *s.* ...	အနောက်မြောက် ...	ă-nowk-myowk ...	ba'yub ...	vaḍamérku, váyumúlai.
Nose, *s.* ...	နှာခေါင်း ...	hnă-kowng ...	nak, bee'nee na'sa, *f.* ...	múkku, nási.
Nósegay, *s.* ...	ပန်းခိုင် ...	pun-kuyng ...	gool-dus'tu, phool-soongh'	chenḍu, púchchenḍu.
Not, *adv.* ...	မ (*as a prefix only*) ...	mă ...	na, ne, nu, nu'hin [nee, ...	illai, alla, inṛu.
Note, *s.* ...	မှတ်သားသည် ...	hmut-thah-the ...	yad-dasht, *f.* ...	kuṛi, aḍaiyáḷam.
Note, *s.* ...	သီချင်းသံ ...	thee-chyin-thun ...	rag ...	suram.
Not'ed, *a.* ...	ကျော်စောသော ...	kyaw-saw-thaw ...	mush'hoor ...	kuṛikkappaṭṭa, peyarpóna.

ENGLISH.	BURMESE.		HINDUSTANI.	TAMIL.
Noth'ing, s. ...	ဘာမျှမရှိ ...	bah-hmyah-m'shee ...	kooch-nu'heen ...	onṛumillai.
Nótice, s. ...	အမှုထားသည် ...	a-hmoo-tah-the ...	ni'gha, f. ...	nókkam, karuttáyppár.
Nótice, s. ...	ကြားပြောခြင်း ...	kyah-pyaw-chyin ...	khub'ur ...	aṛivi, aṛivittal, vilambharam.
Notification, s. ...	သိတင်းကြော်ညာစာ ...	thĕ-din-kyaw-nyah-sah ...	il'am, iz'har ...	kúṛugai, prasittam.
Nótify, v. a. ...	သိအောင်ပြောသည် ...	thee-owng-pyaw-the ...	iz'har-k ...	aṛivi, kúṛu, sáṛṛu.
Nótion, s. ...	အာရုံထင်ခြင်းစိတ်ထင်ခြင်း ...	ah-yohn-tin-chyin-sayt-tin-	fikr, khi'yal, [ur'chi, ...	eṇṇam, ninaivu.
Notwithstanding, v.	သို့သော်လည်း ...	thoh-thaw-lee, [chyin, ...	tud'bhee, tis'pur, go'ki, ug'	ágilum, enṛálum, allámalum.
Noun, s. ...	နာမ ...	nah-mah ...	ism, sung'ya, f. ...	peyar, peyarchchol.
Nour'ish, v. a. ...	ကျွေးမွေးသည် ...	kyoo-ay-moo-ay-the ...	pal'na, pur'wur'ish-k ...	póshi, úṭṭu, payiṛṛu.
Nour'ishment, s. ...	ထိုးပွါးအောင်ပြုစုခြင်း ...	toh-pwah-owng-pyoo-soo-	pur'wur'ish, f. ...	ágáram, bhójanam, uṇḍi.
Nov'el, a. ...	သစ်သော ...	thit-thaw, [chyin, ...	ny'a, nou, hadis ...	puthiya, puthu, navamána.
Nov'elty, s. ...	ထူးဆန်းသောအရာ ...	too-sun-thaw-ă-yah ...	ha'dis'u, huds, hoo'doos ...	núthanam, navasambhavam
Now, adv. ...	ယခု ...	yă-koo' ...	ub, ub'hee, fil'hal ...	ippoḷuthu, innéram.
Now'adays, adv. ...	ယခုကာလတွင် ...	yă-koo-kah-lah-dwin ...	aj-kul, indin'on ...	innáṭkaḷil, ikkálattil.
Nówhere, a. ...	ဘယ်ဆီမှာမရှိ ...	beh-see-hmah-m'shee, [yah..	ku'heen-nu'heen ...	óriḍattilumillai, eṅgumillai.
Nui'sance, s. ...	နှောင့်ရှက်တတ်သောအရာ ...	hnowng-shet-dut-thaw-a-	moo'zee'yu, f. ...	tollai, aluppu, alaṭṭu.
Numb, a. ...	ထုံသောထုံကျဉ်သော ...	toht-thaw ...	thit'hur'a ...	timirpiḍitta, maratta.
Num'ber, s. ...	ရေတွက်သည်နံပါတ် ...	yayt-twet-the, num-but ...	gin'tee, shoo'mar, shoo'maree	kaṇakku, ilakkam, eṇ.
Numerátion, s. ...	ရေတွက်ခြင်း ...	yay-twet-chyin ...	gun'it, f. ...	kaṇakkuppárkkai, eṇmánam
Númerous, a. ...	များပြားသော ...	myah-byah-thaw ...	bu'hoot, wa'fir ...	tiraḷána, vegu, anéka.
Nup'tials, s. pl. ...	လက်ထပ်မင်္ဂလာနှင့်ဆိုင်သော	let-tut-ming-ga-lah-hnin-suyng-thaw ...	ur'oo'see ...	viváhachchaḍaṅgu.
Nurse, v. ...	ထိန်းသည်နို့တိုက်သည် ...	tayn-the, noh-tuyk-the ...	a'ya, f. da'ee, da'ee-khil'a'ee, f.	táthi, kaittáy, áyál.
Nútriment, s. ...	အစာအဟာရ ...	a-sah-a-hah-yah ...	kha'na ...	uṇavu, bhójanam, ágáram.
Oak, s. wood ...	ဝက်သက်ချပင်းသစ် ...	wet-thet-chyah-bin, thit ...	bul'oot ...	karuválimaram.
Oar, s. ...	တက် ...	tet ...	dand, hul'es'a ...	tanḍukkaḷi, tuḍuppu.

Oath, *s.* ...	သစ္စာကျိန်း။ ...	thit-sah-chyun ...	kus'um, *f.* hul'if, hulf ...	áṇai, sattiyam.
Obédience, *s.* ...	နားထောင်ခြင်း။ ...	nah-towng-chyin ...	i'ta'ut, fur'man-bur'dar'ee...	kíḻppaḍivu, kíḻamaivu.
Obédient, *a.* ...	နားထောင်သော။ ...	nah-towng-thaw ...	fur'man-bur'dar ...	kíḻppaḍithaluḷḷa.
Obey, *v. a.* ...	နားထောင်သည်။ ...	nah-towng-the ...	man'na ...	kíḻppaḍi, amai, kéḷ.
Ob'ject, *s.* ...	အရာ။ ...	ă-yah, [khyowng...	muk'sud ...	eṇṇam, karuttu, poruḷ.
Objec'tion, *s.* ...	မနှစ်သက်စရာအကြောင်း။ ...	mă-nit-thet-să-yah-ă-	it'i'raz, gir'ift, *f.* ...	taḍai, átchébam.
Oblátion, *s.* ...	ပူဇော်သက္ကာ။ ...	poo-zaw-th'kah ...	ni'yaz, *f.* zubh ...	káṇikkai, pali.
Oblíge, *v. a.* ...	ကျေးဇူးပြုသည်။ ...	kyay-zoo-pyoo-the ...	ih'san-k ...	dayaichey, kaḍamaipaḍuttu.
Oblique', *a.* ...	ရှုဧသော။ ...	shoo-ay-thaw ...	a'ra, tir'chha, ter'ha ...	kóṇaláṇa, vaḷaintha.
Obliq'uity, *s.* ...	မှားယွင်းခြင်း။ ...	hmah-yoo-in-chyin ...	ter'ha'ee, *f.* ...	vaḷaivu, kóṇal.
Obliv'ion, *s.* ...	မေ့လျော့ခြင်း။ ...	may-lee-aw-chyin ...	nis'yan, muhv ...	marathi, nirchchinthanai.
Obscúre, *a.* ...	မှုန်သော။ ...	hmohn-thaw ...	ta'reek, tee'ru ...	teḷivarra, karugaláṇa.
Obstruc'tion, *s.* ...	အဆီးအတား။ ...	ă-tsee-a-tah ...	rok, rokun, ut'ka'o, *f.* ...	marippu, taḍai, iḍaiyúru.
Obtain', *v. a.* ...	ရသည်။ ...	yah-the ...	pa'na, ha'sil-k ...	koḷ, peṟu, aḍai.
Obtúse, *a.* ...	မချွန်းတုံးသော။ ...	m'chyohn, tohn-thaw ...	bhon'tha, koond ...	kúḻaiyáṇa, maḻukkáṇa.
Ob'vious, *a.* ...	ထင်ရှားသော။ ...	tin-shah-thaw ...	ma'loom ...	veḷiyáṇa, teḷiváṇa.
Occásion, *v. a.* ...	အကြိုးအကြောင်း။ ...	ă-khyo-ă-khyowng ...	dil'a'na, kur'a'na ...	uṇḍákku, ákku, varuvi.
Occur'rence, *s.* ...	ဖြစ်ခြင်း။ ...	pyit-chyin ...	ha'dis'u, it'ti'fak ...	káriyam, sambhavam.
O'cean, *s.* ...	သမုဒ္ဒရာ။ ...	thă-moht-tă-yah ...	dur'ya, sum'oodr, yum ...	áḻi, samudram.
Ode, *s.* ...	လင်္ကာသီခြင်းတမျိုး။ ...	lin-gah-thee-chyin-t'myoh..	ghuz'ul ...	vaṇṇam, sinthu.
O'dious, *a.* ...	မုန်းခြင်း။ ...	mohn-chyin ...	muk'rooh ...	aruvaruppáṇa.
O'dour, *s.* ...	အနံ့။ ...	ă-nun ...	boo, bas, *f.* ...	maṇam, vásanai, náṟṟam.
Of, *pr.* (*affix only*)...	၏။ (*affix only*) ...	ee, (*affix only*) ...	ka, ke, kee, (*affix only*) ...	uḍaiya, uriya, il, in, ál, kuṟittu
Off, *adv.* ...	ကာ။ ...	gah ...	door, doot, tuf'a'woot ...	appál, aṟa, vilagi, viṭṭu.
Off, *interj. begone*,...	သွားဟဲ့။ ...	thwah! heh! ...	chukh'e! hut! ...	pó, agal, oṟṟu.
Of'fer, *v. a.* ...	ပေးသည်။ ...	pay-the ...	urz-k ...	néridu, váy.
Of'fering, *s.* ...	ပူဇော်ခြင်း။ ...	poo-zaw-chyin, [yohn,...	nuzr, ni'yaz, *f.* ...	koḍai, káṇikkai.
Of'fice, *s.* ...	အရာ၊ပြုရသောဝတ်ရုန်း။ ...	ă-yah, pyoo-thaw-woot-	duf'tur-kha'nu ...	toḻil, vélai.

English.	Burmese.		Hindustani.	Tamil.
Of'ficer, *s.*	အရာရှိဗိုလ်။	a-yah-she-boh	mun'sub-dar	talaivan, athikári.
Off'spring, *s.*	သားသမီး။	thah, thum-mee	ou'lad, sun'tan	santathi, vittu, vamisam.
Oft, Oft'en, *adv.*	ခဏခဏ။	kă-nah-kă-nah	bar'ha, bar'bar, uk'sur	aḍikkaḍi, palamuṛaiyum.
Oh, *int.*	အို။အော်။	oh, aw	ya, !	á, aiyó, appá, ó.
Oil, *s.*	ဆီ။	tsee	tel, rou'ghun	eṇṇey, ney, tailam.
Oil'-mill(*or*)press, *s.*	ဆီစက်။	tsee-set	kol'hoo, gha'nee	álai, chekku.
Oil'y, *a.*	ဆီပါသော။	tsee-pah-thaw	chik'na, chik'kun, til'ha	eṇṇeypparṛána.
Oint'ment, *s.*	ဖယောင်းဆီ။	pă-yowng-see	til'a, lep, doohn	tailam, eṇṇey.
Old, *a.*	အိုသော။	oh-thaw	kooh'nu, poor'a'na, bhoor'ha	púrva, kiḻa, paḻamaiyána.
Old'-age, *a.*	အသက်ကြီးခြင်း။	ă-thet-kyee-chyin	boor'ha'pun, bood'dha'pun	múppu, viruttáppiyam.
Old'-man, *a.*	လူအို။	loo-oh	boor'ha, bood'dha	kiḻavan.
Old'-woman, *a.*	မည်းကြီးအို။	mee-gyee-oh	boor'hi'ya, bood'hee, *f.*	kiḻavi.
O'men, *s.*	တိတ်။နိမိတ်။	tayt, ne-mayt	shoo'goon, soo'gun	kuṛi, nimittam, sagunam.
Omis'sion, *s.*	ချထားခြင်း။	chyah-tah-chyin	bhool, koo'soor	viḍugai, oḻivu.
Omit', *v. a.*	ချထဲ့သည်။	chyah-teh-the	bhool'na, chhor'na	viḍu, oḻi, taḷḷiviḍu.
Omnip'otent, *a.*	အနန္တတန်ခိုးရှိသော။	ă-nun-dah-t'goh-she-thaw	jub'bar, ka'dir-i-moot'luk	sarvavallamaiyuḷḷa.
Omnis'cience, *s.*	သဗ္ဗညုတဉာဏ်။	thup-pin-nyoo-tah-nyahn	hum'u-dan'ee, ilm-i-ghyb	sarvaññánam.
On, *pr.*	အပေါ်မှာ။	ă-paw-hmah	oo'pur, pur, bur	mél, míthu.
On, *adv.*	ရှေ့သို့။	shay-thoh	a'ge, ul'a, oo'pur	uyara, dúra, mélé, appuṛam.
Once, *adv.*	တခါ။	t-kah	ba're, ek-bar, yuk-bar	orumuṛai, mun, orutharam.
One, *a.* & *s.*	တစ်။ ၁။	tit	ek, ik, yuk	onṛu, égam, orumai.
On'ion, *s.*	ကြက်သွန်။	khyet-thohn	pi'yaz, bus'ul, kun'da	veṇkáyam.
O'nly, *a.*	တခုတည်း။	tă-koo-dee	ek, ik'la, kha'lee, nir'a	oré, éga, tanimaiyána.
O'nly, *adv.*	သာ။	thah	fuk'ut, sirf, ke'wul	máttiram, taniyé. [viḻugai.
On'set, *s.*	တိုက်ခြင်း။	tuyk-chyin	hum'lu, hul'lu, wuh'lu	ethirppu, pagaivar-mél-
On'ward, *adv.*	ရှေ့သို့။	shay-thoh	ug'a'ree, a'ge	munné, munthi, appál.

English	Burmese	Pronunciation	Hindustani	Tamil
O'nyx, *s.* ...	မဟူရာ။ ...	m'hoo-yah ...	soo'le'ma'nee-put'hur, sung-	kóméthagam.
Open', *a.* ...	ပွင့်သော။ ...	pwin-thaw ...	khool la, [i-soo'le'ma'nee,...	veḷiyána.
O'penly, *adv.* ...	ထင်ရှားစွာ။ ...	tin-shah-swah ...	za'hir'a, za'hir'un ...	veḷiyáy, bahirangamáy.
Operátion, *s.* ...	ပြုလုပ်သည်။ ...	pyoo-loht-the ...	fi'ul, kar ...	kriyai, cheykai, toḻil.
Opin'ion, *s.* ...	စိတ်ထင်ခြင်း။ ...	sayt-tin-chyin ...	ki'yas, da'nist, sum'ujh ...	matham, eṇṇam, karuttu.
O'pium, *s.* ...	ဘိန်း။ ...	bayn ...	uf'eem, uf'yoon, up'heem ...	apini.
Oppónent, *s.* ...	ဆန့်ကျင်ဖက်။ ...	sun-kyin-bet, [pyit-thaw,...	moo'kha'lif ...	ethiri, ethiráḷi, pagaiñan.
Opportúne, *a.* ...	တော်သင့်သောအချိန်ဖြစ်သော။	taw-thin-thaw-a-chayn-	bur-wukt ...	nallavéḷai, tarchamayamána
Opportúnity, *s.* ...	အဆင့်သင့်သောအချိန်။ ...	ă-tsin-thin-thaw-ă-chayn...	da'o, goun, ka'boo ...	samayam, véḷai.
Oppóse, *v. a.* ...	ဆီးတားသည်။ ...	tsee-tah-the ...	moo'ka'bil'u-k ...	ethir, taḍu, viróthi.
Op'posite, *a.* ...	မျက်နှာချင်းဆိုင်။ ...	myet-hnah-chyin-suyng ...	sam'ne, moo'ka'bil ...	ethirána, munnána.
Oppress', *v. a.* ...	နှိပ်စက်သည်။ ...	hnayt-set-the ...	zoolm-k ...	nerukku, oḍukku, chey.
Oppres'sion, *s.* ...	နှိပ်စက်ခြင်း။ ...	hnayt-set-chyin ...	zoolm, zool'mee'yut ...	nerukkam, koḍumai.
Oppres'sor, *s.* ...	နှိပ်စက်သောသူ။ ...	hnayt-set-thaw-thoo ...	zoolm-shi'ar, dust'dur'az ...	kurúran, oḍukkuvón.
Oppróbrious, *a.* ...	အသရေဖျက်ပြုသောအမှု။ ...	ă-thă-ray-pyet-pyoo-thaw-ă-hmoo ...	ma'yoob ...	ninthaiyána, paḷippána.
Oppróbrium, *s. Lat.*	အသရေဖျက်ခြင်း။ ...	ă-thă-ray-pyet-chyin ..	roos'wa ...	paḷippu, ninthanai.
Op'tion, *s.* ...	ရွေးကောက်သောအခွင့်။ ...	yoo-ay-kowk-thaw-ă-kwin..	ikh'ti'yar ...	priyam, viruppam.
Op'ulent, *a.* ...	ဥစ္စာရတတ်သော။ ...	oht-sah-yah-dut-thaw ...	dou'lut-mund ...	chelvamána, válvuḷḷa.
Or, *conj.* ...	သို့မဟုတ်။ ...	thoh-mă-hoht ...	khwah, ky, ya ...	allathu, ágilum, engilum.
Or'acle, *s.* ...	ထူးဆန်းသောပညာ။ ...	too-zun-thaw-pin-nyah ..	a'kash-ban'ee, *f.* ...	devaviḍai, sannatham.
O'ral, *a.* ...	နှုတ်ထွက်စကား။ ...	hnoht-twet-să-gah ...	zub'an'ee, *f.* ...	váymoḻiyána, kéḷviyána.
Orang'-outang', *s.* ...	လူဝံ။ ...	loo-wun ..	bun-ma'noos ...	válillákkurangu.
Or'ange, *s.* ...	လိမ္မော်သီး။ ...	laym-maw-thee ...	kou'la, koun'la, na'runj ...	kichchili, nárttampaḻam.
Or'ator, *s.* ...	မြွက်ဆိုတတ်သောသူ။ ...	myoo-et-soh-dut-thaw-thoo.	khut'eeb, soo'khun'saz ...	sádhuryaván, váchálan.
Or'atory, *s.* ...	အစည်အတုံ့မြွက်ဆိုခြင်း။ ...	ă-tsee-ă-tuyug-myoo-et-soh-chyin,...	soo'khun-saz'ee ...	pirasangam. [paḍuttu.
Or'der, *v. a.* ...	အမိန့်။ ...	ă-mayn, ...	hookm-k, tum'heed-k ...	kaṭṭalaiyiḍu, évu, oḻungu-
Or'derly, *a.* ...	စီစည်သော။ကောင်းသော။ ...	tsee-tsee-thaw, kowng-thaw.	theek, ba-kai'da ...	oḻungána, kiramamána.

ENGLISH.	BURMESE.		HINDUSTANI.	TAMIL.
Or'dinance, *s.*	ဥပဒေ။	oo-bă-day	a'een, ud'a'lut, hoo'koo'mut	niyamam, muṛaimai, chaṭṭam.
Ord'nance, *s.*	အမြောက်စု။	ă-myowk-tsoo	top, *gujanl*	pírangi;perumpírangi.
Or'dure, *s.*	မစင်။	m'sin	bish'tha, gooh, gund, mul	malam, kashṭam.
Or'igin, *s.*	အစ။အဦး။	a-tsah, ă-oo	usl, oon'soor	áthi, múlam, toḍakkam.
Orig'inal, *a.*	အဦးဆုံးသော။	ă-oo-zohn-thaw	us'lee, oon'soo-ree	áthiyána, puráthana.
Or'nament, *s.*	တန်ဆာ။	t'zah,	sing'ar, a'ra'ish, zeb	siṅgáram, chiṛappu.
Ornamen'tal, *a.*	ဆင်တတ်သော တန်ဆား ဖြစ်သော။	tsin-tut-thaw-t'zah-pyit-thaw,	a'ra'ish'ee	chiṛappána, chittramána.
Or'phan, *s.*	မိသဆိုး။	mee-thă-soh	moor'ha, yut'eem	tanthai-táy-yillátha-piḷḷai.
Or'piment, *s.*	ဆေးဒန်း။	tsay-dun	hur'tal, zur'neekh	aritháram, ponnaritháram.
Or'thodox, *a.*	ဟုတ်မှန်သောအယူဝါဒကိုရုံသော	hoht-hmun-thaw-a-yoo-wah-dah-goh-yohn-thaw	ra'shid	véthanúlmuraiyána.
Osten'sible, *a.*	ထင်ရှားသော။	tin-shah-thaw	za'hir	káṭchiyána, tóṛṛamána.
Oth'er, *a.*	အခြား။	a-chyah	doos'ra, our, dee'gur, ghyr	maṛṛa, véṛu, maṛu.
Oth'erwise, *adv.*	အနည်းအခြား။	a-nee-a-chyah	nu'heen-to	maṛṛappaḍi, allávittál.
Our, Ours, *poss. pron.*	ကျွန်ုပ်တို့၏။	kyoon-hnoht-doh-ee	hum'a'ru	namathu, nammuḍaiya, eṅgaluḍaiya.
Out, *adv.*	အပြင်။	ă-pyin,	ba'hur, ba'hir	veḷiyé, puṛambé.
Out'cast, *s.*	နှင်ထုတ်ခြင်းကိုခံရသောသူ။	hnin-toht-chyin-go-cun-yah-thaw-thoo,	kha'rij'ee	pulaiñan, kíḻmagan.
Out'er, *a.*	ပြင်မှာရှိသည်။	pyin-hmah-she-thaw	ba'hir'ee	puṛambána, veḷiyána.
Outside, *s.*	အပြင်။	a-pyin	ba'hur, za'hir	veḷippuṛam, puṛambu.
Ov'en, *s.*	ပေါင်းဖို။	powng-poh	tun'door, tun'oor	aḍuppu, chuḍuchúḷai.
O'ver, *pr.*	လွန်သွားပြီ။	lohn-thwah-byee	oo'pur	mélé, míthu.
O'ver, *adv.*	တဖန်။	t'pun	o'se, par, pur, oo'pur	athikamáy, mélum, táṇḍi.
Overcome', *v. a.*	နိုင်သည်။	hnuyng-the	jeet'na, chit-k	mérkoḷḷu, veṛṛikoḷḷu.
O'verplus, *s.*	အပိုအမို။	ă-poh-ă-moh	ba'kee, zi'ya'du	mélmichcham, sochcham.
Overseer', *s.*	အကြီးအကြပ်။	a-kyee-a-kyut	ni'gah-ban, sur'kob	álóṭṭi, óvarsíru.
Overthrow', *v. a.*	မှောက်လှန်သည်။	hmowk-hlun-the	gir'a'na	kaviḻ, aḻi, nirmúlamákku.

Overturn', *v. a.*	လှည့်သည်။	hlee-the	ool'ta'na, oo'lut'na	aḻi, méṛkoḻḻu, kaviḻ.
Own, *a.*	ပိုင်သည်။	puyng-the	up'na, up'nee, *f.* nij, nij'ka..	tan, sontha, uriya.
Own'er, *s.*	အရှင်ပိုင်သောသူ။	ă-shin-puyng-thaw-thoo	ma'lik, wa'ris, dhun'ee	uḍaiyavan, sonthakkáran.
Ox, *s.* (*pl.* Oxen)	နွားသင်း။	no-ah-thin	byl, go'roo, *m. f.*	eruthu, iḍabam, rishabam.
Oys'ter, *s.*	ကနုကမံ။	kă-noo-kă-mun	kus'too'ra, *f.*	maṭṭi, chippi.
Pace, *s.*	လှမ်းသွားသည်။	hlun-thwah-the	kud'um	naḍai, kathi, pókku.
Pack'age, *s.*	အထုပ်။	ă-htoht	gut'hur, gut'tha, moth	kaṭṭu, chumai, sippam.
Pad'dy, *s.*	စပါး။	să-bah'	dhan	nellu.
Pagóda, *s.*	စေတီ။	zay-dee	dev-sthan, boot-kha'nu	kóvil, dévastánam.
Pain, *s.*	နာခြင်း။	nah-chyin, [thaw,	durd, dookh, ee'za	nó, varuttam.
Pains'taking, *s.*	လုလ္လဝီရိယထုတ်သော။	lohl-lah-wee-ree-yah-toht-	mih'nut'ee	uḷaippu, piṛayásam.
Paint, *s.*	သုတ်ရန်ဆေး။	thoht-yun-tsay	rung	mai, varṇam, niṛam.
Paint'er, *s.*	ဆေးသုတ်သောသူ။	say-thoht-thaw-thoo	rung-saz, chitr-gur	varṇakkáran, chittrakkáran
Pal'ace, *s.*	နန်းတော်။	nun-daw	dou'lut-kha'nu	máligai, araṇmanai.
Palanquin', *s.*	ပါလာရထား။	pă-lah-yit-tah	pal'kee	pallákku, chivigai.
Pantaloon', *s. In pl.*	ပေါင်းဘီ။	bowng-bee	paja'mu, shil'war, sur'wal	kárchaṭṭai.
Papa', *s.*	အဘ။ဖခင်။	ă-pah, pah-khin	ba'ba	appá, pithá.
Páper, *s.*	စက္ကူ။	sek-koo	ka'ghuz	kákitham, kaḍithási.
Par'able, *s.*	ပုံဥပမာ။	pohn-oo-pă-mah	tum'seel, drish'tant, mis'al	uvamai, oppanai.
Par'adise, *s.*	သုခသက်သက်ရှိသောအရပ်။	thoo-kah-thet-thet-she-	fir'dous, jun'nut, bi'hisht	mótcham, parathisu. [gi, *f.*).
Par'amour, *s.*	ရည်းစား။	yee-sah, [thaw-a-yut,	yar, lug'oo'a	kaḷḷappurushan, (chóranáya-
Par'aphrase, *s.*	ထိုသို့ပွင့်ပြသောအချက်။	toh-thoh-pwin-pyah-thaw-	tuf'seel, *f.*	viritturai, payanchollu.
Par'cel, *s.*	အထုပ်ကလေး။	ă-toht-gă-lay, [a-chyet,	gut'hee, gut'i'ya, mot'ree	chumai, múṭṭai, sippam.
Párent, *s.*	မိဘ။	mee-bah	bap, ba'ba, ma, ma'ta	tanthai, táy.
Part, *s.* Portion,	ပိုင်းသည်။ခွဲသည်။	puyng-the, kweh-the	his'su, bhag	paṅgu, págam, kúṛu.
Part'ner, *s.*	လုပ်ဖော်။ဆောင်ဖက်။	loht-paw, sowng-pet	shur'eek, saj'hee	kúṭṭáḷi, paṅgáḷi, tóḻan.
Pas'senger, *s.*	ခရီးသွားသောသူ။	kă-yee-thwah-thaw-thoo	moo'sa'fir, chur'hun-dar	payaṇakkáran, prayáṇi.
Paste, *s.*	မှုန့်ညက်ကော်။	mohn-nyet-kaw	le'yee, mar'nee	pasai, oṭṭu, pisin.

English.	Burmese.		Hindustani.	Tamil.
Pay, *v.* ...	ပေး။ ...	pay ...	de'na, (*wages*, tul'ub, muz'-	koḍu, aḷi, (sambaḷam, kúli).
Peace, *s.* ...	ငြိမ်းခြင်း။ ...	nyain-chyin ...	soolh, sul'ah, leem,[doo'ree,).	sántham, samáthánam.
Pea'cock, *s.* ...	ဥဒေါင်း။ ...	oo-downg ...	mor, moor'ha, moor'la ...	mayil, mayúram.
Pen, *s.* ...	မှင်တံ။ ...	hmin-dun ...	kul'um, likh'nee ...	ilékaṇi, péna.
Pen'cil, *s.* ...	ခဲတံ။ ...	keh-dun ...	kul'um, see'sa-kul'um ...	eḻuthukól, pensal.
Pen'sion, *s.* ...	အငြိမ်းစား။ ...	a-ngyain-sah ...	wuj'ha, bund'han ...	upakárachchambaḷam.
Pen'sioner, *s.* ...	အငြိမ်းစားသောသူ။ ...	ngyain-sah-thaw-thoo ...	bund'han'ee, wuz'ee'fu-dar..	upakárachchambaḷakkáran.
Peo'ple, *s.* ...	လူများ။ ...	loo-myah ...	ad'mee, log, lok ...	janam,prajaigal,kuḍijanam.
Pep'per, *s.* ...	ငရုတ်ကောင်း။ ...	ngă-yoht-kowng ...	mirch, gol-mirch ...	miḷagu.
Perhaps, *adv.* ...	ဖြစ်ကောင်းဖြစ်လိမ့်မည်။ ...	pyit-kowng-pyit-laym-mee.	sha'yud, sha'id ...	oruvéḷai, silavéḷai.[maiyána.
Per'manent, *a.* ...	မြဲသော။ ...	myeh-thaw ...	pae'dar, sa'bit ...	asaiyátha, márátha, nilai-
Permis'sion, *s.* ...	အခွင့်။ ...	ă-kwin ...	ij'a'zut, rookh'sut ...	viḍai, anumathi, uttaravu.
Petit'ion, *s.* ...	လျှောက်လွှာ။ ...	showk-hloo-ah ...	dur'khwast, ni'yaz ...	manu, viṇṇappam.
Petit'ioner, *s.* ...	လျှောက်သောသူ။ ...	showk-thaw-thoo ...	ni'ya'zee ...	manukoḍuppón.
Pet'ticoat, *s.* ...	ထမိန်။ ...	t'-mayn ...	ghun'gher'a, sa'ya, luhn'ga.	páváḍai, peṇgaḷáḍai.
Phrase, *s.* ...	ခေါ်ဝေါ်သည်။ ...	caw-waw-the ...	ib'a'rut, is'til'ah ...	toḍarmoḻi, vachanam.
Pic'ture, *s.* ...	ရုပ်ပုံ။ ...	yoht-pohn ...	tus'weer, nuksh, chitr ...	paḍam, chittrappaḍam.
Piece, *s.* ...	အစကလေး။ ...	ă-tsah-ga-lay ...	took'ra, took'ree ...	tuṇḍu. kaṇḍam, chinnam.
Pig'eon, *s.* ...	ခို။ ...	koh ...	kub'oo'tur, kup'ot ...	puṛá. kabhótham.
Pill, *s.* ...	ဆေးလုံး။ ...	say-lohn ...	go'lee ...	máttirai, kuḷikai.
Pil'low, *s.* ...	ခေါင်းအုံး။ ...	gowng-ohn ...	tuk'i'ya, bal'ish ...	talaiyaṇai, ubáthánam.
Pilot, *s.* ...	ရေကြောင်းမာလိန်။ ...	yay-gyowng-mah-layn ...	ur'ka'tee ...	kappalóṭṭi,áṛukáṭṭi,málumi.
Pious, *a.* ...	ဘုရားကိုရိုသေသော။ ...	pă-yah-go-yoh-thay-thaw...	deen-dar, khoo'dapur'ust ..	dévabattiyuḷḷa.
Pit, *s.* ...	တွင်း။ ...	dwin ...	ghar, gar'a, gur'ha ...	kuḻi, turavu, paḷḷam.
Pit'y, *s.* ...	သနားခြင်း။ ...	th'nah'-chyin ...	dy'a, durd, ruhm ...	irakkam, urukkam.
Place, *s.* ...	အရပ်။ ...	ă-yut ...	jug'uh ..	iḍam, stalam, stánam, nilai.

Plain, *s.*	... ညီညာသော။	... nyee-nyah-thaw	... my'dan	... veḷi, maithánam, samabhú-mi.
Plaintiff, *s.*	... တရားလို။	... t'rah-loh	... fur'ya'dee, mood'dy, *m. f.*	... váthi, vaḻakkáḷi.
Plan, *s.*	... ပုံထုတ်ခြင်း။	... pohn-toht-chyin	... nuk'shu, kha,ka, tus'weed	... oḷuṅgu, paḍam, chaṭṭam.
Plant, *s.*	... အပင်။	... ă-pin	... nub'at, bir'wa, per	... payir, náṟṟu, púṇḍu, cheḍi.
Plan'tain, *s.*	... ငှက်ပျောသီး။	... hngek-pyaw-thee	... ke'la, mouz	... váḻai, kathali.
Play, *s.*	... ကစားခြင်း။	... kah-sah-chyin	... khel	... viḷaiyáṭṭu, áṭṭam, vinótham.
Pleas'ure, *s.*	... ပျော်မွေ့ခြင်း။	... pyaw-mway-chyin	... khoo'shee, *f.*	... inbam, santhósham.
Plen'ty, *s.*	... ပေါများခြင်း။	... paw-myah-chyin	... bu'hoo'tat, fur'a'khee	... púraṇam, éráḷam, miguthi.
Plough, *s.*	... ထယ်။	... teh	... hul, hur, na'gul, kool'bu	... kalappai, ér, uḻupaḍai.
Pock'et, *s.*	... အိတ်။	... ait	... jeb, khee'sa	... chaṭṭaippai, aṅgiyuṟai, pai.
Póem, *s.*	... လင်္ကာတစောင်။	... lin-gah-t'sowng	... kub'it'a, mus'nu'wee	... páṭṭu, kavi, prabantham.
Póet, *s.*	... လင်္ကာဆရာ။	... lin-gah-say-yah	... sha'ir, nuz'mee	... pulavan, kaviráyan.
Póny, *s.*	... မြင်းငယ်။	... myin-ngeh	... tut'too, ya'boo, tan'ghun	... maṭṭam, maṭṭakkuthirai.
Poor, *a.*	... ဆင်းရဲသော။	... tsin-yeh-thaw	... ghur'eeb, kun'gal	... eḷiya, éḻaiyána.
Populátion, *s.*	... ပြည်သူပြည်သား။	... pyee-thoo-pyee-thah	... a'ba'dee, a'ba'da'nee, bustee.	kuḍijanam, janam, pirajai.
Pork, *s.*	... ဝက်သား။	... wet-thah	... soo'ur-ka-gosht	... panṟiyiṟaichchi.
Por'tion, *s.*	... အပိုင်း။	... ă-puyng	... his'su, bhag	... paṅgu, kúṟu, bágam.
Post, *s.*	... တိုင်။	... tuyng	... dak, tup'pal	... tabál, añjal.
Potáto, *s.*	... မျောက်ဥ။	... myowk-oo	... a'loo	... uruḷaikkiḻaṅgu.
Pow'er, *s.*	... တန်ခိုး။	... t'goh	... kood'rut	... vallamai, balam, tiráṇi.
Praise, *v. s.*	... ချီးမွမ်းသည်။	... chyee-mohn-thee	... sun'a, tu'a'reef, sur'ah	... tuthi, tóttiram, pugaḻchchi.
Pray, *v. a.*	... ဆုတောင်းသည်။	... soo-towng-the	... num'az-k, doo'a'kur'nee	... véṇḍuthalchey.
Pray'er, *s.*	... ပဌနာစာ။	... put-ta-nah-sah	... num'az, doo'a	... vinṇappam, pirárttanai.
Preach, *v. a.*	... တရားဟောသည်။	... tă-yah-haw-the	... waz'kuh'na	... pirasaṅgi, póthi.
Preach'er, *s.*	... တရားဟောဆရာ။	... tă-yah-haw-tsay-yah	... wa'iz, khut'eeb	... póthagan, pirasaṅgi.
Prepáre, *v. a.*	... ပြင်ဆင်သည်။	... pyin-sin-the	... ty'ar-k	... áyattampaṇṇu.
Pres'ent, *s.*	... လက်ဆောင်။	... let-sowng	... dan, in'am, dad	... ígai, vegumathi.
Pres'ent, *a.*	... ပါရှိသော၊ယခု။	... pah-she-thaw, yă-koo	... ha'zir, mou'jood	... irukkiṟa, nikaḻugiṟa.

English.	Burmese.		Hindustani.	Tamil.
Price, *s.* ...	အဘိုး။ ...	ă-poh ...	mol, kee'mut ...	vilai, kirayam.
Priest, *s.* ...	မွေဆရာ၊ဘုန်းကြီး။ ...	dum-mah-tsay-yah, hpoon-	berahmun, pad'ree ...	guru, ácháriyan, prógithan.
Prince, *s.* ...	မင်းသား။ ...	min-thah, [gyee,...	rajes'wur, pruj'a-put'i ...	arasan, rájakumáran.
Princess', *s.* ...	မင်းသမီး။ ...	min-thum-mee ...	ranee, raj-kun'ya ...	rájakumáratti, rájátti.
Print, *s.* ...	ပုံနှိပ်သည်။ ...	pohn-hnayt-the ...	chhap, chha'pa ...	achchu, muttirai, chuvaḍu.
Print'er, *s.* ...	ပုံနှိပ်သောသူ။ ...	pohn-hnayt-thaw-thoo ...	chha'pewa'la ...	achchaḍikkiṛavan.
Pris'on, *s.* ...	ထောင်။ ...	htowng ...	kyd- *or* bund-(kha'nu) ...	kával, chiṛaichchálai.
Pris'oner, *s.* ...	ထောင်သား။ ...	htowng-thah ...	kyd'ee, bun'dee ...	kaithi, kávaliliruppavan.
Priv'y, *s.* ...	ရေအိမ်။ ...	yay-ayn ...	pa'e-kha'nu, tut'tee ...	veḷivíḍu, kakkúsu, pruváthi.
Prof'it, *s.* ...	အမြတ်။ ...	a-myut ...	faï'du, ha'sil, labh ...	átháyam, ilábam.
Prom'ise, *s.* ...	ဂတိထားခြင်း။ ...	gă-dee-tah-chyin ...	buch'un, ik'rar, koul ...	vákkuttattam,pirathikkinai.
Promótion, *s.* ...	ရာထူးတိုးခြင်း။ ...	yah-too-toh-chyin ...	bur'ha'o, sur'uf'raz'ee ...	uyarchchi, virutti.
Pronounce', *v. a.* ...	မြွက်ဆိုသည်။ ...	myoo-et-tsoh-the ...	tul'uf'fooz-k, ooch'char'na...	uchchari, chollu, oli.
Pronunciátion, *s.*...	အက္ခရာကျအောင်ဆိုသည်။ ...	ek-ka-yah-chyah-owng-soh-	tul'uf'fooz, ooch'char ...	uchcharippu, uchcháraṇam.
Prop'er, *a.* ...	တော်လျော်သော။ ...	taw-lee-aw-thaw, [the...	laik, moo'na'sib ...	muṛaimaiyána, sariyána.
Proph'et, *s.* ...	ပရောဖက်။ ...	pă-yaw-bet ...	nub'ee, py'ghum'bur ...	tírkkatarisi,munnaṛivippón.
Propríetor, *s.* ...	ပိုင်သောသူ။ ...	hpuyng-thaw-thoo ...	ma'lik, dhun'ee ...	esamánan, áṭchikkáran.
Pros'ody, *s.* ...	လင်္ကာစပ်နည်း။ ...	lin-gah-sut-nee ...	ilm-i-ur'ooz, mee'zan ...	yáppilakkaṇam.
Protec'tion, *s.* ...	ကွယ်ကာစောင့်မခြင်း။ ...	kweh-kah-sowng-mah-chyin	him'a'yut, buch'a'o, *f.* ...	káppu, kával, iraṭchai.
Proud, *a.* ...	မာနထောင်လွှားသော။ ...	mah-nah-towng-hloo-ah-	hun'ka'ree, dum'agh'ee ...	perumaiyuḷḷa,méṭṭimaiyána
Prov'erb, *s.* ...	သုတ္တံစကားပုံ။ ...	thoht-tun-s'gah-pohn[thaw.	mus'ul, zurb'ool'mus'ul ...	paḷamoḷi, níthimoḷi.
Prov'ince, *s.* ...	ကျေးလက်၊ပြည်ငယ်။ ...	kyay-let, pyee-ngeh ...	di'yar, khundh, soo'ba ...	náḍu, mákáṇam.
Publicátion, *s.* ...	လူများကြည့်ဘို့ပုံရိုက်သောစာ။	loo-myah-kyee-boh-pohn-yuyk-thaw-sah ...	ish'ti'har, phy'la'o ...	pirasuram, pirachittam.
Pub'lish, *v. a.* ...	ကျော်ညာသည်။ ...	kyaw-nyah-the ...	ish'ti'har-k, za'hir-k ...	aṛivi, pirachittampaṇṇu.
Pull, *s.* ...	ဆွဲသည်။ ...	tsweh-the ...	kynch, jhut'ka, khich'a'o ...	iḻu, vali.

Pulse, *s.* ...	သွေးထိုးခြင်း။ ...	thway-toh-chyin ...	nubz, na'ree ...	táthu, náḍittuḍippu.
Punc'tual, *a.* ...	အချိန်မလွဲ။ ...	ă-chayn-m'-lweh ...	wa'du-wuf'a ...	tavaṛátha, nérantappátha.
Pun'ishment, *s.* ...	ဒါဏ်။ ...	dahn ...	suz'a, si'ya'sut, ta'zeer, *f.* ...	taṇḍippu, taṇḍanai.
Púpil, *s.* (*of the eye*).	မျက်ဆန်။ ...	myet-sun ...	poot'lee, rut'un, kak ...	kaṇmaṇi.
Púpil, *s. scholar,* ...	တပည့်။ ...	t'-byee ...	sha'gird ...	mánákkan, síshan.
Pur'chase, *s.* ...	ဝယ်သောအရာ။ ...	weh-thaw-a-yah ...	khur'eed'ar'ee, mol-tol ...	koḷvilai, koṇḍaporuḷ.
Purge, *s.* ...	ရှင်းလင်းစေသည်။ ...	shin-lin-say-the ...	jool'lab ...	bhéthimarunthu.
Pur'pose, *s.* ...	အကျိုးအကြောင်း။ ...	ă-kyoh-a-kyowng ...	ir'a'da, ir'a'dut, *f.* ...	karuttu, eṇṇam, abhiprá-
Push, *s.* ...	တွန်းသည်။ ...	toon-the ...	dhuk'el, pel ...	taḷḷu, iḍi. [yam.
Put, *v. a.* ...	ထည့်သည်။ ...	tee-the ...	rukh'na, rukh-d, dhur'na ...	vai, póḍu, iḍu.
Quad'rangle, *s.* ...	လေးထောင့်ပုံ။ ...	lay-downg-pohn ...	moor'ub'bu, chargo'shu ...	nárkóṇam, sathurkkóṇam.
Quar'rel, *s.* ...	ရန်တွေ့သည်။ ...	yun-tway-the ...	jhug'ra, kuz'i'ya, big'ar ...	váthu, chaṇḍai, kalagam.
Quar'ter, *s.* ...	လေးစိတ်တွင်တစိတ်။ ...	lay-sayt-dwin-t'sait ...	pa'o, pou'wa, chouth, *f.* ...	kál, nálilonṛu.
Queen, *s.* ...	မိဖုရား၊ ရှင်ဘုရင်မ။ ...	mee-bu-yah, shim-bu-yin-	be'gum, ra'nee, dev'ee, put-	iráṇi, paṭṭathévi, irákkini.
Quéry, *s.* ...	မေးမြန်း။ ...	may-myun, [mah, ...	su'wal, is'tif-ham, [ra'nee, ...	viná, kéḷvi, aiyaviná.
Ques'tion, *s.* ...	အမေး။ ...	a-may ...	su'wal, is'tif'sar ...	viná, tharkkam, kéḷvi.
Quick, *a.* ...	လျင်မြန်သော။ ...	lee-in-myun-thaw ...	juld, jhut, shit'ab, tez ...	viraiváṇa, turithamána.
Quick'sand, *s.* ...	ကျွံတတ်သောသဲသောင်။ ...	kyoon-tut-thaw-theh-	chor-ba'loo, reg-i-ru'wan ...	kurumaṇal, túvumaṇal.
Quick'silver, *s.* ...	ပြဒါး။ ...	pa-dah', [thowng, ...	pa'ra, zee'buk, ab-i-nook'ru.	irasam, pátharasam.
Quíet, *a.* ...	ငြိမ်းသော။ ...	ngyain-thaw ...	a'soo'du'gee, a'sa'ish, *f.* ...	amaithiyána, sánthamána.
Quill, *s.* ...	အတောင်။ ...	a-towng ...	pur ...	iṛagu, kuruttu.
Quit, *a.* ...	ထွက်သွားသည်။ ...	twet-thwah-the ...	chhor'na, ty'ag'na ...	tír, viḍu, turattu.
Quóta, *s.* ...	အငန်းအတား။ ...	a-ngun-a-tah ...	buh'ru, bih'ree, *f.* ...	paguthi, págam, paṅgu.
Quotátion, *s.* ...	နှုတ်ထုတ်သောအချက်။ ...	hnoht-toht-thaw-a-chyet ...	ik'ti'bas ...	utháraṇam, eḍuttukkáṭṭu.
Quote, *v. a.* ...	သူတပါး စကားကို နှုတ်ထုတ် သက်သေပြသည်။ ...	thoo-ta-bah-s'gah-goh- hnoht-toht-thet-thay-	ik'ti'bas-k ...	eḍuttuchchollu, eḍuttuk- káṭṭu.
Rab'bit, *s.* ...	ယုန်။ ...	yohn, [pyah-the, ...	khur'gosh, khur'ha, ur'nub..	veḷḷaimuyal, símaimuyal.
Rab'ble, *s.* ...	လူရှုပ်။ ...	loo-zoo ...	bheer, hoo'joom, um'boh ...	kaláthikárar, santhaḍikárar.

English.	Burmese.		Hindustani.	Tamil.
Rad'ish, *s.* ...	မုန်လာ။ ...	mohn-lah ...	moo'lee, *f.* foo'jool, toorb ...	mullangi.
Raft, *s.* ...	ဖောင်။ ...	powng ...	be'ra, oo'rup, tap'a ...	ódam, kattumaram, teppam.
Rage, *s.* ...	ပြင်းစွာအမျက်ထွက်သည်။ ...	pyin-swah-a-myet-twet-the.	ghoos'su, ghuz'ub, khushm..	ugram, múrkkam, kurótham.
Rain, *s.* ...	မိုဃ်းရွာသည်။ ...	moh-yoo-ah-the ...	menh, bur'us, bur'us'ta ...	malai, mári.
Rain'bow, *s.* ...	သက်တံ့။ ...	thet-tun ...	kous-i-koo'zu, bo'ro ...	vánvil, inthiravil.
Rank, *s.* ...	မြင့်မြတ်သော။ ...	myin-myut-thaw ...	mur'tub'a, jah, roo'dar'ee, *f.*	vagai, anthastu, vaguppu.
Rap'id, *a.* ...	မြန်သော။ ...	myun-thaw ...	juld, tez, tur'kha, jul'dee ...	viraivána, vékamána.
Ras'cal, *s.* ...	လူဆိုး။ ...	loo-soh ...	hur'am'za'du, hur'um-za'du.	kallan, chandálan, páthagan.
Rat, *s.* ...	ကြွက်။ ...	kyoo-et ...	moos'ra, muchh'un'dur, in'-	eli, múshigam.
Ratan', *s.* ...	ကြိမ်။ ...	chyain ...	bet, bed, *f.* [door,...	pirambu, véttiram.
Rate, *s.* ...	အဘိုး။ ...	a-poh ...	mol, kee'mut, dur, bha'o ...	vilai, vigitham.
Rath'er, *adv.* ...	သာ၍။ ...	thah-yoo-eh ...	a'ge, puh'le, puh'la ...	sarru, il, párkkilum.
Ráven, *s.* ...	ကျီးအ။ ...	kyee-ah ...	jung'lee-kou'wa, dhur-kou'-	andankákkáy, nírkkágam.
Read, *v. a.* ...	ဖတ်သည်။ ...	put-the ...	purh'na, syr-k [wa...	vási. padi.
Read'y, *a.* ...	အသင့်ရှိသော။ ...	a-thin-she-thaw ...	ty'ar, ha'zir ...	áyttamána, ettanamána.
Réally, *adv.* ...	ကေန်အမှန်။ ...	ay-cun-ă-hmun ...	huk'ee'kut'un, such, nis'chy.	ullapadi, unmaiyáy.
Rear, *s.* ...	နောက်ပေ။ ...	nôwk-pay ...	pich'ha'ree, peech'ha ...	pin. pinpuram, pinpakkam.
Reas'on, *s.* ...	အကြောင်း။ ...	a-kyowng ...	ukl, id'rak, sub'ub, was'tu...	yutti, mathi, mukántharam.
Receipt', *s.* ...	ခံယူခြင်း။ ...	cun-yoo-gyin ...	rus'eed, kubz-ool-wus'ool, *f.*	parruchchíttu, kaipparru.
Receive', *v. a.* ...	ခံယူ။ ...	cun-yoo ...	le'na, le-le'na ...	érrukkol, oppukkol, kaikkol.
Recommendátion, *s.*	လက်မှတ်။ ...	let-hmut ...	sif'a'rish, tak'reeb, *f.* ...	sipárisu. [paduttu.
Rec'oncile, *v. a.* ...	သင့်သင့်တင့်တင့်ဖြစ်စေသည်။ ...	thin-thin-tin-tin-pyit-say-	mil'a'na, bun'a'na ...	uravákku, samáthánap-
Recov'er, *v. a.* ...	ပြန်ရသည်။ ...	pyun-yah-the, [the,...	pher-pa'na ...	tirumba-adai, kandadai.
Red, *a.* ...	နီ။ ...	nee ...	lal, soorkh, *pers.* uh'mur, *arab.*	chivappána, chivantha.
Redeem', *v. a.* ...	ရွေးနှုတ်သည်။ ...	yoo-ay-hnoht-the ...	khul'as-k ...	mīl, iratchi, ídérru.
Redúce, *v. a.* ...	ရှုတ်ချသည်။ ...	shoht-chyah-the ...	ghut'a'na, ...	kurai, odukku, surukku.

Refer', *v. a.* ...	ဆိုင်သည်။ ...	suyng-the ...	roo'joo-k ...	kuṛi, oppuvi, chuṭṭu.
Reform', *s.* ...	အသစ်ပြုဖျင်သည်။ ...	ă-thit-pyoo-byin-the ...	doo-'roost ...	tiruttam, chírttiruttam.
Refresh', *v. a.* ...	အားဖြည့်အောင်ပြုသည်။ ...	ah-pyee-owng-pyoo-the ...	ta'zu-k ...	iḷaippáṛṛu, kuḷirappaṇṇu.
Refúse, *v. a.* ...	ငြင်းသည်။ ...	ngyin-the ...	in'kar-k ...	allattaṭṭu, maṛu, taḍuttuch-
Reg'ular, *a.* ...	နည်းဥပဒေအတိုင်း။ ...	nee-oo-pă-day-ă-tuyng ...	theek, ba-kai'du ...	oḻuṅgána, kirama. [chollu.
Regulátion, *s.* ...	ဥပဒေ။ ...	oo pă-day ...	dus'toor,bund-o-bust,tur'eek	oḻuṅgu, chaṭṭam.
Reign, *s.* ...	စိုးစံသည်။ ...	soh-sun-the ...	bad-sha'hee, sha'hee, raj, *f.*	rájarikam, áḷugai.
Rejoice', *v. a.* ...	ဝမ်းမြောက်သည်။ ...	wun-myowk-the ...	bi'hur'na ...	santhóshippi,kaḷikkachchey
Relátion, *s.* ...	ဆွေမျိုး။ပေါက်ဖော်။ ...	sway-myo, powk-paw ...	tuk'reer, by'an, nis'but ...	uṛavu, inam, urimai.
Release', *s.* ...	လွှတ်သည်။ ...	hloot-the ...	khul'as,khul'a'see,chhoot'tee	viḍuthalai, míṭppu, kaḻivu.
Relig'ion, *s.* ...	ဘာသာ။ ...	bah-thah ...	deen, muz'hub, tur'eek ...	matham, márkkam.
Remain', *s.* ...	နေသည်။ ...	nay-the ...	ruh'na, tik'na ...	nilai, tari.
Remark'able, *a.* ...	ထူးခြားသော။ ...	too-chyah-thaw ...	ni'ha'yut ...	kuṛippána, viséshamána.
Remem'ber, *v. a.*...	မှတ်မိသည်။ ...	hmut-mee-the ...	yad-k, -chet, yad'a'wur'ee, *f.*	nínaivukúr, ninai, chinthi.
Remínd, *v. a.* ...	သတိပေးသည်။ ...	th'dee-pay-the ...	yad-dil'a'na ...	ninaippúṭṭu,ñapagapaḍuttu
Renown', *s.* ...	ကျော်ဇော်သည်။ ...	kyaw-zaw-thee ...	nam-wur'ee, *f.* nam'a'wur'ee	kírtti, pugaḻchchi.
Rent, *s.* ...	ငှါးခ။ ...	hngah-kah ...	kir'a'yu, ij'a'ru, khir'aj ...	váḍagai, kuttagai.
Repair', *s.* ...	ဖျင်သည်။ ...	pyin-the ...	mur'um'mut, *f.* ...	marámattu, puthuppippu.
Reply', *s.* ...	ပြန်ပြောသည်။ ...	pyun-pyaw-the ...	ju'wab ...	maṛumoḻi, pirathiyuttaram.
Represent', *v. a.* ...	ပုံသဏ္ဍာန်ပြသည်။ ...	pohn-tha-dun-pyah-the ...	dikh'la'na, dik'ha'na ...	káṇbi, kuṛi, veḷippaḍuttu.
Request', *s.* ...	တောင်းပန်သည်။ ...	towng-bun-the ...	urz, dur'khwast, *f.* su'wal...	manu, viṇṇappam.
Res'idence, *s.* ...	နေရာအရပ်။ ...	nay-yah-a-yut ...	muk'am, muk'an, us'than ...	vásam, víḍu, iḍam, agam.
Resígn', *v. a.* ...	လက်လွှတ်သည်။ ...	let-hloot-the ...	chhor'na, de'na, ty'ag'na ...	viṭṭuviḍu, rásínámá.
Respect', *s.* ...	မျက်နှာကိုထောက်သည်။ ...	myet-hna-go-towk-the ...	ta'zeem, tuk'reem, ud'ub, *f.*	ácháram, mariyáthai.
Respon'sible, *a.* ...	ဝန်ခံသည်အတိုင်းတတ်နိုင်သော။	woon-cun-the-a-tuyng-tut-	ju'wab'dih ...	uttaraváthamuḷḷa.
Rest, *s.* ...	ငြိမ်းသည်။ ...	ngyain-the, [hnuyng-thaw,	a'ram, a'sa'ish, fur'agh, *f.*...	óyvu, áṛṛi.
Result', *s.* ...	အကျိုး။ ...	a-kyoh, [chyin,...	nut'ee'ju, ha'sil ...	palan,muḍivu,káriyasiddhi.
Resurrec'tion, *s.* ...	သေးခြင်းကမြောက်ခြင်း။ ...	thay-gyin-gah-tah-myowk-	ki'ya'mut, hushr, nushr ...	uyirtteḻugai.

ENGLISH.	BURMESE.		HINDUSTANI.	TAMIL.
Revelátion, *s.* ...	ဗျာဒိတ်။ ...	byah-dayt ...	iz'har, kushf, pruk'as ...	velippáḍu, aṛivippu.
Revíse, *v. a.* ...	စာကိုပြုပြင်ခြင်း။ ...	tsah-goh-pyoo-byin-chyin..	nuz'ur-sa'nee-k ...	pi̱laipár, tiruttu.
Reward', *s.* ...	ဆု။ ...	soo ...	bukh'shish ...	veg umathi, vegumánam.
Rice, *s.* ...	ဆန်။စပါး။ ...	tsun, tsa-bah ...	dhan, sha'lee, bir'unj ...	arisi, sóṛu, annam.
Rich, *a.* ...	သဌေး။ ...	th'tay ...	dou'lut-mund, mal'dar ...	aisuvariyamuḷḷa.
Ride, *v. a.* ...	စီးသည်။ ...	see-the ...	su'war'ee-k, su'war-h ...	váhanaméṛichchellu.
Right, *s.* ...	မှန်သော။ ...	hmun-thaw ...	huk, theek, rast ...	niyáyam, taguthi, urimai.
Ríghteousness, *s.* ...	ဖြောင့်မတ်ခြင်း။ ...	pyowng-mut-chyin ...	rast-baz'ee, nek'ee, *f.* ...	níthi, puṇṇiyam, dharmam.
Ríghtful, *a.* ...	ပိုင်ထိုက်သည်။ ...	puyng-tuyk-thee ...	huk-dar, moos'tu'hik ...	niyáyamána, níthiyána.
Ripe, *a.* ...	မှည့်သော။ ...	hmeh-thaw ...	puk'ka, pookh'tu ...	paḻutta, kanintha.
Rise, *s.* ...	ထသည်။ ...	tah-the ...	chur'ha'o ...	uthayam, éṛṛam, virutti.
River, *s.* ...	မြစ်။ ...	myit ...	dur'i'ya, dur'ya, nud, nud'ee	áṛu, nathi.
Road, *s.* ...	လမ်း။ ...	lun ...	ras'ta, rus'tu, rah, *f.* ...	vaḻi, páthai sálai, teru.
Roast, *v. a.* ...	မီးနှာမှာကင်သည်။ ...	mee-nah-hmah-kin-the ...	kub'ab-k ...	pori, vaṛu, tíy, chuḍu.
Rob'ber, *s.* ...	ဓားပြ။ ...	dah-myah ...	da'koo, dak'i'ya, thug, chor..	tiruḍan, kaḷvan, chóran.
Rock, *s.* ...	ကျောက်။ ...	khyowk ...	sil, sil'a, pak'han, pash'an ...	kanmalai, páṛai, pár.
Rod, *s.* ...	တံပျား။နှင်တံ။ ...	t'pyah, hnin-dun ...	chhur'ee, soot'koon, *f.* ...	taḍi, kól, miláṛu.
Roof, *s.* ...	အမိုး။ ...	ă-moh ...	chhut, chhat, pa'tun, sukf, *f.*	kúrai, tá̱lváram.
Room, *s.* ...	အခန်း။ ...	ă-cun ...	jug'uh, muk'an, kum'ur'a...	aṛai, iḍam, stánam.
Root, *s.* ...	အမြစ်။ ...	ă-myit ...	jur, bekh, mool ...	vér, ki̱laṅgu, táthu.
Rope, *s.* ...	ကြိုး။ ...	khyoh ...	rus'see, dor, hubl ...	kayiṛu, vaḍam támam.
Rose, *s.* ...	နှင်းဆီ။ ...	hnin-see ...	goo'lab, wurd, ...	rójápú, muṛchevanthi.
Rósewater, *s.* ...	နှင်းရည်။ ...	hnin-yay ...	gool-ab, gool-ab-neer ...	pannír.
Ros'in, *s.* ...	သစ်စေး။ ...	thit-say ...	dhoo'na, ral, kur'a'yul ...	kuṅgiliyam. [mulla.
Roy'al, *a.* ...	ရှင်ဘုရင်နှင့်ဆိုင်သော။တော်။...	shin-bu-yin-hnin-suyng-	bad'sh'hee, sha'hee ...	rájarikamána, mahatuva-
Roy'alty, *s.* ...	စိုးစံခြင်း။ ...	tsoh-sun-chyin, [thaw, taw,..	bad-sha'hee, bad-sha'hut, *f.*	rájarikam, rájáṅgam.

Rub, *s.*	... ပွတ်သည်။	... poht-the	... ghis'a'o, ghis'a'wut, ma'lish.	ṭuḍai téy, kasakku.
Rúby, *s.*	... ကျောက်နီ။	... khyowk-nee	... lal. ya'koot, man'ik ...	máṇikkam, gembu, pathu-chukkán. [marágam.
Rud'der, *s.*	... တက်မ။	... tet-mah	... sook'kan, put'war, kur'wa'ra	
Rude, *a.*	... ကြမ်းတမ်းသော။	... kyun-dun-thaw	... be-im'ti'az, be-ud'ub ...	tuḍinamána, múḍamána.
Rule, *s.*	... အုပ်ချုပ်သည်။	... oht-chyoht-the	... hoo'koo'mut, um'ul, dus'toor	oḷungu, chaṭṭam, kaṭṭaḷai.
Rúler, *s.*	... အုပ်ချုပ်သောသူ။	... oht-chyoht-thaw-thoo	... ha'kim, wa'lee ...	áṇḍavan, talaivan.
Rum, *s.*	... တင်းလဲကိုချက်သောအရက်။	... tin-leh-goh-chyet-thaw- [a-yet,	... as'uv ...	sáráyam, mastu, loṭṭi.
Run, *s.*	... ပြေးသည်။	... pyee-the,	... dour, bhag ...	óṭṭam, ulá, naḍai, chári.
Rupee', *s.*	... ဒင်္ဂါး။	... din-gah	... roo'pi'yu, (roop, *sans.*) ...	rúbáy.
Rust, *s.*	... မှိုတက်သည်။	... hmoh-tet-the	... zung, zun'gar, mor'chuh ...	karai, kaḷimbu, turu.
Sab'bath, *s.*	... ဥပုသ်နေ့။	... oo-boh-nay	... sun'ee'chur, it'war ...	óyvunáḷ.
Sack, *s.*	... အိတ်ကြီး။	... ayt-gyee	... gon, gon'ee, ghur'a'ru, tung	kóṇi, pai, umal.
Sac'rifice, *s.*	... ယဇ်ပူဇော်သည်။	... yit-poo-zaw-the	... zubh, koor'ban, fid'a ...	bali, naivéttiyam.
Sad, *a.*	... စိတ်မသာသော။	... sayt-m'thah-thaw	... ghum-geen, oo'das, ghumnak	thukkamuḷḷa, visana.
Safe, *a.*	... လုံချုံသော။	... lohn-chyohn-thaw	... sa'lim, sul'um, doo'roost ...	bhattiramána, chémamána.
Sáfety, *s.*	... ဘေးကင်းသော။	... bay-kin-thaw	... sul'am, sul'am'ut, um'an ...	taññjam, átharavu.
Saf'fron, *s.*	... ကုံကမံ။	... kohn-gă-mun	... za'fur'an, ke'sur ...	mañjaḷ, kuṅgamam.
Sage, *s.*	... ပညာရှိသော။	... pin-yah-she-thaw	... huk'eem, gy'an'ee ...	ñáni, vivégi, muni, irushi.
Ságo, *s.*	... သာဂူ။ပင်ပွါး။	... thah-goo, pin-pwah	... sa'goo-da'na ...	savvarisi.
Sail, *s. n.*	... ရွက်။	... yoo-et	... pal, bad-ban, ser'h, sur ...	kappalóḍu, páyvalittóḍu.
Sail'or, *s.*	... သင်္ဘောသား။	... thing-baw-thah	... khul'a'see, mul'lah, ju'ha'zee.	kappalóṭṭi. kapparkáran.
Saint, *s.*	... သန့်ရှင်းသောသူ။	... thun-shin-thaw-thoo	... peer, wul'ee ...	meydévabhaktan, muni.
Sake, *s.*	... အတွက်။	... ă-twet	... kha'tir, wastu, was'te ...	nimittam, poruṭṭu.
Sal'ary, *s.*	... လခ။	... lah-gah	... tul'ub, tun-khwah, *f.* ...	sambaḷam, kúli.
Sale, *s.*	... ရောင်းခြင်း။	... yowng-chyin	... bik'ree, fur'okht, by, *f.* ...	vikkirayam, vilai, virpanai.
Salt, *s.*	... ဆား။	... tsah	... num'uk, lon, non ...	uppu, ilavaṇam.
Salúte, *s.*	... နှုတ်ဆက်ခြင်း။	... hnoht-set-chyin	... sul'am, tus'leem ...	váḷttu. salám, upachára m.
Salvátion, *s.*	... ကယ်တင်ခြင်း။	... keh-tin-chyin	... sul'a'mut, sul'a'mut'ee, *f.* ...	íḍérram, iraṭchai.

English.	Burmese.		Hindustani.	Tamil.
Sand, *s.* ...	သဲ။ ...	theh ...	ba'loo, ret, reg, ret'ul ...	maṇal.
Satisfac'tion, *s.* ...	အလိုပြည့်စုံစေခြင်း။ ...	a-loh-pyee-sohn-say-chyin..	khoosh-noo'dee, kha'tir-	púraṇam, púrtti, sammathi.
Sat'urday, *s.* ...	စနေနေ့။. ...	să-nay-nay ...	sun'ee'chur, shum'bu[jum'a.	sanikkiḻamai, manthaváram
Sauce, *s.* ...	စဲ။ ...	sah-meh ...	chut'nee, chash'nee, *f.* ...	kuḻambu, kaṛi, áṇam.
Sau'cer, *s.* ...	လက်ဖက်ရည်ပုကန်ပြား။ ...	let-pet-yay-pă-gun-pyah ...	pir'ich, tush'tur'ee, *f.* ...	taṭṭaipiṅgán, taṭṭaikóppai.
Sáviour, *s.* ...	ကယ်တင်သောသူ။ ...	keh-tin-thaw-thoo ...	buch'an'e-wa'la ...	iraṭchagan, míṭpan.
Saw, *s.* ...	လွှ။ ...	hlwah ...	a'ra, a'ru, ur'ru, kur'ot ...	váḷ, maramarukkumváḷ.
Saw, *v.* ...	မြင်ပြီ။ ...	myin-byee ...	dek'ha ...	kaṇḍén, párttén.
Saw'yer, *s.* ...	လွှသမား။ ...	hlwah-th'mah ...	a'ra-kush, kur'ant'ee ...	vaṭkáran, válkáran.
Say, *v. a.* ...	ပြောသည်။ ...	pyaw-the ...	bol, bat, bo'lee, *f.* ...	chollu, pésu, urai.
Scent, *s.* ...	အနံ့။ ...	ă-nun ...	bas, bo, boo, *f.* ...	maṇam, vásanai, parimaḷam
Schol'ar, *s.* ...	စာသင်သား။ကျောင်းသား။ ...	sah-thin-thah,kyowng-thah	sha'gird, tul'meez ...	kaṛpón, máṇákkan.
School, *s.* ...	စာသင်ကျောင်း။ ...	sah-thin-kyowng ...	path'sha'la, put'sal,muk'tub	páḍasálai, paḷḷikkúḍam.
Scor'pion, *s.* ...	ကင်းမြီးကောက်။ ...	kin-mee-gowk ...	uk'rub, beech'ha ...	téḷ, teṛukkál.
Screen, *s.* ...	ကွယ်ကာသည်။ ...	kweh-kah-the ...	pur'du, ot, *m.-f.* ...	paḍuthá, maṛaivu, tirai.
Scrip'ture, *s.* ...	ကျမ်းစာ။ ...	kyun-sah ...	kitab-moo'kud'dus, shastr...	vétham, maṛai, dévavákku.
Sculp'tor, *s.* ...	ပန်းပုသမား။ ...	pun-poo-thum-mah ...	boot'tur'ash ...	kottuvélaikáran.
Sea, *s.* ...	ပင်လယ်။ ...	pin-leh ...	dur'ya, buhr ...	kaḍal, samuttiram.
Seal, *s.* ...	တံဆိပ်။ ...	t'sayt ...	moohr, mood'ra, *f.* khutm...	muttirai, aḍaiyáḷam.
Sea'son, *s.* ...	ဥတု။ ...	oo-doo ...	wukt, mou'sim, suma, *f.* ...	paruvam, kálam, néram.
Seat, *s.* ...	ထိုင်ရာ။ထိုင်ခုံ။ ...	tuyng-yah,tuyng-kohn[yah	koorse, *f.* ...	ásanam, píḍam, maṇai.
Sécret, *s.* ...	လျှို့ဝှက်လျက်ရှိသောအရာ။ ...	sho-wet-le-et-she-thaw-a-	raz, bhed, sir, ni'han ...	iragasiyam, antharaṅgam.
Sec'tion, *s.* ...	ပိုင်းဖြတ်သောအရာ။ ...	puyng-pyut-thaw-a-yah ...	kut'u, kand, fusl, *f.* ...	pirivu, kúṛu, paguthi.
Secúrity, *s.* ...	အာမခံ။ ...	ah-mah-cun ...	buch'a'o, um'an, *f.* ...	piṇai, íḍu, uttaraváthan.
See, *v. a.* ...	မြင်သည်။ ...	myin-thee ...	dekh'na, dikh'na ...	pár, káṇ, tharisi.
Seed, *s.* ...	အစေ့။ ...	a-see ...	beej, beerj, bi'hun ...	vithai, koṭṭai, vittu.

Seek, *v. a.*	... ရှာသည်။	... shah-the	... tul'ash-k, dhoondh'na	... tédu, áráy, vichári.
Sell, *v. a.*	... ရောင်းသည်။	... yowng-the	... beech'na, bench'na	... vil, vikkirayaṅchey.
Semi, *a.*	... တဝက်။	... t'wet	... adh-, udh-, ud-,	... arai, páthi, artta.
Send, *v. a.*	... စေလိုက်သည်။	... say-luyt-the	... bhej'na, put'ha'na	... anuppu, pógaviḍu, prayógi.
Sénior, *s.*	... အသက်သာ၍ကြီးသော။	... a-thet-thah-yu-eh-kyee-[thaw	... bur'a, kub'eer	... mútta, jéshṭa.
Sense, *s.*	... ဉာဏ်။	... nyahn	... ukl, sum'ujh, *f.*	... buḍḍhi, aṛivu, mathi.
Sen'timent, *s.*	... စိတ်ထင်။အယူ။	... sayt-tin, ă-yoo	... bha'o	... eṇṇam, abhipráyam.
Sep'arate, *a.*	... ကွာသည်။	... kwah-the	... joo'da, ul'ug, furk	... tanitta, vérána, pṛambhána.
Sep'ulchre, *s.*	... သင်းချိုင်းတွင်း။	... thin-chuyn-dwin	... toor'but, dur'gah, gor, *f.*	... samáthi, préthachémastalam
Ser'mon, *s.*	... ဟောသောဒေသနာ။	... haw-thaw-day-th'nah	... waz, nus'ee'hut, *f.*	... ubhathésam, prasaṅgam.
Ser'pent, *s.*	... မြွေ။	... moo-ay	... surp, samp, uf'a, mar, *pers.*	... pámbhu, nágam, aravam.
Ser'vant, *s.*	... အစေအပါး။အစေခံ။	... ă-say-ă-pah, ă-say-gun	... nou'kur, cha'kur, das	... thásan, vélaikkáran.
Set, *s.*	... ထည့်ထားသည်။	... tee-tah-the	... jur'a'oo, mel, jut'it	... jóḍu, toḍai, aḍukku.
Set'tle, *v. a.*	... ငြိမ်းစေသည်။	... nyain-say-the	... moo'kur'rur-k, thuh'ra'na...	tír, oḻuṅgupaḍuttu.
Set'tlement, *s.*	... ငြိမ်းစေခြင်း။	... nyain-say-chyin	... thuh'ra'o, bund-o-bust, fy'sul	tírppu, tírmánam, nilai.
Sev'eral, *a.*	... ခြားနားသော။	... chyah-nah-thaw	... ky, ky'ee, ba'z	... sila, pala, vegu, paṛpala.
Sevére, *a.*	... အလွန်ကြမ်တည်းသော။	... ă-hlohn-chyut-tee-thaw	... sukht, doo'roosht	... kurúramána, kaḍinamána.
Shad'ow, *s.*	... အရိပ်။	... a-yayt	... zil	... niḻal, cháyai.
Shake, *v. a.*	... လှုပ်သည်။	... hloht-the	... hil'a'na, doo'la'na	... asai, kulukku, áṭṭu, alai.
Shame, *s.*	... ရှက်ကြောက်ခြင်း။	... shet-chyowk-chyin	... push'e'man'ee	... veṭkam, náṇam, kúcham.
Shape, *s.*	... ပုံ။သဏ္ဍာန်။	... pohn-thă-dun	... doul, soo'rut, suj, *f.*	... uru, uruvam, vaḍivu, cháyal.
Share, *s.*	... ခွဲဝေသည်။	... kweh-way-the	... his'su, bant, ban'ta	... paṅgu, págam, kúṛu.
Sharp, *a.*	... ထက်သော။	... tet-thaw	... tez, toond, kur'a	... kúruḻḻa, kúrmaiyuḻḻa.
She, *pron.*	... သူ။အမ။	... thoo, ă-mah	... wo, wooh. yih, yuh, oos'ne...	aval, peṇ.
Shine, *v. n.*	... အရောင်ထွက်သော။	... ă-yowng-twet-thaw	... chum'uk'na, ro-shun-h	... prakási, oḻivísu, tulaṅgu.
Ship, *s.*	... သင်္ဘော။	... thing-baw	... teen-dol'ee-ju'haz	... kappal, marakkalam.
Shoe, *s.*	... ခြေနင်း။	... chyee-nin	... joo'ta, joo'tee, nal	... pátharaṭchai, cheruppu.
Shop, *s.*	... ဆိုင်။	... suyng	... doo'kan, *f.*	... kaḍai, aṅgáḍi, ávaṇam.

English.	Burmese.		Hindustani.	Tamil.
Shore, *s.*	ကမ်း။	oun	kun'a'ru, kin'a'ra	kaḍarkarai, óram.
Short, *a.*	တိုသော။	toh-thaw	sun'chhep, kum, ko'tah	surukkamána, kuṛugina.
Shut, *v. a.*	ပိတ်သော။	payt-thaw	bund-k, lug'a'na	aḍai, múḍu, sárttu.
Shy, *a.*	ရှက်သော။	shet-thaw	bhur'kel	kúchchamána, náṇamuḷḷa.
Sick, *a.*	နာသော။	nah-thaw	bee'mar, a'za'ree, ro'gee	viyáthiyuḷḷa, nóykoṇḍa.
Sight, *s.*	မြင်ခြင်း။	myin-chyin	nuz'ur, dek'ha, drisht, *f.*	párvai, nókkam, káṭchi.
Sign, *s.*	လက္ခဏာ။	lek-kă-nah	nish'an, chinh	aḍaiyáḷam, kuṛi, saigai.
Sig'nature, *s.*	လက်မှတ်။	let-hmut	dust-khut, sun'ud, *f.* chinh.	kaieḻuttu, kaiyoppam.
Sílence, *s.*	မြိမ်းခြင်း။	myain-chyin	choop'kee, khum'osh'ee, *f.*	pésámai, maunam, amaithi.
Silk, *s.*	ပိုး။	poh	resh'um, ub-resh'um	paṭṭu, (*silk thread* paṭṭunúl).
Sil'ly, *a.*	မိုက်သော။	muyt-thaw	un'ar'ee, bhon'doo	bhuddhikeṭṭa, mathikeṭṭa.
Sil'ver, *s.*	ငွေ။	ngway	chan'dee, roop, roop'a	veḷḷi, veṇpon.
Sim'pleton, *s.*	သူမိုက်။	thoo-muyt	sa'da-dil, un'ar'ee	péthai, aṛivillán, manthan.
Sin, *s.*	ဒုစရိုက်။အပြစ်။	doo-sa-yuyt, ă-pyit	goo'nah, joorm, pap	pávam, dósham, paḻi.
Since, *conj.*	လွန်ခဲ့ပြီး။	lohn-geh-byee	jub'se, tud'se	paḍiyáḷ, ágakkoḷḷa.
Sincére, *a.*	လျှို့ဝှက်ခြင်းမရှိ။	shoh-wet-chyin-m'shee	rast, such'cha, sa'dik	uṇmaiyuḷḷa, nérmaiyuḷḷa.
Sing, *v. a.*	သီချင်းဆိုသည်။	thee-chyin-soh-thee	ga'na	gíthampáḍu.
Sing'er, *s.*	သီချင်းဆိုသောသူ။	thee-chyin-soh-thaw-thoo	gu'wy'ya, ga'ne-wa'la	páḍagan, saṅgíthakkáran.
Sin'gle, *a.*	တဦးတည်း။	ta-oo-dee	wa'hid, uk'e'la, ik'la	oṛṛaiyána, tanitta, tani.
Sin'ner, *s.*	အပြစ်ရှိသောသူ။	a-pyit-she-thaw-thoo	goon'nah-gar, a'see	pávi, kuṛṛaváḷi, páthagan.
Sir, *s.*	ခင်ဗျား။	kin-byah	jee, joo, la'la, mi'yan	aiyan, aiyá.
Sire, *s.*	အဘ။	a-pah	bap, ba'ba	pithá, appan.
Sis'ter, *s.*	အမ။နှမ။	ă-mah, hnit-mah	bu'hin, bhan, bhug'in'ee	sahóthari, uḍanpṛanthál.
Sit, *v. n.*	ထိုင်သည်။	tuyng-the	byth'na	uṭkáru.
Situátion, *s.*	အရာ။	a-yah	mou'ku, jul'su	udyógam, iḍam, stiti.
Skel'eton, *s.*	ကိုယ်ခန္ဓာရိုး။	koh-kun-dah-yoh	thuth'ree, *f.*	elumbhukkúḍu, kaliyuḍal.

Skiff, *s.*	[illegible]	thum-bun-ngeh	thuk'thon'wa, *f.*	ódam, tóṇi, teppam.
Skil'ful, *a.*	လိမ္မာသော။	laym-mah-thaw	hoo'nur-mund, hoonur-wur.	sádhuriyamuḷḷa,samarttuḷḷa.
Skin, *s.*	အရေ။အရေပြား။	ă-yay, a-yay-pyah	chum'ra, cham, khal, *f.*	tól, uri, sarumam.
Sky, *s.*	မိုဃ်းကောင်းကင်။	moh-kowng-gin	asman, ful'uk	vánam, viṇ, ákáyam.
Slack, *a.*	လျော့သော။	shaw-thaw	dhee'la	taḷarntha, iḷakkamána.
Slap, *s.*	လက်ဝါးနှင့်ပုတ်သည်။	let-wah-hnin-poht-the	thup'pur, thup'e'ra	aṛai, aḍi, kuṭṭu.
Slate, *s.*	ကျောက်သင်ပုန်း။	kyowk-thin-bohn	put'i'ya, *f.*	kaṛpalagai, órvagaikkal.
Slaugh'ter, *s.*	သတ်ဖြတ်သည်။	thut-pyut-the	kutl, kut'a, *f.*	kolai, vathai, saṅgáram.
Slave, *s.*	ကျွန်။	kyoon	ghoo'lam, bun'du	aḍimai, chiṛai, muṛiyan.
Sleep, *s.*	အိပ်ပျော်သည်။	ait-pyaw-the	neend, nid'ra, so'ta, su'yun.	nittirai, tuyil túkkam.
Slóthful, *a.*	ပျင်းရိသော။	pyin-yee-thaw	soost	chómbhana, timirtta.
Slow, *a.*	နှေးသော။	hnay-thaw	soost, ka'hil, pichh'la	manthamána, támathamána
Small, *a.*	ငယ်သော။	ngeh-thaw	chho'ta	aṛpa, chiṛu, chinna.
Small'-pox, *s.*	ကျောက်ကြီး။	kyowk-gyee	see'tul'a, ma'ta, go'tee, *f.*	vaisúri, ammai, muttu.
Smell, *s.*	အနံ့။အနံ့ခံသည်။	ă-nun, ă-nun-cun-the	bas, bo, boo, soongh, *f.*	maṇam, kantam.
Smoke, *v. a.*	မီးခိုး။	mee-goh	dhoo'an-k, dhoon'an-k	pugaippi, churuṭṭuppiḍi.
Smooth, *a.*	ချောသော။	chyaw-thaw	bur'a'bur, hum-war	methuvána, samamána.
Snuff, *s.*	နှာခေါင်းဆေး။	hnă-kowng-say	nas, soongh'un, *f.*	nasiyam, múkkuttúḷ.
So, *adv.*	ထိုအတူ။	toh-ă-too	is'tur'uh, i-'se, uy'seh, yon	appaḍi, ivváṛu, avvithamáy.
Society, *s.*	အပေါင်းအသင်း။	ă-powng-ă-thin	shirk, shir'kut, fir'ka	sabai, saṅgam, kúṭṭam.
Soft, *a.*	ပျော့သော။နူးညံ့သော။	pyaw-thaw, noo-nyun-thaw.	nurm, moo'la'im, gool-goo'la.	miruthuván, methuvána.
Some, *a.*	အချို့။	ă-chyoh	kooch, ky'ee, tho'ra	sila, koñja, aṛpa.
Some'times, *adv.*	တခါတလေ။	t'kah-d'lay'	kub'hee-kub'hee	silavéḷaiyil, koñjanéṛattil.
Some'where, *adv.*	တစုံတခုသောအရပ်မှာ။	t'sohn-t'koo-thaw-a-yut- [hmah	ku'heen, ku'koon	eṅgéyó, óriḍattil.
Son, *s.*	သား။	thah	bet'a, pootr, soot, pi'sur, bin.	magan, suthan, kumáran.
Song, *s.*	သီချင်း။	thee-chyin	geet, gan	páṭṭu, saṅgítham, kánam.
Soon, *adv.*	ချက်ချင်း။	chyet-chyin	jul'dee, sheegh'ru	viraivil, síkkiramáy.
Sor'row, *s.*	ဝမ်းနည်းသည်။	wun-neh-the	ghum, uf'sos	tukkam, tuyaram, kilésam.

English.	Burmese.		Hindustani.	Tamil.
Sort, *s.*	အမျိုး။	a-myoh	kism, ruk'um	vitham, inam, taram.
Soul, *s.*	ဝိညာဉ်။	wee-nyin	jan, pran, jee	áttumá, jívan, ávi.
Sound, *s.*	အသံ။	ă-thun	a'waz, nu'wa, sud'a. *f.*	sabdam, nátham, ósai, thoni.
Sour, *a.*	ချဉ်သော။	chyin-thaw	khut'ta, toorsh	puḷippána, veḍveḍuppána.
South, *s.*	တောင်။	towng	duk'khun, duk'khin	teṛku, tenṛisai.
Sov'ereign, *s.*	ဧကရာဇ်မင်း၊ရှင်ဘုရင်။	ay-kă-yet-min, shin-bu-yin.	shah, bad-shah	suyáthipathi, chakkaravartti
Sow, *s.*	ဝက်မ။	wet-mah	soo'ur'ee, *f.*	vithai.
Sow, *v.*	မျိုးစေ့ကြဲသည်။	myo-see-kyeh-the	bo'na, rop'na	náṛruppávu.
Spar'row, *s.*	စာငှက်။	sah-hnget	chir'a, chir'ee, chir'i'ya, *f.*	aḍaikkalán- *or* úk-(kuruvi).
Speak, *v. a.*	ပြောသည်။	pyaw-the	bat-k, kuh'na, khu'na	pésu, chollu, moḻi, urai.
Spec'tacles, *s.*	မျက်မှန်။	myet-hmun	chush'mu, chush'muk	múkkukaṇṇáḍi.
Speech, *s.*	စကားပြောခြင်း။	s'gah-pyaw-chyin	zub'an, zoo'ban, soo'khun	péchchu, páshai, prasṅgam.
Spend, *v. a.*	သုံးချေကုန်သည်။	thohn-yoo-eh-kohn-the	khurch-k	chelavu, chelaviḍu.
Spir'it, *s.*	နံဝိညာဉ်။	nun-win-ngin	rooh, nufs, jan, jee	ávi, áttumá, asaríri.
Spir'it, *s.*	အရက်။	ă-yet	shur'ab, ur'uk, mud, da'roo.	mastu, sáráyam.
Spit, *v. a.*	တံတွေးထွေးသည်။	tun-tway-tway-the	thook'na	umiḻ, tuppu, kakku.
Spittoon', *s.*	ထွေးအင်။	tway-ing	peek-dan, oo'gal-dan	echchiṛpaḍikkam.
Spoon, *s.*	ဇွန်း။	zoon	chum'chu, kuf'chu	karaṇḍi, agappai.
Spoon'ful, *s.*	တဇွန်းစာ။	t-zoon-sah	chum'chu-bhur	karaṇḍikoṇḍa-aḷavu.
Square, *a.*	စတုရန်း။	s'doo-yun	char-go'shu, char-ko'na	chathuramána, samamána.
Squint'eyed, *a.*	မျက်စိစောင်းသည်။	myet-see-sowng-the	bhen'ga, ter'a, dhe'ra	órakkaṇ, máṛukaṇ.
Squir'rel, *s.*	ရှဉ့်။	shin	gil'uh'ree, chik'hoo'ree, *f.*	aniṛpiḷḷai, anil.
Star, *s.*	ကြယ်။	kyeh	ta'ra, sa'bit, ta'rik'a	naṭchattiram, táragai.
State, *s.*	ဖြစ်ခြင်း။	pyit-chyin	hal, ha'lut, ky'fee'yut, *f.*	stiti, nilaimai, tanmai.
Státion, *s.*	ရပ်နေရာ။	yut-nay-yah	muk'am, muk'an, ja'e-ga	stánam, iḍam, nilai.
Státioner, *s.*	စက္ကူရောင်းသောသူ။	sek-koo-yowng-thaw-thoo.	ka'ghuz'ee, [lak-, wughuy'ra.	kaḍithamuthaliya-viṛpón.

Státionery, *s.* ...	စာရေးတန်ဆာအမျိုးမျိုး။	... sah-yay-t'sah-a-myoh-moh..	ka'ghuz-kul'um-,si'ya'hee-,-	kaḍithási-iṛagu-muthaliya-
Steam'er, *s.* ...	မီးသင်္ဘော။	... mee-thing-baw ...	bhup'ha'ra-ju'haz, ag-ju'haz.	nírávikkappal. [vai.
Still, *adv.* ...	ငြိမ်သော။	... nyain-thaw ..	ub-tuk, ub-tul'uk, ub-to'ree.	innum, enṛálum, ágilum.
Stink, *s.* ...	နံစော်သည်။	... nun-saw-the ...	bud-bo, bud-boo, gund ...	náṛṛam, durgantam.
Stone, *s.* ...	ကျောက်။	... khyowk ...	put'thur, pa'thur, sung ...	kallu, kal, irattinam.
Stool, s. (low seat).	ထိုင်ခုံ။	... tuyng-kohn ...	mor'ha, mond'ha, tukh'tu...	ásanapíḍam, maṇai.
Stool, *s.* ...	ဝမ်းသုတ်ခြင်း။	... woon-thoht-chyin ...	jha'ra, *pers.*dust,*arab.*bur'az.	malóbhathai.
Stóry, *s.* ...	ဒဏ္ဍာရီစကား။	... dun-dah-ree-să-gah ...	kis'sa, ku'ha'nee, kut'ha ...	kathai, charittiram.
Straight, *a.* ...	ဖြောင့်သော။	... pyowng-thaw ...	seed'ha, bur'a'bur ...	néránа, oḻuṅgána, kóṇátha.
Stream, *v. s.* ...	စီးသည်။ချောင်း။မြစ်။	... see-the, chyowng, myit ...	dha'ra, dhar, nuhr ...	níróṭṭam, nírppáychchal.
Street, *s.* ...	လမ်း။	... lun ...	ras'ta, sur'uk ...	teru, víthi, páthai, sálai.
Strength, *s.* ...	ခွန်အား။	... kohn-ah ...	zor, muz'boo'tee, ta'kut, *f.*...	bhalam, uram, sattuvam.
Strong, *a.* ...	အားကြီးသော။	... ah-kyee-thaw ...	muz'boot, ku'wee, kut'ta ...	bhalamuḷḷa, uramána.
Stud'y, *s.* ...	စာသင်သည်။	... săh-thin-the ...	ta'lib-i-ilm'ee, *f.*seekh,chin'-	paḍippu, kal, avathání.
Stúpid, *a.* ...	မိုက်သော။	... muyt-thaw ...	be-woo'koof,bhud'da,[tun...	múḍamána, péthaimaiyuḷḷa.
Subscrip'tion, *s.* ...	လက်မှတ်ထိုးခြင်း။	... let-hmut-toh-chyin ...	bih'ree, chun'da, mut'hout..	kaiyoppam, kaichchárttu.
Success', *s.* ...	အောင်ခြင်း။	... owng-chyin ...	kam-yab'ee, bur-khoord, *f.*.	anukúlam, palippu, siddhi.
Success'ful, *a.* ...	အကျိုးစီးပွါးတိုးသော။	... a-kyoh-see-pwah-toh-thaw..	kam-yab, kam-ran ...	anukúlamána, sittiyána.
Such, *a.* ...	ဤသို့။	... ee-thoh ...	ty'sa, uy'sa, wy'sa ...	appaḍippaṭṭa, avvithamána.
Sud'den, *a.* ...	ရုပ်ခနဲ။	... yoht-kă-neh ...	na'gah'ee,na'gu'han,ek-a-ek.	saḍithiyána, síkkiramána.
Súet, *s.* ...	အဆီခဲ။	... ă-tsee-keh ...	chur'bee, *f.* ...	koḻuppu, niṇam, neyppu.
Suf'fering, *s.* ...	ခံခြင်း။	... cun-chyin ...	ee'za, uz'ee'ut, dookh ...	páḍu, varuttam, tunbham.
Suffici'ent, *a.* ...	လောက်။	... lowk ...	bus, ka'fee, ka'bil ...	póthumána, tirptiyána.
Sug'ar, *s.* ...	သကြား။	... th'chyah ...	shuk'ur, shuk'kur, chee'nee.	sarkkarai, síni.
Suggest', *v. a. & n.*...	အရိပ်ပေးသည်။	... a-yait-pay-the ...	ish'a'ra-d, chit'a'na ...	chuṭṭich-*or*-kuṛittuch-chollu
Suit'able, *a.* ...	တော်လျော်သည်။	... taw-lyaw-the ...	moo'wa'fik, moo'na'sib, la'ik	taguthiyána, éṛṛu.
Sun, *s.* ...	နေ။	... nay ...	soo'ruj, soor, af'tab, urk ...	súriyan, áthittan, arukkan.
Sun'day, *s.* ...	တနင်္ဂနွေနေ့။	... t'ning-gă-noo-ay-nay ...	it'war, et'war, rub'i-bar ...	ñáyiṛṛukkiḻamai.

English.	Burmese.		Hindustani.	Tamil.
Superinten'dent, *s.*	ေစာင့်ကြပ်သောသူ။	sowng-chyut-thaw-thoo	da'rogh'uh, sur'kob, sur'kar.	athikári, attiyatchan.
Sup'per, *s.*	ညစာ။	nyah-sah	bi'ya'ree, *f.* by'a'loo, ush'a...	iráppójanam,iráchcháppáḍu
Supplication, *s.*	တောင်းခြင်း။	towng-chyin	il'tim'as, il'tij'a, *f.*	véṇḍugai, pirárttanai.
Support', *s.*	ခုသည်။ထောက်သည်။	koo-the, towk-the	pur'wur'ish	átharavu, átháram.
Suppóse, *v. a.*	ထင်မှတ်သည်။	tin-hmut-the	ki'yas-k, jan'na, man'na	uttési, ninai, eṇṇu, karuthu.
Sure, *a.*	ေကန်အမှန်။	ay-kun-ă-hmun	sa'bit	nisamána, nichchayamuḷḷa.
Súrety, *s.*	မှန်ခြင်း။အာမခံ။	hmun-chyin,ah-mah-cun	za'min'ee, zamin, kuf'eel ...	piṇai, uttaraváthi, jámín.
Swear, *v. a.*	ကျိန်ဆိုသည်။	chayn-soh-the	kus'um-kha'na, kus'um-de'-	áṇaiyiḍu, sattiyampaṇṇu.
Sweep, *v. a.*	လှည်းသည်။	hleh-the	jhar'na, boo'har'na, [na,...	perukku, kúṭṭu, viḷakku.
Sweet, *a.*	ချိုသော။	chyoh-thaw	meet'ha	tittippána, inimaiyána.
Symp'tom, *s.*	လက္ခဏာ။	lek-kă-nah	put'a, luch'chhun, ee'ma ...	kuṛi, tóṛṛam, aḍaiyáḷam.
Synon'ymous, *a.*	အနက်တူသော။	ă-net-too-thaw	hum-mu'a'nee,moo'tur'a'dif.	égárttamuḷḷa. [páḍu.
Sys'tem, *s.*	အစီအစဉ်။	a-see-a-seen	ka'i'da	oḷuṅgu,muṛai,matham, kóṭ-
Táble, *s.*	စားပွဲ။	să-bweh	mez	mésai, píḍapalagai.
Tail, *s.*	အမြီး။	a-myee	doom, doom'bal	vál, tógai.
Tail'or, *s.*	အချုပ်သမား။	ă-chyoht-tham-mah	dur'zee, khy'yat, soo'jee ...	taiyaṛkáran.
Take, *v.*	ယူ။	yoo	le'na, man'na, le-le'na, le...	eḍu, váṅgu, paṛṛu.
Talk, *s.*	စကားပြောသည်။	s'gah-pyaw-the	bat-cheet, bol, bat-ku'ha'o...	péchchu, sambháshanai.
Tape, *s.*	ထိုးကြိုးပြား။	toh-khyoh-pyah	fee'ta, na'ra, ni'war	náḍá, kachchu, téppu.
Taste, *s.*	အရသာခံသည်။	a-yah-thah-cun-the	muz'ak, su'wad, za'i'ka	urusi, chuvai.
Tax, *s.*	အခွန်။	a-kohn	muh'sool, khir'aj, kur	vari, tírvai, kappam, iṛai.
Tea, *s.*	လက်ဖက်။	let-pet	cha	téyilai, tétaṇṇi.
Teach, *v. a.* & *n.*	သင်ချသည်။	thin-chyah-the	sik'ha'na,but'a'na,sikh'la'na.	póthi, poḍippi, kaṛppi, óthu.
Teach'er, *s.*	ဆရာ။	tsay-yah	oos'tad, moo'ul'lim	upáttiyáyar,ásán,kaṛpippón
Tear, *s.*	မြက်ရည်။	myet-yee	an'soo, an'jhoo, un'joo	kaṇṇír.
Teat, *s.*	နို့သီး။နို့တိုင်။	noh-thee, noh-duyng	ji'ji'ya, choo'chee	mulaikkaṇ, mulaikkámbu.

Tell, *v. a.*	ပြောသည်။	pyaw-the	kuh'na, kuth'na, bol'na	chollu, aṛivi, urai.
Tem'ple, *s.*	ဗိတ်မှန်တော်။	bayt-hmun-daw	gir'ja-ghur, ma'bid	kóvil, déválayam.
Temptátion, *s.*	သွေးဆောင်ခြင်း။	thoo-ay-sowng-gin	im'ti'han	sóthanai, mayakku.
Tent, *s.*	တဲ။	teh	der'a, tum'boo, chut'ree	kúḍáram.
Term, *s.*	အပိုင်းအခြား။	a-puyng-a-chyah	hud, uj'ul	tavaṇai, taram, keḍu.
Tes'timony, *s.*	သက်သေခံချက်။	thet-thay-cun-chyet	gu'wah'ee, sha'hid'ee	sáṭchi, thirshtántham.
Than, *conj.*	ထက်။	det	se, uz	párkkilum, il, páṛkka.
Thank, *s.*	ကျေးဇူးတင်သည်။	kyay-zoo-tin-the	shookr, goon-man'na, dhun.	vanthanam, nanṛi.
Thank'ful, *a.*	ကျေးဇူးသိသော။	kyay-zoo-thee-thaw	shookr-goo'zar, sha'kir	nanṛiyuḷḷa, nanṛiyána.
That, *pron.*	ထို။ဟို။	toh, ho	o, wo, wooh, wuh, jo, oos...	athu, aṇthu, antha, a.
The, *definite article.*	ထို။သည်။	toh, the	wuh, yuh, yih	antha, intha, untha, a, i, u.
Théatre, *s.*	ဇါတ်ရုံ။	zaht-yohn	tum'ash'u-gah, nach-ghur...	náḍakasálai, abhinayasálai.
Thee, *pron.*	မင်း။သင်။	min, thin	to'hee	unnai, ninnai.
Theft, *s.* [*pron*...	ခိုးမှု။	koh-hmoo	thug'a'ee, cho'ree, dooz'dee..	kaḷavu, tiruṭṭu, chóram.
Their, Theirs, *poss.*-	သူတို့။သူတို့၏။	thoo-doh, thoo-doh-ee	oon'un, oon'o, oon'on	avargaḷuḍaiya, avaigaḷuḍai-
Them, *pron.*	သူတို့ကို။	thoo-doh-goh	in, oon, win, win'hen	avargaḷai, avaigaḷai. [ya.
Themselves', *pron*...	သူတို့ကိုယ်တိုင်။	thoo-doh-koh-duyng	a'pus	táṅgaḷé, ivargaḷaiyé.
Then, *adv.*	ထိုအခါ။	toh-a-cah	tub, tud, oos-wukt, ton	appoḷuthu, ágavé, pinnai.
There, *adv.*	ဟိုမှာ။	hoh-hmah	wu'han, wan, oo'dhur, oot...	avviḍam, aṅgé.
These, *pron.*	သည်ဟာများ။	thee-hah-myah	ye, in, in'on, ee'no, yo	ivai, ivaigaḷ, intha, ivargaḷ.
They, *pron.*	သူတို့။	thoo-doh	wooh, wuh, we, ye, oon'oo...	avargaḷ, tám, táṅgaḷ, avai, avaigaḷ.
Thief, *s.*	သူခိုး။	thoo-koh	chor, huthe'la	kaḷḷan, tiruḍan, chóran.
Thin, *a.*	ပိန်သော။	payn-thaw	put'la, doob'la, sook'ta	melliya, nuṇmaiyána.
Thine, *poss. pron.*...	သင်တို့၏။	thin-doh-ee	ter'a, tir'a	un, unathu, unnuḍaiya.
Thing, *s.*	အရာ။ဥစ္စာ။	a-yah, oht-sah	cheez, bust, vus'too, umr...	poruḷ, vasttu, paṇḍam.
Think *v. a.*	ထင်သည်။	tin-the	khi'yal-k, soch'na	ninai, eṇṇu, karuthu, uṇar.
This, *pron.*	ဤ။သည်။	ee, the	yih, yuh	ithu, intha.

English.	Burmese.		Hindustani.	Tamil.
Those, *pron.*	ထိုဟာများ။	toh-hah-myah	we, wo, win, oon, oon'hen	avaigal, avargal. antha, a.
Though, *conj.*	သို့သော်လည်း။	thoh-thaw-lee	ug'ur'chi, ju'nook, jo'ki	ágilum, áyinum, enṛálum.
Thou'sand, *s. a.*	တထောင်။၁၀၀၀။	t'-towng	huz'ar .	áyiram, srgastiram.
Throne, *s.*	ရာဇပလ္လင်။	yah-zah-pă-lin	tukht, mus'nud, sing'ha'sun.	siṅgásanam, pattirásanam.
Thurs'day, *s.*	ကြာသာပတေးနေ့။	kyah-tha-pa-day-nay	joo'mu-rat, punj-shumbu	viyáḻakkiḻamai, guruváram.
Thus, *adv.*	ဤသို့။	ee-thoh	uy'se, uy'sen, is'tur'uh	ivvithamáy, ivváru.
Tie, *s.*	ချည်နှောင်သည်။	chyee-hnowng-the	bund	kattu, taḷai, piṇai.
Tíger, *s.*	ကျား။	kyah	bagh, sher	puli, véṅgai.
Tígress, *s.*	ကျားမ။	kyah-mah	ba'ghun, bagh'nee, sher'nee.	peṇpuli, pulippiṇavu.
Tile, *s.*	အုပ်ကြွပ်။	oht-chyoht	khup'ra, nur'i'ya	óḍu, sathuraóḍu.
Tim'ber, *s.*	သစ်။	thit	kath, luk'ree, chob	vettumaram, uttiram.
Time, *s.*	ကာလ။အခါ။အချိန်။	kah-lah, ă-kah, ă-chayn	wukt, sum'a	kálam, véḷai, néram, muṛai.
Tin, *s.*	သံဖြူ။	thun-byoo	rang, kul'a'ee	tagaram. [kaṇai.
Títle, *s.*	ဘွဲ့။	bweh	nam, khit'ab	pattam, pattappeyar, vak-
Tobac'co, *s.*	ဆေး။ဆေးရွက်။	say-say-yoo-et	tum'ba'koo	pugaiyilai.
Tod'dy, *s.*	ထန်းရည်။ဓနိရည်။	tun-yee, dă-nee-yee	ta'ree, tar	kaḷ, mathu.
Tomb, *s.*	သင်းချိုင်းတွင်း။	thin-chyuyn-dwin	toor'but, mur'kud	kallaṛai, savakkuḻi.
Tongue, *s.*	လျှာ။	shah	joobh, rus'un'a, zub'an	ná, nákku, (*language* páshai).
Too, *adv.*	လွန်း။	loon	zi'ya'duh, bu'hoot, nip'ut	um, kúḍa, athiga.
Tooth, *s.*	သွား။	thwah	dant, dun'dan	pal, tantham.
Tor'toise, *s.*	လိပ်။	layt	kuch'hoo'a, koorm	ámai, kúrmam.
Tótal, *s.*	အကုန်အစည်။	ă-kohn-a-see	sub, joom'la, poo'ra	mottam, togai.
Town, *s.*	မြို့ရွာ။	myoh-yoo-ah	nug'ur, nug'ur'ee, shuhr	nagaram, nagari, pattaṇam.
Trade, *s.*	ရောင်းဝယ်သည်။	yowng-weh-the	sou'da, by'par	viyáparam, varttakam.
Tráder, *s.*	ရောင်းဝယ်သောသူ။	yowng-weh-thaw-thoo	sou'da'gur, ta'jir, kar'bar'ee	varttakan, viyápári.
Treas'ure, *s.*	ဘဏ္ဍာ။	bun-dah-(p'dah)	khuz'a'na, gunj	thanam, pokkasam.

Treas'urer, *s.* ...	ဘဏ္ဍာစိုး။ ...	bun-dah-soh (p'dah-soh) ...	khuz'an'chee, gun'joor ...	pokkasakkáran.
Tríumph, *s.* ...	အောင်မြင်သည်။ ...	owng-myin-the ...	fee'roz-mund'ee,jy-jy-kar...	verri, vijayam, árpparippu.
True, *a.* ...	မှန်သော။ ...	hmun-thaw ...	such, sut, huk ...	unmaiyána, meyyána.
Trum'pet, *s.* ...	တံပိုး၊ခရာ။ ...	t'boh-ka-yah ...	ban'ka ...	ekkálam, tárai, bhúrigai.
Tune, *s.* ...	တီးမှုတ်သံ။ ...	tee-hmoht-thun ...	rag ...	isai, irágam, suruthi.
Tur'ban, *s.* ...	ခေါင်းပေါင်း။ ...	gowng-bowng ...	pug'ree, dus'tar ...	págai,talaippágai,mundásu.
Tur'key, *s.* ...	ကြက်ဆင်။ ...	kyet-sin ...	feel-moorgh, pe'roo ...	vánkóli, kánánkóli.
Turn, *v. n.* ...	လည်သည်၊လှည့်လည်သည်။ ...	leh-the, hlee-lee-the ...	phir'a'na, ghoom'a'na ...	tiruppu, tirumbu, churru.
Two, *a.* ...	နှစ်ခု။ ...	hnit-koo, [thaw-min,...	do, dwy ...	irandu, inai, iru.
Ty'rant, *s.* ...	ရက်စက်သော အုပ်စိုးသောမင်း။	yet-set-thaw-oht-soh-	mookh'tar-kool, [pun,...	kurúran, nishtúran.
Ug'liness, *s.* ...	အရုပ်ဆိုးခြင်း။ ...	a-yoht-soh-chyin ...	bud-soo'rut'ee, *f.* bhon'da-	avalatchanam, anthakkédu.
Ug'ly, *s.* ...	အရုပ်ဆိုးသော။ ...	a-yoht-soh-thaw ...	bhon'da, bud'soo'rut ...	anthakkédu, avalatchanam.
Umbrel'la, *s.* ...	ထီး။ ...	htee ...	chha'tee, *f.* chhut'tur, chhutr.	kudai, kavigai. [tha-
Unáble, *a.* ...	မတတ်နိုင်။ ...	m'-tut-hnuyng ...	be-muk'door, u'shukt ...	iyalátha, élátha, chaktiyillá-
Unadorn'ed, *a.* ...	တန်ဆာမဆင်သော။ ...	t'sah-m'tsin-thaw ...	be-a'ra'ish ...	alangarikkappadátha.
Unal'terable, *a.* ...	မပြောင်းလဲနိုင်သော။ ...	m'pyowng-leh-hnuyng-	be-bud'ul ...	márrakkúdátha, márátha.
Unassis'ted, *a.* ...	မကူဘဲ။ ...	m'koo-beh, [thaw,...	be-mud'ud ...	tunaiyarra, uthaviyarra.
Unavail'able, *a.* ...	မသုံးမရှောင်နိုင်အောင်ဖြစ်သော။	m'hloo-ey-m'showng-hnuyng-owng-pyit-thaw..	la-bood ...	tavirkkak- *or* vilakkak-(-kú-
Unaw'ed, *a.* ...	မကြောက်ရွံ့။ ...	m'khyowk-yohn ...	be-ib'rut ...	bhayamillátha. [dátha).
Unbelief, *s.* ...	မယုံခြင်း။ ...	m'yohn-chyin ...	be-it'i'kad'ee, *f.* be-ee'man'ee	avvisuvásam, avanambikkai.
Unbeliev'er, *s.* ...	မယုံသောသူ။ ...	m'yohn-thaw-thoo ...	be-ee'man ...	nambháthavan, avvisuvási.
Unbid', Unbid'den *a.*	အမိန့်မရှိဘဲ၊မခေါ်မပိတ်ဘဲ။ ...	ă-mayn-m'she-beh, m'caw-m'payt-beh ...	be-ne'o'ta ...	karpikkappadátha.
Unblámable, *a.* ...	အပြစ်တင်ဖွယ်မရှိ။ ...	ă-pyet-tin-bweh-m'she ...	nir-dokh'ee, be-goo'na ...	kurramarra, pilaiyarra.
Unborn', *a.* ...	မဖွားမမြင်သေးသော။ ...	m'pwah-m'myin-thay-thaw.	na-pyd, na-py'da, un-jun'a.	pravátha, urpattiyágátha.
Unboun'ded, *a.* ...	အနန္တ၊အဆုံးအဆမရှိသော။ ...	a-nun-dah, a-sohn-a-sah, m'shee-thaw ...	be-hud ...	alavarra, ellaiyarra.

English.	Burmese.		Hindustani.	Tamil.
Unbróke, *a.* ...	မကျိုး၊မကွဲ၊မပဲ့သော၊ ...	m'kyoh,m'kweh,m'peh-thaw	un-too'ta, na-shik'us'ta ...	uḍaiyátha,aṛátha,negiḻátha.
Unchángeable, *a.*...	မပြောင်းလဲနိုင်သော။ ...	m'pyowng-leh-hnuyng-thaw ...	be-tub'deel ...	máṛátha, iyalbhána.
Unchar'itable, *a.*...	မေတ္တာစိတ်မရှိသော၊ ...	myit-tah-sayt-m'she-thaw...	be-fyz ...	tharumachinthaiyilláiha.
Un'cle, *s.* ...	ဘကြီး၊ဦးရီး။ ...	bah-gyee, oo-yee ...	*maternal uncle, mother's brother, sans.* ma'ma, ma'moo, ma'moon,ma'tool,*arab.*khal *mother's sister's husband,sans* sou'sa, *arab.* kha'loo,*a husband's or wife's mother's brother, sans.* mum'i'ya-soos'oor:—*paternal uncle, father's brother, hin.* chuch'a, ka'ka, *sans.* pit'i'ya, *arab.* kuk'a, um,um'moo:—*father's elder brother, hin.* ta'oo ...	*maternal uncle, mother's brother*,máman, *mother's sister's husband*, chiṛiyatagappan, *paternal uncle, father's brother*, chiṛiyatagappan, *father's elder brother*, periyappan.
Unclean', *a.* ...	ညစ်သော၊ညစ်ညူးသော။ ...	nyit-thaw, nyit-nyoo-thaw.	na-pak ...	asutta, aḻukkána, tíḻppána.
Uncom'fortable, *a.*..	မချမ်းသာသော။ ...	m'chyun-thah-thaw ...	uch'uyn ...	kalakkamuḷḷa, áṛuthalaṛṛa.
Unconnec'ted *a.* ...	မစပ်သော။ ...	m'sut-thaw ...	be-lug'a'o, [bak,...	printha, isaiyátha.
Undaun'ted *a.* ...	မကြောက်သော။ ...	m'khyowk-thaw, [thaw,...	be-dhur'uk, be-dhur'ka, be-	tiḍamuḷḷa, añchátha.
Undenîable, *a.* ...	ငြင်းခုံရန်မရှိသော။ ...	ngyin-kohn-yun-m'she-	la-rud ...	maṛukkappaḍátha.
Un'der, *a.adv.& pr.*	အောက်မှာ။ ...	owk-hmah ...	nee'cheh, *less than* kum ...	kíḻána, kíḻáy, kíḻé, il.
Understand', *v. a.*...	နားလည်သည်။ ...	nah-leh-thee ...	sum'ujh'na, puh'chan'na ...	aṛi, uṇar, teḷi, tér. [thi.
Underval'ue, *v. a.*...	တန်ဘိုးကပြုတ်သည်။ ...	t'boh-gah-pyut-the ...	kum-kudr-k, be-kudr-k ...	vilaikuṛaittuppár,taṇiyama-
Undesígned, *a.* ...	အကြံအစည်မရှိဘဲဖြစ်သော။ ...	a-kyun-a-seen-m'she-beh-	be-bich'ar ...	eṇṇátha,karuthátha.[muḷḷa.
Undistur'bed, *a.* ...	ငြိမ်းသော။ ...	ngyain-thaw, [pyit-thaw,...	be-kur'ar ...	kalakkamilláthe, sántha-

Udoubt'edly, *adv.*	ယုံမှားရန်မရှိ။ ...	yohn-hmah-yun-m'shee ...	nis'un'deh ...	nichchayamáy, santhégami-
Undress', *v. a.* ...	အဝတ်ကိုချွတ်သည်။ ...	ă-woot-goh-choht-the ...	kup're-oo'tar'na ...	uḍaikaḷaṛṛu, uḍaiyuri. [nṛi.
Unemploy'ed, *a.*...	အလုပ်အစောင်မရှိ။ ...	ă-loht-ă-sowng-m'shee ...	be-kaj, be-kar, be-kam-ka...	toḷillillátha, víṇána.
Unéqual, *a.* ...	မညီမျှသော။ ...	m'nyee-m'hmyah-thaw ...	na-hum'war, be-mel ...	ovvátha, ékathésamána.
Unfaith'ful, *a.* ...	သစ္စာပျက်သော။ ...	thit-sah-pyet-thaw ...	be-wuf'a ...	nambhikkaikkéḍána.
Unfávourable, *a.*...	မပြုစုတတ်သော။ ...	m'pyoo-soo-dut-thaw ...	na-mihr'ban ...	uthaviyaṛṛa, sahàyamaṛṛa.
Unfeel'ing, *a.* ...	မကြင်နာတတ်သော။ ...	m'kyin-nah-dut-thaw ...	be-durd, be-dy'a ...	irakkamillátha.
Unfit', *a.* ...	မတော်သော။ ...	m'taw-thaw ...	na-la'ik, na-ka'bil, na-rus'a.	tahátha, aḍátha. ovvátha.
Unfriend'ly, *a.* ...	ရန်ဘက်ဖြစ်သော။ ...	yun-bet-pyit-thaw,[m'thay.	na-mihr'ban, be-ool'fut ...	snéhamaṛṛa. satturuthana-
Ungod'ly, *a.* ...	ဘုရားသခင်ကိုမရိုမသေ။ ...	pă-yah-th'kin-goh-m'yoh-	na-khoo'da-turs ...	deyvabhattiyillátha. [mána.
Ungrácious, *a.* ...	ကျေးဇူးပြုခြင်သော သဘောမရှိ သော။ ...	kyay-zoo-pyoo-chyin-thaw- th'baw-m'shee-thaw ...	be-seel ...	iraṅgátha, krubhaiyaṛṛa.
Unhealth'y, *a.* ...	မကျန်းမာသော။ ...	m'khyun-mah-thaw ...	be-a'ram ...	sugamillátha, viyáthiyuḷḷa.
Unheard', *a.* ...	မကြားသော။ ...	m'khyah-thaw ...	un-soo'na ...	kéḷvippaḍátha, núthanamá-
Unhóly, *a.* ...	မသန့်ရှင်းသော။ ...	m'thun-shin-thaw ...	na-moo'kud'dus ...	asutta,parisuttamillátha[na
Uninhab'ited, *a.*...	နေသောသူမရှိ။ ...	nay-thaw-thoo-m'shee ...	na-a'bad, nir-jun,[it'ti'fak,).	kuḍiyillátha, nirmánushiya
U'nion, *s.* ...	ပေါင်းစပ်သည်။ ...	say-sut-the ...	wusl,(*concord* mel, mil'ap,*f.*-	isaivu, aikkiyam.
U'nit, *s.* ...	အစ်။တစ်။တခု။ ...	it, tit, t'koo ...	ek'un, ek'ka, yuk'a'ee, *f.* ...	ékam, onṛu, tanimai.
Unite, *v. a.* ...	ပေါင်းသည်။ဆက်သည်။ ...	powng-the, tset-the,[thaw,..	jor'na, mil'a'na, sut'a'na,-	isai, kúṭṭu, chér, iṇai.[haga.
Univer'sal, *a.* ...	အလုံးစုံနှင့်ဆိုင်သော။ ...	ă-lohn-sohn-hnin-suyng-	ja'mi, kool'lee, [wusl-k,...	eṅgumniraintha,sarvaviyáb-
U'niverse, *s.* ...	စကြာဝဠာ။ ...	sek-kyah-wah-lah ...	a'lum-tum'am, tri-lok ...	sarvalóham, prapañjam.
Unjust', *a.* ...	မတရားသော။ ...	m'tah-yah'-thaw, [thaw,...	be-a'dil, be-in'saf, na-in'saf..	aniyáya, aníthamuḷḷa.
Unkínd, *a.* ...	ကျေးဇူးမပြုခြင်သော။ ...	kyay-zoo-m'pyoo-chyin-	be-mihr, be-shuf'uk'ut, be-	urukkamillátha.
Unknown', *a.* ...	မသိသော။ ...	m'thee-thaw ...	un-ja'na, na-ma'loom,[lootf.	aṛiyátha, aṛivukkeṭṭátha.
Unlaw'ful, *a.* ...	မတရားသော။ ...	m'tah-yah'-thaw ...	hur'am, khil'af-shu'ra ...	aniyáyamána,níthikkéḍuḷḷa.
Unlearn'ed, *a.* ...	စာမတတ်သော။ ...	sah-m'tut-thaw ...	na-khwan'da, un-sikh ...	kallátha, paḍiyátha.
Unless', *conj.* ...	မ။လျှင်။ ...	hlin,*prefix or* yin,*affix*[thaw.	mug'ur, *pers.* il'la, *arab.*	oḻiya, allámal, anṛi, tavira.
Unlim'ited, *a.* ...	အပိုင်းအခြားမရှိသော။ ...	ă-puyng-ă-chyah-m'shee-	be-hud, [bin, *sans.*...	maṭṭillátha, ellaiyillátha.

ENGLISH.	BURMESE.		HINDUSTANI.	TAMIL.
Unload', *v. a.* ...	ဝန်ကိုချသည်။ ...	woon-goh-chyah-the ...	oo'tar'na ...	bháramiṛakk...
Unluck'y, *a.* ...	ကံဆိုးသော။ ...	cun-soh-thaw ...	bud-bukht ...	athirshṭamaṛṛa.
Unmar'ried, *a.* ...	လက်မထပ်သော။ ...	let-m'tut-thaw ...	un-bi'ya'ha ...	viváhamillátha, onṛiyána.
Unmean'ing, *a.* ...	အနက်မရှိသော။ ...	ă-net-m'shee-thaw ...	be-ma'nee, be-tuh ...	payanaṛṛa, nókkamaṛṛa.
Unnec'essary, *a.* ...	အသုံးမရှိ။ ...	ă-thŏhn-m'she ...	na-zur'oor ...	véṇḍátha,ávasiyagamillátha
Unoc'cupied, *a.* ...	လွတ်လပ်သော။ ...	loht-lut-thaw ...	ghyr-muk'booz ...	páḷána, kuḍiyiráthá.
Unpar'donable, *a.*...	မလွှတ်နိုင်သော။ ...	m'hloht-hnuyng-thaw ...	ghyr-uf'oo ...	mannikkapaḍátha.
Unpleas'ant, *a.* ...	မသာယာသော။ ...	m'thah-yah-thaw ...	na-khoosh ...	veṛuppuḷḷa,santhóshamaṛṛa.
Unprepáred, *a.* ...	အသင့်မရှိသော။ ...	ă-thin-m'she-thaw ...	na-ty'yar ...	ettanappaḍátha, áyattamaṛ-
Unprotec'ted, *a.* ...	အစောင့်အမမရှိသော။ ...	ă-sowng-ă-mah-m'she-thaw.	be-sa'ya ...	kávalillátha,átharavaṛṛa.[ṛa
Unpun'ished, *a.* ...	ဒဏ်မခံရသော။ ...	dun-m'cun-yah-thaw ...	be-suz'a ...	taṇḍikkappaḍátha.
Unquíet, *a.* ...	မငြိမ်းသော။ ...	m'ngyain-thaw ...	be-chyn ...	amaithiyaṛṛa, asaivuḷḷa.
Unread', *a.* ...	မဖတ်သော။ ...	m'put-thaw ...	un-pur'ha, na-khwan'da ...	vásiyátha, kallátha.
Unreas'onable, *a.*...	မညီလျော်သော။ ...	m'nyee-lee-aw-thaw ...	na-mu'u'kool ...	aniyáya.
Unreward'ed, *a.* ...	ဆုမရသော။ ...	soo-m'-yah-thaw ...	be-ujr, [gar,...	kaimáṛillátha.
Unríghteous, *a.* ...	မဖြောင့်မတ်သော။ ...	m'pyowng-mut-thaw ...	be-a'dil, be-in'saf, goo'nah-	níthiyaṛṛa, anítha, tíya.
Unrípe, *a.* ...	မမှည့်သော။ ...	m'hmeh-thaw ...	kuch'cha, up'uk ...	muṛṛátha,paḷátha,*fruit* káy.
Unsáfe, *a.* ...	မလုံချုံသော။ ...	m'lohn-chyohn-thaw ...	be-sul'a'mut ...	mósamána, bhattiramillátha
Unsat'isfied, *a.* ...	သဘောမကျသော။ ...	thă-baw-m'-chyah-thaw ...	na-ra'zee, na-a'soo'du ...	tirptiyillátha.
Unsávoury, *a.* ...	အရသာမရှိသော။ ...	ă-yah-thah-m'she-thaw ...	be-muz'u, be-za'i ka ...	sáramaṛṛa, urusiyaṛṛa.
Unsea'sonable, *a.*...	မတော် သင့်သော အချိန်၌ ဖြစ်	m'taw-thin-thaw-ă-chayn-	be-wukt, be-mou'sim ...	akálaorsamayabhétha-mána
Unseen', *a.* ...	မမြင်သော။ [သော။...	m'myin-thaw,[hnuyt-pyit-	un-dek-ha, na-dee'du ...	káṇátha, atharisanamána.
Unskil'ful, *a.* ...	မတတ်သော။ ...	m'tut-thaw, [thaw,...	be-hik'mut, be-hoo'nur ...	sámárttiyamaṛṛa,puttiyaṛṛa
Unsuccess'ful, *a.* ...	အကြံမထမြောက်သော။ ...	ă-kyun-m'tah-myowk-thaw.	na-kam'yab ...	kúḍátha, sittiyágátha.
Unthank'ful, *a.* ...	ကျေးဇူးမသိသော။ ...	kyay-zoo-mee-thaw ...	na-sip'as, na-shookr ...	nanṛiketta.
Unthrif'ty, *a.* ...	မချွေတာသော။ ...	m'khyoo-ay-tah-thaw ...	be-kif'a'yut ...	útháriyána, áráthúriyána.

Untie, *v. a.* ...	ဖြည်သည်။ ...	pyee-the ...	khol'na ...	avil, kalarru pri, kulai.
Until', *pr.&conj.* Till	ထိုင်အောင်။ ...	tuyng-owng ...	lug, jud-lug, tuk, jud-tul'uk.	mattum, alavu, varaiyil.
Un'to, *pr.* To ...	ကို။ ...	goh ...	ko, koo, koon, kee, ke-tu'een.	idattirku, ku.
Untried, *a.* ...	မစုံစမ်းသော။ ...	m'sohn-sun-thaw ...	na-az'moo'du ...	sóthiyátha, visáranaiyarra.
Untrue', *a.* ...	မဟုတ်မမှန်သော။ ...	m'-hoht-m'hmun-thaw ...	us'ut, jhoo'ta, ka'zib ...	meyyallátha, poyyána.
Unúsual, *a.* ...	တခါတလေသာဖြစ်သော။ ...	t'kah-t'lay-thah-pyit-thaw..	be-dus'toor ...	apúrva, navamána.
Unwell', *a.* ..	မကျန်းမမာသော။ ...	m'khyun-m'mah-thaw ...	na-doo'roost, *v. sick* ...	suhavínamulla, viyáthiyulla.
Unwil'ling, *a.* ...	အလိုမရှိသော။ ...	ă-loh-m'she-thaw ...	na-raz, na-ra'zee, na-khwah.	manasillátha, támathamulla.
Unwor'thy, *a.* ...	မထိုက်တန်သော။ ...	m'tuyk-tun-thaw ...	na-la'ik, na-rus'a ...	tahátha, páttiramarra.
Up, *adv.* ...	အပေါ်သို့။ထသည်။ ...	ă-paw-thoh, tah-the ...	oo'pur, *pers.* bala, oot'ha, oot.	mélé, uyara, míthu.
Upon', *pr.* ...	အပေါ်မှာ။ ...	ă-paw-hmah ...	oo'pur, pur, *pers.* bur ...	mél, míthu, tattu.
Up'right, *a.* ...	မတ်သော။ဖြောင့်မတ်သော။ ...	mut-thaw, pyowng-mut-	khur'a ...	nimirntha, nérmaiyána.
Upset', *v. a.* ...	မှောက်သည်။ ...	mowk-the, [thaw, ..	ool'ta'na ...	kavil, purattu.
Up'ward, *adv.* ...	အထက်သို့တက်သော။ ...	ă-tet-thoh-tet-thaw ...	oo'pur ...	mélága, mélé. [mána.
Ur'gent, *a.* ..	ကြိုးစားအားထုတ်သည်။ ...	kyoh-sah-ăh-toht-the ...	la zim. zur'oor ...	ahattiyamána, ávasiyaga-
U'rine, *s.* ...	ကျင်ငယ်။ရေဟောင်း။သေး။ ...	khying-ngeh, yay-howng,	pesh-ab, pish-ab, moot, boul	sirunír, múttiram, amari.
Us, *pron.* ...	ကျွန်ုပ်တို့ကို။ ...	kyoon-hnoht-doh-goh[thay	hum, hum'en, *duk.* hum'un,-	engalai, nammai.
U'sage, *s.* ...	ထုံးစံ။အလေ့။ဓလေ့။ ...	tohn-zun, ă-lay, dă-lay ..	dus'toor, ru'waj, [hum'na,...	nadappu, valakkam, mámúl.
Use, *v. a.* ...	အလေ့ရှိသည်။ ...	ă-lay-she-the ...	is'ti'u'mal, kam, khid'mut, *f.*	valangu, kaiyálu.
U'seful, *a.* ...	အသုံးဝင်သော။ ...	ă-thohn-win-the ...	kam'ka, moo'feed, na'fi ...	palanulla, ubhayóhamána.
U'seless, *a.* ...	အသုံးမဝင်သော။ ...	ă-thohn-m'win-thaw ...	na kar'u, na-buk'ar, uk'aj'ee	uthavátha, viyarttamána.
Uten'sil, *s.* ...	အသုံးအဆောင်။ပရိက္ခရာ။ ...	ă-thohn-ă-tsowng, pă-rayk-	a lut. *f. vessel,* bur'tun ...	tattumuttu, panimuttu.
Ut'terly, *adv.* ...	အကုန်အစင်။ ...	ă-kohn-ă-tsin, [kă-yah,...	ui ha'yut ...	muluthum. parichchéthamáy
U'vula, *s. Lat.* ...	လျှာခင်။ ...	shah-kin ...	lar, kag, lu'hut, lo'la, kuw'wa.	unnákku, ilam, annákku.
Uxórious, *a.* ...	မယားကိုချစ်လွန်းသော။ ...	ma'yah-goh-chyit-lohn-thaw	zun-pur'ust, kur-lug'oo'a ...	manavikkamaintha.
Va'cancy, *s.* ...	လစ်သောနေရာ။ ...	lut-thaw-nay-yah ...	shig'af, jug'uh, *f.* khul'a ...	káli, verumai.
Vacant, *a.* ..	လစ်သော။ ...	lut-thaw ...	kha'lee, na'gah, [ja'ee,...	veru, káliyána.
Vag'abond, *s.* ...	လူဝင်။ ...	loo-wing ...	koo'cha-gurd, bu het'oo, hur'-	kávâli, pókkiri, tirivón, vínan

English.	Burmese.		Hindustani.	Tamil.
Vague, *a.*	မသေချာသော။	m'thay-chyah-thaw	ghyr-moo'kur'rur	kuriyátha, víṇána, payanaṛṛa
Vain, *a.*	အချည်းနှီးသက်သက်။	ă-chyee-nee-thet-thet	ti'hee, ba'til, ub'us	víṇána, viruthávána.
Vain'ly, *adv.*	အလကား။	ăh-lă-gah	ba'til'se	víṇáy, viruthávay.
Vale, *s.*	ချိုင့်။	chuyng	wa'dee, *f.* nich'an	paḷḷathákku, paḷḷanilam.
Valetudinarian, *s.*	မကျန်းမမာသောသူ။	m'kyun-m'mah-thaw-thoo	jun'um-ro'-gee, [roost,	viyáthiyána.
Val'iant, *a.*	ခွန်အားကြီးသော။	kohn-ăh-kyee-thaw	bu'ha'door, dil'er, dil'chul'a,-	víra- *or* parákkirama-muḷḷa.
Val'id, *a.*	ခိုင်ခံ့သော။	kuyng-eun-thaw	sa'bit, oos'too'war	perumathiyána, stiramána.
Val'our, *s.*	သူရဲခြင်း။	thoo-yeh-chyin	bu'ha'doo'ree. dil'chul'ee, *f.*	víram, súram, sauriyam.
Val'uable, *a.*	အဘိုးထိုက်သော။	ă-poh-tuyk-thaw	kee'mut'ee, gir'a'mee	vilaiyuyarntha, sréshṭamána
Val'ue, *s.*	အဘိုး။	ă-poh	kee'mut, kudr, *f.* bha'o, urz, sar	vilai, perumathi, arttam.
Van, *s.*	တပ်ဦး။	tut-oo	mooh'ra ug'a'ree	murpaḍai, munnaṇichchénai
Van, *s. cart,*	လှည်းကြီး။	hleh-gyee	chhuk'ra, ga'ree	banḍi.
Váriable, *a.*	မတည်တုံ။	m'tee-tun	be-kur'ar	vérupaḍugira, márugira.
Varíety, *s.*	ထူးခြားသောအမျိုး။	too-chyah-thaw-ă-myoh	ruk'um-ruk'um, ruk'um	palavitham, vigarpam.
Várious, *a.*	အမျိုးမျိုး။	ă-myoh-myoh	mookh'tul'if, joo'da-joo'da...	pala-*or*-náná-(-vithamána.)
Var'nish, *s.*	ချိတ်ဆေး။	chyait-tsay	look, kab'i's, choo'pur'na	minukkeṇṇai, varṇattailam.
Vast, *a.*	ကြီးကျယ်သော။	kyee-kyeh-thaw	bur'a, wus'ee, kul'an	éráḷamána, aḷavirantha.
Veal, *s.*	နွားကလေးအသား။	no-ah-gă-lay-ă-thah	buch'reh-ka-gosht	pasuvinkanṛiraichchi.
Véda, *s.*	ဗေဒင်ကျမ်း။	bay-din-khyun	ve'du, ved, *or* bed	vétham.
Veer, *v. a.*	လှည့်သော။	hlee-thaw	phir'na, ghoom'na, [a'tee,...	tiruppu, tirumbhu, vilagu.
Veg'etable, *s.*	ဟင်းသီးဟင်းရွက်ပင်။	hin-thee-hin-yoo-eh-pin	nub'-at, roos'tun'ee, nub'at'-	púḍu, púṇḍu, távaram.
Vel'vet, *s.*	ကတ္တီပါ။	kud-dee-bah	mukh'mul, mukh'mul'ee, *a*...	sûriyakánthippaṭṭu.
Vend, *v. a.*	ရောင်းသည်။	yowng-the	bech'na, bik'a'na, by-k	vil, vilaikkukkoḍu.
Ven'der, Ven'dor, *s.*	ရောင်းသောသူ။	yowng-thaw-thoo	fur'o'shin'da, ba'i'u	virkiravan.
Ven'ison, *s.*	ဒရယ်သား။	dă-yeh-thah	hur'un-ka-gosht, mirg-mans	mániraichchi.
Ven'om, *s.*	အဆိပ်။	ă-tsait	bis, bish, *arab.* zuhr	nañju, visham.

Ven'omous, *a.* ...	အဆိပ်ပါသော။ ...	ă'-tsait-pah-thaw ...	bis'el'a, bis'ha, bis'i'yur ...	nañjulla, vishamulla.
Verb, *s.* ...	ကြိယာ။ ...	kă-ree-yah ...	kri'ya, *f. arab*, fi'ul ...	vinai, vinaichchol.
Ver'dant, *a.* ...	စိမ်းလန်းသော။ ...	sayn-lun-thaw ...	subz, sur-subz, hur'a ...	pasumaiyána, talaitta.
Ver'ily, *adv.* ...	စကန်။အမှန်။ ...	ay-oun, ă-hmun ...	tuh'keek, such, wa'ki'ee ...	meyyáy, unmaiyáy. [ya·
Vernac'ular, *a.* ...	ဇာတိ အမျိုး ဘာ သာနှင့် ဆိုင် သော။ ...	zah-dee-ă-myoh-bah-thah-hnin-suyng-thaw ...	des'ee, mool'kee ...	suthésa, janmathésattirkuri-
Verse, *s.* ...	လင်္ကာ။အပုဒ်။ ...	ling-gah, ă-poht ...	mis'ra, furd, *f.* took ...	páttu, kavi, vasanam, slógam.
Ves'sel, *s.* ...	ခွက်။ ဖလား။ ပုကန်လုံး။ အိုး။ အင်တုံး။သင်္ဘော။ ...	kwet, palah, pă-gun-lohn, oh, in-dohn, thing-baw...	bur'tun, kish'tee, *f.* ju'haz, na'o, suf'ee'na ...	páttiram, tálam, énam, tóni, marakkalam, kappal, uru.
Vex, *v. a.* ...	စိတ်ထွက်သည်။ ...	sayt-twet-the ...	chir'a'na, chher'na, dik-k...	alakkali, kilésappaduttu.
Vexátion, *s.* ...	စိတ်ထွက်ခြင်း။ ...	sayt-twet say-chyin ...	chher, dik, moo'zee-gur'ee, *f.*	tontharai, alaichchal.
Víal, *s.* ...	ပန်ဘူးငယ်။ ...	pun-boo-ngeh ...	shee'shee, *f.* ...	kuppi, kinnan. [nam.
Víand, *s.* ...	အစား။ ...	ă-sah ...	kha'na ...	bhójanam, samaittabhója-
Vicegérent, *s.* ...	မင်းကိုယ်စားလည့်တော်။ ...	min-koh-sah-leh-daw ...	na'ib, ja-nish'een, wul'ee-uhd	prathinithi, bhathilál.
Vicéroy, *s.* ...	ရှင်ဘုရင်ကိုယ်စားပြုခွံအုပ်ချုပ်သောမင်း။ ...	shin-boo-yin-koh-sah-pyoo-yoo-eh-oht-soh-thaw-min...	nou'wab, soo'bu'dar ...	prathiyarasan, thésáthipathi
Více-Ver'sa, *adv.*...	အပြန်အလှန်။ ...	á-pyun-ă-hlun ...	bil'uks, pher-bud'ul ...	ethiráy, máráy, manuthalai-
Vic'tim, *s.* ...	ယစ်ကောင်။ ...	yit-kowng ...	koor'ban, nich'ha'wur, ma'ra.	bhali, rattabhali, irai. [yáy·
Vic'tor, *s. Lat.* ...	နိုင်သောသူ။ ...	nuyng-thaw-thoo ...	ghal'ib, gha'zee, zuf'ur'yab.	verriyadainthavan, vijayan·
Victórious, *a.* ...	အောင်သော။ ...	owng-thaw ...	futh-mund, futh'yab, fee'roz.	verrikonda, verriyulla.
Vic'tory, *s.* ...	အောင်မြင်ခြင်း။ ...	owng-myin-chyin ...	futh, zuf'ur, fee'roz-mund'ee.	verri, jayam, kelippu.
Victu'als, *s.* ...	စားစရာ။ ...	sah-sah-yah ...	kha'na, seed'ha, bho'jun ...	bhójanam, ágáram.
View, *s.* ...	ကြည့်ရှုခြင်း။ ...	kyee-shoo-chyin ...	nuz'ur, li'haz, drisht, *f.* ...	kátchi, tórram, párvai, kannu.
Vig'our, *s.* ...	အား။ခွန်အား။ ...	ăh, kohn-ăh ...	tun'door'oos'tee, zor ...	ánmai, víran, thairiyam.
Vile, *a.* ...	ယုတ်မာသော။ ...	yoht-mah-thaw ...	kum-zurf, bud, boo'ra ...	pálána, ilivulla, arppa.
Vil'la, *s.* ...	အိမ်ကလေး။ ...	ayn-gă-lay ...	ba'ti'ka ...	singáravídu, náttumáligai.
Vil'lage, *s.* ...	ရွာ။ဇနပုဒ်။ ...	yoo-ah, ză-nă-boht ...	bus'tee, *f.* ga'on, gram, teh'ra.	úr, grámam, kuppam.
Vil'lager, *s.* ...	ရွာသူ။ ...	yoo-ah-thoo ...	bus'tee-wal, dih'kan ...	grámattán, úrán.

English.	Burmese.		Hindustani.	Tamil.
Vine, *s.*	စပျစ်နွယ်ပင်။	să-byit-noo-ay-bin	un-goor-ka-dur'ukht	dráḍchakkoḍi.
Vin'egar, *s.*	ပုံးရည်။	pohn-yee	sir'ka, *arab.* khull, lys	káḍi.
Vine'yard, *s.*	စပျစ်ဥယျာဉ်။	tsă-byit-oo-yin	un'goor-is'tan	dráḍchattóṭṭam.
Violence, *s.*	ပြင်းထန်ခြင်း။	pyin-tun-chyin	jubr, zub'ur-dust'ee, *f.* zor...	koḍumai, bhalátkáram.
Violent, *a.*	ကျမ်းဒမ်သော။	kyun-dun-thaw	zub'ur-dust, *vehement* sukht.	balapanthamuḷḷa, koḍiya.
Violin', *s.*	တယော။	t'yaw	be'la, sa'rung'ee, *hin.*	víṇai, kiṇṇáram, sáraṅgi.
Viper, *s.*	မြွေဆွေ။	moo-ay-bweh	uf'a. *pers.* teer-mar	viriyanpámbhu.
Vir'gin, *s.*	အပြိုကညာ။	ă-pyoh-kah-nyah, [thaw,...	ko'ree, do'shee'zu, kun'ya, *f.*	kanni, kanniyástiri, kumari.
Vir'ile, *a.*	ယောက်ျားနှင့်ဆိုင်သော။	yowk-kyah-hnin-suyng-	mur'da'nu	áṇmaiyuḷḷa. víramuḷḷa.
Vir'tue, *s.*	တန်ခိုး။ပါရမီ။	t'goh. pah-ra-mee	di'ya'nut, fuzl, dhurm, poon'-	oḷukkam, aṛam, puṇṇiyam.
Vis'ible, *a.*	ထင်ရှားသော။	tin-shah-thaw	za'hir, uy'an, [yu,...	tóṛṛamuḷḷa, káṅgiṛa.
Vis'ion, *s.*	ရူပါရုံ။	yoo-pah-yohn	nuz'ur	párvai, káṭchi. tharisanam.
Vis'it, *s.*	အကြည့်အရှုခြင်း။	ă-kyee-ă-shoo-chyin	moo'la'kat, *f.* bhent, mil'ap.	póychchanthikkai, póykkáṇ-
Vis'itor, *s.*	အကြည့်အရှုသွားလာသောသူ။	ă-kyee-ă-shoo-thwah-lah-	moo'la'kee, mil'ap'ee, za'ir...	póychchanthikkiṛavan[ugai
Viz, Videl'icet, *adv.*	ဟူသည်ကား။	hoo-thee-gah, [thaw-thoo,...	*that is* ja'no, ya'neh, ya'nee.	athávathu, ennaveṇil.
Voice, *s.*	အသံ။	ă-thun	a'waz, nu'wa, sud'a, sout *f.*...	kural, sattam, ósai, nátham
Volcáno, *s.*	မီးထွက်သောတောင်။	mee-twet-thaw-towng	jwa'la-mookh, jul'ta-pu'har.	agnimalai, erigiṛamalai.
Vol'ume, *s.*	အခွေ။စာအုပ်။	ă-kway, sah-ohk, [thoo,...	duf'tur, *f.* durj, too'mar ...	pustagachchuruḷ, parumam.
Volunteer', *s.*	အလိုအလျောက်ဝင်သောသူ။	ă-loh-ă-lyowk-win-thaw-	ek'ka, oop'ka'ree, nuj'eeb ...	sambhaḷaminṛichchévippón.
Volup'tuary, *s.*	ကာမဂုဏ်မှုနှင့်ပျော်မွေ့သော။	kah-mah-gohn-hnin-pyaw-	yar-bash, rus'i'ya	kámi, kámavigáran. [thura.
		moo-ay-thaw	yar-bash, jush'nee	kámavigáramuḷḷa. kámá-
Vom'it, *v.*	အန်သည်။	un-the	chhant. *f.* *sans.* bum'un	kakkal, vánthi.
Vouch, *v. a.*	တိုင်တည်သည်။	tuyng-teh-the	sha'hid'ee-d, gu'wah'ee-d ...	sáṭchikkaḷai sáṭchichollu.
Vouch'er, *s.*	သက်သေ။	thet-thay	dul'eel. *f. v.* *Document*	sáṭchichollugiṛavan. [kaḍan.
Vow, *s.*	သစ္စာပြုသည်။	thit-sah-pyoo-the	nuzr, *f.* *sans.* sun-kulp, prun,	poruttanai, nómbhu, néṛ-
Vow'el, *s.*	သရ။	thah-yah	swur, mat, mut'ra, nook'tu...	uyireḷuttu, uyir, ávi.

Voy'age, *s.*	ရေပေါ်မှာခရီးသွားခြင်း။	yay-baw-hmah-kă-yee-	dur'i'ya'ee *or* juh'az'ee-suf'ur.	kaḍarpirayáṇam, yáttirai.
Vul'gar, *a.*	အခွဲဂကျာန်း။	ă-kweh-gah-nun [thwah-	am, sa'man'yu, neech, pa'jee.	kíḻmaiyána, níchan, eḷiya.
Vul'ture, *s.*	လင်းတ။	lin-dah, [chyin,...	giddh,geedh,run'git,kur'gus	irásáḷi, valiyán.
Wag, *s.*	နန့်သည်။လှုပ်သည်။လူပြက်။	nun-the, hloht-the,loo-byet.	thut'heh-baz, thut'hol'i'ya...	kómáḷi, tiruvan, chuḻiyan.
Wáger, *s.*	လောင်းစားသည်။	lowng-sah-the	hor, *f.* da'o, gir'ou	panthayam, sabhatham.
Wáges, *s. pl.*	အခ။လက်ခ။	ă-kah, lek-kah	tul'ub, mih'nut'a'na	sambhaḷam, kúli.
Wail, *s.*	ငိုကျွေးမြည်တမ်ခြင်း။	ngoh-kyoo-ay-myee--tun-	na'lish, nou'hu, kook, *f.*	aḻu pulambhu, pralábi.
Waist, *s.*	ခါး။	kah, [chyin,...	kum'ur, *sans.* kut'ee, *f.*	iḍai, arai, iḍuppu, naḍu.
Waist'belt, *s.*	ခါးပတ်။	kah-but	*pers.*kum'ur-bund,*hin.*phent	araippaṭṭigai.
Waist'coat, *s.*	လက်တို။	let-toh	cho'lee, kum'ree-un'gur'kha.	márbhuchchaṭṭai, iravikkai.
Wait, *v. a.*	ဆိုင်းသည်။စောင့်နေသည်။	suyng-the, sowng-nay-the.	subr-k, ruh-ja'na	káttiru, ethirpár.
Wákeful, *a.*	နိုးသည်။	noh-the	be-dar, hosh'yar	viḻippána, túṅgátha.
Walk, *v. a.*	လမ်းလျှောက်သည်။	lun-showk-the	chul'a'na, phir'na	naḍa, chel.
Wall, *s.*	ဖုတ်ရိုး။	oht-yoh	dee'wal,dee'war *sans.*bheent	chuvar, mathil.
Wal'let, *s.*	လွယ်အိတ်။	loo-eh-ayt	zum'beel. khoor'jeen, *f.*	sámánpai, aḍaipai, pothi.
Wal'nut, *s.*	သစ်ကျားသီး။	thit-khyah-thee	ukh'rot, uk'root	kaḍukkáy, kaḍu.
Wand, *s.*	လှံတံ။	hlun-dun	chhur'ee, chhik'oo'nee, *f.*	taṇḍam, cheṅgól. [lagu.
Wan'der, *v. n.*	အရပ်ရပ်လှည့်လည် သွားသည်။	ă-yut-yut-hlee-lee-thwah-	rum'na, phir'na	alai ulai, tiri, uḻalu, vaḻivi-
Want, *s.*	လိုသည်။	loh-the, [the ...	chah, ha'jut, ih'ti'yaj, *f.*	tévai, virumbhu, véṇḍu.
War, *s.*	စစ်တိုက်ခြင်း။	tait-tuyk-chyin	lur'a'ee, *f.* joodh, run	pór, chaṇḍai, yuttam.
Ward, *s.*	စောင့်နေခြင်း။	sowng-nay-chyin	pa'ra,*hin.* mu'hul'luh, *arab*...	kával, mariyal, taḍai.
War'den, War'der,*s*	စောင့်ထိမ်းသောသူ။	sowng-tayn-thaw-thoo	dur'wan, dur'waz'ee	káppavan, kávarkáran. [án.
Ware, *s.*	ကုန်စည်။	kohn-see	mal, us'bab	sarakku, viyábhárachchám-
Wárehouse, *s.*	ကုန်လှောင်ရာတိုက်။	kohn-hlowng-yah-tuyk	kot'hee, bar-kha'nu, go'dam.	paṇḍasálai, kalañjiyam.
Warm, *a.*	နွေးသော။	noo-ay-thaw	gurm, ta'tul, tup'ut	analána, veppamána.
Warmth, *s.*	နွေးခြင်း။	noo-ay-chyin	gur'mee, gur'ma [na,...	veppam. chúḍu.
Warn, *v.a. caution.*	သတိပေးသည်။	th'dee-pay-the	jut'a'na, chit'a'na, kan-khol'-	echchari, bhayamuruttu.
Warn'ing, *v. n.*	သတိပေးခြင်း။	th'dee-pay-chyin	chit'a'o'nee, khub'ur, *f.*	echcharikkai, uṛuthichchol.

English.	Burmese.		Hindustani.	Tamil.
War'rant, *s.* ...	ဝါရန်စာ။	... wah-run-sah	... pur'wa'nu, hookm-na'mu...	kaṭṭaḷai, athigárapattirikai.
War'rior, *s.* ...	ရဲသောသူ။	... yeh-thaw-thoo	... jun'gee, hur'bee, jo'dha, bhut.	pórvíran, súran.
Wáry, *a.* ...	သတိပြုသော။	... th'dee-pyoo-thaw	... chou'kun'na, [shoo-k,...	echcharippuḷḷa, viḻippuḷḷa.
Wash, *v. a.* ...	ဆေးကြောသည်။	... say-kyaw-the	... dho'na, nu'ha'na, shoost-o-	kaḻuvu, kuḷi, kasakku, tuvai.
Wash, *face, v. a.* ...	မြက်နှာသစ်သည်။	... myeh-hnah-thit-the	... moonh-dho'na ...	mukham *or* múñchi-kaḻuvu.
Wash, *hands, v.a.*...	လက်ဆေးသည်။	... let-say-the	... hath,- *or* dust,-(-dho'na) ...	kai-(*or*)-kaiyai-kaḻuvu.
Wash, *clothes, v.a.*...	အဝတ်ဖွတ်သည်။	... ă-woot-polit-the	... kup'ra-dhona, *or* pheench'na,	tuṇi-(*or*)-véshṭi-(-tuvai, *or*
Wash, *houses, v.a.*...	အိမ်ဆေးသည်။	... ayn-say-the	... ghur-dho'na, [dhob...	víṭṭai-kaḻuvu. [kasakku.)
Wash'er-man, *s.* ...	ခဝါသည်။	... kă-wah-the	... dho'bee, ruj'uk, bur'et'ha ...	vaṇṇán, égáli.
Wasp, *s.* ...	နကြည်။	... nă-gyee	... birnee, bur, boor'la, hud'da...	kuḷavi, vaṇḍu.
Waste, *s.* ...	ပြုန်းတီးသော။	... pyohn-tee-thaw	... is'raf, (nook'san. *loss*) ...	víñchelavu, kéḍu, páḻ.
Watch, *s. time piece.*	နာရီ။	... nah-yee	... ghur'ee, sa'ut, *f.* [san'kur, *f.*	kai-kaḍiyáram.
Watch-chain, *s.* ...	နာရီကြိုး။	... nah-yee-khyoh	... ghur'ee-yal'-ka-san'kul, *or*	kaḍiyárasangili.
Watch, *s.* ...	အစောင့်။	... a-sowng	... ja'gut, puh'ra, ni'guh-ban'ee.	kával, kávarkárar.
Watch, *v.* ...	စောင့်နေသည်။	... sowng-nay-the	... chow'kee-d, puh'ra-d [dar...	kávalchey, ká.
Watch'ful, *a.* ...	စောင့်နေသော။	... sowng-nay-thaw	... hosh'yar, chou'kus, khub'ur'-	viḻippuḷḷa, jákkrathaiyuḷḷa.
Watch'-house, *s.* ...	ကင်းတဲ။	... kin-teh	... chou'kee-kha'nuh ...	kávalvíḍu.
Wat'er, *s.* ...	ရေ။	... yay	... pa'nee, pun'i'ya, jul, neer ab.	taṇṇír, jalam.
Wat'ercourse, *s.* ...	ချောင်းငယ်။	... khyowng-ngeh	... nuhr, *f.* ...	níróṭṭam, nírppáyohchal.
Wat'erfall, *s.* ...	ရေတံခွန်။	... yay-t'goon	... ab-shar, *f.* ...	aruvi, nírvíḻchchi
Wat'er-lily, *s.* ...	ကြာပွင့်။	... kyah-bwin	... kunj, sur'oj kum'ul ...	nírámbal.
Wat'er-man, *s.* ...	လှေသား။	... hlay-thah	... dand'ee, mul'lah ...	tóṇikkáran, paḍavukkáran.
Wat'er-mill, *s.* ...	ရေယန္တရားစက်။	... yay-yun-dă-yah-set	... pun-chuk'kee, a'si'ya, *f.* ...	jalayanthiram.
Wave, *s.* ...	လှိုင်းတံပိုး။	... hluyng-t'boh	... mouj, mou'juh, hil'kor ...	alai, tirai, tarangam.
Wax, *s.* ...	ဖယောင်း။	... pă-yowng	... mom, shum, *lac* lukh ...	meḻugu, arakku.
Way, *s.* ...	နည်း။ခရီး။လမ်း။	... nyee, kă-yee, lun	... tur'eek, *f.* ras'ta, rus'tu ...	vaḻi, páthai, márkkam.

We, *pron.* ...	ကျွန်ုပ်တို့။ ...	kyoon-hnoht-doh, ngah-doh.	hum, hum'a're, hum'un ...	nángal, nám, yám.
Weak, *a.* ...	အားနည်းသော။ ...	ah-nee-thaw ...	be-zor, kum'zor, **be-ta'kut**...	bhalavínamulla, melintha.
Weak'ness, *s.* ...	မသန်စွမ်းသော။ ...	m'thun-sohn-thaw ...	kum-zor'ee, **be-ta'kut'ee** *f.*...	bhalavínam. chórvu.
Wealth, *s.* ...	စည်းစိမ်ခြင်း။ ...	tsee-sayn-chyin ...	sum-put, dou'lut, *f.* durb ...	chelvam, válvu.
Wean, *v. a.* ...	နို့ခွဲသည်။ ...	noh-kweh-the ...	doodh-chhoo'ra'na ...	pálmarakkappannu.
Wear, *v. a.* ...	ဝတ်သည်။ ...	woot-the ...	pin'ha'na ...	ani, tari, púnu.
Weath'er, *s.* ...	ဥတု။ ...	oo-doo ...	rit'oo, *f.* (yam, *arab.*) uy'yam.	kálasubhávam, kálabétham.
Weave, *v. a.* ...	ရက်သည်။ ...	yet-the ...	boon'na, bin'na, goondh'na..	ney, nesavupannu.
Weav'er, *s.* ...	ရက်သောသူ။ ...	yet-thaw-thoo ...	tan'tee, ko'lee, joo'lah ...	nesavukáran, kárugan.
Web, *s.* ...	ရက်ကန်းသား။ပင့်ကူမျှေး။ ...	yet-kun-thah, pin-goo-	baft, *f.* ...	neyyappattathu.
Wed, *v. a.* & *n.* ...	လက်ထပ်သည်။ ...	let-tut-the, [hmyay,...	sha'dee-k, by'ah-k ...	viváhamudi, kaliyánañchey.
Wed'ding, *s.* ...	လက်ထပ်မင်္ဂလာပွဲ။ ...	let-tut-min-gă-lah-poo-ey..	sha'dee, *f.* by'ah ...	viváham, kaliyánam.
Wedge, *s.* ...	အတုံး။သပ်။ ...	ă-tohn, thut ...	phun'ee, mekh, puch'chur, *f.*	áppu, *of metal* pálam.
Wednes'day, *s.* ...	ဗုဒ္ဓဟူးနေ့။ ...	bohd-dhoo-nay ...	boodh, char-shum'bu ...	bhuthankilamai.
Week, *s.* ...	ခုနစ်ရက်။ ...	koh-hnit-yet ...	huftu, *sans.* uth'wa'ra ...	váram, kilamai.
Weep, *v.* ...	ငိုသည်။ ...	ngoh-the ...	ro'na, bil'la'na, too'suk'na...	alu, pralábi.
Weigh, *v. a.* ...	ချိန်သည်။ ...	chain-the ...	tol'na, toul'na, jokh'na ...	niru, túkku, edu.
Weight, *s.* ...	အချိန်။ ...	ă-chayn ...	toul, jokh ...	nirai, bháram, edai.
Weight'y, *a.* ...	လေးသော။ ...	lay-thaw, [chyin,...	bha'ree ...	kanamána, prathána. [ram.
Wel'come, *s.* ...	ဝမ်းမြောက်စွာလက်ခံခြင်း။ ...	wun-myowk-swah-let-cun-	moo'ba'ruk-bad, mur'hub'a..	váltu, sóbhanam, ubachá-
Wel'fare, *s.* ...	ကောင်းမွန်စွာနေခြင်း။ ...	kowng-mohn-swah-nay-	bhul'a'ee, koo'sul, *f.* chhem.	sugam, kshémam.
Well, (*water*) *s.* ...	ရေတွင်း။ ...	yay-dwin, chyin,...	koo'a, ba'o'lee, *f.* chah ...	kinaru, kúvam.
Well, (*in health*) *a.*	မာသော။ ...	mah-thaw ...	uch'chhee-tur'uh, sul'a'mut..	sugamulla, sugamána.
"Are you well?,". How do you do?...	မာ၏လား။ ...	mah-ee-lah ...	toom-uch'chha-ho, (*respectfully*, ap-uch'chha-hyn...	sugamá. eppdi-yiurkkiráy.
Well, *adv.* ...	လျောက်ပတ်စွာ။ ...	lee-owk-put-swah ...	tun'door'oost, nee'ka ...	sugamáy, kettiyáy, nanráy.
West, *s.* ...	အနောက်။ ...	ă-nowk ...	puch'chhum, ghoo'roob ...	mérku, mérrisai.
Wes'tern, *a.* ...	အနောက်အရပ်။ ...	ă-nowk-ă-yut ...	ghurb'ee, mugh'rib'ee ...	mérkilulla, mérrisaiyána.

ENGLISH.	BURMESE.		HINDUSTANI.	TAMIL.
Wet, *a.* ...	ရွဲသော။ ...	tsoh-thaw ...	bhee'ga, bhee'na, gee'la, num.	nanaintha, íramána. [turai-
Wharf, *s.* ...	တန်တား။ ...	tun-dah, (*pron.* t'dah) ...	(ghat, *sans.*) wharf ...	éṟṟiṟakkumathi-cheyyum-
Wharf'age, *s.* ...	တန်တားခ။ ...	t'dah-kah ...	ghut'war'ee ...	éṟṟiṟakkumathi-kúli.
What, *interrog.pron*	ဘယ်ဟာ။ ...	beh-hah, (*pron.* bhah) ...	ky'a ? ku'ha ? jo, jis, joun...	enna, ethu, yáthu.
Whatev'er, *pron.* ...	ဘယ်အရာမဆို။ ...	beh-a-yah-m'soh ...	jo-jo, jis-tis, jo-kooch ...	ethágilum, yáthenilum.
Wheat, *s.* ...	ဂျုံစပါး။ ...	jyohn-să-bah' ...	gun'doom, ge'hoon ..	kóthumai.
Wheel, *s.* ...	ဘိန်း။ ...	bayn ...	chuk'kur, chukr, puh'i'ya ...	uruḷai, sakkaram.
When, *adv.* ...	ဘယ်သောအခါ။ ...	(*pron.*) beh-daw-a-kah ...	jub, jis-wukt, jub-ki, jud ...	eppoḻuthu, ennéram.
Whence, *adv.* ...	အဘယ်အရပ်က။ ...	a-beh-a-yut-gah ...	ju'han'se, ku'han'se, kid'hur'-	eṅgé, evviḍattil, eṅgirunthu.
Whenev'er, *adv.* ...	ဘယ်အချိန်မဆို။ ...	beh-a-chain-m'soh ...	jub-jub, jub-kub'hee, [se,...	eppoḻuthágilum.
Where, *adv.* ...	ဘယ်မှာ။ ...	beh-hmah ...	kid'hur, ? ku'han, ? ju'han,	eṅgé, evviḍam, avviḍattil.
Whereabout', *adv*...	အရပ်အနီးအပါးတွင်။ ...	ă-yut-ă-nee-a-pah-dwin ...	kis-tur'uf ? [jid'hur...	evviḍattil. eṅgé. [ṟálum.
Whereas', *adv* ...	သို့ဖြစ်၍။ ...	thoh-pyit-yoo-eh ...	bur-uks ...	áthalál, appaḍiyirukka, en-
Whereat', *adv.* ...	သောအရပ်မှာ။ ...	thaw-ă-yut-hmah ...	tis-pur ...	ethinál, athinál.
Where'fore, *adv.* ...	အကြောင်းကြောင်း။ ...	ă-kyowng-chyowng ...	is-was'te, kis-was'te, ka,heko?	etharkága, ethanál, áthalál.
Wheresoev'er, *adv*...	ဘယ်အရပ်မဆို။ ...	beh-ă-yut-m-tsoh ...	ju'han-ju'han, jis-tur'uf ...	evviḍattilágilum, evviḍatti-
Whereupon', *adv*....	အရာအပေါ်မှာ။ ...	ă-yah-ă-paw-hmah ...	tispur ...	athanál, athaippaṟṟi. [lum.
Wheth'er, *adv.* ...	ကို။ ...	goh, [goh,...	ki, ky'a kim ba, [kis?kaun'sa.	ethuvágilum.
Which, *interrogpron*	ဘယ်သင်းကို၊ ဘယ်အရာကို။ ...	beh-thin-goh, beh-ă-yah-	jo, joun, joun'sa, je, jis, koun ?-	ethu, yáthu, entha, athu.
While, *s.* ...	စဉ်တွင်၊အခါ။ ...	see-dwin, ă-kah ...	be'la, *arab.* ur'su, mood'dut, *f.*	véḷai, poḻuthu, néram.
Whim, *s.* ...	အခြင်း။ ...	ă-khyun ...	khi'yal, mouj, tur'ung, *f.* ...	eṇṇam, kóṭpáḍu, ninaippu.
Whim'per, *v. n.* ...	ငိုသည်။ ...	ngoh-the ...	bi'soor'na ...	chiṇuṅgu, vimmiyaḻu.
Whip, *s.* ...	ကြိမ်လုံးတဖျား။ ...	chain-lohn-t'byah ...	cha'book, ko'ra, ta'zi'ya'nuh	chavukku, jáṭṭi.
Whip, *v. a.* ...	ရိုက်သည်။ ...	yuyk-the ...	cha'book-mar'na ...	chavukkináḷaḍi, kasaiyáḷaḍi.
Whirl, *v.* ...	ချာချာလည်သည်။ ...	chyah-chyah-lee-the ...	gur'dish *f.* ...	chuḻi, chuḻalvu.
Whirl'pool, *s.* ...	ဝဲ။ ...	weh ...	gird-ab, ghurk-ab ...	nírchchuḻi.

Whirl'wind, *s.* ...	လေဘွေ။ ...	lay-bweh ...	gird-bad, *f.* chukr, bug'oo'la.	chulalkárru, chulikárru.
Whis'ker, *s.* ...	ပါးမုန်း။ ...	pah-mohn ...	moochh, moench, *f.* ...	kannamísai.
Whis'per, *v. a.* & *n.*	တိုးတိုးပြောသည်။ ...	toh-doh-pyaw-the, [gă-lay.	kan-men-kuh'na, ka'na-	irakasiyampésu, kusukusu.
Whis'tle, *s.* ...	လေချွန်သည်။ပြွေကလေး။ ...	lay-chyohn-the, pă-loo-ay-	see'tee, sit'tee *f.* [ka'nee-k,...	síkkárakkulal ísaladikkum-
White, *s.* ...	ဖြူသော။ ...	pyoo-thaw ...	suf'ed, soo'fyd chit'ta, ou'dat	venmai, vellai. [karuvi.
White-lead, *s.* ...	ခဲဖြား။ ...	keh-byah ...	suf'eda, soo'fy'da ...	vellíyam.
Whitewash, *s.* ...	ထုံးဖြူရည်။ ...	tohn-pyoo-yee ...	kul'ee-choon ...	kulaichunnámbhu.
Whith'er, *adv.* ...	အဘယ်အရပ်သို့။ ...	ă-beh-ă-yut-thoh ...	jidhur, *adv.* kid'hur,? khooja,?	engu, engé.
Who, *rel. pron.* ...	ဘယ်သူ။ ...	beh-thoo(*colloquially* b'doo.)	jo, joun, jis, koun,? ki,? kin,?.	ár, yávan, evar, evan, eval.
Whoev'er, *pron.* ...	မည်သူမဆို။ ...	mee-thoo-m'tsoh ...	jo-ko'ee, jo-jo, jo'ee-ko'ee ...	árágilum, evanágilum, evanó
				evaló. [tam, mulumai.
Whole, *s.* ...	အားလုံး။ ...	ă-lohn ...	tum'am'ee, kool lee, *f.* sub,	muluvathum, ellám, samas-
Whólesale, *s.* ...	ဖောက်သည်ချ။ ...	hpowk-the-chyah ...	thok-dar. [su'ra,...	mottavilai, órottu.
Whólly, *adv.* ...	အကုန်အစင်။ ...	ă-kohn-ă-sin ...	tum'am'tur, kool lee, bil kool.	égattukku tíra, muluthum.
Whom, *pron.* ...	ဘယ်သူကို။ ...	beh-thoo-goh, (*colloquially*	jis *pl.* jin, (kis ? *pl.* kin ?)...	árai. yárai, evanai, evalai.
Whoop, *v. a.* ...	အော်ဟစ်သည်။ ...	aw-hit-the, [b'doo-goh,)...	lul'kar-na ...	kúvenal, kúvili, kúval [agal.
Whore, *s.* ...	မိမ္မရှင်။ ...	maym-mah-shwin ...	chhin'al, lo'lee, pa'toor, *f.*...	vési vésai, parattai vilaim-
Whose, *pron.* ...	ဘယ်သူ၏။ ...	beh-thoo-ee ...	jis-ka, jis-kee, kis-ka? kis-kee?	árudaiya, evarudaiya [gilum
Whosoev'er, *pron.*...	ဘယ်သူမဆို။ ...	beh-thoo-m'soh ...	jo-ko'ee, jo-jo. jo'ee-ko'ee ...	evanágilum, evanum, evali.
Why, *adv.* ...	အကြောင်းကြောင့်။ အဘယ်	ă-kyowng-gyowng, ă beh-	ka'he? ka'he-ko? ky'oon?	
	ကြောင့်။ဘာဖြစ်လို့။ ...	khyowng, bah-pyoo-loh...	kis-was'te ? ...	én, ennattinál, éthu.
Wick, *s.* ...	မီးစာ။ ...	mee-sah ...	but'tee, *f.* (ful'ee'ta, *arab.*)...	vartti, vilakkuttiri.
Wick'ed, *a.* ...	ဆိုးသော။ ...	soh-thaw, [ă-khyin ...	bud, khub'ees, uk'ur'mee ...	tudukkulla, pollátha.
Wick'edness, *s.* ...	ဆိုးသောအရာ။ဆိုးသောအကျင့်။	soh-thaw-ă-yah, soh-thaw-	bud'ee, boo'ra'ee, uk'urm, *f.*..	pollángu, tívinai ágámiyam.
Wide, *a.* ..	ကျယ်သော။ ...	khyeh-thaw ...	chou'ra, chuk'la ...	aganra, agalamána, viriváná
Wid'ow, *s.* ...	မုဆိုးမ။ ...	moh-soh-mah ...	be'wa, *pers.* vid huv'a, *f.* ...	kaimpen, vithavai, kaimai.
Wid'ower, *s.* ...	မုဆိုးဖို။ ...	moh-soh-boh ...	run'doo'a, *sans.* ...	táramilanthón, vithuran.
Wid'owhood, *s* ...	မုဆိုးမ၏အဖြစ်။ ...	moh-soh-ee-ă pyit ...	be'wa'gee, *pers.* run'da-pur'o.	vithavaittanmai kaimai.

English.	Burmese.		Hindustani.	Tamil.
Width, *s.* ...	အနံ။ဗျက်။ ...	ă-nun, byet ...	chou'ra'ee, puh'na'ee, *f.* ...	agalam, virivu, parappu.
Wield, *v. a.* ...	လက်စွဲ၍သုံးသည်။ ...	let-sweh-yoo-eh-thohn-the..	chul'a'na ...	iyaṟṟu, naḍattu, cheluttu.
Wife, *s.* ...	မယား။ ...	mă-yah ...	jo'roo, put'nee, (zou'ja, *arab.*).	manaivi, pári, manaiyáṭṭi,
Wild, *s.* ...	မယဉ်။ရိုင်းသော။ ...	m'yin, yuyng-thaw ...	jun'gul, by'a'ban, wuh'shut, *f.*	káḍu, vanántharam. [illáḷ.
Wil'derness, *s.* ...	တော။ ...	taw ...	wuh'shut, *f.* ...	vanam, vanántharam, káḍu.
Wile, *s.* ...	လိမ်မာခြင်း။ ...	laym-mah-chyin ...	hee'lu ...	tanthiram, chúthu, kapaḍam.
Wil'ful, *a.* ...	သဘောရှိသည့်အတိုင်း။ ...	th'baw-she-the-ă-tuyng ...	hut'hee, khood-sur ...	tanmúppána, aḍaṅgátha.
Will, *s.* ...	အလိုရှိခြင်း။သဘော။ ...	ă-loh-shee-chyin, th'baw ...	mush'ee'yut, *f.* ikh'ti'yar,	chittam, manam, karuttu.
Wil'ling, *a.* ...	သဘောရှိသည်။ ...	th'baw-shee-the ...	ra'zee, moo'reed, [cha'ha...	priyamuḷḷa, manamuḷḷa.
Wily, *a.* ...	လိမ်မာသော။ ...	laym-mah-thaw ...	hee'lu-baz, hee'lu-gur ...	tanthiramuḷḷa, máyamána,
Win, *v. a. & n.* ...	နိုင်သည်။အောင်သည်။ ...	nuyng-the, owng-the ...	jeet'na, ba'zee-le'ja'na, le'na.	vellu, keli, jayi.
Wind, *s.* ...	လေ။လက်လုံး။ ...	lay, let-lohn ...	hu'wa, reeh, *f.* pu'wun *sans.*..	káṟṟu, váyu. [thiram.
Wind'mill, *s.* ...	လေယန္တရားစက်။ ...	lay-yun-dă-yah-set ...	pu'wun-chuk'kee, *f.* ...	káṟṟáliyakkappaḍumyan-
Win'dow, *s.* ...	ပြတင်းပေါက်။ ...	pyah-din-powk ...	khir'kee, *f.* dur'ee'chu, *pers.*	palakaṇi, jannal.
Wind'pipe, *s.* ...	အသက်လေ ထွက်ဝင်ရာ လည်	ă-thet-lay-twet-win-yah-	gul'oo, goo'loo, nul'ee, nul'da..	kuralvaḷai miḍaṟu.
Wine, *s.* ...	စပျစ်ရည်။ [ချောင်း။...	sa-byit-yee, [lee-chyowng...	shur'ab, my, dookh'tur-i-roz.	dráḍcharasam.
Wing, *s.* ...	အတောင်။ ...	ă-towng ...	pur, *pers.* puchh, pukh, *sans.*	chiṟai, chiṟagu, cheṭṭai.
Wing'ed, *(swift) a.*..	လျင်မြန်သော။ ...	lyin-myun-thaw ...	pur'in'du, pur'un'du ...	iṟaguḷḷa, chiṟaguḷḷa.
Wink, *s.* ...	မျက်တောင်ခတ်သည်။ ...	myet-downg-cut-the ...	jhup'kee, chush'muk, *f.* ...	imai, chimiṭṭu.
Win'now, *v. a.* ...	လှေ့သည်။ ...	hlay-the ...	oo'sa'na, dhoo'ri'ya'na ...	muṟam, chuḷagu.
Win'ter, *s.* ...	ဆောင်းကာလ။ ...	sowng-kah-lah ...	ja'ra, thund-ka'la, shit'a ...	márikálam, sítaḷakálam.
Wire, *s.* ...	နန်းကြိုး။ ...	nun-khyoh ...	*pers.* tar, *m. f.* ...	kambi, saraḍu, tanthiri.
Wis'dom, *s.* ...	ပညာ။ ...	pin-nyah ...	*arab.* ukl, *f.* woo'koof, da'nish.	ñánam, aṟivu, vivékam.
Wise, *a.* ...	ပညာရှိသော။ ...	pin-nyah-she-thaw ...	ukl-mund, a'kil, ul'eem ...	ñánamuḷḷa, aṟivuḷḷa.
Wish, *s.* ...	အလို။ ...	ă-loh ...	*arab.* ir'a'da, ish'ti'yak ...	viruppam, ásai, ával, avá.
Witch, *s.* ...	စုန်းမ။ ...	sohn-mah ...	ja'doo-gur'nee *f.* ton'ha'ee...	kusalakkári, mánthiriyastiri.

With, *pr.* ...	နှင့်။နှင့်အတူ။ ...	hnin, hnin-ă-too ...	se, sen ...	kúḍa, uḍan, óḍu, kiṭṭa, ál.
Withal', *adv.* ...	အတူ။ ...	ă-too ...	sath-is'ke ...	kúḍa, um.
Withdraw', *v. a.* ...	ထွက်သွားသည်။ ...	twet-thwah-the ...	le-lena ...	níkku. piri, eḍu, pókku.
With'er, *v a.* ..	ညှိုးနွမ်းသည်။ ...	nyoh-no-un-the ...	sookh'na, moor'jha'na ...	váṭṭu, ularttu, váḍu, ular.
Within', *pr.* ...	အထဲမှာ။ ...	ă-teh-hmah ...	bhee'tur, un'dur, un'dur'oon.	uḷ, uḷḷé, il, iḍaiyé.
Without', *pr.* ...	အပြင်မှာ။ ...	ă-pyin-hmah ...	be'roon, be, bi'la, bin, bin'a, nir, la ...	illámal, inṛi, oḷiya anṛi.
Withstand', *v. a.* ...	ရပ်ခံသည်။တားသည်။ ...	yut-cun-the, tah-the ...	bur'a'bur'ee-k ...	ethir, maṛi, viróthi, taḍu.
Wit'ness, *s.* ...	သက်သေ။ ...	thet-thay ...	gu'wah'ee,shu'had'ut,gu'wah	sáṭchi, sákshi.
Wit'ness, *v. a.* ...	သက်သေခံသည်။ ...	thet-thay-cun-the ...	gu'wah'ee-de'na ...	sáṭchichollu.
Woe, Wo, *s.* ...	အမင်္ဂလာ။ ...	ah-min-gă-lah ...	ghum, la'nut, *f.* phit'kar ...	tukkam, sábam, tímoḷi.
Wolf, *s.* ...	ဝံပုလွေ။ ...	woon-poo-loo-ay ...	bu'her'a, hoon'dar, bik ...	ónáy, tóṇḍán.
Wom'an, *s.* ...	မိမ္မ။ ...	maym-mah ...	ou'rut, *f* ...	stri, peṇ, manushi.
Wom'anhood, *s.* ...	မိမ္မအဖြစ်။ ...	maym-mah-ă-pyit ...	ou'rut-pun'a ...	peṇmai.
Wom'anish, *a.* ...	မိမ္မကဲ့သို့ဖြစ်သော။ ...	maym-mah-geh-thoh-pyit-	zun'a'nuh ...	peṇmaiyána, strikkaḍutta.
Wom'ankind, *s.* ...	မိမ္မမျိုး။ ...	maym-mah-myoh. [thaw...	rin'dee-zat, stree-jun, *f.* ...	peṇ, uyartiṇaippeṇbárpothu
Womb, *s.* ...	သားအိမ်။ဝမ်း။ ...	thah-ayn, woon ...	rihm, ru him, pet, ghur'i'ya,-	karuppai, karukkuḷi.
Won'der, *s.* ...	အံ့ဩသည်။ ...	un-aw-the ...	uj'ub, ij'az, shig'ift,[kokh,...	athisayam,áchchariyam.[ra.
Won'derful, *a.* ...	အံ့ဩသော။ထူးဆန်းသော။	un-aw-thaw, too-sun-thaw.	oo'joo'ba, na'dir, uj'ub ...	vichittramána,bramippikki-
Wont, *s.* ...	အလေ့ရှိသော။ ...	ă-lay-she-thaw ...	a'dut, *f.* a'dee, kur'na, ruh'na.	vaḷakkam, payiṛchchi.
Wood, *s.* ...	သစ်။ ...	thit ...	luk'ree, *f.* kath ...	maram.
Wood, *(jungle) a.*...	သစ်တော။ ...	thit-taw ...	ka'nun, jun'gul, bun ...	tóppu, vanam, chólai.
Wood'pecker, *s.* ...	သစ်တောက်။ ...	thit-towk ...	kuth-pho'ra, put'thur-phor..	tachchankuruvi.
Wool, *s.* ...	သိုးမွေး။ ...	thoh-moo-ay ...	oon, ro'an, pushm, soof ...	chemmaṛiyáṭṭu-rómam.
Wool len, *s.* ...	သိုးမွေးကိုလိတ်သော။ ...	thoh-moo-ay-goh-lait-thaw.	bun'at, ba'nat ...	áṭṭumayiráláya.
Wool'len-Cloth, *s.*...	သက္ကလပ်။ ...	thek-ka-lut ...	bun'at, -ban'nat-kup'ra ...	áṭṭumayiráláya-tuṇi.
Word, *s.* ...	စကား။ ...	s'gah' ...	bat, buch'un, bol, kul'i'mu, subd, koul ...	chol, várttai moḷi, patham.

ENGLISH.	BURMESE.		HINDUSTANI.	TAMIL.
Work, *s.* ...	လုပ်သည်။အလုပ်။ ...	loht-the, ă-loht ...	mih'nut, kam, kar, kaj ...	vélai, panividai, cheygai, tolil
Work, *v. a.* ...	ပြုသည်။ ...	pyoo-the ...	kam-kur'na, kam-k ...	vélaichey, tolirchey, chey.
Work'man, *s.* ...	အလုပ်သမား။ ...	ă-loht-thum-mah ...	ka'ree-gur, dust-kar, koo'lee.	vélaikáran.
World, *s.* ...	လောက။ကမ္ဘာ။ ...	law-kah kub-bah ...	doo'ni'ya, a'lum, jug'ut, lok.	ulagam, bhúmi, puvanam.
World'ly, *a.* ...	လောကီနှင့်ဆိုင်သော။ ...	law-kee-hnin-suyng-thaw...	doo'ni'ya'dar, bis'wee ...	laugiha, ulagattirkadutta.
Worm, *s.* ...	ပိုး။ ...	poh ...	kirm, kee'ra, je'o'ree, kir'muk.	pulu, krumi, pottu.
Worse, *a.* ...	သာ၍ဆိုးသော။ ...	thah-yoo-eh-soh-thaw ...	bud-tur, boo'ra, our-boo'ra...	athigakédulla, athigakédáy.
Wor'ship, *s.* ...	ကိုးကွယ်သည်။ ...	koh-gweh-the ...	pur'us'tish, poo'ja, ib'a'dut...	áráthanai, namaskáram.
Wor'ship, *v. a.* ...	ပူဇော်သည်။ ...	poo-zaw-the ...	ur'chun'a, pooj'na, pur'us'na.	vanangu, áráthi, tolu.
Wor'shipper, *s.* ...	ကိုးကွယ်သောသူ။ ...	koh-gweh-thaw-thoo ...	pur'us'tin'duh, a'bid, pur'ust.	toluvón, tondan.
Worst, *a.* ...	မကောင်းဆုံး။ ...	m'kowng-sohn ...	hud-bhur-boo'ra'ee, riz'a'lu..	arakkédáy, níchamána.
Worth *s.* ...	အဘိုးတန်သော။ ...	ă-poh-tun-thaw ...	kudr, jou'hur, li'ya'kut ...	perumathi, perumánam.
Worth'less, *a.* ...	အဘိုးမတန်သော။ ...	ă-poh-m'tun-thaw ...	kum-kudr, be-kudr ...	abháttiramána, tálvána.
Wor'thy, *a.* ...	ထိုက်သော။ ...	tuyk-thaw ...	nek'o'kar, laik, suz'a'war ...	páttiramána, mukkiyamána
Would, *pret of* Will	လိမ့်မည်။ ...	laym-mee ...	chu'ha, chuh'ta ...	virumbhu, ási.
Wound, *s.* ...	အနာ။ ...	ă nah ...	zukhm, gha'o, jur'a'hut, chee'ra ...	káyam, iranam, úru.
Wrath, *s.* ...	အမျက်ဒေါသ။ ...	ă-myet-daw-thah ...	ghuz'ub ...	krótham, kadunkóbham.
Wres'tle, *v. n.* ...	လက်ပွတ်တိုက်သည်။ ...	let-pwet-tuyk-the ...	koosh'tee-k, hath-mil'a'na...	mallukkattu, malluppidi.
Wres'tler, *s.* ...	လက်ပွတ်တိုက်သောသူ။ ...	let-pwet-tuyk-thaw-thoo ...	koosh'tee-geer, puh'lu'wan..	mallan.
Wretch, *s.* ...	အလွန်ယုတ်ညံ့သောသူ။ ...	ă-hloon-yoht-nyun-thaw-thoo ...	be-cha'ra, kum-bukht ...	nirppanthan, páthagan, ínan
Wrist, *s.* ...	လက်ကောက်ဝတ်။ ...	let-kah-woot ...	pu'hoon'cha, kul'a'ee ...	manikkattu, kaikkaradu.
Writ, *s.* ...	စာ။မှတ်ချက်။ ...	tsah, hmut-chyet ...	kit'ab, tul'ub-na'muh ...	eluthappattathu, sáthanam.
Write, *v. a.* ...	စာရေးသည်။ ...	tsah-yay-the ...	likh'na, likh'le'na, tuk'reer-k	eluthu, títtu, varai, pori.
Wri'ter, *s.* ...	စာရေးသောသူ။ ...	tsah-yay-thaw-thoo ...	likh'ne-wa'la, likh'nee-das...	ligithan, ilékkan, ásiriyan.

Writing, *s.* ...	လက်ရေး။ ...	let-yay ...	likh ha'o, lik ha'wut ...	eḷuttu, prabandham.
Wrong, *s.* ...	မတရားခြင်း။ ...	m'tă-rah-chyin ...	chook, ghul'ut, nook'san, zur.	tíṅgu, kuṛṛam, piḷai, tavaṛu.
Wrong, *a.* ...	မမှန်သော။ ...	m'hmun-thaw ...	na-moo'na'sib, na-huk, ghul'ut ...	tappithamána, kuṛṛamuḷḷa.
Wrong, *v. a.* ...	ပြစ်မှားသည်။ ...	pyit-hmah-the ...	boo'ra-k ...	tíṅguchey, aniyáyañchey.
Wroth, *a.* ...	ဒေါသ။ ...	daw-thah ...	ghoos'sa, khu'fu ...	kóbikkiṛa, kuróthamuḷḷa.
Wrought, *pret&p. p.*	လုပ်ပြီ။ ...	loht-pyee ...	bun'na ...	cheyyappaṭṭa cheytha.
Wry, *a.* [of Work...	ကျစ်သည်။ ...	khyit-the ...	ter'ha, kuj ...	kóṇaláṇa, vaḷaintha.
Xiph'ias, *s. sword fish*	ငါးမန်း။ ...	ngah-mahn ...	a'ra-muchh ...	komban-churá, katti-mín, *or*
Yam, *s.* ...	မျောက်ခေါင်း။ ...	myowk-kowng ...	a loo ...	íyámichchikkiḷaṅgu. [véḷá.
Yard, *s.* ...	သုံးပေ။ ...	thohn-pay ...	guz ...	gajam, múnṛadikoṇḍa-aḷa-
Yard, *s.* ...	ဝင်း။ ...	wing ...	an'gun, ung'na, uj'ir ...	muṛṛam, vásal. [vu.
Ye, *pron.* ...	သင်တို့။ ...	thin-doh ...	toom ...	nír, níṅgaḷ.
Year, *s.* ...	နှစ်။ ...	hnit ...	bur'us, bur'ush, sal, sun ...	varuḍam, varusham áṇḍu.
Yel'low, *a.* ...	ဝါ။ ...	wah ...	zaf'ur'a'nee, pee'la, us'fur ...	mañjaḷniṛamuḷḷa.
Yes, *adv.* ...	ဟုတ်ကဲ့။ ...	hoht-keh ...	han, hoon, jee, bul'e, a're ...	ám. ámám, óm.
Yes'terday, *s.* ...	မနေ့က။ ...	mă-nay-gah ...	kul, dee-roz ...	néṛṛu, néṛṛaiyathinam.
Yet, *conj.* ...	သို့သော်လည်း။ ...	thoh-thaw-lee ...	lek, lek'in, pur, um'ma ...	allámalum, enṛálum.
Yield, *v. a.* ...	သီးသည်။ပေးသည်။ ...	thee-the, pay-the ...	de'na, dee'na ...	í, koḍu, viḷaivukoḍu.
Yoke, *s.* ...	ထမ်းပိုး။ ...	tă-boh ...	joo'a, joo'ath. jooh, ur'dun'da.	nugattaḍi, nugam, iṇai.
Yon, Yon'der, *a. & adv.* ...	ဟိုမှာ။ ...	hoh-hmah ...	wooh, oo'dhur-ka ...	athó, anthaṇḍai. [gaḷai.
You, *pron.* ...	သင်။သင်တို့။ ...	thin, thin-doh ...	toom, ap ...	ní. nír, níṅgaḷ, unnai, uṅ-
Young, *s.* ...	အသက်ငယ်သော။ ...	ă-thet-hngeh-thaw ...	buch'a, pat'ha, put'hi'ya, *f.*...	kuñju, kanṛu, piḷḷai.
Young, *a.* ...	ပျိုသော။ ...	pyoh-thaw ...	ju'wan. joo'ba, khoord ...	iḷaiya, yauvana, bháliya.
Your Yours *poss. pron*	သင်တို့၏။သင်၏။မင်း၏။ ...	thin-ee, thin-doh-ee, mín-ee.	toom'ha'ra, toom'ha'ree, up'na, upnee, ap'ka ...	un, unnuḍaiya, unathu, uṅgaḷ, umathu.
Yourself, *pron.* ...	သင့်ကိုယ်တိုင်။ ...	thin-koh-duyng ...	toom, ap, ap'hee ...	níré, níyé, ummaitáné.

ENGLISH.	BURMESE.		HINDUSTANI.	TAMIL.
Youth, *s.* ...	ပျိုသောအရွယ်။ ...	pyoh-thaw-ă-yoo-eh ...	ju'wan'ee, ju'wan, ju'wan-pun, jo'bun,...	iḷamai, iḷamparuvam, yauvanam.
Youth'ful, *a.* ...	ပျိုသော။ ...	pyoh-thaw ...	ju'wan,	válibha, yauna.
Zeal, *s.* / Zeal'ous, *a.* } ...	စိတ်အားကြီးသော။ ...	{ sayt-ah-kyee-thaw ...	gur'mee, hur'a'rut, sur-gurm	ával, uṛchágam, vairákkiyam
Zébra, *s.* ...	မြင်းကြောင်း။ ...	myin-chyowng ...	Africa *or* bil'ad-i-soo'dan-ka-khuch'chur, *or* ustur, *or*	varik-kuthirai. *or* káṭṭuk-kuthirai.
Zinc, *s.* ...	သွတ်ပြား။ ...	thoht-pyah ...	dus'ta, jun'gul-ka-us'tur...	tuttanágam, vaṅgam, nágam

FINIS.

PART II
USEFUL SENTENCES.

USEFUL SENTENCES.

PART II.

I.—On Breakfast.

Get the breakfast equipage ready.
နံနက်စာစားရန်ကရိယာတန်ဆာတို့ကိုအသင့်ယူထားပါ။
na-net-tsa-tsa-yan ka-ree-yah tă-zah-doh-goh ă-thin yoo tah-bah.
hazree ka saman tyar ku'ro.
kálai sáppáṭṭukku véṇḍiya thellám tayárpaḍuttu.

Toast some bread, and butter it properly.
ပေါင်မုန့်ကိုမီးကင်၍ထောပတ်နှင့်ကောင်းမွန်စွာလူးလိုက်ပါ။
powng-mohn goh mee-kin you-ey taw-but-hnin kowng-mohn-zwah loo-luyt-bah.
kooch rotee sen'ko, our oos'pur uch'chhee tur'uh muk'khun lug'a'o.
koñjam roṭṭiyai neruppilé káychchi sariyánapaḍi veṇṇey taḍavu.

Does the water boil?
ရေနွေးရှိလား။
yay noo-ay-yeh-lah?
pa nee khoul ta hy?
taṇṇír kothikkiṛathá?

Give me a clean cup and saucer.
ကျွန်ုပ်ကိုပုဂံလုံးကလေးတလုံးနှင့်လက်ဘက်ရေပုဂံပြားတချက်ပေးပါ။
kyoon-hnoht-goh pă-gan-lohn-gă-lay-tă-lohn-hnin let-pet-yay-pă-gan-byah-tă-chet pay-bah.
ek saf pi ya la our tha li mooj'he de.
suddhamána oru kóppaiyum taṭṭum koḍu.

Give that gentleman another cup of tea.
ထိုသခင်ကိုလက်ဘက်ရေတခွက်ထပ်၍ပေးပါဦး။
toh-th'kin-goh let-pet-yay-tă-kwet tut-yoo-eh pay-bah-ohn.
ek our pi'ya la cha-ka oos sa'hib ko de
antha turaikku innoru kóppai tétaṇṇír koḍu.

Bring the cold meat.
အေးသောအမဲသားကိုယူခဲ့ပါ။
eh-thaw-ă-meh-thah-goh yoo-geh-bah.
thun da-gosht la o.
palaṅkaṛi koṇḍu vá.

Give me a cup of coffee and a little more sugar.
ကျွန်ုပ်ကိုကော်ဖီရေတခွက်နှင့်သကြားနည်းနည်းထပ်၍ပေးပါဦး။
kyoon-hnoht-goh kau pee-yay tá-kwet-hnin tha-jyah-neh-neh tut-yoo-eh pay-bah-ohn.
ek pi ya la kuh'wa mooj'he de, our tho'ree see shuk'ur zia'da de.
enakku innoru kóppai káppiyum koñjam sarkkaraiyum koḍu.

Set the egg-cups and salt-cellar on that side.
ဥပုဂံလုံးနှင့်ဆားခွက်ကိုဟိုဘက်ကထား။
oo-pă-gan-lohn-hnin tsah-kwet-goh hoh-bek-kah-tah.
un'don ke pi'ya'le our num'uk-dan oos tur'uf rukh'o.
muṭṭai kóppaiyum uppénamum anthappakkattil vai.

Bring bread, biscuit, sweetmeats, cake, &c.
ပေါင်မုန့်။ဘီစကွတ်။ကိတ်မုန့်အစရှိသောသရေစာတို့ကိုယူခဲ့ပါ။
powng-mohn bee-skut kait-mohn ă-tsah-shee-thaw thă-yay-zah-doh-goh yoo-geh-bah.
ro'tee, koo'lee'cha, mit'ha'ee, kak, wu'ghuy'ra la'o.
roṭṭi, biskóttu, miṭṭáy, paṇikáram muthaliyavai koṇḍuvá.

You know I cannot drink tea without cream.
ငါသည်မလိုင်မပါဘဲလက်ဘက်ရေမသောက်နိုင်ကြောင်းကိုမင်းသိသည်။
ngah-thee mă-luyng-mă-pah-beh let-pet-yay-ma-thowk-hnuyn-gyowng-goh min-thee-thee.
toom jan'te ho ke myn mul'a'ee ba'ghyr cha na pee-suk'ta.
éḍu illámal nán téttaṇṇír kuḍikkamáṭṭén enṛu unakku teriyum.

The bread is very bad, and full of sand.
သည်ပေါင်မုန့်သည်အလွန်ညံ့လျက်သဲလည်းများစွာရှိ၏။
thee-powng-mohn-the ă-hloon-nyun-hlyet theh-lee myah-zwa-shee-ee.
ro'tee nihayat bur'ee, our ba'loo bhur'ee hu'ee hy.
roṭṭi mettak-keṭṭu pónathu, veṛumaṇṇáy irukkiṛathu.

II.—On Dinner.

Tell the cook to have the dinner ready at three o'clock.
၃နာရီအချိန်တွင်ညစာအသင့်ရှိအောင်ထမင်းချက်သွားတစ်ဦးသူကြီးကိုပြောလိုက်ပါ။
thohn-nah-yee ă-chain-dwin nyah-zah ă-thin-shee-owng ta-min-chyet-thum-mah (*or* oh-thoo-gyee-goh) pyaw-luyt-bah.
ba'wur'chee se kaho ki teen baje kha'na ty'ar howe.
múnṛu maṇikku pagal sáppáḍu tayáráy irukkumbaḍi kusinikkára-nidattil chollu.

Sir, dinner is ready.
ညညစာစားရန်အသင့်ရှိပါပြီခင်ဗျား။
nyah-zah-tsah-yan ă-thin shee-bah-byee kin-byah.
sa'hib kha'na ty'ar hy.
aiyá, sáppáḍu tayáráy irukkiṛathu.

Where are the soup and the soup-spoon?
စွပ်နှင့်စွပ်သောက်သောဇွန်းဘယ်မှာရှိသည်လဲ။
soop-hnin soop-thowk-thaw-zohn beh-hmah shee-thee-leh?
shor'ba ku'han hy, our shor'ba pee'ne-ka chum'cha?
irasamum irasakkaraṇḍiyum eṅgé?

Bring a hot-water plate.
ရေနွေးပုဂံပြားတချပ်ယူခဲ့ပါ။
yay-noo-ay-pă-gan-byah-tă-chat yoo-geh-bah.
gurm pa'nee-ka ba'sun la'o.
suḍutaṇṇír píṅgáṇonṛu koṇḍuvá.

Let me have a clean plate.
ပုဂံပြားစင်စင် or စင်ကြယ်သောပုဂံပြားတချပ်ပေးပါ။
pă-gan-byah-sin-zin (*or* sin-kyeh-thaw-pă-gan byah) tă-chat pay-bah.
ek saf rik'ab'ee mooj'he de.
suddhamána píṅgán oṇṛu enakku véṇum.

Let me have of every sort of vegetable on the table.
ဟင်းသီးဟင်းရွက်အမျိုးရုံကိုကျွန်ုပ်ထံစားပွဲသို့လာခဲ့ပေးပါ။
hin-thee hin-yoo-eh ă-myo-zohn-goh kyoon-hnoht tsah-bweh-thoh lah yoo-ey-pay-bah.
mez pur ek tur'ah kee tur'ka'ree kooch kooch rukh'o.
sáppiḍugaiyil ovvoru marakkaṛi pathárttamum enakku koṇḍu vanthu vai.

Tell me the name of each.
အသီးသီးသောအမည်ကိုကျွန်ုပ်အားပြောပါ။
ă-thee-thee-thaw ă-myee-goh kyoon-hnoht ah-pyaw-bah.
ek-ek ka nam mooj he but'a'o.
ovvonṛukkum pér chollu.

What do you call that vegetable?
ထိုဟင်းလျာပင်ကိုဘယ်နှယ်ခေါ်သလဲ။
toh-hin-hlya-pin-goh beh-hneh-kaw-th'leh?
oos tur'ka'ree-ko ky'a ku'ha'te ho?
antha marakkaṛikku pér enna?

Bring some beef.
အမဲသားကိုယူခဲ့ပါ။
ă-meh-thah-goh yoo-geh-bah.
kooch ga'e-ka-gosht la'o.
koñjam máṭṭukkaṛi koṇḍuvá.

What fruits are in season now?
ယခုရာသီနှိုက်ဘယ်သစ်သီးများပေါ်သလဲ။
yă-koo yah-thee-hnuyt beh-thit-thee-myah paw-th'leh?
kis-kis mewu kee ab fusl hy?
intha kálattilé ennenna paḻam agappaḍum?

Bring me some of each sort.
သစ်သီးအမျိုးထဲကတဆိပ်စီယူခဲ့ပါ။ or တမျိုးစီတမျိုးစီတဆိပ်ယူခဲ့စန်ပါ။
thit-thee ă-myo-deh-gah tă-myo-zee tă-myo-zee yoo-geh-bah.
hur kism se tho'ra tho'ra mer e pas la'o.
thinisukku koñjam koṇḍuvá.

III.—On Naming, Telling, Speaking, &c.

What is the name of this?
သည်ဟာ၏အမည်ပါလဲ။ or ဘည်ဟာဘယ်နှယ်ခေါ်သလဲ။
thee-hah-ee ă-myee bah-leh (or thee-hah-beh-neh-kaw-th'leh?)
is-ka ky'a nam hy?
itharkku pér enna?

What do you call this thing?
သည်အရာကိုဘယ်နှယ်ခေါ်သလဲ။
thee ă-yah-goh beh-neh-kaw-th'leh?
is cheez ko ky'a ku'ha'te ho?
ithai enna enṛu chollugiṛathu?

What do they call that in Burmese?
ထိုဟာကိုမြန်မာဘာသာအားဖြင့်မည်ခဲ့သို့ခေါ်သလဲ။
toh-hah-goh myum-mah bah-thah-pyin myee-geh-thoh kaw-th'leh.
oos ko Bur'ma zub'an men ky'a ku ha te hyn?
Bramá bháshaiyil itharku enna pér?

Can you tell me where Moung Bah Thain lives?
မောင်ဘသိန်းဘယ်မှာနေသည်ကိုမင်းပြောနိုင်သလား။
Moung Bah Thain beh-hmah nay-the-goh min-pyaw-hnuyng the-lah?
toom kuh-suk te ho ki Moung Bah Thain ku'han rah ta hy?
Moung Bah Thain enbavar engé yirukkiṛár teriyumá?

Tell him he is a great rogue.
သူသည်လိမ်လည်တတ်သောသူဆိုးဖြစ်ကြောင်းကိုသူအားပြောကြားလိုက်ပါ။
thoo-thee lain-lee-dat-thaw loo-zo-pyit-khyowng goh thoo ăh-pyaw-khyah-luyt-bah.
oo se ku bo ki too sukht dugh'a baz hy.
avan ketta tiruṭṭuppayal enṛu chol.

He said he had business.
သူမှာကိစ္စရှိကြောင်းကိုပြောပြီး။
thoo-hmah kayt-sah shee-gyowng-goh pyaw-byee.
oos'ne ku ha ki mer e hath men kam hy.
avan tanakku vélai yirukkirathága chonnán.

Yes, I did ask.
ဟုတ်ကဲ့ကျွန်ုပ်မေးခဲ့ပြီ။
hoht-keh, kyoon-unoht may-geh-byee.
han, poochh a tha.
ám, nán kéṭṭén.

They speak English among themselves.
သူတို့သည်မိမိတို့အချင်းချင်းနှင့်အင်္ဂလိပ်စကားပြောတတ်ကြသည်။
thoo-doh-the mee-mee-doh ă-chin-gyin-bin-hlin Ingalait-t'sa-gah-pyaw-dut-gyah-thee.
we a pus men ung'rez'ee bol'te hyn.
avargaḷ tangaḷukkuḷḷé ingilishil pésikkoḷḷugiṛárgaḷ.

Could I speak Burmese I would with pleasure.
ကျွန်ုပ်မြန်မာစကားပြောနိုင်လျှင်နှစ်သက်စွာပြောပါလိမ့်မည်။
kyoon-unoht myum-mah-t'sa-gah-pyaw-hnuyn-hlyin hnit-thet-swah-pyaw-bah-laym-mee.
ug ur myn Burma zub'an bol'suk'ta to khoo'shee se bol'ta.
Bramá bháshai terinthirunthál santhóshamáy pésuvén.

They will know him to be a foreigner, though he speaks the Burmese language very grammatically.
မြန်မာစကားကောင်းကောင်းပြောတတ်သော်လည်း၊ သူတို့သည်တတိုင်းတပြည်သား ဖြစ်ကြောင်းကိုသိကြပါလိမ့်မည်။
myum-mah-tsă-gah-kowng-gowng pyaw-dut-thaw-lee, thoo-doh-thee-tă-duyng-tă-pyee-thah-pyit-gyowng-goh thee-gyah bah-lay-mee.
we oo se pur des ee janenge, ug ur chi wooh Burma bu hoot ba ka ida bol ta hy.
avan bramá-bháshai nalla ilakkaṇa muṛaiyáy pésiuálum, avan anniyan enṛu avargaḷukku teriyum.

IV.—On Visiting, Shopping, &c.

Bring the carriage near me.
ရထားကိုအနီးသို့ယူခဲ့ပါ။
yit-tah-goh ă-nee-thoh yoo-geh-bah.
ruth *or* ga ree me re pas la o.
vaṇḍiyai en kiṭṭa koṇḍuvá.

Bring the carriage close to the door.
ရထားကိုတံခါးနှင့်နီးနီးယူခဲ့ပါ။
yit-tah-goh tă-gah-huun nee-nee-yoo-geh-bah.
ga ree dur wa zu se bhi ra do.
vaṇḍiyai kathavukiṭṭa koṇḍuvá.

Go as fast as you can.
မင်းတတ်နိုင်သမျှမြန်မြန်သွားပါ။
min-tat-hnuyn-thă-hmyah myun-myun-thwah-bah.
jitn ee jul dee ja suk o ja o.
kúḍiya maṭṭum viraiváy pó.

Ask if the gentleman has gone out.
သခင်လယ်ပတ်ရန်ထွက်သွားသည်ကိုမေးစမ်းပါ။
th kin-let-put-yun twet-thwah-the-goh may-zuu-bah.
poooh o ki sa hib ba hur gu ye hyn ki na heen.
durai irukkiṛárá veḷiyé póyviṭṭárá enṛu kéḷ.

When will he return?
သူအဘယ်သောအခါမှပြန်လာပါလိမ့်မည်လဲ။
thoo beh-thaw-ă-kah-hmah pyan-lah-bah-lay-mee-leh?
kub phir awenge?
eppó tirumbi varuvár?

Give my compliments to your master.
ငါ၏မေတ္တာစကားကိုမင်သခင်အားပြောကြားလိုက်ပါ။
ngah-myitta-taă-gah-goh min-th kin-ăh pyaw-khyah-luyt-bah.
toom up ne sa hib se me ra sul am kuh na.
un esamánukku nán vanthanam chonna thága chollu.

Give this note to him when he returns.
သူပြန်လာသောအခါသည်မှာစာကလေးကိုပေးလိုက်ပါ။
thoo-pyun-lah-thaw-ă-kah the-hmah-tsa-gă-lay-goh pay-luyt-bah.
yih chit thee oon ko dee jo jub wo phir awen.
avar tirumbi vantha yuḍané intha kaḍithattai avar kaiyil koḍu.

Bring the umbrella to this side.
ထီးကိုသည်ဘက်သို့ယူခဲ့ပါ။
htee-goh thee-bek-thoh yoo-geh-bah.
chha'ta is tur'uf la'o.
koḍaiyai intha pakkam konḍuvá.

Do not go near the carriage.
ရထားနားကိုမသွားပါနှင့်။
yit-tah-hleh-nah-goh mă-thwah-bah-hning.
ga'ree ke pas mut ja'o.
vanḍikkiṭṭa pógáthé.

Put down the mat.
ဖျာခင်းလိုက်ပါ။
pyah-kin-luyt-bah.
chu'ta'ee nee'che rukh'o.
páyai kíḻé vai.

Stop, I am going to this shop.
နေပါဦး၊ကျွန်ုပ်သည်ဆိုင်သို့သွားဆဲဖြစ်ပါသည်။
nay-bah-ohn kyoon-hnoht the-tsuyng-thoh thwah-zeh-pyit-bah-the.
ru'ha'o, myn is doo'kan men ja'ta hoon.
nillu, nán intha kaḍaikku pógiṛén.

What is the price of this book?
ဤစာအုပ်၏အဘိုးမည်မျှလဲ။
thee-t'sah-ohk-ee a-poh-mee-hmyah-leh.
is kit'ab kee kee'mut ky'a hy?
inthapustakam enna vilai?

I will not give so much.
ဤမျှလောက်ကျွန်ုပ်မပေးဘူး။
ee-hmyah-lowk kyoon-hnoht mă-pay-boo.
myn it'na na doo'nga.
nán avvaḷavu koḍukka máṭṭén.

I have no cash.
ကျွန်ုပ်မှာကြေးငွေမရှိဘူး။
kyoon-hnoht-hmah chee-ngway-m'shee-boo.
me're pas nukd na'heen hy.
en kaiyilé kásillai.

Bring the book with you, and then receive its price.
စာအုပ်ကိုမင်းယူခဲ့ပြီးသည်နောက်၊၎င်းအဘိုးကိုခံယူလိုက်ပါ။
tsa-ohk-goh miu-yoo-geh-pyee-the-nowk lă-gowng ă-poh-goh-kun-yoo-luyt-bah.
kit'ab ko up'ne sath la'i'o, tub oos'kee kee'mut lee'jo.
unnóḍu pustakattai konḍu vanthu piragu athin vilaiyai váṅgik-koḷ.

v.—On Walking, Riding, &c.

He is gone out walking somewhere.
သူသည်လယ်ပတ်ရန်အခြားသို့ထွက်သွားပြီ။
thoo-thee-leh-put-yun-ă-chyah-thoh-twet-thwah-byee.
wooh phir'ne ko ku'heen ba'hur gu'ya hy.
avar eṅgéyó ulátta póyirukkiṛár.

I shall go out also.
ကျွန်ုပ်လည်းလယ်ပတ်ရန်ထွက်သွားအုံးမည်။
kyoon-hnoht-lee-leh-put-yun-twet-thwah-ohn-mee.
myn bhee ba'hur ja'oon'ga.
nánum veḷiyé póvén.

Can you walk much ?
မင်းလမ်းများများလျှောက်နိုင်သည်လား။
min-lun-myah-myah-showk-hnuyng-the-lah ?
toom bu'hoot chal suk'te ho ?
ní athigam naḍakka kúḍumá ?

Do not walk among the grass.
မြက်ပင်ထဲတွင်လမ်းမလျှောက်ပါနှင့်။
myet-pin-deh-dwin-lun-m'showk-bah-hnin.
ghas pur mut phir'o.
pullu mélé naḍanthu tiriyáthé.

Is the horse ready ?
မြင်းအသင့်ပြင်ဆင်ပြီးပြီလား။
myin-ă-thin-pyin-zin-pyee-byee-lah ?
gho'ra ty'ar hy ?
kuthirai tayárâchchá ?

Put the saddle on well.
ကုန်းနှီးကိုကောင်းကောင်းတပ်ပါ။
kohn-zee-goh-kowng-gowng-tut-bah.
uch'chhee-tur'a zeen bund'o.
jíniyai nanṛáy kaṭṭu.

Hold the horse.
မြင်းကိုကိုင်ထားပါ။
myin-goh-kuyng-tah-bah.
gho'ra puk'ur.
kuthiraiyai piḍi.

Take care !
သတိပြုပါ။
thă-dee-pyoo-bah !
khub'ur'dar !
battiram !

VI.—With a Head Servant.

Do you speak our language?
မင်းငါတို့ဘာသာစကားကိုပြောတတ်သည်လား။
min-ngah-doh-bah-thah-tsă-gah-goh-pyaw-dut-thĕ lah?
toom hum'a'ree zub'an bol'te ho?
eṅgaḷ páshai unakku pésa teriyumá?

Yes, Sir, I can speak a little English.
ဟုတ်ပါခင်ဗျား။ကျွန်တော်အင်္ဂလိပ်စကားကိုအနည်းငယ်မျှပြောတတ်ပါသည်။
hoht-bah-kin-byah-kyoon-daw-Ingalait-tsă-gah-goh-ă-nee-ngeh-hmyah-pyaw-dut-bah-thee.
han, sa'hib, myn ung'rez'ee kooch kooch bol suk'ta hoon.
ám aiyá, ingilísu koñjam pésuvén.

I have not yet learned to speak Burmese.
ကျွန်ုပ်သည်မြန်မာစကားကိုမသင်ကြားရသေးပါ။
kyoon-hnoht-the-myum-mah-tsă-gah-goh-m'thin-kyah-yah-thay-bah.
myn ne ub-tul'uk Bur'ma zub'an bol'nee na'heen seekh'ee.
Bramá páshaiyai innum pésa kaṛṛukkoḷḷa villai.

Where do you now live?
ယခုမင်းဘယ်မှာနေသည်လဲ။
yă-koo-min-beh-hmah-nay-the-leh?
toom aj-kul ku'han ruh'te ho?
ippó eṅgé yirukkiṛáy?

What is your name?
မင်းနာမည်ဘယ်နှယ်ခေါ်သည်လဲ။
min-nah-meh-beh-neh-kaw-thee-leh?
toom'ha'ra nam ky'a hy?
un pér enna?

Let me know also your master's name.
မင်းသခင်၏အမည်ကိုလည်းကျွန်ုပ်သိပါရစေ။
min-th'kin-ă-myee-goh-lee-kyoon-hnoht-thee-bah-yah-zay.
up'ne sa'hib-ka nam bhee but'la'o.
enakku unnuḍaiya ejamán pérkúḍa koñjam chollu.

How long have you been in that gentleman's service?
မင်းသည်ထိုသခင်၏အမှုကိုထမ်းရွက်လုပ်ဆောင်ခြင်းနှင့်မည်မျှကြာပြီလဲ။
min-thee-toh-th'kin-ă-hmoo-goh-tun-yoo-eh-loht-tsowng-gyin-hnuyt-mee-hmyah-khyah-byee-leh?
kub se oos sa'hib ke han nou'kur ruhe ho?
antha duraiyiḍattil ovvaḷavu kálam vélai cheygiṛáy?

Are your parents alive or not?
မင်း၏အမိအဘတို့အသက်ရှင်လျက်ရှိနေသေးသည်လား။သို့မဟုတ်သေကုန်ကြပြီးလား။
min-ee-mee-bah-doh-ă-thet-shin-hlyet-shee-nay-thay-the-lah, thoh-mă-hoht-thay-kohn-gyah-byee-lah?
toom ha're ma bap jee'te hyn ky na'heen?
unakku perrár irukkiṛárgaḷá, illaiyá, (*or*) unakku táy tanthai irukkiṛár-gaḷá illaiyá?

VII.—Between a European Doctor and a Native Patient.

Tell me what is the matter with you.
မင်းဘါဖြစ်သည်ကိုငါအားပြောစမ်းပါ။
min-bhah-pyit-the-goh-ngah-ah-pyaw-sun-bah.
ku'ho toom'ha'ra hal ky'a hy.
unakku enna paṇṇuthu chollu.

How long have you been ill?
မမာသည်၊ဘယ်လောက်ကြာပြီးလဲ။
m'mah-the-beh-lowk-khyah-the-leh?
toom kub'se bee'mar ho?
evvaḷvu kálamáy unakku savukkiyam illai?

How did the fever attack you at first?
ဘယ်နှယ်စ၍ဖျားသလဲ။
beh-neh-sah-yoo-eh-pyah-the-leh?
puh'le toom'hen tup ke'on-kur a'ee tee?
muthalil juram eppaḍi tuvakkiṛṛu?

Did you feel very cold?
မင်းအလွန်ချမ်းသည်လား။
min-ă-hloon-chyun-the-lah?
toom ko bu'hoot thundah ma'loom kee'ya?
athigamáy unakku kuḷir eḍuttathá?

What medicine have you taken?
ဘယ်ဆေးကိုစားသလဲ။
beh-tsay-goh-tsah-the-leh?
toom'ne ky'a du'wa kha'ee hy?
enna marunthu sappiṭṭáy?

None with any regularity.
မည်သည်ဆေးကိုမျှစွဲမြဲစွာမစားသေးပါ။
mee-thee-tsay-goh-hmyah-tsweh-myeh-swah-m'tsah-thay-bah.
ma'mool se kooch na'heen kha'ee.
ethuvum kiramamáy sáppiḍa villai.

You must-take some strong medicine.
မြန်မြန်ပျောက်စေတတ်သောဆေးကိုမင်းစားရမည်။
myun-myun-pyowk-say-dut-thaw-tsay-goh-min-tsah-yah-mee.
ko'ee moo'ku'wee du'wa toom'ko kha'nee pureg'ee.
ethávathu taguntha aviḻtham sáppiḍa véṇum.

I suppose you have no appetite.
မင်းစားသောက်ချင်သောစိတ်ရှိမည်ကိုငါမထင်။
min-tsah-thowk-chyin-thaw-sayt-sh-myee-goh-ngah-m'tin.
myn sum'ujh'ta hoon ki toom'ko kooch bhookh na'heen.
unakku pasi yillai pólirukkiṛathu.

Let me feel your pulse.
သွေးစမ်းပါရစေ။
thoo-ay-tsun-byah-say.
toom'ha'ree nubz dekh'oon.
un náḍiyai párkkaṭṭum.

Put out your tongue.
လျှာထုတ်စမ်းပါ။
shah-toht-tsun-bah.
up'nee (zub'an *or* jeebh) ba'hur ni'kal'o.
un nákkai níṭṭu.

Are your bowels regular?
ဝမ်းမှန်သလား။
woon-hmun-the-lah?
toom'ha'ra untree ky'a uch'chha hyn?
mala suddhi sariyáy águthá?

Let me well examine you.
ကျွန်ုပ်မင့်ကိုကောင်းမွန်စွာကြည့်ရှုစမ်းပါရစေ။
kyoon-hnoht-min-goh-kowng-mohn-swah-kyee-shoo-sun-bah-yah-say.
um toom'ko uch'chhee'tur'uh pur'ukh kur'e'ga.
nán unnai nanṛáy sóthikkaṭṭum.

I will send you some medicine which you must take regularly.
မင်းကောင်းကောင်းသောက်ရမည့်ဆေးကိုငါပေးလိုက်မည်။
min-kowng-gowng-thowk-yah-myee-tsay-goh-ngah-pay-luyt-mee.
um toom'ko be'je'gha tho'ra du'wa yih toom bur'ra'bur le'oo'ge.
nán unakku koñjam avilṯham koḍuttu anuppugiṛén athai ní kiramamáy sáppiḍa véṇum.

Be careful what you eat and drink.
အစားအသောက်နှင့်သတိပြုပါ။
ă-tsah-ă-thowk-hnuyt-th'dee-pyoo-bah.
kha'ne pee'ne se toom khub'ur'dar ru'ho.
sáppiḍugiṛathilum kuḍippathilum gavanamáy iru.

VIII.—On Housekeeping.

Butler, have you brought a cook?
စားပွဲထိုး၊ အိုးသူကြီးတယောက်ခေါ်ခဲ့ပြီးလား။
tsă-bweh-tain-oh-thoo-gyee-t-yowk-goh-kaw-geh-byee-lah?
khan'sa'man, toom ba'wur'chee la'e'o?
boṭlór, kusinikkáranai konḍu vantháyá?

Yes, sir, (*or* madam!)
ဟုတ်ပါသခင်။ (Madam, သခင်မ။)
hoht-bah-th'kin- (*madam*, th'kin-mah!)
han, sahib, (*madam*, mam sa'hib!)
ám, aiyá (*madam*, ammá!)

One has come to-day.
ယနေ့တယောက်လာပြီး။
yă-nay-t'yowk-lah-byee.
aj ek a'ya hy.
oruttan inṛaikku vanthán.

Can you cook well?
မင်းကောင်းကောင်းချက်တတ်သည်လား။
min-kowng-gowng-chyet-dut-the-lah?
toom ky'a uch'chhee tur'e kha'na puk'a suk' te?
unakku nanṛáy samaikka teriyumá?

I can prepare twenty-five dishes.
ဟင်းလျာအစိတ်လောက်ကျွန်တော်ချက်နိုင်သည်။
hin-hlyah-ă-sayt-lowk-kyoon-daw-chyet-hnuyng-the.
puch'ees bur'tun ty'ar kur suk'ta hoon.
irubattainthu vagai kaṛi tayár cheyvén.

Have you any certificates?
မင့်မှာတစုံတခုသောသက်သေလက်မှတ်စာရှိသည်လား။
min-ḥmah-t'sohn-t'koo-thaw-thet-thay-let-hmut-tsah-shee-the-lah?
toom'ha're pas chit'thee hy?
yókkiyá pattiram ethávathu unakku irukkiṛathá?

I have certificates from three gentleman and four ladies.
သခင်သုံးယောက်နှင့်သခင်မလေးယောက်ကလက်မှတ်များရှိပါသည်။
th'kin-thohn-yowk-hnin-th'kin-mah-lay-yowk-gah-leh-hmut-myah-she-bah-the.
me're pas teen sa'hib-lok'on our char mam sa'hib-lok'on kee chit'thee'an hyn.
múnṛu duraigaḷum nángu duraisáṇigaḷum koḍuttathu irukkiṛathu.

Your certificates are good.
မင့်လက်မှတ်များကောင်းပါသည်။
min-let-hmut-myah-kowng-bah-the.
toom'ha'ree chit'thee'an to uch'chhee hyn.
un naṛ sáṭchi pattiram ṇérttiyáy irukkirathu.

But I will not give you such high wages just now.
သို့သော်လည်းယခုပင်သည်လောက်များသောလခကိုမပေးသေးဘူး။
thoh-thaw-lee-y'koo-bin-thee-lowk-myah-thaw-lah-gah-goh-m'pay-thay-boo.
pur ub'hee hum it'nee tun'khwah na dengeen.
ánálum taṛ kálattilé unakku avvaḷavu uyarntha sambhaḷam koḍukka máṭṭén.

I will try you for a month.
မင့်ကိုတလငါစမ်းအုံးမည်။
min-goh-t'lah-nga-sun-ohn-mee.
ek mu'hee'ne hum toom'ha'ra kam de'khengeen.
oru másam unnai párkkiṛén.

I will work well.
ကျွန်ုပ်ကောင်းကောင်းကြီးလုပ်ပါမည်။
kyoon-hnoht-kowng-gowng-gyee-loht-bah-mee.
myn uch'chhee tur'o kam kur'oon'ga.
náu nanṛáy vélai choyvén.

The curry is very good.
သည်ဟင်းတယ်ကောင်းပါသည်။
the-hin-teh-kowng-bah-the.
sal'un to uch'chhee hy.
kaṛi metta nanṛáy irukkiṛathu.

The butcher has not brought mutton to-day.
သိုးသတ်သမားယနေ့သိုးသားကိုမယူခဲ့သေးပါ။
thoh-thut-thum-mah-yă-nay-thoh-thah-goh-m'yoo-goh-thay-bah.
aj kus'a'ee bher-ka-gosht na'heen la'ya.
kasáppukkáṛan inṛaikku áṭṭukkaṛi koṇḍu-varavillai.

Has not the baker come yet?
ပေါင်မုန့်သည်ယခုမလာသေးဘူးလား။
powng-mohn-the-y'koo-m'lah-thay-boo-lah ?
ro'tee-wa'la ub-tuk na'heen a'ya?
roṭṭikkáṛan innum varavillaiyá?

Make two or three slices of toast.
ပေါင်မုန့်နှစ်လွှာသုံးလွှာကင်လိုက်ပါ။
powng-mohn-hnit-hlwah-thohn-hlwah-khin-luyt-bah.
do teen phank ko toast bun'a'o.
iraṇḍu múnṛu roṭṭi tuṇḍai neruppilé káychchu.

Nurse bring the baby.
အာယာ၊ ခလေးကိုယူခဲ့ပါ။
ah-yah-kă-lay-goh-yoo-geh-bah.
a'ya, ba'ba ko la'o.
áyá, kuḻanthaiyai koṇḍuvá.

Master is going out, and wants to kiss it.
သခင်ထွက်သွားမည်ဖြစ်၍သူကိုနမ်းချင်သည်။
th'kin-twet-thawh-mee-pyit-yoo-eh-thoo-goh-nun-chyin-the.
sa'hib ba'hur ja'ta hy, kis'ee de'ne mang'ta.
aiyá veḷiyé pógiṛár, athai muttiyiḍa véṇumám.

Nurse, see what the child is doing.
အာယာ၊ ခလေးဘာလုပ်၍နေသည်ကိုကြည့်လိုက်ပါ။
ah-yah-kă-lay-bah-loht-yoo-ey-nay-the-goh-kyee-luyt-bah.
a'ya, dekh'o ba'ba ky'a kur'ta hy.
áyá, piḷḷai enna paṇṇugiṛathu páṛ.

Tell the groom to get the buggy ready.
မြင်းထိန်းသမားကိုရထားအသင့်ရှိရအောင်ပြောလိုက်ပါ။
myin-tain-thum-mah-goh-yit-tah-ă-thin-shee-yah-owng-pyaw-luyt-bah.
sa'ees ko bol'o bug'gee ty'ar kur'e.
kuthirai-káṛanai baggi-vaṇḍiyai tayár paṇṇa chollu.

Master is going out.
သခင်ထွက်သွားဆဲဖြစ်သည်။
th'kin-twet-thwah-seh-pyit-the.
sa'hib ba'hur ja'ta hy.
durai veḷiyé pógiṛár.

Groom, bring the horse quickly.
မြင်းထိန်းသွား၊ မြင်းကိုမြန်မြန်ယူခဲ့ပါ။
myin-tain-thum-mah-myin-goh-myun-myun-yoo-geh-bah.
sa'ees, gho'ra jul'dee la'o.
kuthiraikkáṛá, kuthiraiyai síkkiram koṇḍuvá.

I am saddling it, Sir.
ကုန်းနှီးတပ်လျက်နေပါသည်သခင်။
kohn-nyeen-tut-lyet-nay-bah-theo, th'kin.
sa'hib! zeen kheench'ta hoon.
athaṛkku jíni vaikkiṛén aiyá.

His horse goes both in the saddle and in a carriage.
သူ၏မြင်းသည်စီးခြင်းနှင့်ရထားတပ်ခြင်းနှစ်မျိုးစလုံးကိုသွားတတ်သည်။
thoo-ee-myin-the-tsee-gyin-hnin-yit-tah-tut-gyin-hnit-myo-să lohn-goh-thwah-dut-the.
is'ka gho'ra zeen-suwa'ree bheo de'ta our ga'ree men bheo lug'ta.
avaruḍaiya kuthirai éṛ savárilum vaṇḍiyilum pógiṛathu.

The horse has dropped a shoe; send for the farrier.
မြင်းသည်သံခွာကိုချပြစ်ခဲ့ပြီး။ သံခွာတပ်သမားကိုခေါ်လိုက်ပါ။
myin-the-thun-kwah-goh-chyah-pyit-koh-byee, thun-kwah-tut-thum-mah-goh-caw-luyt-bah.
gho're'ka na'l gir'gu'ya na'l-bund ko boo'la'o.
kuthiraikku láḍam viḷunthu póchchuthu láḍakáṛanai kúppiḍu.

Shoe the horse.
မြင်းကိုသံခွာတပ်လိုက်ပါ။
myin-goh-thun-kwah-tut-luyt-bah.
gho're ke na'l-lug'a'o.
kuthiraikku láḍam tai.

Has the saddle been mended?
ကုန်းနှီးကိုဖာရှုပြီးပြီးလား။
kohn-nee-goh-pah-yoo-eh-pyee-byee-lah?
zeen kee mur'um'mut kur'a'o?
lagánai paḷuthu párttiyá?

Sweeper, clean the place.
တံမြက်လှဲသမား၊ သည်နေရာကိုလှဲလိုက်ပါ။
t'byet-hlee-thum-mah, the-nay-yah-goh-hleh-luyt-bah.
mih'tur, jha'roo do.
perukkugiṛavané, iḍattai perukku.

Sweeper! come here.
တံမြက်လှဲသမား၊ သည်ကိုလာခဲ့ပါ။
t'byet-hlee-thum-mah, thee-goh-lah-geh-bah.
mih'tur! ee'dhur a'o.
perukkugiṛavané! iṅgé vá.

See how filthy this room is.
သည်အခန်းဘယ်လောက်ညှစ်သည်ကိုကြည့်စမ်းပါ။
thee-ă-cun-the-beh-lowk-hnit-thee-goh-kyee-sun-bah.
dekh'o yih kum'ur'a ky'sa my'la hy.
intha aṛai enna asaṅgiyamáy irukkiṛathu pár.

Washerman, you are very careless.
ခဝါသယ်၊ မင်းအလွန်သတိမဲ့သည်။
kă-wah-theh, min-ă-hloon-th'dee-meh-the.
dho'bee, toom bur'a soost hy.
vaṇṇán, ní metta ajákkiṛathai-yuḷḷavan.

You have not even done the ironing well.
မင်းမီးပူအောင်ကောင်းကောင်းမတိုက်ဘူး။
min-mee-boo-owng-kowng-gowng-m'tuyk-boo.
is'tir'ee bhee uch'chhee na'heen kee.
isttiri kúḍa nanṛáy póḍavillai.

Tailor, how have you sewn this?
အပ်ချုပ်သယ်၊ မင်းသည်ဟာကိုဘယ်နှယ်ချုပ်သည်လဲ။
ut-chyoht-theh, min-the-hah-goh-beh-neh-chyoht-the-leh?
dur'zee yih toom ne ky'sa see'ya hy?
taiyakáṛá, ithai ennamáy ṭaittáy?

Stitch nicely.
ကောင်းကောင်းချုပ်ပါ။
kowng-gowng-chyoht-bah.
toom bukh'i'ya uch'chha laga'ya kur'o.
nanṛáy tai.

Who is going round the bungalow?
ဗိုလ်တဲကိုမည်သူလှည့်ပတ်၍သွားသည်လဲ။
boh-deh-goh-mee-thoo-hlee-put-yoo-eh-thwah-th'leh?
bung'le kee cha'ron tur'uf koun ghoom'ta hy?
baṅgaḷávai churri pógiṛathár?

What gentleman's house is that?
ဘယ်သခင်အိမ်လဲ။
beh-th'kin-ayn-leh?
wooh kis sa'hib kee kot'hee hy?
athu entha duraiyuḍaiya víḍu?

Bring a cheroot, and some fire.
ဆေးလိပ်တလိပ်နှင့်မီးတဆိတ်ယူခဲ့ပါ။
tsay-layt-t'layt-hnin-mee-t'sayt-yoo-geh-bah.
choo'root la'o our ag.
suruṭṭum neruppum koṇḍuvá.

Let the gentleman come in.
သခင်ဝင်ပါစေ။
th'kin-wing-bah-say.
sa'hib ko a'ne do.
durai uḷḷé varaṭṭum.

Give him my compliments.
ကျွန်ုပ်မေတ္တာစကားကိုသူအားကြားပြောလိုက်ပါ။
kyoon-hnoht-myit-tah-tsa-gah-goh-thoo-ah-pyaw-luyt-bah.
oos'ko 'me'ra sul'am bo'lo.
avarukku en vanthanam chollu.

Bring a chair.
ကုလားထိုင်တခုယူခဲ့ပါ။
kŭl-lah-tuyng-t'koo-yoo-geh-bah.
ek koor'see la'o.
oru nárkkáli konduvá.

Where is the punkah puller gone?
ရပ်ဆွဲသ္မားဘယ်ကိုသွားသလဲ။
yut-tsweh-thum-mah-beh-goh-thwah-th'leh?
punk'he-wa'la ku'han gu'ya?
pańgá iḻukkiṛavan eńgé póy irukkiṛán?

IX.—MISCELLANEOUS SENTENCES.

Who are you?
မင်းအဘယ်သူလဲ။
min-ă-beh-thoo-leh, (*colloquially* b'doo-leh?)
toom koun ho?
ní ár?

What is your name?
မင့်နာမည်ဘယ်နှယ်ခေါ်သလဲ။
min-nah-myee-beh-neh-kaw-the-leh?
toom'ha'ra nam ky'a hy?
un pér enna?

How are you?
မာကြီးလား။
mah-ee-lah?
toom ky'se ho?
eppaḍi irukkiṛáy?

What are you saying?
မင်းဘာကိုပြောဆိုသည်လဲ။
min-b'hah-goh-pyaw-tso-the-leh.
toom ky'a kuth'e ho?
enna chollugiṛáy?

He is a fool.
သူလူမိုက်တယောက်ဖြစ်သည်။
thoo-loo-muyt-t'yowk-pyit-the.
wooh be-woo'koof hy.
avan múḍan.

What is your age?
အသက်ဘယ်လောက်ကြီးပြီးလဲ။
ă-thet-beh-lowk-kyee-byee-leh ?
toom'ha'ree oomr ky'a hy ?
unakku vayasu enna ?

He is a great drunkard.
သူသည်အရစ်ထုပ်တယောက်ဖြစ်သည်။
thoo-the-ă-yet-toht-t'yowk-pyit-the.
wooh bur'a shur'ab'ee hy.
avan keṭṭa kuḍiyan.

Where is his shop?
သူဆိုင်ဘယ်မှာရှိသည်လဲ။
thoo-suyng-beh-hmah-she-the-leh ?
oos'kee doo'kan ku'han hy ?
avan kaḍai engé irukkiṛathu ?

He charges very high.
သူအလွန်အဘိုးဆိုသည်။
thoo-ă-hloon-ă-poh-soh-the.
wooh bur'ee kee'mut le'ta hy.
athiga vilai chollugiṛán.

He is always coming with complaints.
သူသည်ပြောဆိုတိုင်းကြာရန်ကိစ္စနှင့်အခါတိုင်းလာတတ်သည်။
thoo-the-pyaw-śoh-tuyng-chyah-yun-kayt-sah-hnin-ă-kah-duyng-lah-dut-the.
wooh hum'esh'a na'lish kur'ta a'ta hy.
ivan óyámal priyáthu koṇḍu varugiṛán.

What must I do?
ကျွန်ုပ်အဘယ်သို့ပြုရမည်လဲ။
kyoon-hnoht-ă-beh-thoh-pyoo-yah-mee-leh ?
hum'a'ra ky'a kur'na la'zim ?
nán enna cheya véṇḍum ?

I have no friends.
ကျွန်ုပ်မှာမိတ်ဆွေမရှိဘူး။
kyoon-hnoht-hmah-mait-sway-m'shee-boo.
ko'ee me'ra dost na'heen hy.
enakku snégithar illai.

I feel very cold.
ကျွန်ုပ်အလွန်ချမ်းပါသည်။
kyoon-hnoht-ă-hloon-chyun-bah-the.
mooj'he ja'ra bu'hoot lug'ta hy.
enakku metta kuḷirugiṛathu.

This land is cultivated.
သည်လယ်မြေသည်ထွန်လုပ်ပြီးပြီး။
thee-leh-myay-thee-tohn-loht-pyee-byee.
yih zum'een bo'ee gu'yee hy.
intha nilam ságupaḍiyágiṛathu.

Why are you afraid?
ဘယ်ကြောင့်ကြောက်ရွံ့သလဲ။
beh-gyowng-chyowk-the-leh?
toom ky'oon dur'te ho?
én bhaya paḍugiṛáy?

This road is very muddy.
သည်လမ်းမှာအလွန်ရွှံ့များသည်။
thee-lun-hmah-ă-hloon-shoon-myah-the.
yih rah bur'ee (chih'lu'ha *or* gud'la) hy.
intha páthai metta chéṛáy irukkiṛathu.

He has a large family.
သူမှာသားသမီးအလွန်များသည်။
thoo-hmah-thah-th'mee-ă-hloon-myah-the.
wooh bur'a koo'toom-dar hy.
avanukku periya kuḍumbam.

They are very dishonest.
သူတို့သည်အလွန်မသမာသောသူများဖြစ်ကြသည်။
thoo-doh-the-ă-hloon-mă-thum-mah-thaw-thoo-myah-pyit-gyah-the.
we bur'ee kha'in hyn.
avargaḷ mahá ayógyar.

I cannot disobey his orders.
သူ၏အာဏာကိုမပယ်ရှားနိုင်ဘူး။
thoo-ee-ah-nah-goh-m'peh-shah-hnuyng-boo.
oos'ka hookm myn radd na'heen kur-suk'ta.
avar uttaravukku nán kīḻpaḍiyámal irukka kúḍáthu.

He is a doctor.
သူဆေးသမားဖြစ်သည်။
thoo-say-thum-mah-pyit-the.
wooh huk'eem hy.
avar vaidiyar.

File these papers.
သည်စက္ကူများကိုတွဲထားလိုက်ပါ။
thee-sek-koo-myah-goh-tweh-tah-luyt-bah.
oon ka'ghuz'on ko nutth'ee-kur'o.
intha kákithangaḷai kambiyilé máṭṭivai.

Don't forget to tell him what I said to you.
မင်းကိုငါပြောသောစကားများကိုသူအားပြောဆိုရန်မမေ့ပါနှင့်။
min-goh-ngah-pyaw-thaw-să-gah-myah-goh-thoo-ah-pyaw-soh-yun-m'may-bah-hnin.
jo myn ne toom se kuh'a hy, so oos se kuh'na, mut bhool'ja'na.
nán avarukku chollumpaḍi unniḍattil chonnathai cholla maṛanthuviḍáthé

His hair is white.
သူဆံပင်ဖြူသည်။
thoo-sä-bin-pyoo-the.
oos'ke bal soo'fyd hyn.
avanukku narai mayir, *or* avanukku mayir veḷḷaiyáy irukkiṛathu.

Give me a handkerchief.
ကျွန်ုပ်ကိုလက်ကိုင်ပဝါတထည်ပေးပါ။
kyoon-hnoht-goh-lek-kuyng-pä-wah-t'teh-pay-bah.
ek roo'mal mooj'he do.
enakku oru kuṭṭai koḍu.

Do you know whose hand-writing this is?
သည်ဟာမည်သူ၏လက်ရေးဖြစ်ကြောင်းကိုမင်းသိရှိလား။
thee-hah-mee-thoo-leh-yay-pyit-gyowng-goh-min-thee-the-lah?
toom jan'te ho ki yih kis-ka khutt hy?
ithu yáruḍaiya kaieḻuttu teriyumá?

He is very helpless.
သူသည်အလွန်ကိုးရာမဲ့ဖြစ်သည်။
thoo-thee-ä-hloon-koh-goh-yah-meh-pyit-the.
wooh bu'hoot la-char hy.
avan evvaḷavum uthaviyaṛṛavan.

Bring some hot water.
ရေနွေးတဆိတ်ယူခဲ့ပါ။
yay-noo-ay-t'sayt-yoo-geh-bah.
tho'ra gurm pa'nee la'o.
koñjam yennír konḍuvá.

She is a naughty girl.
သူသည်ဆိုးသော မိန်းခလေးဖြစ်သည်။
thoo-thee-soh-thaw-maym-mah-gä-lay-pyit-the.
wooh chhok'ree natkhat hy.
avaḷ keṭṭa peṇ.

I must obey his orders.
သူ၏အမိန့်အမိုင်းကျွန်ုပ်ဖြူရမည်။
thoo-ee-ä-mayn-ä-tuyng-kyoon-hnoht-pyoo-yah-mee.
mooj'he oos'ka hookm man'na ho'gä.
avar uttaravukku ñáñ kíḻpaḍiya véṇum.

Open the door.
တံခါးကိုဖွင့်လိုက်ပါ။
t'gah-goh-pwing-luyt-bah.
dur'wa'za khol'o.
kathavai tiṛa.

Who is that man?
ထိုလူဘယ်သူလဲ။
toh-loo-beh-thoo-leh?
wooh ad'mee koun hy?
antha manushan ár?

Whose house is this?
သည်အိမ်ဘယ်သူ့အိမ်လဲ။
thee-ayn-beh-thoo-ayn-leh?
yih kis-ka ghur hy?
ithu yár vídu?

I will go out.
ကျွန်ုပ်ထွက်သွားလိမ့်မည်။
kyoon-hnoht-twet-thwah-laym-mee.
myn ba'hur ja'oon'ga.
nán veḷiyé póvén.

Bring my shoes.
ကျွန်ုပ်ဖိနပ်များကိုယူခဲ့ပါ။
kyoon-hnoht-pĕ-nŭt-myah-goh-yoo-goh-bah.
me'ree joo'tee la'o.
en jóṭṭai koṇḍuvá.

Who is he?
ထိုသူမည်သူလဲ။
toh-thoo-mee-thoo-leh?
wooh koun hy?
athu yár?

Let him go.
သူသွားပါလေစေ။
thoo-thwah-bah-lay-say.
oos'ko ja'ne-do.
avar pógaṭṭum.

Are you able to read my writing?
ကျွန်ုပ်လက်ရေးကိုမင်းဖတ်နိုင်သည်လား။
kyoon-hnoht-let-yay-goh-min-put-hnuyng-the-lah?
toom me'ra lik'ha purh-suk'te ho?
en eḷuttai ní vásikka kúḍumá?

Bring my book.
ကျွန်ုပ်စာအုပ်ကိုယူခဲ့ပါ။
kyoon-hnoht-sah-oht-goh-yoo-geh-bah.
me'ree kit'ab la'o.
en pustakattai koṇḍu vá.

Be careful.
သတိပြုပါ။
th'dee-pyoo-bah.
khub'ur'dar ho.
pattiramáy iru.

Is this your house?
သည်အိမ်မင့်အိမ်လား။
the-ayn-min-ayn-lah?
yih toom'ha'ra ghur hy, *or* ky'a yih toom'ha'ra ghur hy?
ithu un víḍá?

Who is there?
ဟိုမှာမည်သူလဲ။
hoht-hmah-mee-thoo-leh?
koun hy?
ár añgé?

House-rent is very high in Rangoon.
ရန်ကုန်မြို့အိမ်ခအလွန်ကြီးသည်။
yan-goon-myo-hnuyt-ayn-kah-ăhloon-kyee-the.
Ram-goon men ghur ka kir'a'ya bu'hoot hy.
Rañgónil víṭṭu váḍagai vegu athigam.

Where are you going?
မင်းဘယ်ကိုသွားမည်လဲ။
min-beh-goh-thwah-mee-leh.
toom ku'han ja'te ho?
ní eñgé pógiṛáy

He is allowed to come.
သူလာဘို့အခွင့်ရပါသည်။
thoo-lah-boh-ă-kwin-yah-bah-the.
wooh a'ne-pa'ta hy.
avan vara uttaravuperrán.

I wish to write a letter.
ကျွန်ုပ်စာတစောင်ကိုရေးချင်သည်။
kyoon-hnoht-sah-t'sowng-goh-yay-chying-the.
myn ek chit'thee lik'ha-cha'ta hoon.
oru kaḍitham eḻutha virumbhugiṛén.

Go away.
သွားတော့။
thwah-daw.
chul'e ja'o.
dúra pó.

He is very clever.
သူအလွန်လိမ္မာသည်။
thoo-ă-hloon-laym-mah-the.
wooh bu'hoot cha'lak hy.
avan metta geṭṭikkáran.

What do you wish to say?
မင်းဘာပြောချင်သည်လဲ။
min-bhah-pyaw-chyin-the-leh?
toom ky'a kuh'a-cha'te ho?
nír enna cholla virumbugiṛír?

You must go home.
မင်းအိမ်ကိုပြန်ရမည်။
min-ayn-goh-pyun-yah-mee.
toom'ko ghur ja'na ho'ga.
ní víṭṭukku póga vénḍum.

Has the gun fired?
အမြောက်ပြစ်ပြီးပြီးလား။
ă-myowk-pyit-pyee-byee-lah?
ky'a top dag ga'ee?
kuṇḍu póṭṭu viṭṭathá?

He is a carefnl man.
သူသည်သတိပြုတတ်သောလူဖြစ်သည်။
thoo-the-th'dee-pyoo-dut-thaw-loo pyit-the.
wooh hosh'yar ad'mee hy.
avan jákkrathai yuḷḷavan.

They are great rogues.
သူတို့သည်လိမ်လည်လှည့်ဖြားတတ်သောသူဖြစ်ကြသည်။
thoo-doh-the-layn-pyah-dut-thaw-thoo-pyit-gyah-the.
we bur'e dugh'a-baz hyn.
avargaḷ mahá tiruṭṭu payalgaḷ.

Why have you come?
မင်းအဘယ်ကြောင့်လာသည်လဲ။
min-ă-beh-gyowng-lah-thee-leh?
kis-was'te a'e ho?
ennattukku vantháy?

Call my steward.
ကျွန်ုပ်ဘဏ္ဍာစိုးကိုခေါ်လိုက်ပါ။
kyoon-hnoht-p'dah-soh-goh-kaw-luyt-bah.
me're khan'sa'man ko boo'la'o.
en ukkiráṇakkáṛanai kúppiḍu.

Bring dinner.
ညစာယူခဲ့ပါ။
nyah-sah-yoo-geh-bah.
kha'na la'o.
pagal sáppáḍu koṇḍuvá.

Bring my clothes.
ကျွန်ုပ်အဝတ်များကိုယူခဲ့ပါ။
kyoon-hnoht-ă-woot-myah-goh-yoo-geh-bah.
me're kup're la'o.
en uḍuppugaḷai koṇḍuvá.

Please come quickly.
ကျေးဇူးပြု၍အလျင်အမြန်လာပါ။
kyoo-zay-pyoo-yoo-eh-ă-hlyin-ă-myun-lah-bah.
ap jul'dee a'iye'ga.
thayai cheythu jelthiyáy várum.

Bring the newspaper.
သတင်းစာကိုယူခဲ့ပါ။
thă-din-sah-goh-yoo-geh-bah.
ukh'bar la'o.
várttamána pattirikkaiyai koṇḍuvá.

They are all there.
သူတို့အားလုံးဟိုမှာရှိကြပါသည်။
thoo-doh-aḥ-lohn-hoh-hmah-she-gyah-bah-the.
wu'han sub'ee hyn.
avargaḷ ellárum añgé irukkiṛárgaḷ.

Is any one there ?
ဟိုမှာတစုံတယောက်သောသူရှိသလား။
hoh-hmah-tă-zohn-t'yowk-thaw-thoo-she-the-lah ?
wu'han ko'ee hy ?
añgé yárávathu irukkiṛárgaḷá ?

Say that again.
တဖန်ထပ်၍ဆိုပါအုံး။
tă-pun-tut-yoo-eh-tsoh-bah-ohn.
wooh phir kuh'o.
athai tirumbavum chollu.

Has the master risen ?
သခင်ထပြီးလား။
th'kin-tah-byee-lah ?
sa'hib ooth'e hyn ?
durai eḻuntháṛá ?

This is a very fine fruit.
သည်သစ်သီးအလွန်လှပသည်။
thee-thit-thee-ă-hloon-hlah-bah-thee.
yih bu'hoot khoob mewu hy.
ithu metta nalla paḻam.

Is your business now completed ?
မင်းကိစ္စယခုပြီးပြီးလား။
min-kay-tsah-yă-koo-pyee-byee-lah ?
toom'ha'ra kam ub tum'am hoo'a hy ?
ippó un vélai muḍinthathá ?

He is very impudent.
သူသည်အလွန်ဆဲတတ်သည်။
thoo-thee-ă-hloon-tseh-dut-the.
wooh bur'ee (goos'takh *or* be-hu'ya) hy.
avan veṭkam keṭṭavan.

These are very mischievous children.
သည်ကလေးများသည်၊အလွန်အကျိုးကိုယုတ်လျော့စေတတ်ကြ၏။
the-ka-lay-myah-the-ă-hloon-ă-chyo-goh-yoht-hlyaw-zay-dat-gyah-ee.
we lur'ke bu'hoot nut'khut hyn.
ivargaḷ metta keṭṭa piḷḷaigaḷ.

Who is making a noise ?
မည်သူညံ၍နေသလဲ။
mee-thoo-nyun-yoo-eh-nay-the-leh ?
koun shor kur'ta hy ?
sattam póḍugiṛathár ?

Put us on shore.
ကျွန်ုပ်တို့ကိုကမ်းပေါ်သို့တင်ပါ။
kyoon-hnoht-doh-goh-kun-baw-thoh-tin-bah.
hum'un kin'a're pur oo'ta'ro.
eṅgaḷai karaiyilé viṭṭu viḍu.

Who lives there?
ဟိုမှာအဘယ်သူနေသည်လဲ။
hoh-hmah-ă-beh-thoo-nay-the-leh?
wu'han koun ruh'ta hy?
aṅgé yár kuḍi irukkiṛathu?

Tie their hands and feet.
သူတို့၏လက်ခြေများကိုတုတ်နှောင်လိုက်ပါ။
thoo-doh-ee-let-chay-myah-goh-toht-hnowng-luyt-bah.
oon ke hath pa'on bund'o.
avargaḷuḍaiya kai kálgaḷai kaṭṭu.

Bring some wine and water.
စပျစ်ရည်နှင့်ရေတစ်ဆိတ်ယူခဲ့ပါ။
tsu-byit-yee-hnin-yay-tă-sayt-yoo-geh-bah.
kooch shur'ab our pa'nee la'o.
koñjam dráḍcha irasamum taṇṇírum koṇḍuvá.

The dinner is on the table.
ညစာစားရန်စားပွဲပေါ်တွင်ရှိသည်။
nyah-zah-tsah-yan-tsă-bweh-baw-dwin-shee-the.
kha'na mez pur a'ya.
pagal sáppáḍu mésai mél vaittáyiṛṛu.

Wake me very early.
ကျွန်ုပ်ကိုနံနက်စောစောကြီးနှိုးပါ။
kyoon-hnoht-goh-nă-net-tsaw-zaw-gyee-hnoh-bah.
mooj'he bur'ee fuj'ur jug'a'o.
athikálaiyilé ennai eḻuppu.

He has made confession.
သူသည်ဝန်ချပါပြီ။
thoo-thee-woon-chyah-bah-byee.
oos ne ik'rar ky'a hy.
avan aṛikkai cheythán.

Put those Rupees in the bag.
ထိုငွေများကိုအိတ်ထဲသို့ထည့်လိုက်ပါ။
toh-ngway-zah-myah-goh-ayt-teh-thoh-teh-luyt-bah.
oon roo'py'on ko thy'lee men bhur'o.
rúbáyai paiyilé vai.